Please remember that this is a library book,
and that it belongs only temporarily to each
person who uses it. Be considerate. Do
not write in this, or any, library book.

☙ Campesino

Campesino

The Diary of a Guatemalan Indian /

[Ignacio Bizarro Ujpán]

Translated and edited by

JAMES D. SEXTON

The University of Arizona Press

Tucson, Arizona

970.3
T999b
1985

About the Editor

JAMES D. SEXTON has worked with Ignacio Bizarro Ujpán (a pseudonym) since 1970, when Sexton first traveled to Guatemala as part of an anthropological team. He translated and edited Ignacio's story up to 1977 in *Son of Tecún Umán: A Maya Indian Tells His Life Story* (The University of Arizona Press, 1981); he also has written a monograph and several articles on modernization and culture change in highland Guatemala. Since 1973 Sexton has been a professor of anthropology at Northern Arizona University, where in 1982 he received the NAU President's Award for excellence in teaching, research, and service. He holds a Ph.D. in cultural anthropology from the University of California at Los Angeles.

THE UNIVERSITY OF ARIZONA PRESS

Copyright © 1985
James D. Sexton

This book was set in 10/12 Linotron Caledonia.
Manufactured in the U.S.A.

Library of Congress Cataloging in Publication Data

Bizarro Ujpán, Ignacio.
    Campesino : the diary of a Guatemalan Indian.

    Sequel to: Son of Tecún Umán.
    Bibliography: p.
    Includes index.
    1. Bizarro Ujpán, Ignacio.   2. Tzutuhil Indians—
Biography.   3. Tzutuhil Indians—Social conditions.
4. Indians of Central America—Guatemala—Social conditions.   I. Sexton, James D.   II. Title.
F1465.2.T9B588   1985   972.81'00497 [B]   85-1115

ISBN 0-8165-0814-3

Contents

The Guatemalan Crisis

❧The Guatemalan Crisis

Although international attention in Central America has focused primarily on El Salvador, there is an equally intense civil war waging in Guatemala. Many analysts believe the real battle for Central America will be won or lost in Guatemala—the country with the largest natural resources, including significant deposits of oil; important U.S. business interests; the largest population, more than half of which is Maya Indians; and a geographic and strategic location second only to Panama.

❧ The Importance of Central America

As the United States incrementally deepens its economic and military support for El Salvador, a rapidly growing number of people in the U.S. and abroad are asking whether El Salvador will become another Vietnam and whether Guatemala will become another El Salvador. Since Son of Tecún Umán was published in 1981, to which Campesino is a sequel, Central America has begun to receive the same kind of intense coverage in the electronic and printed media that Southeast Asia once commanded in the 1960s and 1970s for essentially the same reasons—the explosion of insurgency and counterinsurgency in relatively small, economically impoverished nations and the U.S. government's responding in essentially the same manner, that is, viewing civil instability as an East-West confrontation that requires a combined

3

economic and military solution but which emphasizes the latter without negotiations with the left. The rationale for not pushing negotiations is that the leftists should not be allowed to shoot their way into power, even though the ruling elites have done so, and that if the Communists are given a toehold in politics they will soon take over the whole government, despite the example to the contrary in Mexico.

There are a number of obvious differences between the situations in Southeast Asia and Central America. Central America's proximity to the United States and the predominance of a Latin-American language and culture make it more familiar to North Americans than Southeast Asia, an area of many national languages and cultures and a hemisphere away. While both regions have an agrarian economy, Southeast Asia's is based on rice whereas Central America's is based on corn. Also, with substantial business and trade interests and a geography adjacent to Caribbean shipping lanes, Central America is more vitally important than Southeast Asia ever was. However, although heightened involvement of the U.S. in Central America is coming at a different time and in a different place, there are numerous, fundamental similarities. For example, the U.S. is backing infighting, ruling elites, who, while professing their anti-communism, are too often incompetent or corrupt and who largely ignore or brutally repress the socioeconomic needs of a woefully impoverished, peasant majority. Central America, like Southeast Asia, has a prolonged history of a persistent, vehemently anti-imperialistic movement of guerrillas who are strongly nationalistic, though not as experienced and hardened as the Viet Cong at the time of the arrival of U.S. military advisers (Tuohy 1983). Nevertheless, the Central American guerrillas are growing in numbers and effectiveness in combat operations, especially in jungles and mountains, with an apparently higher morale than the U.S.-supported government troops. Both insurgents and counterinsurgents are capable of savage attacks on combatants and noncombatants alike; military and paramilitary forces have received most of the blame for civilian deaths, including the elimination of political moderates, although there are increasing signs that the guerrillas are stepping up their attacks on civilians as pacification programs are implemented. The pacification programs in "zones of conflict" are designed to win the hearts and minds of peasants, who are rational and will listen to any armed group, but who have little love for either side and stand little chance of enjoying cultural plurality and prosperity if either the extreme right or extreme left prevails (Schwartz 1983; Gossen 1983). The U.S. is gradually deepening its military commitment while voicing reassurances of limited involvement. For instance,

President Reagan's claim that there is no parallel whatsoever of El Salvador to Vietnam and his declaration, "Only Salvadorans can fight this war," is hauntingly similar to President Johnson's promise that American boys would never fight an Asian boys' war (Tuohy 1983). The U.S. is pushing for free national elections in nations where national democracy is little more than a slogan (Tuohy 1983). Disputes are focusing on body counts and on charges that the U.S. administration is withholding vital information in order to maintain military support from Congress (Lewis 1982; McManus 1984; Roderick 1984). And there is mounting moral outrage in the U.S. and among its allies against the Americans, who, although not directly responsible for the destruction, killing, and creation of refugees, are increasingly being blamed for not stopping the conflict (Lewis 1982).

Although a growing number of people are asking whether we have learned anything from history and whether we are making the same mistakes in Central America as we did in Southeast Asia, not everyone agrees on the lessons that we should have learned. Two polarized conclusions are dominant: one is that the U.S. military was not allowed to use enough force to win, and the other is that we never could have won because we teamed up with the wrong side—a government that never had a broad, popular base.[1]

There are both liberals and conservatives in the United States who do not wish Central America to go Communist (White 1982) and who worry that dominoes in Central America may fall faster than in Southeast Asia because of greater cultural homogeneity. Thus, Morton Kondracke warned that the situation in Central America was like that of Indochina in 1975, when Congress denied funds to South Vietnam. He wrote, "We liberals cannot avert our eyes from what ensued: 3 million murders in Cambodia, total deprivation of human rights in Viet Nam and a falling of dominoes" (Kondracke in Isaacson 1983:27). Officials of the Reagan administration are echoing the fears of earlier officials involved with Vietnam who did not want to be responsible for losing the country. For example, Brecher et al. (1982:17) quoted a close Reagan aide as saying, "We can't afford to have Ronald Reagan be the President who let Central America go Communist." Yet some senior officials concede they may be in a no-win situation. Another familiar statement by one American official in El Salvador was, "We thought it would be so easy. The place was so little and we were so big" (Brecher et al. 1982:17).[2]

President Reagan has made it clear that he does not wish to lose Central America to communism. In an unprecedented appearance before a joint session of Congress, on 27 April 1983, he stressed that the security of the Americas is at stake in Central America and that Democratic opponents of his policy could be held responsible for losing El Salvador in the 1984 elections (Toth 1983). The implication was clear that with Cuba, Nicaragua, and El Salvador communistic, Guatemala, Mexico, and even Venezuela would be threatened. The latter three countries have significant oil deposits, and Panama, of course, has a strategic canal. Moreover, Mexico has a two-thousand-mile border with the U.S. Reagan declared:

> *I do not believe that a majority of the Congress or the country is prepared to stand [by] passively while the people of Central America are delivered to totalitarianism and we ourselves are left vulnerable to new dangers. Who among us would wish to bear the responsibility for failing to meet our shared obligations? (Toth 1983:1)*

The argument that Central America is crucial to the security of the Americas emphasizes that the region is a strategic and commercial artery for the U.S. and its Latin-American allies. The Reagan administration states that nearly half the U.S. trade and over half of our imported strategic minerals pass through the Panama Canal or the Gulf of Mexico (Pastor 1982). And even though the Panama Canal has become obsolete for more efficient large ships and aircraft carriers (Girling and Goldring 1983), it has become critical for such Latin-American nations as Panama, Ecuador, Colombia, Costa Rica, and Nicaragua (Pastor 1982). Certainly the U.S. does not wish the canal to fall into unfriendly hands that might interfere with its traffic (Karlstrom 1983).

Perhaps because a number of analysts have pointed out that Central America accounts for less than two percent of both U.S. investments abroad and U.S. trade (Pastor 1982:30; Girling and Goldring 1983), Reagan has not made U.S. financial interest a manifest concern of his administration in Central America. Nevertheless, Central America is one of the most Americanized economies in the world (Hanley 1983), and what may be more important than the relative quantity of business in the area is the relative influence of the companies concerned with various U.S. governments.[3] In any case, more than a thousand companies have a minimum direct investment of $4 billion, which may reflect only a fraction of the true stake they have in the area, and some of these companies are among the world's most powerful multinationals (Nairn 1983). Furthermore, the region owes some $10 billion to foreign banks, most of them American.

It is precisely the overshadowing presence of U.S. businesses in Central America that has fueled hatred among leftists who view it as abusive, laissez-faire, Yankee imperialism, especially to the extent that it blocks labor movements and encourages the expansion of agribusiness that pushes peasants off the land and forces them to work as low-paid farm laborers (Partido Guatemalteco del Trabajo 1982, 1983). Also, liberals in the U.S. point out that American businesses have been coexisting happily with tyranny for years in Central America and have supported martial law to restore order (Cockburn 1983).

In a Democratic rebuttal to President Reagan's speech of 27 April 1983 before Congress, Senator Christopher Dodd warned that the administration is leading the U.S. into a Vietnam-type quagmire in Central America. Essentially agreeing with Contadora (a synonym for Mexico, Colombia, Panama, and Venezuela, who are also seeking a solution but who, like the Spanish Prime Minister, Felipe González, believe the root causes are poverty and injustice), Dodd stated:

> *Instead of trying to do something about the factors which breed revolution, this Administration has turned to massive military buildups at a cost of hundreds of millions of dollars. Its policy is ever-increasing military assistance, endless training, even hiring our own paramilitary guerrillas. This is a formula for failure. And it is a proven prescription for picking a loser. The American people know that we have been down this road before—and that it only leads to a dark tunnel of endless intervention. . . .*

> *We believe the Administration fundamentally misunderstands the causes of the conflict in Central America. We cannot afford to found so important a policy on ignorance—and the painful truth is that many of our highest officials seem to know as little about Central America in 1983 as we knew about Indochina in 1963 (Houston 1983).*

The senator went on to argue that the U.S. should negotiate a settlement with the rebels, and a number of analysts back this position (Pastor 1982; Fagen and Pellicer 1983:11).[4] However, the Reagan administration opposes negotiated settlements that would give leftists power they have not won in elections. But such elections often have small turnouts—even in Guatemala, where voting is mandatory. In El Salvador during the March 1982 elections other shortcomings included numbered ballots and transparent voting urns, and no place on the ballot for any group more left of center than the Christian Democrats (White 1982).

Responding to such criticism, President Reagan created a bipartisan commission headed by Henry Kissinger to recommend a policy toward Central America. The commission has proposed the Jackson Plan (a kind of Marshall Plan for Central America), which recommends $8 to $12 billion in economic and development aid to the friendly Central American countries over the next five years, beginning in fiscal 1985. However, the commission endorsed the view that vital U.S. security interests are at stake and that substantial military aid is needed to supplement the economic assistance and to reinforce diplomatic efforts (Skelton 1984). The commission specifically recommended that Congress enact legislation that would require U.S. military aid to be conditional on "demonstrated progress toward free elections, freedom of association, the establishment of the rule of law and an effective judicial system, and the termination of the activities of the so-called death squads, as well as vigorous action against those guilty of crimes and the prosecution to the extent possible of past offenders," and that "these conditions should be seriously enforced."[5]

The Jackson Plan is bound to be compared to the Alliance for Progress, an earlier variant of the Marshall Plan founded by President Kennedy in 1961 to eliminate social and economic poverty in Latin America within ten years. When Kennedy announced his program, he stated his now haunting and famous refrain, "Those who make peaceful revolution impossible, make violent revolution inevitable." There is much discussion as to why this earlier program failed to meet its goals.

According to James Wilkie (1983:656), in order for the Alliance to have been equivalent to the Marshall Plan, the amount of external funding for Latin America should have been doubled and made available in a much shorter period of time because in Latin America there was the need to build factories, not just reconstruct them, and to educate the manpower necessary to run them. Robert White (1982) adds that Kennedy's successors were preoccupied with Vietnam and that they reverted to the policy of the 1950s, in which a feckless mix of economic and military assistance did more to prop up military dictatorships than to improve the lives of the poor.

Certainly the Jackson Plan is a step in the right direction toward a lasting solution to the complex problems of Central America. Indeed military aid to these countries should be tied to certification of progress in human rights. The major challenge of such a plan will be to insure, perhaps through a team of international auditors, that the neediest—the impoverished lower class—will receive substantial portions of the economic aid. There must be adequate safeguards against the widening of the gap between the rich and the poor[6] and against corruption among the officials administering the aid, from the lowest to highest levels of office. If fraud or embezzlement is detected, Congress should respond by isolating offenders, not by cutting off the entire package, an action which denies help to those who need it the most.

In addition to concern over Central America's geopolitical and economic interests, there is growing worry in the U.S. that is more permanent in nature—that the country is becoming Caribbeanized (Pastor 1982; Karlstrom 1983). The total number of people who have migrated to the U.S. from the region is about 8.5 million—more than half of the people who have come to live in the U.S. since 1960. Largely because of immigration, the Hispanic community is one of the fastest growing ethnic groups in the U.S. Many who were considering a move to the U.S. for economic reasons finally decided to leave because of the political violence. Thus, there is more reason to come and more reason to stay. As Pastor (1982:35–37) points out, the Central American conflict is not just an abstract foreign policy issue to be debated in the state department and universities. Rather, it is a real concern to departments of health and human services in cities such as Miami, Los Angeles, Boston, and Chicago. Also, Latin American exiles have imported some of the turmoil of their homelands to cities such as New Orleans, where old-line conservative immigrants have violently clashed with more recent immigrants who support rebel factions. Unlike Southeast Asia, which is halfway around the world from the U.S., the proximity of Central America only heightens its emotional impact in the U.S. (Beck et al. 1982).

Similarly, Mexico is being forced to become more actively involved in dealing with the fire burning next door in Guatemala. In 1982 the Mexican Interior Ministry estimated that there were 120,000 Guatemalan refugees. In 1983 an estimated additional 35,000 fled from Huehuetenango and Quiché, known as zones of conflict (Schuster 1983). Mexico is hard pressed to provide for and protect these refugees. Some refugees are making their way to Puerto Rico, Honduras, Belize, and Canada, making the Central American problem more than an abstraction for these countries as well.

ᕗ The Significance of Guatemala

Guatemala is the ultimate prize in Central America, and the battle for that region may be fought there (Sanders 1982; Frank 1982). With an estimated population in 1980 of 7,262,400 (3,181,200 of them Indians) (Dirección General de Estadísticas 1980), it is the most populous of the Central American states. Guatemala's GNP in 1980 of $7.5 billion was the largest in the region. With some five billion barrels of untapped oil, significant deposits of nickel and other minerals, and a sizeable agribusiness that exports coffee, bananas, sugar, and beef, it is potentially the richest Central American nation.[7] In addition, more than 190 U.S. firms, including Bank of America, Del Monte, Goodyear, Coca-Cola, and Reynolds, have invested $300 million in Guatemala, and several firms such as IBM and NCR have an export economy of $400 million (Tobis 1974:170–174; Latin American Regional Reports Mexico & Central America 1981a; Preston 1981; Nairn 1983).[8] In short, the U.S. has greater economic interests in Guatemala than in any other Central American country now in crisis.

Guatemala's 108,900 square kilometers make it the third largest country in Central America. Its relatively large size and its strategic position on the southern Mexican border, making it the last domino in Central America, give it a geopolitical importance surpassed only by Panama, which, of course, has the Panama Canal (and which also has the greatest concentration of U.S. wealth in Central America) (Hanley 1983).

With an international reputation for brutal dictatorship, Guatemala poses one of the most serious dilemmas for U.S. foreign policy (Rohter 1982). Civil instability clearly predates Castro's Cuba (1959) and Ortega's Nicaragua (1979). Among the Maya of the highlands, where much of the disturbance is now concentrated, there had been communal landowning patterns and communistic value systems for thousands of years before the world ever heard of Karl Marx (Melville and Melville 1971:285). Most observers agree that poverty and social injustice are clearly root causes of the present instability and that the U.S. has played a murky, if not dark, historical role in supporting the military and ruling elites, mainly because they were favorable to U.S. business interests and claimed to be anti-communistic.

Since 1954, when the CIA engineered a coup that overthrew a freely elected, reformist government, Guatemala has had as high as an estimated 90,000 politically motivated killings (Toriello Garrido 1983:xv). Both Amnesty International (1981) and the American Embassy (Press 1982a) have stated that most of the murders have been carried out by death squads of the extreme right. Amnesty International linked the Lucas government to such squads, who have been responsible for eliminating lawyers, politicians, professors, students, teachers, priests, and pastors. Until recently, guerrillas have been more selective in their targets and have limited their assassinations to *wealthy landowners, managers of farms, national policemen, military personnel, military commissioners, mayors, and governors. However, by 1982 there was evidence that both sides were changing tactics, with the guerrillas becoming more indiscriminate and the army more discriminate (Torgerson 1982b). In both cases, scores of noncombatants have been caught in the middle.*

❧ Inequities in Guatemala

Walter LaFeber (1982) points out that in 1962 (a year after Kennedy began the Alliance for Progress) nine out of ten rural families in Guatemala had lives of poverty, malnutrition, sickness, and illiteracy. While 68,000 rural families scratched out a living as tenants or low-wage laborers without any land of their own, half the country's best farmland was owned by 1,100 families. While these elite groups used Alliance funds to expand production of export crops, especially sugar, food shortages threatened starvation in some areas. Finally, the government had to pay top prices to import such staples as corn, beans, and rice from the U.S. and Colombia. LaFeber concludes that, despite more than $100 million in U.S. government aid and private investment during the 1960s, the Alliance was unable to execute any agrarian reforms for 80 percent of some 5 million Guatemalans who eked out a living on the land.

Unlike Pastor, who argues that the main cause for civil instability in Central America is the inconsistent status of people with new wealth but little or no power, Edelberto Torres-Rivas (1983), a Costa Rican sociologist, argues that in Guatemala the principal problem is that the majority in the lower class have become relatively even poorer as the gap between them and the rich has widened. According to Torres-Rivas, the sustained economic growth that improved the overall GNP of Guatemala also exacerbated the gap between the rich and poor. Agricultural exports such as coffee, cotton, bananas, and beef favor those who have concentrated land ownership, capital, and marketing networks. Industrial development favors those who by birth are able to monopolize channels to foreign capital (such as loans from Bank of America). Adding the fact that the state is definitely on the side of private enterprise, inequities and social tensions between the abysmally poor and the ostentatiously rich were bound to grow. Under such conditions, this disparity increases despite the emergence of an expanding middle class.

In 1980 the per capita income in Guatemala was $1,067; the GNP *was $7.5 billion, with about 26 percent of it coming from agriculture (Bacheller 1983:579). However, as LaFeber (1982) and others point out, such aggregate figures are misleading. For example, between 1960 and 1980, Guatemala's economy grew at an average rate of 5.7 percent. But by the mid-1970s, 5 percent of the population received more than $2,000 per year while 70 percent tried to live on only $74 per year. Citing a U.S. embassy report, Raymond Bonner (1982a) illustrates the disparity in slightly different terms—2 percent of the population received about 25 percent of the income while the bottom 50 percent received only 10 to 15 percent. Andrea Brown (1983:232) illustrates the gross economic disparities with yet another criterion— land ownership. She notes that 2.1 percent of the landowners own 62 percent of the arable land, and 87 percent of landowners own 19 percent of the arable land.[9]*

Although in 1980 Guatemala had the largest GNP of the Central American countries and a per capita income surpassed only by Costa Rica and Panama (Bacheller 1983), the quality of life for the most populous nation was the lowest. Not surprisingly, Costa Rica and Panama, the two most stable countries in the region, had the highest scores on a quality-of-life scale devised by Wilkie and Haber (1983:2– 3). The composite scale includes 12 indicators of three different types of variables: (1) health (life expectancy at birth, infant mortality rates, persons per hospital beds, population per physician, and persons per dentist); (2) education (percentage of population age 15 and over who are literate; percentage of school-age population, ages 7 to 14, enrolled in primary school; students enrolled in secondary school as percentage of school-age population, ages 13 to 18; college enrollment, including professional, technical, and vocational schools, as percentage of primary school enrollment); and (3) communication (newspaper circulation, copies per 1,000 persons, number of telephones per 100 persons, and number of persons per motor vehicle of autos, buses, and trucks in use).

Wilkie and Haber (1983) report other revealing statistics. In 1975 Guatemala had the lowest number of teachers per population (ages 7–14) in Central America (107.6 per 10,000). Not surprisingly, it also had the highest rate of illiteracy of population over 15 years of age (in 1973, 53.9 percent). In 1973 (the year of the last census) only 42.3 percent of the population had access to piped water (inside the house, on the lot, or no more than 100 meters away). Only Nicaragua had less access. Only 17.9 percent of the population had access to sewerage or septic tanks in Guatemala. Only in Honduras was the percentage smaller. Diarrhea, flu, and pneumonia were the leading causes of death. And infant mortality was the highest in Central America (in 1978, 69.2 per 1,000 live births).[10]

Using more current estimates, Bonner (1982a) points out how statistics indicating quality of life among Indians, who comprise about half the population, are more grim than for non-Indians. About 80 percent are illiterate in Spanish; life expectancy for them is about 50 years, compared to about 60 for Ladinos; infant mortality is almost twice as high in the rural areas, where most Indians live, as it is in the cities; and four out of every five peasant children are malnourished.

A Maya and His Story

With the debate intensifying in the United States as to whether El Salvador will become the next Vietnam and Guatemala the next El Salvador, there is an urgent need to know more about what life is really like for the peasants who make up the majority of these people. Despite some ethnographies on Vietnam, we knew very little about the peasants from their own perspective (Butterfield 1983). And to my knowledge, not a single autobiographical account emerged from a peasant despite the fact that this class bore the brunt of the destruction inflicted from both sides.

Although there is a fairly extensive anthropological literature on highland Guatemala, there are few autobiographical studies of the Maya. As a sequel to the first full-length life history of a Mayan Indian, Campesino *continues a personal account of daily life during a period of upheaval never before paralleled in Guatemala's history.*

In Campesino *the story of the life of Ignacio Bizarro Ujpán (a pseudonym, like most of the other proper names except Panajachel, Lake Atitlán, and Solola) continues from 1977 to 1983.*[11] *The same major themes that emerged from* Son of Tecún Umán *continue in* Campesino: *grinding poverty, recurrent illness, reliance on drink, family and community solidarity, and sensitivity to agents of change. However, beginning in 1978 a new, alarming theme surfaces and remains dominant throughout rest of the book—political violence and turmoil.*[12]

Ignacio is not necessarily representative of everyone in his community or culture in every respect in a statistical sense. He is not a famous shaman or a political official of high office. However, in the last few years of his life, he has grown in social stature in his community through service as president of his cooperative and as head of the cofradía, or religious brotherhood, of the Virgin Mary, and through attracting government training programs to his town. Although he shares the language, culture, and low socioeconomic status of his fellow Maya, Ignacio is more acculturated in some respects than many of his townspeople: he speaks Spanish fluently, has taught himself to type, and is more exposed to Ladino culture through work as a labor contractor for coastal farms and through radio, travel, military service, and printed media.

Although Ignacio has lived just one life and some of his opinions may change, his position in two worlds—indigenous and Ladino—makes him uniquely qualified to describe life in rural Guatemala. His diary gives us a remarkably candid, personal perspective on the physical and psychological impact of insurgency and counterinsurgency. Thus, the story offers a human dimension to the terror and tension of revolution and repression in Central America.

A Campesino's Diary

✎A Campesino's Diary, 1977-83

✎Reflections about Publishing My Life History
26–27 SEPTEMBER 1978

Today I was in the capital city. On 26 September 1978 I cashed a check that my great friend James D. Sexton sent me in the Banco Agrícola Mercantil, without any problems. Wednesday, 27 September, dawned very peacefully. I am very grateful to God and to the good-natured James D. Sexton. This señor has tried to help me with my diary. Also, I am thankful that all of this work is going well for publication. Soon they are going to publish this sad story of a humble peasant.[13]

Previously I said [in *Son of Tecún Umán*] that my parents did not give me birth. I was an adopted child of my aunt, my real mother's sister. When I was a baby, I did not know my real mother. I knew my aunt more as my mother. But the husband of my aunt was very mean, and he punished me cruelly. He liked liquor, and when drunk, he beat me bitterly.

After drinking his liquor, he ordered me to go to San Martín in the late hours of the night to buy more. I went with much fear to San Martín from San José, which is only two kilometers away. But two kilometers for a small child is a lot. Sometimes I would be asleep by 8–9:00 P.M., but suddenly I would have to get up at 11–12:00 at night to go look for the husband of my aunt, who was out drinking with his friends. I was very cold. My typical [Indian-style] trousers were very short, and I did not have a pair of *cayetes* [open-toe sandals]. My feet could not stand the cold, but I had to bear it because, if I did not, they did not give me food. I remember it well; I will never forget these things.

The señor who was the spouse of my aunt liked being a *zanjorín* [shaman]. For him it was a good business, especially about the time of the Day of the Dead, 2 November. On 30 October 1952 this man took me and my aunt to a farm called Santo Tomás near Totonicapán. The three of us went to this farm to say prayers for the dead. Well, the inhabitants of that place crowded together when they saw that Señor Martín was able to perform a service for the redemption of souls from purgatory. Each one wanted purgatory for his dead kin.

Well, the people were very satisfied because he told them that with this prayer the dead would reach paradise. Then the people began to give *tragos* [drinks] of liquor to the petitioner, and eventually he became drunk. That is the way it was on 30 October.

In the afternoon and all day of 31 October, this señor earned many dollars, but it made him drunk. On 1 November, we left the farm and returned to San José, but Señor Martín continued to drink on the road.

When we arrived in the village of Patzilín, this señor and his friends became staggering drunk. When night fell, my aunt and I were very grieved, but the señor made us continue to San José. Finally, he left his friends, and we began to walk toward San José. Unfortunately, it was a dark night, and it was difficult to walk. It was intensely cold because of the mountainous region, but it did not matter to the señor because the alcohol numbed his senses.

When we arrived at the summit of Chocojomché, just four kilometers from home, he began to hit my aunt. Because I defended her, he began to hit me, too. Since it was dark, it was impossible for us to run. This man hit my aunt and me hatefully. I was unable to walk because of the blows. He beat us as if we were animals.

My aunt and I did not get to the bottom of the Hill of Chocojomché until about 3:00 A.M., walking carefully along the road because there were barrancas [ravines] and we ached. At 5:00 A.M. we arrived home. We had lost Señor Martín, who returned to Patzilín with his friends. When we arrived home, he was not there. When daylight came, we could see the results of his blows. My aunt's face was bruised, and her arms were black and blue. I was the same.

During the day, my aunt went to look for her spouse in the town of San José, but she could not find him. In vain, she looked for a friend who would go to Patzilín to bring him back. She paid no attention to the beating she had received during the night. She asked me to go with her, but I did not want to go—I was trembling with fear from the beating the señor had given me.

Because my aunt feared that her husband might be killed in Patzilín, where he had many enemies, she went to look for him. During this time Señor Martín was the secretary-general of the Unión Campesina [Peasant Union]. It is certain that many were on his side, but the Tuc brothers, who are the richest [in the area], did not want the agrarian reform to affect their property, and for that reason they said they were going to kill the leader of the campesinos.

On this day the Tuc brothers gathered to torture Señor Martín, taking advantage of him when he came during the night. While the señor was good and drunk, his enemies beat him until it hurt. They tied him up and took away his shotgun and delivered him into the hands of the *comisionado militar* [military commissioner], who escorted him to jail in San José. I was sleeping when my aunt came to tell me what had happened. It made me very happy because I still hurt from the beating he had given me.

That is what happened to Señor Martín. After beating him, they threw him in jail. The next day they made the false accusation that he had been brandishing arms in the villages with the intent to kill the Tuc brothers. In the end Señor Martín received blows of his own, and he was sentenced to 30 days in jail or a $30 fine.

He was unable to pay the fine. But he had spent only six days in jail when a deputy of Colonel Arbenz arrived. I well remember that the deputy was named *licenciado* [licensed, graduate, or lawyer] Marino Cruz Aguilar. It was he who paid the $30 fine, and not until then did the señor secretary-general of the union of peasants realize his freedom. However, there was nothing the deputy could do about the wounds. For that reason, since that time as a child, I learned by experience not to be bad. I knew very well that one night earlier this man hit us a lot and the next night he was hit doubly hard by others and then imprisoned.

And that is the way it was. When I was a boy, I suffered a lot. My aunt was poor, and her husband liked liquor and women. My aunt and I had to go fish in the lake, and by selling the little fish we were able to buy tortillas. At times we could not eat breakfast until we sold the fish in San Martín. It did not matter that they gave us tortillas that were two to three days old, because we were hungry.

But when there was a lot of wind, we were not able to fish in the lake. We suffered hunger. Sometimes we could nourish our stomachs with only a few herbs. There was no money to buy things to eat, and I was still too small to work. It is true that I gathered firewood and took care of some bulls. But the bulls belonged to the husband of my aunt. When the animals were fattened, he would sell them and go on drunken sprees.

Much later my aunt sent me to the coast on Saturdays and Sundays to sell *jocotes* [a green fruit]. Thus I made 60 centavos each trip for two days. But when she sent me to the coast, she sent me with a señora called Paula whom she trusted to take care of me and to sell my *jocotes*. During the trip I spent 10 centavos, and I arrived home with 50 centavos. With these centavos my aunt bought a pound of meat and a little corn. In those days a pound of meat cost only 14 centavos. For me none of the money was spent on sweets. It was well accounted for. We ate bread two times a month, meat one or two times a month.

My goodness, I remember well the fiestas of my town! The other children drank their *frescos* [drinks] and bought toys and ate fruit in front of me. I had nothing. During these fiestas, they gave me three centavos to spend, and I wanted to buy toys, but who can buy toys with just three centavos? What I did was to take care of those three centavos, and in the afternoon I would spend them on something mediocre to eat—a centavo's worth of rice in milk and a centavo of candy, and it was good-bye fiesta.

Also, I remember well the year of 1953, when I was a delivery boy at the Guatalón farm in Santa Elena Río Bravo. There were inhabitants of San José who got parcels on these farms [during the agrarian reform]. But afterwards they were discouraged and afraid because the *finqueros* [farm owners or administrators] threatened them with death. They gave up the struggle. The only thing they took advantage of were the 20 little bulls they were granted, one for each *Joseño*, to be paid on credit over a period of ten years. Depending on the size, the price of each bull was from $15 to $20. Because my aunt's husband was secretary-general of the Unión Campesina, the Confederación Nacional Campesina [National Confederation of Campesinos, or Peasants], gave him a very large young bull for $20 whose value was to be paid back in 10 years.

Can you explain a little more what was happening during this time?

There are some things that I did not write about in the first book [*Son of Tecún Umán*]. It was not because I did not want to include them in the first book. Rather, it is because I just now remember them, and I think they still should be mentioned. Señor Martín, who is now deceased, was the secretary-general of the Unión Campesina in the year of Jacobo Arbenz Guzmán [president from 1951–1954]. During this time the governing body decreed that the farm owners must rent vacant lands at 5 percent of the annual value of the crops. For instance, at harvest time, the campesino might pay 5 centavos for each *cuerda* [.178 acre], or 5 pounds of corn per *cuerda* for rent. I was still little, not a man, but I remember these things well.

Then many people of San José traveled to the coast to claim their parcels of land, but many lost their lives. Not just people of San José died, people of San Luis, San Martín, and other towns also died. When other *Joseños* saw that their townsmen were dying for these parcels, they did not go. The only thing that they did was to bring 20 young bulls, all from the Guatalón farm. Each one took his bull, some not paying and others paying from $5 to $20. I refer to these things because they are very important—there was much suffering for *Joseños*.

Also, in the village of Pachichaj, the Unión Campesina was exploiting the land of the Tucs. Some of the campesinos were using the land without the authorization of the owners. Indeed, they planted for a year and harvested the milpa. But the following year they were not able [to continue doing this] because the Arbenz government fell and the owners of the farms recouped their lands.

I had to pasture the bull that they gave my aunt's husband. When it got good and fat, he dispatched it to sell the meat during a fiesta, as it was the custom to kill bulls two days before the fiesta. And thus the people bought their meat. However, when Señor Martín sold the first pound of meat, he marched to the cantinas to sip liquor. He finished selling the meat and spending the money. One could see neither a single part of the bull nor its value.

I do not know if anything was gained because when the government of President Jacobo Arbenz Guzmán fell, all was lost. The landowners were in power again, and many peasant leaders died. Those who were not killed spent a lot of time in jail as political prisoners. I know these things well because Señor Martín was imprisoned for several days. They tied him up and carried him away to jail in Sololá.

All his companions were scared, and no one wanted to go visit him. Before, he had plenty of friends. But the new right-wing authorities humiliated Señor Martín and threw him in prison.

He was waiting in the jail of Sololá when the notice came that all the prisoners were going to Petén for cruel punishment. Many poor peasants were sent to this place, and it was a blessing that he was not sent also.

   What kind of cruel punishment was there in Petén?

   Because a lot of people died in this period when Castillo Armas took over, there is a saying, "*Al que el mal entra, el mal sale* [Evil begets evil]." When Armas took over, he punished a lot of people. They said it was a liberation, but they indeed killed a lot of people. They killed a lot of people here by a farm called Memoria below Tiquisate. In a ravine they shot a lot of persons.

   They sent many to Petén for dark tortures, accusing them of being Communists and asking them why they were lying about it. They removed the soles of their feet and made them walk over salt. Do you understand? They made them walk on salt! They cut off their fingers, and then they cut off their hands, little by little. But they did not kill a person in one day. One day they would cut off the fingers, the next day the hands, until a person died. Some of the people who went there returned, and brought back the news of what happened. They talked about the horrible punishments they witnessed. A lot of people were lost. Many from San Martín, San Luis, and Sibinal died, including their friends and their close kin. A lot of people perished because of this Carlos [Castillo Armas]. But it was not because these poor people were guilty, they just wanted to work the parcels. They did not know that what they were accused of meant death. The only thing they thought of was to sow land to get bread to feed their children. In all it was a very savage thing because when the Arbenz government fell, the farm owners, the rich, approved of the killings. They approved of killing so many! And when the farm owners took back their land, the leaders of the campesinos were the first they killed. For this there was no law—to kill a Communist, there was no law. A lot of people lost their lives.[14]

   And this was what was happening to Señor Martín. But thanks to God, my deceased aunt and I fought to keep them from sending him to Petén.

   There was no way to contact Señor Martín or to know how much time he would spend in prison. My aunt and I spent days in Sololá appealing to the governor to set Señor Martín free. I wrote three letters daily with the signature of Señor Martín explaining to the governor that Martín was a man who worked in the countryside, planting corn and beans. Finally, the governor in the afternoon called Señor Martín to meet him and ask him whether he really was a Communist. We entered the office of the governor to ask him the favor of giving liberty to the señor captive. After all our pleading, the señor governor set Martín free on Wednesday at 6:00 P.M.

When the señor was freed, we went to eat a little in the market. The next day we took the road to San José on foot. When we arrived in San José, some people visited us; others did not—they feared the penalty of death.

It cost a little money for us to get Martín set free. Because my aunt did not have children, I had to go with her to Sololá. We had some centavos to go there and buy things like gifts for the governor because it was not judicial—it was political! Only the governor could determine whether to give Martín his liberty or send him elsewhere. Gradually we began to figure this out, and to save Señor Martín from death, we had to go three times. None of his companions went, and there were plenty of people in the peasant union with all the committees and leaders. But when Señor Martín fell, none of them helped, just his wife and I. No one even went to talk to him, because talking to a Communist was being an accomplice. His companions would tell us that, if they were seen with him, they would be killed too. More than anything else they hid. It was an incredible situation. This señor always got along poorly. After this incident, he spent three more times in jail. His enemies helped to put him in jail because now he could not rely on the government to help him. But we did everything possible to free him. We struggled a lot and suffered hunger and thirst because we had no money, but after all our efforts, he remained unappreciative.

After this man obtained his freedom, he abandoned my aunt and took as a concubine my aunt's niece, the daughter of my aunt's brother. Señor Martín was a shaman and told the girl that, if she did not join him, he would bewitch and kill her. Because she did not want to lose her life, the niece agreed. They lived in a rented house, which was a small house with a straw roof. When the girl realized that the man did not have any money, she abandoned him and went to work in San Luis.

Señor Martín did not want to live alone in the small house, so he returned to the house of my aunt for some months. He continued to be a dedicated shaman. Many people from other towns arrived to visit him.

He was the godfather of many children of San Benito, San Jorge, and Santa Ana la Laguna. As such, if the children became sick, he was in charge of seeing that they got ceremonies to save their lives. That is, he invoked the gods of the hills to take away their sicknesses.

In this manner, the señor fell in love with one of his *comadres* [mother of a son to whom he was godfather] in Santa Ana la Laguna. He abandoned the house of my aunt and went to live in Santa Ana, taking the *comadre* as his woman. They had a baby. He was stepfather of his godson, godfather to his son. Later, because of his drunkenness, he stopped living with his *comadre*, and he came to live again in San José with my aunt.

This man knew how to make canoes in the mountains of Santa Ana. One day he was working at this when he won the heart of a young woman of Santa Elena. The man was famous for seducing girls. By then he was about 48 years old, but he was still good for making love to girls. So the señor took the girl from Santa Elena for his woman. But this woman had a sister who also became Martín's woman. They were two women with one husband, and each one had children. The children were siblings of only one father and also first cousins since their mothers were sisters.

This is the story of Señor Martín. He wanted me to go with him for his work, but I did not like his attitude. When he saw that I did things against his advice, he looked for *calumnias* [calumnies, or false accusations] to put me in prison. On specific occasions, he accused me in court, but he was unable to have me thrown in jail.

What calumnias *did he make in court?*

Imagine, he was living in the same homesite where we were living. He said the homesite was his. But the truth is that it belonged to my grandmother. When I was on the coast, he went to the homesite to fight with the women because he claimed the homesite was his.

One night when I came back from the coast, he arrived to threaten us. He tried to hit me with a machete, but I took it away from him because he was trying to kill people. After I took it away from him, he grabbed the point, the sharp edge, and cut his hand. It bled a lot!

In court he claimed that I cut him. He also said that I struck his woman, who was pregnant. It was a delicate situation for me because he said he was going to take action against me. Then I told the mayor, "Examine these things well. Where is the wound?"

"In the hand," he answered.

"How is it that he is able to say that I put the machete in his hand? If I had done this, I could have cut him anywhere, not just in the hand. Señor Judge, consider these things well. Yes, I took away the machete because he wanted to kill a woman, my mother or my grandmother."

"But he said it was you who cut him," the judge responded.

"Señor Judge, imagine how could it be that when I drew a machete I put it in his hand? It is not possible. If I had done this, I could have cut him anywhere and not in the palm of his hand. Look, that is where the machete cut him."

It turned out that it was he who lied before the law. He just wanted to slander me. Earlier I had suffered with him, and then he did this to me. But that is life. When I told the judge that I could have cut him anywhere other than just in his hand, he lost the case.

❧ Organizing Cooperatives
7 FEBRUARY 1977

Before 1976, hardly anyone was familiar with Caritas of Guatemala, the committee for the development of the western highlands. Because of our ignorance, we *Joseños* were unable to get a loan from this institution. Some *Joseños* had been able to get a loan from the Banco Nacional de Desarollo Agrícola (BANDESA), but this institution wanted the campesino to use the title to his property (as collateral). However, we poor people scarcely have our *ranchos* [rustic homes], and we are unable to deposit our titles in the bank. Some persons have the the deeds to their houses, but some still live with their parents, who have not yet transferred ownership. And at times those who have deeds have a value written on them that is below the value of a loan they wish [to obtain]. For example, if they want a loan of $150, but their deed says that their property is worth only $100, the bank does not grant the loan because the property does not cover the value of the loan. But thanks to the radio station, La Voz de San Luis [The Voice of San Luis], we were introduced to Caritas through the radio's literacy program.

On 7 February 1977 Caritas granted us campesinos a loan of $2,677.50. Twenty-five of us with limited means received the loan with the low interest of 3 percent annually.

At this time we campesinos organized ourselves into a pre-cooperative named Los San Joseños, after a saint of our town. [They had chosen the name of their group on 19 October 1976.] Señor Mario Ramos Pop and the rest of the companions who were on the board of

directors were named by Don Domingo Quic Tzal, a resident of San
Luis. They say that this señor is the social promoter of the committee
of the western highlands. He was invited to the towns of San José, San
Jorge, San Benito, and San Martín la Laguna to organize groups of
countrymen.

I am going to talk a little about the arrival of Señor Domingo
Quic Tzal. This señor did not have acquaintances in San José when he
arrived. Earlier, when some señores first came from San Luis, they
looked for a voluntary teacher to be in charge of their literacy program
over the radio. They talked to a lot of people, but no one accepted
because of the need to work in the fields. I know this is true because
they asked me if I would teach, but I refused because of my poverty.
By the grace of God these men were able to convince Señora Lucía
Sánchez, who in turn convinced Señorita Alicia Reyes. Both of these
women were full-blooded Tzutuhils. They began to teach some señoritas to read and write. For some months they received the lessons
over the radio from the channel La Voz de San Luis, and then they [in
turn] gave them to the students.

Thus, this was how La Voz de San Luis was introduced to San
José. Don Diego, the advisor of Caritas, first talked with Señora Lucía
Sánchez, who began to talk to others. Unfortunately, the señora began
to spread word in town that some men of San Luis were offering
money with low interest but that the money belonged to the gringos,
who were giving it as payment for our sons who would go to North
America as food (human flesh). Thus, instead of encouraging the
people, she frightened them. And no one accepted the promotion of
the radio.

However, thanks to God, the other literacy teacher, Alicia
Reyes, clarified the purpose of the loan and alleviated the fears of the
people. Don Domingo communicated with Señorita Alicia, and in
turn she passed the information on to many other men and women.
However, the men did not believe her. They said she was lying because they were unaccustomed to women advocating their borrowing
money. Nevertheless, Señorita Alicia organized a number of women
into a group called Las Tamajales.

Later, when we received the loan [on 7 February 1977], we were
very appreciative. The president of the group of borrowers gave us
certain recommendations—that the money lent serve only for buying
onion seedlings, fertilizer, insecticide, and fungicide—not for buying
clothing. And he also said that every three months each one of the
borrowers has to account for his actions to Caritas, including the price
received for the onions [when they were sold]. My loan was $170.10,

but I used it to plant corn because I thought it better to sow corn first and onions later.

What is the difference between a pre-cooperative and a co-operative?

A pre-cooperative is a group in the process of becoming a cooperative. A pre-cooperative becomes a cooperative when it is legalized, or when it has legal capacity. That is, it has its formal principles signed and registered in the Instituto Nacional de Cooperativas. Before it has all of these papers, it is still a pre-cooperative.

❧ Working on the Coast
12 MARCH–2 APRIL 1977

From 12–26 March I was working on the coast preparing eight *cuerdas* [about 1.42 acres] of land to sow corn. I was working on the La Noria farm in Totonicapán. In total 42 *Joseños* were sowing milpa on this farm. Three hundred *cuerdas* [about 53.4 acres] I rented from Señor Antonio Cholotio Canajay, who was in charge of contracting the land from the farm. He divided it into parcels for each renter.

For the rent of the land each *Joseño* has to plant African Star grass. The larger the milpa one has for planting corn, the more grass one has to plant [between the rows of corn], with the provision that if the *Joseño* has not cultivated the grass well, he will not be able to harvest his corn.

During these days, I was working very hard with my helper, whom I paid $1.50 daily plus meals. But it was extremely hot, and one could make little progress in the middle of the day.

How long does the grass last, and what happens to the land after the grass is planted?

The grass lasts for about 7 to 8 years. After the corn is harvested, there is just grass. The corn is for the campesino, and the grass is for the owner of the farm. It is as if the worker were renting the land because he is poor and does not have money to pay for the use of the land, so he pays for it by sowing grass.

Isn't the amount of land for sowing corn reduced if the land is planted permanently in grass?

The land remains for the livestock, but the farm owners have a lot of land. In another year one rents another piece of land that is not planted in grass. After planting this land, one rents another piece of land and so on.

On 1 April all of us renters of land went to burn the dry grass and the trees so that we would be ready to sow when it rains. We left San José at 2:00 A.M. to catch the bus in San Martín. At 6:00 A.M. we arrived in Cocales, where I had a bus take us about an hour's walking distance. We ate a breakfast of day-old tortillas, but we drank water from the river instead of coffee. Then we left to work together.

First we fixed the edges so that we would not start a fire on adjacent farms. Each person struggled to burn his plot, but I did not finish burning mine. Instead I paid Agustín María $2.00 to finish my burning.

On Saturday, 2 April, at 5:00 A.M. I left to go to Santa Lucía Cotzumalguapa to wait for Ricardo Tziac Sicay, who was bringing a bus for a *cuadrilla* [work crew] which was working on the Ipalita farm [an annex of Ipala].

Ricardo and I arrived on the bus in Ipalita at 2:00 P.M., and the people were waiting for us. The administrators paid them, and we left, arriving in San Jorge at 12:00 midnight. The people were from San Benito, so they got off in San Jorge. They worked for only 20 days, not the usual 30, because the heat is unbearable. We had brought them to the farm on 10 March, and they earned an average wage of $2.50 to $3.00 daily, depending on their ability. My commission was $50.

❧ A Fire in Chocojomché
8–11 APRIL 1977

Holy Friday was very pleasant. At 1:00 P.M. my friend Diego came to talk about two *tablones* [carefully squared and terraced garden plots] of onions. We agreed on the price of $50 because the price is low these days.

During the same day, there was a big fire in the place called Chocojomché. The one responsible for the fire was Señor Coché Pantzay, who had burned [the vegetation] on his land [to make fertilizer]. Three days after his burning his land, there was a big fire in this place.

Although we *Joseños* never work on Holy Friday, many people went to try to put out the fire. But it was impossible because the fire had advanced until it covered the Hill of Chocojomché. It reached a summit where Señor Rubén Rímola had two houses, and both burned with everything in them.

On Holy Friday many Catholics did not go to the [reenactment of] the crucifixion of Jesús. Instead, on order of the mayor, they went to fight the fire. During the night the voracious fire illuminated the entire town until Saturday dawned.

On Saturday, 9 April, the fire continued to advance to the jurisdiction of San Martín. Both towns sent workers to try to contain the fire, but it was impossible.

On Saturday the mayor of San José went to inspect the losses of Señor Rubén Rímola. I was told to accompany the mayor, but when we arrived in Chocojomché where the two houses had burned, we found the owner quite drunk. He wanted to hit the mayor with a stick, but the mayor was compassionate. Little by little he consoled this man until he began to declare his losses—two houses with cane walls and straw roofs, bedding, corn, beans, hoes, and machetes—more than $150 worth of property.

This man said he was left with only the image of San Simón that he had taken out of the house three days before the fire. He had put it in another shed. He said that San Simón had told him in a dream that it would be better to remove his possessions from these houses because something bad was going to happen. But the man took out only San Simón, not the other things—he did not think what he had dreamed was important.

Then the mayor went to where the people were working. I did not go. Instead, I stayed behind with the man to try to console him a little more. A little afterwards many people arrived from the village of Patzilín carrying a lot of clandestine *aguardiente* [sugarcane liquor, or firewater], or *cusha* [bootleg rum].

Easter Sunday is a holy day for us Indians, but the people had to go to fight the fire. However, they could not control it. Buses from San Martín brought hundreds of people to fight the blaze.

It was the same thing on Monday, 11 April.

Here Ignacio reports another trip to the coast to plant corn with the permission of the mayor to be absent from fighting the fire. Although he was sick with headaches and fever in April and June of 1977, he continued to work, even on 1 May, the international day of labor. His face swelled with pain from mosquito bites on the coast. The weariness, bad food, and insufficient sleep made it nearly unbearable. His wife supported the planting in May with money she earned from weaving and selling typical fabrics.

*From 21 June to 2 July he and his friend Agustín María earned
$33 each by selling 50 cases of beer, 28 cases of soft drinks, 7
cases of* aguardiente, *and many cigarettes during a fiesta. When
he returned to the coast on 3 July, he discovered that animals
had eaten what he had planted. It was his son José's first trip to
the coast. Ignacio reported that he returned again to the coast
and harvested 3,000 pounds of corn from 23 July to 13 August,
his birthday, for which there was no party—just weariness and
bad food.*

❧ An Accident in the Field
16–30 AUGUST 1977

We went to work in Tamalaj to prepare a *tablón* to make an *al-mácigo* [nursery] for coffee. We prepared the plot in four days, but to finish the job we had to cover it with a lot of sticks and cane to shade the coffee plants. Don José sold me the sticks, but I had to buy the cane from a man in Xesucut.

How does one make a nursery of coffee sprigs?

There are two ways to make a nursery. The way that was used in the past was to prepare *tablones* by tilling 10–15 inches deep. When all was ready, one planted the sprigs about 8 inches apart in the pure earth. Thus, this was a nursery in the earth. The second method that we use more today is to make a nursery with the sprigs in a *pilon* [pylon] of earth inside plastic bags. The roots develop better before transplanting and the sprigs' roots grow freer. It is more difficult to extract the pylon of earth, but it is more efficient.

On Monday, 21 August, I set out for Xesucut to get cane, but before arriving, I slipped on a stone and fell, receiving a great blow which nearly cut to the bone of my shin. I could not go on for the cane. Because of the bleeding, I had to return. First I went to the health clinic, where Marta Rincón Rivas, the nurse, treated me. By the afternoon I was unable to walk because of the pain. My bone became infected, and I could not walk for three days.

On 24 August Uncle José, my wife, José, and María went to bring the cane from Tamalaj.[15] I also went, but just to tie it. It was difficult for me to make it back home.

On 25 August I asked a friend, Benato, to plant the grove of coffee. He did the work, but it was very expensive. For planting 1,200 sprigs of coffee, he charged $8 for one day. He did this because I was sick with my foot. I do not think being able to plant coffee is a divine attribute, but this friend is very arrogant because he is famous for his coffee-planting ability.

By 30 August my infected foot was somewhat better. During this time [from 21–30 August] I received five injections.

❧ My Grandma Breaks Her Hip
17 SEPTEMBER–13 OCTOBER 1977

We ate lunch on Saturday, 17 September, contentedly without knowing what was going to happen later. After lunch my wife went to the lake to wash clothing. About an hour later I went to bathe in the lake.

While I was bathing, my son José came shouting that my grandma, Isabel, had fallen in her *sitio* [homesite] and broken her hip. I did not pay any attention to the youngsters, and I continued bathing and chatting with another friend. Immediately, however, another child came to call me home. I dressed and ran to the house. When I arrived, my grandma was spread out on the ground crying in pain. She could not get up. I carried her in my arms and put her in her bed, but she was dying of pain.

Then I ran to advise my uncle Bonifacio what had happened. Only then did he and another uncle, my grandma's two sons, come to visit. When she is well they hardly ever come. My grandma stays mostly with me, and for that reason when she fell she called me. She did not want any other person.

I thought we could give her medicine, but hardly anything could be done because her hip bone was broken. She could not get up. Nor could she eat or drink for many days. All she could do was to take a shot of liquor to alleviate the tormenting pain. Five days and nights passed while we tended to her constantly (day and night), but no one could do anything for her. Finally we called a señor who cures bones. He was not able to effect a change in her condition, and he said that her broken hip could not be cured. Furthermore, he said that her death was certain. Two days later we called another bone curer who said the same thing. It was difficult to take care of her. She did not improve; she only suffered more. We called the priest to recommend her spirit to God because death seemed certain, but she did not die.

I fell sick again because of the lack of sleep and decent food. I had money, but the other relatives gave me the main responsibility

of tending to my grandma. It was my wife who suffered the most
with her.

I continued to be sick, but I did not understand why. I had to
sell more *quintales* [, or 100-pound measures, of corn] to buy medicine and some things to eat. But my sickness continued. Some of my
friends told me I should drink (liquor). They claimed that my body
was accustomed to alcohol and that the absence of liquor was making
me sick. But I was able to resist ingesting alcohol. Instead I bought
medicine from the pharmacy that I swallowed and received as
injections.

Thus ended the month of September. On 4 October, I felt a little
better, but I was worried that I had not cleaned the milpa. However,
I had no money for traveling to the coast. I offered to sell people corn,
but they wanted to buy it very cheaply. People are opportunistic when
one is in a difficult situation. To get some money, I had to sell a pump
for spraying insecticide and fungicide on plants. It cost me $22, but I
had to sell it for $12. I sold it so I could go to the coast. I need the
corn, and selling the pump made it possible to go.

On 8 October I returned to the coast, but Uncle José did not go
with me. Instead, he stayed caring for my grandma. I had to take a
friend, Eduardo, to help me. Because of worry over my grandma, I
returned home on Wednesday, 13 October. Eduardo remained for
three days to finish the work. When I returned home, my grandma
was the same.

*What happened to your grandma? How is her hip now and how
many months was she in bed after the fracture? What kind of
medicine did you use to cure her?*

When my grandma broke her hip, she was cared for by my wife
and my mother. They washed her for almost three months because
she was bedfast. Her skin tore in the region of the hip, and it was tied
in a bandage. Material came out of the wound. It was bathed in hot
water and salt, and gradually it healed. Then we went to Señor Ricardo Tziac of San Martín la Laguna who is a bone curer. It was he
who cured the bone. She was in bed three months, and three months
after that Ricardo cured the bone. Then she was able to get up. Now
she can walk. I do not know how or why the bodies of old people have
so much resistance. We were surprised, because she is already advanced in age. Still she was able to recover her health. You saw yesterday [during my visit to San José in 1982] that she is able to walk.
But when it happened, she was in critical condition because it was a

severe fracture. Today we ask her if she aches, and she says that she does not hurt at all—the fracture is completely healed. She also broke a bone in her hand, and it was Ricardo Tziac who cured it.

> *Here Ignacio reports another trip to the coast on 21 October 1977. He and Andrés went to spray Bolaton on the growing points of the corn, or* cooyos, *to control for worms. They also looked for work for crews, turning down one farm administrator who offered them only a verbal contract. They thought too much of their fellow Indian workers to agree to detrimental working conditions. On the Xebacu farm, they accepted work for Andrés at $1.50 per day and the workers at $1.25 per 100 pounds of picked cotton. When Ignacio returned to the coast on All Saints' Day, his crew complained about their tortillas tasting like diesel because they were cooked not on a stove but over a lamp with a wick. The farm administrator finally agreed to contract firewood with which to cook the tortillas and beans, but he stated he would deduct from Ignacio's commission $6 per* tarea, *or day's work.*

℧ Señor Manuel Flores Tziac Dies of Drunkenness
16 NOVEMBER 1977

On this day I worked very peacefully, not thinking of the people on the coast. Suddenly the news of the death of Señor Manuel Flores Tziac spread throughout the town. He is one of three brothers who are shamans and who have the *cofradía* [religious brotherhood] of Maximón. We did not believe he had died, because he had not been sick. When everyone confirmed his death, I ran to investigate. When I arrived at the municipality, they informed me that it was certain that Señor Manuel had died, but not of sickness—of drunkenness. They said that he began to drink on Wednesday in the afternoon with his wife. Because he drank so much, his wife went home. She did not realize that her husband continued drinking. By daybreak on Thursday, he had not appeared. They looked in all the cantinas; they looked to see if he was with their friends; they looked to see if he was with his other children. But they could not find him. They looked for him in San Martín and among the coffee groves, but still they did not find him.

Manuel prophesied that he would die by drowning. Miguel, his eldest son, remembered what his father had said before. He took the path to the shore of the lake, and when he arrived at the pier below the place where the launch docked, he saw the clothing of his father. When he arrived, he found his father dead. Then he ran to advise the justice of the peace. From there the news traveled that Don Manuel had drowned. This surprised the people because earlier he had said that he had to die by drowning. And because of his drunkenness, he went to the lake, took off his clothing and drowned. They found his corpse at 6:00 P.M.

By law he had to be transported to the amphitheater [a room with a gallery] of the hospital of Sololá, but it was difficult to transport his dead body. His children tried to obtain a canoe or a launch, but both were impossible. Then his son Miguel and I went with some friends to San Martín to look for a car or a truck, but no one wanted to make the trip. We were offering $50 just to take the cadaver and return it. We met Señores Rudy Rivera and Luis Alberto Zelaya. With these two I was hopeful because they are preachers of the Assembly of God Church. But when we arrived at the place where they preach the gospel, Miguel could hardly speak because his heart was suffering so much. Then I asked these two señores, and the answer they gave me was, "No, Ignacio, we are not able to make this trip. We are afraid to carry the dead in our car. The car is only for carrying *creyentes* [believers, church members] to the other towns, not a dead person. Moreover, we have to preach until 11:00 P.M., so, Ignacio, we are not able to serve you—perhaps some other time. We can always help you when you have a trip for *cuadrillas*. Then we can do business with you gladly." This is what the two *Martineros* told me. We returned from them without consolation.

Then in the street I met my friend Luis Có, the owner of a truck. He does not live in San Martín la Laguna; he is from San Pedro Cutzan Sibinal. I told him that we were looking for a transport to carry a dead person. He agreed to take the body to Sololá for the autopsy and bring it back to San José.

> *Here Ignacio writes about another trip to the coast, in which he and his crews faced discrimination on the Xebacu farm. His Indian crews had to pick in the green fields while the Ladinos picked in the riper fields. Also, the Ladino pickers looked upon the Indians with scorn. On payday, the administrators deducted $96 for allegedly stolen sacks and $207 for firewood for cooking. Disheartened, Ignacio stated, "Always the rich never lose anything—they always live off the poor." Consequently, he took his*

crews to the Ipalita farm, where there was less oppression. He reported that during this period he was still sick and that he treated himself with reconstituent injections of 1 cc of vitamin B-12 and 1 cc of liver abstract.

ᕙ Christmas and New Year's Day
25 DECEMBER 1977–1 JANUARY 1978

Before Christmas, I received greetings from special friends like Dr. Sexton, *licenciado* Jorge Carlos Morales Marroquín, General Fernando Romeo Lucas, *licenciado* Donaldo Alvarez Ruiz, and my *compadre* [friend] Julián Hugo Martínez. I received greetings from these honorable persons, but it was impossible for me to send cards to them because I had no money.

Ignacio later changes his mind about Alvarez Ruiz and Romeo Lucas García being special friends.

We poor people sometimes think of sending a card to greet a friend, but we are not able because we are short of money. But we Indian people have a very good custom. As a tradition on Christmas and in the middle of the night on the first day of January, everyone in the church or in his home kneels down, burns some candles and a little incense, and asks God to bless his family, his work, and his kin and friends who are distant. Only in this way are we able to satisfy our desires, because, as I have said, we poor people are not able to give to others. We only ask God to give rich blessings. After doing these things our hearts are filled with happiness for not having forgotten such persons. The distance is unimportant; it is as if we have talked with them. This is what we Indians of San José do.

If one is only in the cantinas drinking with another, one is not in accordance with God or his friends. As I have said earlier, I have passed Christmas and New Year's Day drinking and relaxing with others in the cantinas. Then I did not appreciate my life and my family, much less remember my dear friends. I only thought of who would give me a beer to calm my thirst. But now, by the grace of God, I think I am better than in previous years. Only now have I joined Alcoholics Anonymous. It is true that I do not speak of having economic resources. I am still poor, but I have learned how to stay sober in Alcoholics Anonymous, and now I also understand that I have great responsibilities—I have a wife, five children, and many expenses at home. I do not have permanent work; only at times do I earn money. Before, when I was working with *cuadrillas*, when I took a lot of *Joseños* to pick cotton, I earned a good commission. But when I returned to my town, the first thing I did was visit the cantinas and buy firewater, beer, and soft drinks for the pleasure of my friends. All of this was because of my not having control of myself. Drinking was more important than work. Well, I always liked to work, but I was working in order that others would enjoy all the money I earned with my suffering. It all went to the pockets of the barmen. One suffers a lot because of drinking.

Also, when I lost my composure, my helpers took advantage of it. As I have written, I work in the contracting of crews, and for that reason I must look for assistants in the places where people live. The helpers are in charge of looking for people and giving them money for their expenses, but this money is contingent upon their fulfilling a contract to work in a crew. They always owed me money that I gave them to carry out my work.

These helpers lost $530, and I had to pay another quantity of money before this was lost. My assistant from Tzancuil, Gabriel Celado, lost $280; my helper from Santa Ana, José Quic Toc, $60; my aide from Santa Rosa, Luciano Manuel Estrada, $100. I also gave $90 to a family for the death of their mother, and they said they would pay me later when they went to work in my crew. All of this money was lost. I thought that perhaps little by little I would get this money back, but it was futile. I gave the money to the assistants in confidence, without receipts. Later these men went to work for other contractors from Santa Elena, and I remained in this hell of owing the sum of $530. It has been so from the time of my joining Alcoholics Anonymous until now. God willing, I have to finish paying for this debt. I do not want to continue owing the rich. My main intention is to maintain my sobriety. Because of alcoholism, I have suffered a lot. I have some bad memories. Now, it is sufficient for me not to continue to drink.

I still have one vice, which is the cigarette. I do not smoke during the day, but in the afternoons. After 6:00 P.M. I spend some of my earnings to smoke any brand of cigarettes. I do not quit until the hour I go to sleep. There are nights when I have the urge to smoke 15 to 20 cigarettes—but after smoking a lot I begin to think many things, as if I am impetuous. It must be the intensity of [the nicotine in the] smoke of the cigarette. It does not allow me to sleep. I have thought a lot about giving up cigarettes, but for me it is very difficult. I ask

God that some day he will free me from this vice that is affecting my health. Sometimes I think it is because of the cigarettes that I am sick these days.

Christmas was very tranquil, and the people of San José ate and drank without any problems in the town. The only thing that I have been able to notice is that San José exists in the most profound ignorance. We Indians drink more than we eat. There are many drunks in the streets and cantinas. In the Catholic religion all the faithful go to the church to see the scene of the birth of Jesucristo. After much prayer and devotion, the hour of 2–3:00 A.M. arrives, but it is cold in the month of December in Guatemala with a lot of mist and frost. Well, they allow a great cold to permeate the church, and then they go to the cantinas to drink their shots of liquor. Then others arrive, and they begin to have a great drunken party. Thus the effect of alcohol begins.

We also have the custom of giving a drink instead of a gift to someone. For us alcohol is the best gift. But we are at fault because, if we thought more about it, we would realize it is better not to oblige someone to drink. When one forces another to drink, it is certain that one wants only the destruction of the family, because after the drunkenness come the fines and the disgust. I know from experience. For that reason, I never offer a drink or a beer to a friend. It is certainly true that I have a lot of friends, and I like to walk around with them. But for this Christmas we are drinking only Coca-Cola and fruit juices. It is very pleasant.

My family and I passed Christmas very peacefully. My wife and children appreciate me more than before. I am spending Christmas without ingesting any kind of liquor.

In the middle of the night of New Year's Eve, it was very nice. I was in the group of Alcoholics Anonymous. We had a little party. We bought a case of sodas and a little bread. We ate very happily, recounting our suffering caused by alcoholism. By the grace of God and the program of Alcoholics Anonymous, we had been able to counter the desire to drink, if only for 24 hours. After this meeting we went to our homes. When I arrived, my wife was waiting for me with chocolate to drink and bread to eat.

I slept very peacefully, and when I arose on the first day of the year, I gave thanks to God, remembering my good friend, James D. Sexton, and asking God that all be well with his work and with his family. During the day, I left town to look for a few workers to pick cotton who would leave on Tuesday, 3 January, but we had not arranged a truck or money. We first have to determine the number of people who want to go to the coast.

During the year of 1977, not many *Joseños* left for the southern coast compared to previous years. Around the months of July and August they begin to go to the coast to work on the cotton plantations to earn money to sustain their families. In October, November, and December of each year, they also go. The only ones who remain in the town are the ones who have their own land—about 20 percent remain in town while about 80 percent travel to various farms on the coast. Because I am a contractor, I know very well the mobility of the *Joseños*. But in 1977 *Joseños* did not leave until October. I did not begin to work with Andrés until November, when we took trucks to the Xebacu farm. And we went only to this farm, not others. However, in previous years, about 5–6 November, we took as many as 5 to 7 truckloads.

These days it seems that we are witnessing certain changes. The workers who normally go to the coast are preoccupied with the planting of onions. They have rented land in the jurisdiction of San José, but the land remains in the hands of the *Martineros*. The *Joseños* have to pay high rent to cultivate their lands. The *Martineros* ask a rental fee of $30 to $40 per *cuerda* annually. The land for cultivating onions produces four harvests because the time from planting to harvesting is 90 days. The *Martineros* say they are the richest, but they take their riches from San José. Most of the *Martineros* extract great quantities of corn, beans, chick-peas, peanuts, and other crops like coffee and avocadoes.

In 1950, when Señor Navichoc Ajpop was mayor, a municipal tax was levied. Then the *Martineros* began to pay 5 centavos for each *quintal* [100 pounds] of corn, beans, and other things. However, this was not very much. So in 1968, when Señor Nicolás María Mendoza was mayor, the municipality decreed a 100 percent increase. *Martineros* began to pay double the tax. For cutting firewood, they had to pay 40 centavos for each *tarea* and 10 centavos for each *quintal* of produce taken out of the jurisdiction of San José. From that time, it was difficult for the *Martineros* who extracted goods to avoid paying the tax. Thus, they sold the products in San José, or, even better for them, they rented their land as they are doing now. Also, some *Martineros* are selling their land into the hands of the *Joseños*. It is good that San José has five brooks for watering vegetables and San Martín does not have a single river for irrigation. Now I have said a little about San Martín.

ᘛIllness Among Us Indians
1 JANUARY 1978

From the night of 1 January until it dawned 2 January, I did not sleep at all because my son Ignacito suffered from a stomachache. But we did not have any medicine to give him. We just gave him coffee without sugar but with plenty of lemon. Afterwards he became a little better.

We Indians never have medicine in our houses because we do not have money to buy any. Yet we always have problems with our health. At times during the night we get a stomachache, body-ache, or a temperature because of the hard work and bad food. At times we awake sick, but we are not able to take care of our bodies because we have a lot of responsibilities for our families. Although sick, we must go to work.

Ignacito continued to be sick, but I had to wait until dawn to be able to buy some pills to kill his pain. During the day, his health improved.

On this first day of the year I planted some seedlings of coffee to be able to transplant in the month of May, if God is willing to permit me to do so. In the afternoon I left town to organize a crew. God willing, the first thing in the morning I will go to the coast.

Here Ignacio tells another lengthy account of a trip to the coast on 3 January 1978. He had to bribe both the national police and the military mobile police because he can't afford to comply with all the many regulations of the transit law. Also, he noted that Jorge del Paz, the owner of the Ipala farm, prefers Joseño laborers because they are humble and obedient. They don't explode with their machetes in hand when asked to do something. In this episode, Ignacio also stated that the farm provides each worker a daily ration of two pounds of corn, four ounces of beans, and salt and lime for hulling corn into nixtamal *(kernels of corn softened and hulled by boiling in limewater to make hominy, which is easy to grind into* masa, *or dough, for tortillas). Furthermore, Ignacio stated that the farm pays a woman four cents per worker to make tortillas. She has a helper, or* flonque, *usually her husband, who washes and cooks the beans and apportions lunch to workers in the field. Finally, Ignacio noted that on the return trip home a truck ran his bus off the road and caused it to overturn. It scared him and the rest of the passengers, but no one was hurt.*

Problems with the Mayor
JANUARY 1978

During a night in early January, some señores, who were councilmen, arrived to tell me of problems caused by the mayor, Juan
Mendoza Ovalle. The councilmen told me that the municipality had a
corn sale. But the money used to buy the corn was that of a *Martinero*.
When the mayor and councilmen finished selling the delivery of corn,
they began to count the money so that they could have more corn
delivered to sell. However, the councilmen say that they were short
$81. They believe the mayor has concealed the money, but the mayor
accuses them of hiding it, which is to say that they had stolen it. Five
councilmen are accusing the mayor. They say that in January $21 was
lost. Moreover, a municipal water outlet was installed on the property
of a North American without consulting the council. The mayor did it
by himself. The councilmen say he did it because he was given a sum
of money.
    Also, the councilmen complained that the mayor gave a stone
sculptured as a toad by the [ancient] Mayas to a *Martinero*. The councilmen had wanted to conserve it as part of their Mayan heritage, but
the *Martinero* gave a sum of money to the mayor in his house. The
councilmen also protested that two months ago a donkey was stolen in
the jurisdiction of Santa Apolonia Carcha and that it was found in an
aldea [village] of San José. This theft was never clarified, and the
mayor took the burro to the owner without prosecuting the thief because the thief is a friend of the mayor.
    All of these things were related to me in my house. For these
reasons, the councilmen do not wish to continue working with the
mayor—they want a new mayor. But I told them no because they
were very much in accord with the mayor when I was *síndico* [syndic,
or legal representative]. When I stood up to the mayor for behaving
improperly, they did not help. If these men had supported me, it
would not have been necessary for me to resign. For that reason, I do
not want to compromise myself further. Moreover, the mayor is sac-
rificing the people, and I do not want to be responsible for these
things. Only God can help them.
    At 5:00 A.M. on 8 January I left my house to take the launch for
Panajachel to attend a political meeting of the Partido Institucional
Democrático (PID). *Licenciado* Donaldo Alvarez Ruiz, the [interior]
minister of government, gave me the invitation. Everything went
well, and we dealt with political matters. He gave money for passage
to each party director from each town in the department of Sololá. He

did not come as minister but as a political representative because he is the national director-general of the PID.

On 15 January at 9:00 P.M. the councilmen came to my house to tell me of the problems they were having with the mayor. They were considering removing the mayor and asking for a new municipal election. They wanted to know whether my party would help. I told them that the party does not get involved in lawsuits. The only thing I told them was that if they did not support the mayor, the best thing for them to do would be to resign, one by one, until the mayor is left alone. Only in this manner could the party summon the town to elect a new corporation.

I told this to these men, but I am not certain what they are going to do about it. I can see that they are very weak—they lack the manliness to do what I recommended. I know them well because when I was with them in the municipality they did not back up what they said.

All day, 16 January, I was working on some pages in my house to send to Señor Sexton. In the afternoon of the same day I went to San Martín with a friend to process the resignation of Señor Bernardino Ujpán Flores, the second councilman of the municipality, who no longer wants to occupy his post because of the problems the councilmen have been confronting with the mayor for the last few months. The secretary of San Martín executed the resignation of this señor for me without charging any fees. In the night of the same day, I continued writing until midnight to clarify [edit] my pages.

❧ The Fiesta of San Jorge and Listening to a Politician
25–27 JANUARY 1978

I went to San Jorge to see the fiesta, but the whole day turned out to be annoying to me. I did not enjoy it. A lot of people went in trucks, but my family and I went on foot.

On 27 January my small son Ramón and I went to Sololá to meet with *licenciado* Jorge C. Morales, a candidate for representative from Sololá. The *licenciado* presented a long list of offerings to all present. But I do not believe a word of what the señor said. I have been in the party for some time now, and all of them pretend. They offer things, but they never deliver them. They are just lying. They want to win our confidence so that they can win the election. As the sacred Bible says, "*Se visten con piel de cordero pero por dentro son lobos voraces* [They are voracious wolves in sheep's clothing]." These señores make offers, but later they forget the poor. Politics for me is of no interest; it is just a sport—just to see and know how they speak.

> *Here Ignacio describes another trying trip to the coast to pre-pare snake-infested land for planting corn from 11 to 19 March 1978. The intense heat and humidity caused him and his uncle to sweat profusely and drink three gallons of dirty river water a day, which, together with the poor food, made them sick. Since he had to prepare his own meals, he regretted having been fussy at home with his wife. He wished his parents had not lost their farm land in San José. Although he likes to work in the country-side, at times like these he thinks about looking for a government job. The fatigue and anxiety resulted in a fitful dream about his deceased best friend, Felipe, who was killed by a car on the same farm where Ignacio was working. In the dream, Felipe was beat-ing two bullocks in the same spot where the car hit him. When the bullocks fell on their backs, Felipe burst out laughing like a madman. Ignacio surmised that the dream meant that something else would happen on this farm. Sure enough, he cut his finger with his machete while fixing a hoe. As he wrapped the profusely bleeding finger, he remembered his grandmother's advice that one should not work when one has no will.*

❧ The Pre-Cooperative Chooses Officers
THURSDAY, 30 MARCH 1978

In the morning of this day, I went to San Martín to buy meat to eat on the coast, and during the night I went to the beach to pick tomatoes to take with me to the coast. During the night we shelled corn seed to plant on the coast. In the morning, God willing, I will be there.

At 9:00 P.M. I had a meeting with a group from the cooperative to arrange a loan that we had solicited to cultivate onions. On 17 Jan-uary of this year, they made me president of a group of countrymen who received a loan from Caritas of Guatemala. I have said previously that the former president was Mario Ramos Pop. But because the boys did not want to attend the meetings, Señor Ramos did not want to continue as president of the group. He did not have the patience. During one of our discussions, no one wanted to to be president be-cause of the responsibility. Some of the boys were not acquainted with the capital, and they were afraid to enter the offices of Caritas. In addition to borrowing the money, the president has the responsibility of supervising the workers who receive the loan. Because I have needs like [those of] the other members of the group, I agreed to accept the presidency. At the same time we drew up an *acta* [memorandum of action, official document] making a solicitation for a loan of $3,135 to buy seed and fertilizer. Each of the 19 campesinos in this group would receive $165. God willing, Caritas will help us. The group knew that I am going to the coast, and for that reason we needed to take measures to procure the loan. I told them to trust in God and to have the patience to wait for the month of April. Thus concluded the session on this night.

All day I worked a lot. I am very tired.

❧ Good News Arrives While I Am Working on the Coast
FRIDAY, 31 MARCH 1978

While [Uncle José and I were] resting [after finishing planting H-3 White corn seed, an experimental seed imported from El Salvador], my friend José Hernández Toc arrived to tell me that we had received the loan in Guatemala City. I was very pleased! Because Uncle José Bizarro cannot speak [he is mute] and has a bad back, I sent him to San José with others. Then Miguel and I left for Guatemala City, arriving about noon. We ate a light lunch and caught a taxi to the office of Caritas.

Why is your uncle, José Bizarro, unable to speak and why does he have a bad back?

My uncle José is a full brother of my mother. Because he is older than I, I am not really sure [why he is afflicted]. But according to my aunt, or—better said—according my grandma, José was born normal. When he was a baby, José's father began drinking with a shaman, a *brujo* [witch]. Then the shaman and José's father entered the house where José was. The shaman believed José, who was still a baby, had a *virtud* [ability or power] to be a strong shaman. For that reason, the shaman bewitched him.

They say that the shaman bewitched José, because before the visit he was healthy and spoke in a strong voice. After the shaman's visit, José fell sick. Part of his head gave in and his hip was bent. He spent many days sick, but there was no doctor to cure him. They had to take José to another shaman to cure him [to counter the black magic]. However, little José did not recover well. His little bones were soft and tender, and his head and hip remained affected. Gradually, with many expensive ceremonies that required lots of alcohol, the shaman cured him. But José lost part of the function of his back, and he was not able to speak. Today, he is not completely mute—he can say a few understandable words. But at times he speaks, and no one can understand him. His condition is very strange.

Why did the shaman want to bewitch him?

The *virtud* that José was born with would enable him to become a powerful shaman, equal to the old shaman. Thus, the old shaman felt weakened in José's presence. For revenge, he bewitched him. It is as if you saw another professor copying [plagiarizing] your work. To keep him from harming you, you would have to do something to stop him. Only in the case of José and the older shaman, it was not just a supposition.

At 3:00 P.M. we signed the contract for a loan of $2,850. Although we had asked for $3,135, the central committee approved only $2,850, and they told me that they would not give me the check until the next day.

In the afternoon we ate and went to a lodge in San Luis. During the night I had a stomachache, which must have been from the food that I ate on the coast.

The fifth of April dawned, and we paid ten centavos for two centavos' worth of bread. After eating it, we walked to the bus terminal to eat some tortillas with meat. It is true that early in the morning we ate some bread with coffee, but for us Indians, bread has little nourishment. In contrast, tortillas are nourishing, and if we do not eat tortillas we feel weak.

At 10:00 A.M. we arrived in the office of Caritas. We spoke with the administrator to see if he would give us the check before the indicated hour, but it was impossible. At 11:00 A.M. they gave me the check, and I ran to the Banco de Londres y Montreal in Zone 9. After cashing the check, I ran to the bus terminal to take the bus to San Martín, but by the time I arrived, the bus had already left. Then I caught a bus of the Flor de Mi Tierra line that travels to Ipala. The driver is a friend of mine, and he told me that the road goes to the point where a bus runs to San Martín. Thus one could go to Escuintla and catch the bus and then transfer to the one that runs to San Martín. I was afraid to walk around in Guatemala [City] with all that money.

At 7:00 P.M. I arrived in San José. Then I sent to call everyone in the group to distribute the borrowed money. Each one signed a receipt for my security. We finished at 11:00 P.M. I recommended that they take care and work with the money but not fail to repay it.

I went to San Martín to finish paying a debt to Señora Elena Ixtamer, money that Luciano Manuel Estrada received but did not pay back. I certainly paid this debt. I did not want to blemish myself by continuing to owe the money. Señora Ixtamer told me I had received $100 but that with interest I owed $250. The señora had no compassion for me. Certainly it was another person who spent this money, but in the end it was I who had to agree to pay it back.

On this date I was to owe $60 more before I would finish paying it all off. She gave me a receipt. For this debt, I suffered a lot. Also, my wife suffered—eating and dressing poorly to pay it back. I asked Señora Elena to excuse me from paying the interest, but she would not. However, I am thanking God that I am paying off my debts. God will help me repay them because I know that I never have tried to swindle people.

More Troubles with the Mayor
28 APRIL–2 MAY 1978

On 28 April my wife and I went to bring firewood from Chimucuní. On this same day I received a written invitation from the president of the committee to improve the village of Tzarayá. In previous years, when Señor Juan Mendoza was candidate for mayor, he offered all his support to improve the villages saying, "When I am mayor, everything will improve." We drew up an act endorsing all the points of help he was offering. But when he took office at the tribunal, he forgot all that he had offered.

The inhabitants of the village do not have potable water. Previously they got it from the source [headstream] of a river in Santa Ana. [That is,] the people of Santa Ana donated the source [of the river to the people of Tzarayá] for their potable water. Because of the great dryness, the source dried up, and now two villages, Tzarayá and Patzilín, remain without potable water. For that reason the poor women have to carry water a distance of two kilometers, which is very dangerous among the barrancas.

The men of the village negotiated with Caritas to obtain potable water. Caritas agreed and completed the work necessary to bring the water a distance of 12 to 14 kilometers. However, the señor mayor decided to impose a tax when he saw that the residents were able to get their water. He is always ready to collect taxes, but they do not help the residents. And the men of the village do not wish to pay the taxes in the municipality of San José. They agree to pay the taxes, but they want the money to stay in the village so that they can maintain the system; that is, so that they can buy supplies of pipe when it breaks in the winter [rainy season, from May through October in most of the region; actually summer in terms of the sun] and thus repair the water system when needed.

The committee of the village of Tzarayá knew very well that we had drawn up a document in which Señor Juan Mendoza offered his help. I have the document, and they asked me for a copy to present to the departmental government of Sololá so that they could receive benefit from the municipal tax.

With much pleasure I certified a copy of the act for the committee to improve Tzarayá. The members of the committee were very appreciative.

On 30 April there was a meeting in the town hall. First, the director of the school spoke about forming a sports committee in accordance with the instructions of a technical supervisor of the department of Sololá. Some of the people supported his proposition. Second, the mayor spoke about demarcating the landmarks of the town in the month of May. He says that then he will apportion the communal lands to all the people of San José. Third, Señor Benjamín Bizarro spoke about the three villages—Pachichaj, Patzilín, and Tzarayá. He wanted to know whether the municipality plans to give the people of these villages [which are under the municipal jurisdiction of the town of San José] part of the land. The mayor said that they would be taken into account but that they would receive the land on the slopes.

The declarations of the mayor are lies. He is not able to apportion land to the residents. Both Benjamín Bizarro and I know that San José does not have communal land. Perhaps there is a little, but it is not fit to cultivate since it is all barrancas (land with deep gullies). The mayor said that there is no money with which to continue the negotiations. Again he asked each person to give $2 to insure that they will receive their *cuerdas* of land. I said, "I certainly am not going to give a single centavo. It's a shame that the people of my town continue to lose their money." I also said that it was possible for the people to contribute $2 each but that the mayor should legalize the committee for improvements and that each contributor should receive a receipt to show how the money is spent.

It has already been a year that a provisional committee for improvement has been functioning, but the committee still has not been legalized [that is, obtained written endorsement signed by the governor of Solalá]. Instead everything is manipulated by the mayor. For that reason, I asked that he legalize the committee in order to safeguard the funds. But the señor insists on illegally exploiting the people for money. The committee is in charge of taking care of the money, and then they give it to the mayor, who is in charge of spending it.

ꙮMother's Day
10 MAY 1978

Mother's Day was celebrated in this town, but we Indians did not give anything to our mothers because we do not have the means with which to give gifts. On the radio we hear that the Ladino people are giving things of value, but that is because they have jobs and they receive money monthly—we do not. We truly struggle to earn our daily sustenance. Mother's Day is celebrated in this town, but those who celebrate are the schoolchildren. They invited their mothers to come receive bouquets of flowers. That was what my two children, María and José, did also. They invited their mother, offering her their affection with branches of wild flowers. This indicates eternal love— love that comes from the heart. The monetary value is not important—just the significance [of the day].

ꙮA Visit to the Dentist and a Fire
11–14 MAY 1978

Because I had an intense pain in my mouth, I stayed inside all day. Two bad teeth bothered me constantly. The pain was the same as when I was working on the coast—a lot of suffering. These days, however, the ache is incessant. I have not been able to eat or sleep peacefully.

My teeth ached all night long. For that reason, I realized it was necessary to go to Santa Bárbara to have the teeth extracted. When I arrived in this town, they told me that the dentist was out gathering firewood in the forest. I had to wait nearly two hours. When he arrived, he pulled my two teeth and charged me very little—35 centavos for each extraction.

At 11:00 A.M. I left Santa Bárbara for San José. The pain and the heat of the sun exhausted me. I arrived at 1:00 P.M., but because of the heat and the pain I had a temperature in the afternoon. I lay down in my hammock, and I was only able to drink sodas. I did not go anywhere else.

Early in the morning about 12:45 A.M. on 14 May, I was lying in bed but not sleeping when suddenly I heard the clamor of alarm bells in the church. Nearly the whole town was asleep, but the bells continued. Then the *alguaciles* [runners and policemen] ran throughout the streets to wake up the people and tell them to help the family of Gerardo Alberto Ujpán V., whose two houses were on fire. The *alguaciles* said that the children were burned. Although I had a great pain in my mouth, I managed to go see what was happening.

When I arrived at the homesite, the fire was consuming the houses. Nearly all townspeople were there with jugs and vats of water trying to control the flames, but it was impossible. Everything in the house was burned. All of the belongings and clothing of the entire family. The children were in their underclothing without bedclothes. Twelve hundred pounds of chemical fertilizer was burned, along with hundreds of pounds of corn, beans, and chick-peas. Moreover, a gasoline motor for irrigating onions was destroyed. Also, Señor Gerardo Alberto burned a hand while removing some things from inside the house. However, all of his family was well; they were just crying because everything they owned had burned.

Many people were asking why the houses had burned. There was quite an uproar. Señor Gerardo Alberto told the authorities that his enemies had burned his house. But his wife contradicted him. She said that the señor was drinking in the house and smoking near the gasoline motor when the fumes ignited. When he saw that the house had caught fire, he got all the children out. Some of the members of the family went to sound the church bells, and others went to tell the *alguaciles*. They said that they lost $3,000.

The people were asking the family about their losses when suddenly at 3:45 A.M. a big quake jolted everyone. Nearly all of us had left our children at home, and because of the quake we ran home. No one stayed with the unfortunate family. The rest of the night I did not sleep. The ache in my mouth intensified because I had talked a lot and the cold affected it.

❧ A Meeting for a Cooperative
14 MAY 1978

I did not go out the entire day. My wife went to San Martín to buy two *ponchos* [blankets] to give to Señor Gerardo. It was a little help for him because he does not have any bedclothes. This man whose house burned is my first cousin on the side of my father.

On this day some men and women met in my house. I invited them to discuss organizing a cooperative because I see that each day the *Martineros* exploit us *Joseños* more. San José is ignorant to emphasize individuality. If we were able to work together we could resolve problems that we have confronted since the time of our ancestors, who could not help themselves because they had neither knowledge nor support. But we *Joseños* do not want to continue being a party to the profits of the *Martineros* who have manipulated all of the agriculture and business of our beautiful town. It is for that reason that I had sent an invitation eight days earlier to the señores of San Luis—Domingo Quic, the social promoter of Caritas of the western highlands; his first cousin, Señor Pedro Tzal, the announcer of the San Luis radio station, La Voz de San Luis; and Señor Ricardo Pantzay Toc, president of the cooperative Cajá of San Luis.

These men accepted the invitation that I sent them, and they arrived in my house to guide us toward organizing a cooperative by overcoming individualism [and collectivizing]. There was much good discussion. It was midnight before we realized it. The señores from San Luis left for their town, but we stayed and chatted for a half hour more. We agreed to meet in three days, and both the men and women left content. They were very appreciative of my efforts.

I am continuing to think a little about doing something for the good of my townspeople. For this reason, I want to form an agricultural cooperative for various services. I have faith in God; I have to stimulate my dear *Joseños*. I do not want to die without doing something worth remembering in my dear San José. It is true that in this town the Catholic religion dominates, but the priest never helps us organize. The only thing important to him is the value of the masses that he conducts daily. But he never guides the indigenous people. Maybe he thinks that if the Indians begin to discover things, he will become unsuccessful with his business with the mass. He is the priest of San Martín, and he always comes to make mass in San José, collecting $8 to $12 for a half hour he spends making a mass. He makes in 30 minutes what the poor Indian makes in an entire week. And he never thinks about arousing the Indian from his ignorance. But God willing, we are going to fight. This is not contrary to the religion, because we are very Catholic; each one of us is baptized and has received Holy Communion. We want to fight against the poverty that is oppressing us!

❧ Another Meeting About Forming Cooperatives
17 MAY 1978

On this day we met again to discuss the forming of a cooperative, but not all of the groups who had participated three days ago arrived. The only ones who came were Abraham Có M., president of the group Nueva España Sembradores de Maíz [New Spain Corn Growers], and Señor Benjamín Bizarro Temó, president of the group Juan Evangelista. We talked about many important things, such as how an agricultural cooperative should be organized. Before we realized it, the hour of midnight arrived. We agreed to meet again within a few days to formalize our discussion.

However, when the day of our next meeting arrived, not one group came. The only one who came was one of the boys from my group, Señor Agustín María Bizarro Toc. For that reason, we did not settle a thing!

On Sunday, Agustín María Bizarro and I set out to go to each house to inform everyone of a meeting to arrange the matters concerning the cooperative. Still not all of them came. Only four of us were there—Abraham Có, Benjamín Bizarro Temó, Agustín María, and myself. We four began to complete the organization. We planned to borrow money to put up a small shop in front of the municipality to try to make a little money. We considered installing the shop on the main day of the fiesta (24 June). But nothing came of it. My three companions weakened and failed to take our plans seriously. They forgot completely.

❧ Heavy Rains Cause Severe Damage
1–16 JUNE 1978

After lunch, José, Ramón, and I went to Xesucut to clean onions. While we were returning at 4:00 P.M., it began to rain heavily on us. It continued to rain heavily until 7:30 P.M. My wife was not able to cook dinner because water leaked into the kitchen. We ate a little bread with coffee, but there was very little bread because I did not have any money.

Wednesday, 7 June, dawned very sad because it had rained too much. At 6:00 A.M. my youngster and I went to Panasajar to check our coffee grove, but when we arrived in Pachichiyit, we could not recognize Panasajar—everything had been swept away by the torrential rain of last night.

We could reach only the side of Panasajar. When we reached the place where we had planted the coffee, there was nothing—it was buried and washed out by the current of the river. A lot of people lost coffee [trees] and *cuerdas* of onions. When the municipality investigated, it calculated that *Joseños* and *Martineros* lost about $20,000. Panasajar is very level, and they do a lot of cultivating there. But it is dangerous because of the water that flows in the winter [the rainy season] from the hills and the Volcano of San Martín. When it rains heavily, there is flooding. About 12 years ago the same thing happened.

Also, Señor Gerardo Ujpán, who just lost his house in a fire, lost all of his onions. He was hoping to recover his losses from the fire with his crop of onions. Now he has hardly anything, and he does not know what he is going to do.

⌘ José Is Ill
16 JUNE 1978

José, my eldest son, began to suffer with a stomachache. I thought it was only a simple illness, but it turned out not to be so. Each day he became worse. We gave him many kinds of medicine from the pharmacy until I ran out of money, but he continued to be seriously ill. When he woke up today, he was in critical condition. His whole body was bloated. He was unable to get out of bed, and he passed out—he was at the point of dying!

My wife and I were very sad because the boy is still sick and we have no money. As I have said many times, we Indians are not accustomed to having medicine in the house because we do not have the money. I needed to buy medicine, but I am without money.

My wife then heard the news that in San Martín there is a man who is able to cure without making ceremonies as the shamans do. Well, my wife, her mother, and a sister carried the boy on their shoulders to San Martín. They did not return to San José until 6:00 P.M. My wife said that the man kneeled down and asked God to touch the sick person. And he did it—he touched the the patient, made him move a lot, and anointed him with oil. He said the the boy was about to die because the sickness he had was not the kind that could be cured by medicine from a pharmacy. He said that the child suffered from an inward blow he had received when he fell from a tree. When they asked the boy questions, he said it was true that he had fallen from a tree while cutting firewood. Everything the man said was true! Also, he said that he was going to cure the boy little by little. He said, "I am not a shaman, nor do I practice magic. God, the King of the universe, heard my prayer asking for a cure for someone who is a human being." This man is an Indian of humble appearance, dressed in typical clothing, and he did not charge for the cure.

At 11:00 P.M. my wife came back [from another trip to the curer in San Martín]. Because I was very busy, I had not gone with them. I worked all day, and at 8:00 P.M. I had to go to a celebration of the second anniversary of the founding of Alcoholics Anonymous.

What this man did was strange to me. I asked my wife whether they bought candles and other things. She told me no!

On 19 June my wife and I wrapped the child and carried him again to San Martín to the señor who was curing him. I also wanted to see whether he had some book. But he does not have a book, nor does he burn candles. The only thing he did to make the cure was to kneel and beseech God to grant good health for the child. I did not much believe my wife when she told me, but when I saw it, I believed it. This man has a great ability to make cures. He told me that it would not be necessary to bring him again and that the sickness will gradually disappear. He did not want to charge me, but I insisted that he accept a few dollars [as a token of appreciation] for his work.

And that is the way it was. Little by little, the child regained his health. Nevertheless, we passed the fiesta of San Juan Bautista sadly because we had a sick child.

❧ Corn Is Scarce
15–23 JULY 1978

The whole town is alarmed due to the absence of corn. Many people are asking for it. Unfortunately, we also ran out of corn. We wanted to buy some, but it was impossible because there is none anywhere.

From 18–23 July three of us—Señor Agustín, Uncle José, and I—were on the coast harvesting corn. We worked very hard bundling the corn. Because of the loads of corn, it was difficult to cross the river, which had risen very much because of the heavy rains. Under the heavy load of corn, my uncle and I fell into the water two times. Soon our shoes were soaked.

The following is a list of all my expenses on the coast from planting the corn:

(1) From 11–19 March, travel and refreshments..............$ 11
(2) Payment to José   12
(3) 31 March–4 April, travel and refreshments..............   10
(4) Value of H-3 Salvadoreño seed..........................   100
(5) 11–17 April 1978, travel and other expenses.............   10
(6) H-3 Salvadoreño seed to reseed   6
(7) Value of chemical fertilizer   21
(8) First hoeing and second hoeing and fertilizer............   22
(9) Travel to inspect the milpa   5
(10) 20 June, travel to knock down the field   4
(11) 27–29 June, planting grass for using land   8
(12) 11 July, travel to inspect the field......................   5
(13) 18–23 July, travel for harvesting.......................   15
(14) Assistants for harvesting.................................   20

In total my expenses were $159 for travel, food, fertilizer, seed, and paying helpers. They do not include my daily wages. At home I calculated 26 *quintales* valued at $7 a *quintal*, or $182. But I spent $159, which means a difference of $23. I earned hardly anything because I lost many days of work. But in all endeavors that's the way it is— sometimes one gains and sometimes one loses.

❧ Alcohol at My Birthday Party
13 AUGUST 1978

Thanks to God for my having completed 37 years of life. I have suffered a lot, but I always give infinite thanks to the King of the universe for having granted me a year more of life.

My wife and I arranged to prepare a little lunch for my family and friends—José Smith and his wife, Josefa García, and Ignacio Cuéllar Chacón and his wife, Gloria Sicay. While my wife was preparing lunch, I went for a walk with José and Ignacio. When we returned, my wife had lunch ready. While we were gone, Josefa had given my wife a beer, and she drank it. At 1:30 P.M., which is about the usual time for us Indians, my wife served us lunch.

During lunch my wife and our guests drank some shots of liquor that José had brought. Then Ignacio went to buy more liquor. After lunch José was the first to drink the first gulp, and then they all began to drink until everyone got drunk. Then my wife's parents, who were very drunk, came to our house. They did not eat lunch, but they brought more liquor. Then José and Ignacio bought more bottles.

At first it was very nice, but later for me it was distressing because they all wound up drunk. Worse, my wife became very drunk out of her mind, losing control and acting foolish. I had to watch her.

At 7:00 P.M. my friends left for their houses, but others arrived, although they did not stay long. At 10:00 P.M. my wife began to suffer a stomachache from so much alcohol, which bothered me a lot. I was alone in the house, and our children had already gone to sleep. I ran to the tienda to buy mineral water and a beer. When I arrived, my wife had fallen from her bed and was spread out on the floor, which scared me very much. I picked her up and put her on her bed and gave her mineral water, but she continued to suffer. None of the children wanted to sleep with her. Finally my wife woke up aching, but she had her senses. She told me she did not remember anything, and she asked me what happened.

Thanks to God I did not drink or smoke a cigarette. All day I was sober. My heart was telling me to stick forever to the program of Alcoholics Anonymous, which had changed me, because before I was a man who was not able to keep himself from drinking. I am realizing that alcohol is not good for an alcoholic. When I drank the first swallow, I could not stop until I was drunk. But God has changed my life, because now I can be at a party without drinking because I first think of the program of Alcoholics Anonymous. I have not forgotten what a disgrace I was earlier.

On 14 August I did not leave for work all day long. We suffered a little because we had already arranged to go to work in Chimucuní. However, my wife was not able to cook breakfast or make lunch, and it was impossible for me to leave. María warmed some tamalitos for breakfast. For lunch José went to borrow a little dough for the tortillas. María made them. My wife did not eat all day long.

❧ Señora Irma Tuc de Velásquez Is Raped
16 AUGUST 1978

Señora Irma Tuc de Velásquez is an auxiliary nurse who works for INCAP [Nutritional Institute of Central America and Panama]. She is working in the village of Tzancuil, where she stays on some days, but on other days she returns to her town of San Martín la Laguna. To get back to San Martín, she has to go through San José by a place called Panasajar. That is where the unruly Héctor Có Muñoz, a native of San José, was hiding. When Irma, the nurse, passed by this place, Héctor surprised her and carried her to the thickets. As it was night and no one could help her, Héctor pinned her down and violated her. The poor woman entered the town of San José crying. I witnessed when she arrived at the commissary to demand that Héctor be punished for the evil deed.

Then the guards of the municipality went to capture him, but they could not find this villainous man. They then called on his father, who said it was true that Héctor was at Panasajar at that hour. Then they made sure that Héctor had committed the crime, and about 10:00 P.M. he presented himself before the commissary. At that instant, the woman recognized him and hit him in the face with her fist saying, "You are the one!" They then locked Héctor up in jail. Much alarm spread throughout the town because never before in the history of the town had *Joseños* seen such abuse.

It all turned out strangely because the father of the violated nurse is one of the famous *huizaches* [pettifoggers] of San Martín, called Renato Tuc Sicay. For many years he has been working with lawyers in many kinds of trials. He said that the man who had violated his daughter was going to be locked up for many years because he has a good knowledge of the laws. On the contrary, the girl's destiny was to have Héctor locked up for only a day and night in the jail of Sololá. Everyone was surprised when they saw Héctor drinking liquor in a cantina. For certain, no one knows why he did not stay in jail.

Now all of the indigenous women of my town are afraid to walk alone because they may be violated by other wicked men, and the authorities will not help. They saw well that the villainous Héctor was in jail only 24 hours. Everyone condemns this kind of abuse. Unfortunately, our wives are left in charge of irrigating our tomato and onion fields when we go to the coast. And now none of them feels safe.

❧News of Nicaragua on the Radio
23–24 AUGUST 1978

At noon, I was listening to the news when the National Palace of Nicaragua was taken by the guerrillas of the country, demanding liberty for the political prisoners.

On 24 August I was listening to the radio when the political prisoners were set free. At 10:00 A.M. they were sent to an airplane of the Hercules de Caracas Venezuela line. Then the guerrillas headed in the direction of Panama. This is what the Radio Mundial of Guatemala announced.

❧A Farm Administrator Hides from Us
11–12 SEPTEMBER 1978

In Santa Lucía we ate breakfast and caught a bus that took us to Cerro Cristalinas. From there we traveled on foot, passing through many farms until we reached Ipalita. When we talked to the administrator, he told us that it was possible to begin work on 25 August, but with the condition that the people would have to work by the piece. However, I did not want that because I did not want bad working conditions for the people of my race. We continued to look for work for the people, but at a reasonable daily wage [by the pound]. From Ipalita we went on foot to San Carlos. When we arrived at this farm, the administrator hid because he thought we were members of some underground group. He did not want to receive us. The field boss told us that the administrator has been threatened with death. I told him not to be afraid of us because we were just humble persons looking for work for a crew of *Joseños*. Only then did the señor tell us that the farm needed people but not until cotton-picking time in November.

❧Torrential Rains and Sleeping Like Pigs on the Coast
18–23 SEPTEMBER 1978

On 18 September, Andrés arrived in San José with a crew at 11:00 A.M. We loaded the people onto the trucks and left for the San Marcos Niza farm.

At 4:00 P.M. we ran out of asphalt. On a very bad road, we arrived at 8:00 P.M. on this farm. It was almost raining. The owner of the truck was very angry because of the long distance we had to travel on a very bad road. Sunup of 19 September came, but the people did not work because of the rain. The people of Tzancuil left for the Cellbilla farm, and those of San José remained in San Marcos Niza. It rained slowly all morning. Then from 11:00 A.M. until nightfall it rained torrentially, and the wind blew hard. It was frightening. I slept on some planks very uneasily because of the hurricane winds. It rained all night until sunrise, 20 September.

In the morning we passed around a list of workers. The administrators ordered that, if we were going to participate, the crew must go to work because the farm cannot afford to feed so many people. It was possible for the people to go to work under a light rain. I ate beans and tortillas with Andrés.

At 7:45 we left San Marcos for the Cellbilla farm, where the people of Tzancuil were working. It is very far, and there were a lot of landslides and rain. We traveled six kilometers on a muddy road. Then we crossed a river with our clothing wet and our shoes muddy. I was feeling very regretful for having placed myself in such circumstances. One cannot endure more unbearable suffering than walking through this plantation. Finally we reached the Cellbilla farm.

We wanted to look for the place where the people were working, but it was impossible. We were too tired from so much walking, and worse—our clothing was muddy on both sides. We reached a river where I washed my trousers, shoes, and feet. I had been walking barefoot because I could not stand the weight of the shoes with mud on the sides. As I was walking barefoot, a wire punctured my right foot. I lost blood, and the ache was severe.

When we arrived in La Cellbilla, we wanted to find a tienda where we could drink some sodas and eat some bread to satisfy our hunger and quench our thirst, but on this farm there was nothing. We asked a señora to sell us lunch. First she told us she had none. Later she had a little sympathy for us and gave us five tortillas and a little broth, but she charged each of us 75 centavos.

We remained there in the sheds. It continued to rain until nightfall. At 7:00 p.m. I caught a bad cold because of my wet trousers and shirt. I wanted to get near a fire and dry out, but I could not light the wet firewood. We slept in the sheds with some old sacks like pigs and very dejected. We had left our bedding in Niza, but due to the torrential rains and our weariness, it was impossible to go back to that farm. The rain did not let up, and all night long Andrés and I suffered.

On 21 September at 4:45 a.m. we left La Cellbilla looking for the road back to San Marcos Niza. We walked a long distance to reach a road, but it was not the same road that we had taken yesterday. At 7:00 a.m. we passed a tienda where we ate bread and water. Immediately we continued walking until we reached San Marcos Niza.

At 9:00 a.m. we ate tortillas with salt. Still it continues to rain. I regret having brought the people. I am mainly worried about the women and children, because they are weak. The radio said that no one is able to travel on the roads because they are obstructed. I am worried about my family and the families of the workers who are in San José.

At 1:00 p.m. we ate the tortillas that they gave us. At 7:00 p.m. I gathered some planks in a tractor shed the same as I did last night. All night there was wind and rain until dawn Friday, 22 September.

The workers went to work under the rain. During the three days from Wednesday to Friday, they could work only two hours each day because of the rain. But working two hours under rain is the bitterness of a poor person.

When the sun came up, it was raining, and I do not know whether it is going to clear. I am very worried. Also, the workers are very distressed about their families because on the radio the news said that the department of Sololá was also affected by the torrential rains and that the road from San Luis to San Martín is blocked.

Andrés and I are not able to leave this farm, and there is no way to communicate with the people at home. We are completely isolated, but by the grace of God, we are all alive. My worry is for the families of the people and my family, but who knows whether we will be able to go home this week. It is important for me to go to San José to advise the families of the workers.

At 10:00 A.M. they attended to us on the farm. They paid me the travel money and the advance that I had given the people, but only in receipts. In effect they are going to give us the money in Retalhuleu. We considered walking to Palo Gordo, but it could have taken about three days to reach the asphalt road. The administrator suggested taking the road via the small parcel, La Máquina, to Cuyotenango. But it would still be difficult to cross the Can River.

We waited until 1:30 P.M., and then we crossed the river in a canoe, but with much fear because the river is immense. After crossing the river, we had to try to find an unfamiliar road, and there was no one to give us information. All the people were closed up in their houses because of the rain. We continued on the road until we reached the asphalt, which is located at the B-14 [road marker] in the middle of La Máquina. There we caught a bus of the Soto Figueroa line which let us off in Cuyotenango. From Cuyotenango we walked until we reached the Sis River. The bridge had been swept away by the water, and hundreds of vehicles were on both sides.

At 6:30 P.M. we arrived in Retalhuleu and looked for the office of the international agent. This is where we actually received the money for the travel and the advance.

At 8:00 P.M. we arrived in Mazatenango, and then we entered the San Luis Inn. Unfortunately, we had to pay $2 each for a place with lots of mosquitos. I did not sleep at all.

On 23 September we ate breakfast in Mazatenango, and immediately afterwards we took a streamlined bus for Cocales. From there we took another bus to San Luis. But when we arrived in this town, they told us that the road from San Luis to San Martín had collapsed. There also were no launches to cross the lake. Together with some *Martineros* we had to pay a man of San Luis to take us in his canoe in the rain. From each of us he collected $2.

When we arrived in San Martín at 5:00 P.M. under bursts of rain, we were giving thanks to God. My family was very worried. Then I went to the houses of the people to tell them their kin are alive. They were pleased.

ॐ Rains in San José
24 SEPTEMBER 1978

I am resting a little. Because of the rain one is unable to work. In the jurisdiction of San José there have been a lot of losses of different kinds of planted fields—corn, onions, chick-peas, and most of the coffee. My friend Andrés lost 85 coffee sprigs he was producing. Others lost more. In San José alone the damage was about $3,000. Also, a lot of onion seeds were lost, and most *Joseños* live by cultivating onions. The damage of the storm will cause us to suffer in these times.

ॐ Another Meeting to Form a Cooperative
MID-OCTOBER 1978–17 JANUARY 1979

In the middle of October I discovered that my friend Abraham was forming a pre-cooperative of artisans, but earlier we had agreed that the cooperative would be an agricultural one. I do not know why my friend took another path [changed his mind]. When I realized what he was doing, I decided to tell my companions that we should meet with Abraham and his companions to keep them from taking another direction. We needed them to remain with us to have more strength.

We had the meeting in the lounge of the school. About 30 men arrived, and we discussed many things. However, in this meeting there were three oppressors [who belong to a group of dissidents]. I believe perhaps these persons think they are rich, but the truth is that they do not have anything. I will never forget all the bad things these dissidents said about us. It seems that this group is always in opposition. However, this afternoon, we were able to discuss matters a little better.

As I have said earlier, we had already designated who would be on the board of directors, but when we found out that Abraham wanted to form another cooperative, we decided to give the presidency to him so that he would not lead away his followers and we would gain a larger number for a better functioning of the cooperative.

This afternoon, we prepared the [list of persons] for the board of directors. In the same afternoon we agreed to have the next meeting on 2 November, because it seemed that everyone would be home resting on that day.

We continued chatting with the boys to insure a greater number of members for the 2 November meeting. We had set the hour at noon, but it did not turn out to be so. The boys did not begin to arrive until 2:00 P.M. Unfortunately, they did not give us permission to meet in the assembly hall of the school. The person who had the key is a son of the Cojs, who always were resentful when they heard of the organization. Thus we met in front of the municipality under a ceiba tree. Because it was a fiesta [All Souls' Day], some of my companions took off to drink, but the majority attended the meeting.

In this meeting we agreed to contribute $60 [each]. The first part of this contribution would be $15 each. We agreed to use this money to put up a tienda for selling basic grains and other consumables. We also said that we will rent a house for the tienda and will agree with whoever is able to contract the house.

After the meeting the boys began to come to my house for some weeks with their $5-to-$10 contributions. We allowed the months of November and December to raise the money because giving the whole $15 at once would put the families in arrears. It was my idea to give the contributions gradually so as not to feel the blow.

In these first days of January, Antonio Cholotio Canajay, with another boy, went to ask Señora Virginia Miranda to rent a house for the tienda. She did not refuse them, and she said the price was $12. We had some doubts because the husband of the señora lives outside of town because of work. At an opportune moment when he came, we asked him, and he told us the same thing. For us it was good. Then we told the rest of our companions.

This house is not in the center of town. We wanted it that way so that it would not interfere with the business of other tiendas already existing. Thus, the central tiendas would not feel bothered.

On 12 January of 1979 my companions ordered some things to sell. But it was very little. Unfortunately they lost a *quintal* of *panela* [unrefined sugar] (which was not found until two months later). Three days later they ordered another load of *panela* with the same luck. The truck in which it was coming broke down on the road. The truck spent about 20 days in the repair shop of San Miguel Cotz. The *panela* sat in the truck all of that time.

On 14 January, a day when I had to go to the coast to inspect a crew, my companions decided to open the tienda. To sell sugar, they had to go and ask Señor Pedro Ixtamer in San Martín to lend us a *quintal* of sugar. Because the boys did not have much money, they could not bring back much in the way of little things for the shop.

They decided to open the shop, although it was not completely ready. We did not have a counter or shelves on which to display the things for sale. However, Antonio Cholotio Canajay was enthusiastic, and he found some boxes on which to place the items for sale. The board of directors obtained some planks to make a counter. We did not have the money to pay a carpenter, but one of us was something of a carpenter, although his carpentry was somewhat a joke. He worked hard, but we had to help him, and, for lack of experience in carpentry, it was almost the middle of the night before we finished the counter.

On 15 January the tienda dawned with its counter, but it still lacked shelves. Later these were made, too.

When the tienda opened at noon on 14 January, Antonio Cholotio Canajay was the companion in charge of selling. On this afternoon the tienda sold $15 worth of merchandise. On Sunday, Antonio also was the salesman, and the tienda sold a little more. On this day we organized turns to sell in the tienda.

On 16 January it was my turn to sell, beginning at 6:00 P.M. until the same hour of the following day. After my turn, I took another turn for my wife, who also is enrolled in the cooperative.

❧ A Child's Cry Is an Omen
24 JANUARY 1979

On this day we went to the Ipalita farm to bring back a crew. At 2:00 A.M. Andrés and I left my house to catch the bus in San Martín headed for the coast. It happened that when we were passing the place called Xechumil, which is near my town, suddenly I heard a child crying out in pain. I heard the cry clearly, close to my house. Then I asked my traveling companion if he had heard the cry too, and he had. It was very strange for us because the hour was quiet and almost all the people were sleeping. The cry bothered me a lot because I thought it was the spirit of someone who was going to die.

By the time we arrived in San Martín, I had forgotten what I had heard. Then we boarded the bus for the coast.

At 6:00 A.M. we arrived at Santa Lucía Cotzumalguapa, where we ate breakfast. However, while we were eating I remembered the crying that we had heard. I worried that one of my children would suffer some misfortune because the crying was very near my house. I entrusted myself to God, and we continued toward the farm. When we arrived at this place, the boys began to settle the accounts, and I forgot what I had heard earlier.

At 6:00 P.M. the workers received their pay. We ate dinner on the way to Cocales. Then we boarded the truck at midnight. When we reached San Martín, we let four workers off. When we arrived in San José, we finished unloading the traveling bags, and then we went to Andrés's house to settle our accounts. We finished about 4:00 A.M., and then I went home. My wife prepared something to eat, and this is how 25 January dawned.

❧ A Car Hits My Sister and Her Children
25–26 JANUARY 1979

In the episode that follows, Ignacio not only typed out the account but he also gave me copies of two certified legal documents concerning the accident of his sister and her children. From these documents I have added details in brackets that Ignacio omitted in his written account.

In the morning my wife told me that we should go to the fiesta in San Jorge because a lot of neighboring towns would be visiting. I told her, "Let's go." My children got up and ate breakfast, changed their clothing, and got ready to go.

I do not know why, but I began to regret having told my family we were going to the fiesta. Then I began thinking about the cry that I had heard in the morning of the previous day. I was annoyed, and finally I did not go. My wife became a little angry with me because I first said yes and then no.

But if my wife and children wanted to go to the fiesta, they would have to go in a truck. My wife left somewhat upset. But I had hardly slept the whole night, and I had agreed that my children could go to the fiesta. The house was silent during the day, and I slept well.

When I arose, I was very hungry. I went to a tienda of the cooperative to eat some bread and drink Pepsi-Cola. After eating I gave some big sighs as if something was going to happen—I felt very heavyhearted!

At 3:00 P.M. my wife and children arrived home uneventfully. I gave thanks to God that they had returned without anything happening to them. My wife and I sat down on the porch, and she told me all that they had seen at the fiesta. We ate a little fruit that they had brought from San Jorge. My wife felt like drinking a beer, and this was what she was drinking when my brother, Jaime, arrived to tell me that my sister, Julia, had had an accident between the boundaries of San Jorge and San José.

I was completely relaxed on the porch of the house without my shoes and wearing only a T-shirt. At this moment I thought a lot of things because my sister did not want me as a brother—she nearly despised me. Finally, with a softer heart, I took the road for the commissary to advise them of the accident.

I found the commissary closed, the tribunal closed, and the secretary's office closed. It was impossible to tell a single authority. Also, no one would give me information regarding which car had injured my sister and her children. I asked many people, but no one would say. I could get no response.

Finally, a friend from San Diego la Laguna gave me the legal information. He said that the car, a blue Toyota pickup, belonged to Señor [Roberto Lionel] Cojbx [Sosa] of San Martín la Laguna. Then I took the road to San Jorge. In a place called Chuachoj I found Señor Cojbx driving his car, good and drunk. He did not want to stop, but fortunately a truck was obstructing the narrow road. Then I got into the car with this señor, who told me he was driving to the commissary.

When we arrived, they asked him if he was guilty of causing the serious accident. He said that he was unaware of such an accident, and that he knew only that a few hours earlier his son, [Enrique] Roberto Cojbx Trujillo had had the keys to the car. While we were in the middle of this conversation, news came that no one wanted to help the injured.

Then I told Señor Cojbx that we would appreciate his helping us get to the health center in either San Jorge or San José. We went to the place where the accident happened, but when we arrived the injured had already been taken by launch to San Jorge. We headed to San Jorge in the same car.

When we arrived in this town, only a few people were able to enter the place where they had the injured. We were able to get inside. My nephew, Angel Alfredo, was unconscious with a wound to the head and with the flesh of a leg pulverized by the tire of the car. My sister had lesions on her arms. My niece, Luciana Elvira, had fractures in her body. But the eldest child, Roberto Félix, was not there. He had been thrown into a pasture when the accident occurred. He was found, thanks to some boys who were checking to see that nothing had been lost at the place of the accident. They carried him to San Jorge. But at the time we had not yet seen him. The situation of these kin of mine was very grave. Only one of the youngsters of the family had not been hurt.

After the initial treatment, they were transferred to the hospital in Sololá. I wanted to accompany them, but, as I said before, I was barefoot and without a shirt, and I did not have a single centavo in my pocket. Thus, I did not go with them. I returned to my town, and the injured were taken to the doctors of INCAP.

When I arrived home, a lot of people were there to visit my sister, but I told them that she and her children had gone to the hospital at Sololá. Then I walked to San Martín to the head of the national police to ask the favor of communicating with Panajachel to have them advise my sister's father of the accident. The señores of the police did me the favor of sending a message by radio. In a half hour the news came back that my sister's father had been told that his daughter was in the hospital with all her children.

When I arrived home, the kin and other neighbors were very sad. They drank their bottles of liquor sadly because of what we had suffered. Many of them wanted to visit my sister, but the distance is far and they were not able because there are no cars in San José. We are almost isolated by Lake Atitlán. Many of them were crying because we Indians are very weak when our people suffer a misfortune. We become very sad. We begin to drink liquor, which is a means for calming our sadness. But the bottle solves nothing. It only makes the situation worse. Instead of becoming disheartened, the visitors become drunk and forget all about it.

Thus arrived the middle of night. I was still very much awake because of the bother with those who were now drunk. I was involved with them when suddenly a car arrived. I ran to see who it was. It was my sister's husband [Roberto Monroy Peneleu], who works in the health clinic of San Diego la Laguna. He said that a friend of his sent him a telegram stating that his family had been injured. For sure it was not us who sent the advice to my brother-in-law because I did not want to alarm him. He said that when he received the news he ran to the parish asking the priest for a car to get his family to take to the hospital. However, I told him that his family already was in the hospital. Then he began to cry bitterly and wanted a *trago*. But I advised him not to, and he took my advice.

Then we left in the car for San Diego la Laguna. I went with him to keep him from getting more depressed. We arrived in this town at 3:00 A.M., and we rested there until 5:00 A.M.

Then we boarded the bus for Sololá. At 7:00 A.M. we entered the hospital where Roberto's entire family was under treatment. One of his sons was was in critical condition, and the doctors could do nothing to cure him. Thus, at 10:00 A.M. they transferred him to the Roosevelt Hospital in Guatemala [City]. The son was between life and death.

Luis went to Guatemala [City] to accompany his family to the hospital. He gave me the entire responsibility of pursuing an *acusación* [indictment under Article 11 of the Código Procesal Penal, or Code of Criminal Procedure] against Señor Roberto Cojbx [Trujillo], who caused the accident. Roberto [Monroy] gave me the legal authority to represent him in the presence of a lawyer. I had to accept for my kin.

In the afternoon of the same day of 26 January, I arrived home. About an hour later, Señor Roberto Cojbx [Sosa, a primary teacher in San Martín] arrived, accompanied by two respected men, [Juan Catalina Tziac of San Martín and *profesor* Arnulfo Gustavo Córdova Guzmán of San Martín la Laguna], to arrange an *arreglo amistoso* [friendly settlement] so that I would not pursue the matter before the tribunals. When these men were talking to me, I began to conclude that a person should not be imprisoned when he is remorseful for such a crime. Then I asked Señor Cojbx what he proposed to do to make amends.

He told me that we could reconcile the case because it was not he who had committed the accident but his son, Roberto Cojbx Trujillo. This boy [who is 18 years old] is finishing his studies in the teaching profession. What he told me bothered me because it does not pay for one to behave poorly. Then I told Roberto Cojbx that, if he agrees to pay for the expenses of the injured, and that, if someone dies in the hospital, he will pay for all the funeral expenses, we could settle the case. Señor Cojbx told me that he would accept all the expenses because he wanted to save his son from going to jail. As I said before, it bothers me to persecute a person, so I promised Señor Cojbx to settle it in a peaceful manner. Not until then did the señor become consoled, because his son had been detained by the justice of the peace of San Jorge.

On 27 January I went to San Jorge to appear before the justice of the peace. Señor Cojbx told me to go in his car, but I replied that it was better for me to go on foot so that the people wouldn't think that I was doing this for money. When we arrived, we entered the courthouse to dismiss the claim and draw up an act [which stated the following points for Roberto Lionel Cojbx Sosa, father of the culprit Roberto Cojbx Trujillo and owner of the Toyota: (1) to pay all of the expenses caused by and credited to the accident such as (a) treatment of the mother and two children, who are under the care of Dr. Hernández in Panajachel, and for the child Angel Alfredo, who is in the

Roosevelt Hospital in Guatemala City, (b) a trip to visit the injured and their parents on a day to be arranged, (c) expenses for an express trip and back from San Diego la Laguna to San José la Laguna by the father of those affected, (d) to pay the salary of Señora Julia Martínez during the necessary time, (e) to pay all the expenses of food, lodging, and others necessary because of the accident, (f) in case of the death of the minor Angel Alfredo to pay all funeral expenses, (g) in case of the child's becoming an invalid, to pay for his care, food, and maintenance; and (2) to settle the matter by trial before whatever appropriate tribunal if faithful execution of the present agreement is not upheld]. We did this without the necessity of jail for the son. At noon on Saturday they set Roberto Cojbx Trujillo free. We arrived together in San José, and these two señores went on to their town of San Martín.

In the afternoon of this same day, a lot of people began to talk badly about my not having prosecuted the culprit. They said I had been given money, but this is not true because I was not given a single centavo. Many murmured about me. But it is certain that I thought a lot about my sister, because, if I had prosecuted Señor Roberto Cojbx, my sister would have had to spend a lot of money for making her children better. For that reason, I thought it best to drop the suit so that the situation would not get worse. I thought this way because in this world we are never free from danger. But the rest of the townspeople did not think this way. They thought only that I was unsuccessful with those who owned the car. But when one puts everything into perspective, we are all in danger.

In the afternoon of the same day, Señor Roberto Cojbx came to bring money. By the grace of God, my sister's husband came to secure the house. Roberto gave him $190. My brother-in-law was very appreciative for the agreement I had made with Señor Cojbx. The latter said that on the next trip he would bring money to cover [more of] the expenses.

❧ Visiting My Sister's Family and Reflecting about a Dream
MONDAY, 29 JANUARY 1979

At 2:00 A.M. I left my house for San Martín, where I caught a bus for Guatemala [City], arriving at 7:00 A.M. I did not know the address of the hospital, and I had to pay a taxi to take me. When I arrived, I located my sister, who was stable. However, her child, Angel Alfredo, continued to be in critical condition. He was still unconscious. The doctor told my sister that, if he could hold up for three days, they could save his life. My brother-in-law gave me $30 to give my sister to buy food. Because she did not know the city, she was accompanied by another person, and for that reason it cost more money.

On the following day, I arrived home, and I told the kin that my sister was all right. Only then were they consoled a little. I did not tell them that the boy continued to be critical because I did not want to alarm them more.

On this day I remembered the cry that Andrés and I had heard in the early hours of morning on 24 January when we were going to the coast. I had heard the cry very near my house. I am certain that the spirit of my nephew, Angel Alfredo, was what we heard. Our spirits advise our bodies when they are going to suffer misfortunes. This is affirmed because our house is very near the cry we heard, and their house is not far away. I repeat that it is certain that the spirit of a person feels and knows what his body is going to suffer. The body is still well when the spirit begins to fly. This I say because I have heard many things like this and days afterwards someone dies or someone falls sick.

We Tzutuhils believe very much in God and the spirit. Many others deny the existence of God, but we do not because we have seen our dreams become reality.

I am going to relate a dream that I had on 17 May 1966. It was a Thursday, when there were only 11 days left before the death of my child, Ana María. My dream was sacred. I dreamed that my wife and little daughter and I passed in front of the church. But when we passed in this place, the baby let go of me and her mother and went running for the church. We waited in front of the church for her, but she did not return from there.

In my dream I saw very well that the *cofrades* [fraternity members] entered the church carrying the dead body of a man in a coffin. The *cofrades* told me that the person who died was Señor Abraham Bizarro González. But in the dream I well remember that this person had already died about three years ago. In the dream, my wife and I drew near the church to see the remains, but when we entered the church we saw a strange thing—the image of Señor Jesucristo had been taken out of the place where it was kept and had been spread out over a big table in the middle of the church. But from that point I did not see my daughter, Ana María, anymore.

The *cofrades* took the corpse in the direction of the cemetery. Suddenly I saw two women dressed in typical clothing, one called María and the other called Nicolasa. Each woman carried under her arms many small funeral things. That is to say, each woman carried under her arms small boxes containing small dead ones. And each went toward the cemetery. With them went my daughter, Ana María. In the dream my wife remained where we were. Then in the dream I told my wife it was time to go, and we went home. But in the dream I felt disheartened.

When I woke up up it was 3:00 A.M. Then I got up and woke my wife and told her what I had dreamed. At the same time we sent a prayer to God asking for a clarification of the meaning of the dream. I did not sleep anymore. I began to think many things, and it made me sigh. I felt profoundly sad the whole day.

In the night we continued sleeping, but at 4:00 A.M. I began to dream again. I only heard a voice. I did not see anyone. The voice told me, "Take much care because your daughter is going to die. And after her, more will die." But I did not want to answer, and then the voice returned to me to say the same thing.

When I awoke, I began to think about what the dream meant. Well, I did not give it much importance; I thought perhaps it was the madness of dreams.

Incredibly, when the next Thursday, the 24th of the same month, came, eight days after the dream, the baby fell sick. She neither ate nor slept. She was like that the whole day. From dusk to dawn, she had a high fever. The next day she was worse.

We gave her homemade remedies, but they did not help her. All day Saturday her temperature was elevated. At 11:00 A.M. measles broke out, but only on part of her body. We made medicine to give her to rid the measles from all her body, but it was impossible. On Sunday in the afternoon she died because of the high temperature.

When the baby died, I was walking to San Martín to buy medicine. On the road they told me the news that my daughter had already died.

On Monday, they buried my daughter, Ana María, but it is the custom of us Indians that, when a person dies, his body has to be put in the church for the final [homage] to God. Then, as was the custom, they carried the little body of my daughter to the church. When they arrived in the church, the image of Señor Jesucristo was in the center positioned over a table, the same as I had dreamed 12 days earlier. The image was just as I had dreamed! Also, it was true that my daughter was the first victim of the measles. Three days later another child died, and thus began the daily plague in the town. We witnessed many deaths. During the month of June to the middle of July, more than 50 children died. My town is small, and when the bad illness broke out, it infected most of the children in town.

During this time the *cofrades* regretted having accepted their offices in the *cofradía* because they are the ones in charge of digging the graves of the dead. There were many deaths, so many that the *cofrades* did not have time to gather their firewood.

However, it was strange that only the sons and daughters of Catholic families died. The evangelists outwitted the Catholic people, for bad luck did not touch a single Protestant family. That is to say, children of Protestant families did not die. These things are true!

A Little More about Dreams
19 FEBRUARY 1979

I am going to say a little more about the thing of dreams. It pertains to a dream I had at 5:30 A.M. on 19 February 1979. On this day, I had a strange dream that turned out to be true. In my dream I met two persons who have been dead for about 18 years. These señores were named José Sicay and Fernando Tuc. They played the marimba for the deer dance. Don José played the marimba of gourds, and Don Fernando played the flute of cane. In previous years there were many in San José who were still performing the deer dance. I knew them when I was a child because I liked to follow the dances. In the *cofradías* they drank *atol* [a ritual drink of corn *masa* or of rice, wheat or corn flour, boiled and served hot]. The *mayordomos* [members of the *cofradías*] would not give me *atol*. What I would do was to stay near Don José and Don Fernando, and these señores, seeing that I did not wish to bother the *mayordomos*, gave me *atol*. They gave me what they had left over. They were very respected, and each fiesta I always accompanied them along with the other youngsters. For that reason, I knew these señores well when they were living.

Later, however, they quit doing the dances. The last year of the dance of the deer was 1952, when Diego Bizarro Ramos, brother of my grandfather, Ignacio Bizarro Ramos, God rest their souls, was tutor of the dance.

Thus, when I was dreaming, the two dead persons appeared, Don José playing the gourd marimba and Don Fernando playing the cane flute. In the dream I was dancing while they were performing with their instruments, but I was dancing in a strange place. Then the two men spoke to me, telling me not to continue dancing because they played *el son* [6/8 time] only for the dead, not for the living. Only then did I stop dancing.

In the dream I asked them where they were in order to know whether there is suffering in the afterlife, but the two dead ones told me that no one is interested in telling me about the other life where they are—only that they are obliged to play music for the dead. And they told me that I ought to take care because some campesinos of San Martín are looking for me to kill me. This is what the two dead men told me. But from there I did not say good-bye to them. The dream ended, and I woke up because it was dawn.

At 6:00 A.M. I told my wife what I had dreamed. She had dreamed the same thing! Well, in her dream the two dead men were Don José Sicay and Don Fernando Tuc. The only difference in my wife's dream was that the two dead men did not play the marimba or the flute. My wife dreamed that these two men gave me a great quantity of sheets of colored paper, but more red than other colors. And they told my wife to take care because some persons are looking for us to kill us. My wife dreamed at the same hour as I dreamed, and there were very few differences in the two dreams. We thought a lot about our dreams, but I gave them almost no importance. Later our dreams turned out to be true.

❧ The Bitter Life That I Am Suffering
20–22 FEBRUARY 1979

There are things that a man suffers in life only because of the lying tongues of the people. Now, I well realize that, when a man thinks a little better about how to improve his town, always there are others who look for a way to try to persecute that person. Those of the middle class of San Martín treat us as if we were irrational animals. They have us very oppressed, and they are very contemptuous of us. They do not want San José to have some organization. For that reason, they are making *calumnias* to the point of trying to get us killed.

However, for us poor people there is a God, pure, true, and wonderful, who indeed defends His children from the destruction of their enemies. I believe firmly in God, who is right in all things, who is owner and master of all things on earth. It happens that sometimes man thinks he is superior, but that is not true. God is the Señor of the visible and the invisible. I am learning many very marvelous things that God is able to do. During this bitter taste of life, God freed me from the persecutors who tried to kill me just because I organized a small agricultural cooperative that we need so much in this town.[16]

I am going to tell the dark and bitter story of a poor man who is innocent of a crime about which those of San Martín slandered and lied. They are people who have surrendered to the devil in order to betray a poor person.

It happened that in San Martín a boy died who had been involved in the vice of witchcraft. It is not certain whether they killed him, he committed suicide, or if the hand of a criminal killed him. According to rumors, the corpse was discovered at 8:00 A.M. on 19 February. He was found hanging from the branch of a tree by his belt and with his tiptoes in the dirt, about three *cuadras* from his house in San Martín la Laguna.

Fear ran through all the neighboring towns because never have we seen fatal things like this, and we did not know what might happen in the future. They took the cadaver to the hospital in Sololá for the autopsy. After the autopsy they brought his remains back to his town, and it was already night. There was much fear in San José because it is only two kilometers from San Martín, and it was not clear how the boy died. The person who told me the news was Señor Don Ignacio Yojcom, who has a field of onions in Xesucut where I also have *tablones* of onions. I was watering onions when this man arrived and later told me what had happened in his town. When I arrived in my town, all the people were alarmed over such a casualty.

Tuesday, 20 February, when the dead person still had not been buried, Andrés and I confidently went to the coast to fetch a crew on the Ipalita farm. From our town we left at 2:00 A.M. to take the bus in San Martín. In this town we waited until 3:00 A.M. without any fear and very content because we had not done anything bad. In Santa Lucía Cotzumalguapa we got off the bus and ate breakfast and then took another bus to the farm.

When we arrived on this farm we spoke to the señor administrator regarding the pay of the *cuadrilla*. The administrator told us that the pay of the crew was not scheduled for this day. That was our first failure. They told us the pay of the crew was not until tomorrow, but we had already contracted a truck to take the people back to our town. In order not to lose the money spent for the truck, Andrés agreed to wait for the pay of the crew while we took them back to San José.

When we arrived in the vicinity of Cocales, the workers were very content. We gave each worker a few dollars to buy food because no one had money since their pay was pending until tomorrow. After dinner we got back into the truck and headed for home.

At midnight we arrived in San Martín and left some workers

there without anything special happening. We came confidently to my dear town, San José. The workers headed for their houses, and I headed for mine.

When I was close to my house, I noticed that the lights on the porch were on. This worried me because I was afraid one of my children had died. Inside my house were many people and much noise.

When I opened the door, all of my close kin began to weep. I asked which of my children had died, and they responded that they were crying for me. Then they told me the reason—the justice of peace of San Martín la Laguna had sent an order to capture Andrés and me. The news was confirmed that the police are looking for us. They want to imprison us because the mother of the deceased accused us of the death of her son.

When they told me this, my entire body felt weak—it nearly paralyzed me. It was very strange that, when I passed San Martín, everything was tranquil. The substation of the national police was open, but the police did not capture me.

Well, when I heard this dark news, I felt very sad in my heart. But little by little I regained my composure. Then I began to think what I would do for my defense.

Andrés's family came to ask me about him, and I told them he was waiting for the crew's pay. Only then did they calm down, because they thought he had been captured.

When the people of my town realized what had happened, they came to my house to console me. Almost the entire town came, and it was not possible to talk to all of them. When I regained my senses, I began to think many things to prevent them from taking me and Andrés prisoner. In the same night I planned a trip to Guatemala [City] to consult with my best friends because for sure I did not know anything about defending myself from such a dark *calumnia*.

At 1:30 A.M. I took the road for Santa Ana to catch the bus. My good friend Roberto accompanied me from San José. Many others went with me as far as the Hill of Chuitinamit, where they said goodbye. A lot of them offered me beer, but I thought more about my situation than drinking. I climbed the slope like an idiot and felt a great dismay, as if I could walk no further. I was very thirsty, but we did not carry any water. We continued until we finally reached Santa Ana at 4:00 A.M. It took two and one-half hours to climb the slope. All night long we suffered.

At 5:00 A.M. the bus left, and at 8:00 A.M. we arrived in the capital. Roberto ate breakfast, but I did not. Then we caught an urban bus for Zone 6, where we looked for the house of our friend, Edgar

Mario Mazariegos Quiroa, to consult about my dark situation. When we arrived at his house, he received us well. He is in charge of advising me with matters of the court of the first instance and of the court of the second instance. However, he said that first he would have to study the law and talk to his friends who know the law. He said that he is going to give me some ideas, but not until after he goes to work. I stayed, waiting for this friend to return from work.

In the afternoon, *licenciado* Zelada gave me a letter to give to a friend in Congress. In the afternoon I ate a little, but not peacefully. I was worried that in a little while or later the police would capture me.

At 6:00 P.M. I left the house of this friend to look for a pension in Zone 1. When I arrived at the inn, I intended to sleep. Weak with exhaustion from the previous night, I slept a lot.

Daylight came on 22 February. Again I could think only about the same problems. At 6:00 A.M. the señor who was accompanying me left me in Guatemala [City] and returned to San José to arrange for witnesses to testify on my behalf. If I should return to San José, I would certainly have problems. At 9:00 A.M. I went to the Congress to look for my friend, but I did not find him.

At 1:00 P.M. I left Guatemala [City] and arrived in Sololá at 4:00 P.M. In the park I waited for my uncle Benjamín. Later he told me that my friend Andrés was in the house of a friend, Señor Raimundo Ramírez Ralon, in Sololá, safe from the police, who have the order to capture him. When I arrived in Sololá, I became very cautious. I went to the telegraph office to send a telegram to my family, signed by Benjamín, that everything was well and that I had encountered policemen but they did not capture me because I have a clean conscience.

In this afternoon I intended to inquire in the hospital about the cause of death of the *Martinero*. The man in the hospital told me he would give me the information but not until another day because he had to look in a book. More or less he gave me a negative response.

Immediately I went to the house where my friend Andrés was staying. When I entered, my friend began to weep. I told him not to cry and to be patient. But this friend is very weak, and he only wept. I was staying in this house because unfortunately they had accused me of being a criminal. I am a humble person, and I do not have the heart to do something evil to someone else. For me these things are very strange. I must, however, cope with them, because that is the way my enemies want it.

Later the owner of the house gave us much consolation. He is a person whom I have known for many years. In contrast, Andrés does not have friends outside his town. By the grace of God, I have a lot of friends all over Guatemala. I consulted with this man about the case. When this friend realized our situation was serious, he went to look for a lawyer.

On this day, Thursday, the *diligencias del crimen* [formalities of the felony] arrived in the courthouse of Sololá, sent by the justice of peace of San Martín. But no one would explain the nature of the accusation against us. Andrés just cried all afternoon. He took no interest in the investigation. To calm his sadness, he began to drink *tragos* until he became drunk. I did not want to drink, because I was interested in the investigation of the lawyers. All night long I slept well because my great friend provided a bed for me and another for my companion.

❧Hiding Out in Sololá and Legal Proceedings
23 FEBRUARY–11 MARCH 1979

Not knowing what was going to happen to us, we awoke with much grief. At eight o'clock some campesinos of San José arrived to visit us in jail, thinking that we already were incarcerated. However, they did not find us in jail. Gradually they began to ask in which house we were staying. When they saw us, they were filled with joy. It also made us feel a little better. These countrymen came to tell us that the situation continues to be unfortunate. Later they went to the park as a disguise to protect us from being discovered.

At 9:00 A.M. we met two lawyers, Don Arnoldo Mejía and Don Emilio, who asked if we needed their professional help for our defense. They told us that, if we needed them, they would defend us from such a dark accusation. These *licenciados* then went to the *juzgado de primera instancia* [court of the first instance] to examine the formalities about us. Within an hour they came back to tell us a little about the case. These lawyers were able to investigate some, but they had limited results because the law prohibits seeing a *proceso* [a file of papers in an action] before the end of 15 days. For that reason, the lawyers were not able to obtain much information, but what they got was important.

The lawyers did not want to present us before the court. They told us we had to wait until the accusing party presented their witnesses. Then they could present our witnesses. They told us that Monday for sure they would present us before the judge of the first instance, with the condition that we might remain some months in jail until they would be able to investigate it well. What they foresaw for us made us very sad, because we had never been imprisoned even for a few hours.

At 2:00 P.M. our countrymen said good-bye to us, and Andrés continued drinking because he was greatly tormented. That was the way it was all afternoon.

Saturday dawned, and we were still in the house of Señor R.R.R. His wife did us the favor of selling us meals, but Andrés did not eat without drinking a bottle. Thus we spent Saturday grieved because we were hiding from the police. Sunday was the same, enduring great pains.

We did not present ourselves before the señor judge because, if he locked us up, we would not be able to do anything for our defense. While we were in seclusion, Señor R.R.R. was in charge of running our errands with the lawyers. This friend was like a father to us. He kept very busy trying to improve our situation.

In the afternoon of this same day, Sunday, 12 close kin from San José arrived. They came to testify for us on Monday, the date of the *indagatoria* [inquiry]. I felt little sadness, and at times I felt happiness in my heart. All night I did not feel sad because my countrymen consoled me very much, telling me how my grandparents and great-grandparents also suffered false accusations from other persons. They told me that the Bizarro family has a history of being persecuted by slanderous tongues.

Monday dawned. I got up very early and began to think a lot of things. It crossed my mind to flee to Mexico or El Salvador and leave behind these false accusations. But later I collected my wits because my conscience is clean. What I did was to entrust myself to God for a rapid solution to the difficulties that I was suffering. I examined my conscience. It is certain that I am a poor person but a worker who is responsible for a family. Never have I tried to damage another person. On the contrary, I have actually saved persons from going to jail, and I have given up my time to help people from [suffering] grave consequences. I do not know why these things have happened to me.

At 7:00 A.M. the señores of San José went to the market to eat breakfast while waiting for the *indagatoria*. The lawyers began to arrange matters in the courthouse for when they would conduct the *indagatoria* and notify the witnesses who saw me Sunday afternoon and Monday. But nobody knew what questions would be asked.

What happened on that Sunday afternoon was that I had seen 30 active members of the cooperative, because at 7:00 P.M. the president of administration, Abraham Có Bizarro, had declared an open session of the group to find out the business results from 14 January to 14 February. Because of other tasks, it had not been done until that day. We did not finish the meeting until 10:00 P.M., when we signed the memorandum indicating that everything had been carried out properly. The majority went to their houses, but Señor Antonio, the president of the *junta de vigilancia* [committee of control], left me four persons to help guard the tienda. The reason is that the house in which the tienda was located was not secure, and always 5 to 6 persons remained guarding the merchandise all night. This was all the witnesses knew, and all of this is what they declared on our behalf.

Later, in the middle of the day, they did not receive us in the courthouse for the *indagatoria* because they were too busy. At 4:00 P.M. the lawyers went in their car to the courthouse. But the officials still did not want to question us.

Conscientiously, the señor judge did not send us to jail. Again he placed us in the hands of the lawyers, charging them to make sure we did not run away. The judge told us that, if we fled, the situation would be aggravated. To prevent us from being captured by the police, the lawyers took us in their cars to our hiding place, and they told us to be very careful.

Again we became very sad because there had been no way to gain our liberty. Again we were secluded in the same house. In the afternoon our countrymen said good-bye to us. They returned to our town, but they left some bottles of liquor for Andrés, who drank a half bottle before dinner. I had gone 28 months without touching a *trago*. Lamentably, only the two of us were [shut up] in a small house. There was nobody there to give me support. I do not know why I gave into the temptation of drinking a swig of liquor. Perhaps it was due to my worry, never resting, thinking day and night. I had no feeling when I drank the [first] shot of liquor, nor did I sense the taste. When I realized what was happening, I had already finished a whole bottle. When my companion saw that I was drinking, he gave me shots until I was inebriated. I was unaware what hour I fell asleep. When I came to my senses, it was already Tuesday. But I needed more liquor to calm my thirst. Then I asked a stranger the favor of fetching me a drink.

At 9:00 A.M. two of my fellow members of Alcoholics Anonymous arrived to visit me. When these friends saw me drunk, they became very sad. They were aware that I suffered from this sickness, and one of them cried for me. For the need of alcohol I asked these friends to buy me another bottle to calm my hangover and thirst. One of them did not much want to buy the liquor, but because he understood my situation, he finally did me the favor. Now good and drunk, I forgot totally this dark situation.

All day Tuesday I was drinking. The same thing Wednesday. Not until Thursday did I come to my senses. But everything was to the contrary. Instead of calming my situation, everything worsened. Now I had three problems—first, I was preoccupied with the false accusations; second, I was worried about my family; and third, I was worried about my sickness of alcoholism. The only thing liquor did was to make the situation worse.

Friday dawned with my having hardly any self-control. When I realized that already it was Friday, 2 March, I began to think hard about solving my problem. I was preoccupied with this when the witnesses arrived anew to testify on my behalf. This consoled me a little, but I was still so upset that I did not want to eat breakfast. When the lawyers arrived, they told me that the *indagatoria* and declarations of the witnesses were certain to take place today. We waited until noon, but it was not to be. Sadly, the same thing happened in the afternoon. In the courthouse they were very busy. They said it was possible that they would receive us next week. The witnesses were demoralized because they did not want to lose a lot of time.

In the afternoon of the same day my kin told me that we should go to San José to visit my family. I told them no, because the police might capture me. It is true that the señor judge was aware that we were in the custody of the lawyers, but the police do not respect lawyers. My friends insisted that I should go home. Finally, they convinced me, and I ran to advise our lawyers. They told me that I could travel to my town but with the condition that I be very careful of the police and my enemies, who could make the *calumnia* worse for me.

Then I got my traveling bag with my bedding. As we were leaving, our lawyer told us to be sure to return on Monday because Tuesday could be the day of making the *notificaciones*. That is the way it was, and we later left in the street with much pain.

We caught a bus for Panajachel, but it was already too late to catch the regular launch [to San José]. We had to contract an express launch that charged $25. We all divided the cost. It was already 6:00 P.M., and when we got into the launch, I was worried and thought it better not to go because I had more protection in Sololá. I felt sad. My friends consoled me, but I did not go calmly. I felt that something more grave was going to happened to me. I had a premonition of what was happening in the town.

When the boat arrived next to the shore, I saw some persons

standing on the pier who I thought were policemen. When the launch was below the pier, I began to leave, when suddenly I saw my friend Benjamín Peña Letona coming to advise me not to go to my house because the *Martineros* had gone to fetch the *policía judicial* [judicial police] to punish us cruelly.

Are there policía judicial *in Sololá?*

There are no *policía judicial* in Sololá. I cannot say that a *jefe* [leader] sent for them. My enemies in San Martín were the ones who wanted the *policía judicial* to submit us to their harsher punishments. They were the villains because they paid these police $300 to $500. These police go to administer justice, and they do not respect the laws; they themselves are the ones who execute.

Don't they need a court?

No, they are the third power of the state. There are three powers: the executive, the Señor President of the Republic; the legislative, the Congress; and the judicial, the Supreme Court of Justice, all that which is judiciary [comprising the three branches of government]. These police are powerful because they are the third power of the state. For them there are no tribunals. They are the judges and the law, too. They torture mainly for bribes. They apply their tortures or death to a person. They take him outside the town, hang him up, throw *ganiexcan* [a strong insecticide] in his eyes, or hang him up by the testicles. After torturing him, they shoot him. A lot of cases have happened this way. This is not a lie; many captured by the *policía judicial* do not reappear, not in their homes or elsewhere. They kill them once and for all.[17]

My friend Benjamín told me that the police had searched Andrés's house and the houses of other *Joseños*, but that they did not enter my house. They only walked by it in the street. The judicial police came because Ignacio Puzul Robles brought them. And it is not even certain that the men he brought were policemen. They may be impersonators paid by my enemies in San Martín because, when they came into town, they went to search the houses without informing the local authorities. The whole town stirred when it realized that *desconocidos* [unknowns, or strangers] were looking for us.

We talked about these things in a coffee grove. I did not want to enter the town because I am a person of a very simple heart, and I was afraid of the sinister punishment that they wanted to give me. At this moment when Benjamín was talking to me, I wanted to return to Sololá the same night. Already, I was not thinking of my family. Finally I reflected a little, and I entered the town. But I did not go to my house. What I did was to go to Benjamín's house, because it is not in the middle of town. There I stayed hidden with Andrés until midnight. My family had not been aware that we were in town.

At 2:00 A.M. I left this house and went to the house of my brother-in-law for more protection. From there my family could be told that we were in town. When we left Benjamín's house and went in the direction of my brother-in-law's house, we met a group of vigilantes who were patrolling the street. I thought they were coming to capture me, but it was not so. Everything was okay. They told us they were guarding the town to find out if those who were entering the houses were really policemen. Also, they asked whether we wanted to have a drink with them. We said yes, and we went to a cantina where we drank many drinks, but with haste because in a little while or so the men who were looking for us might come again. After finishing our drinks, we entered the house and spent the rest of the night.

Saturday dawned in hiding. We were not able to leave because notice could reach San Martín. In the morning they brought us food because we did not want other persons to see us. They scarcely told my family or anyone else. Everyone knew that we were here, but no one knew exactly where. Saturday night some family and friends arrived to console us a little. But we were still worried because the police could discover us. By the grace of God, it was not so. We were worried that our return to Sololá would be more difficult. We wanted to leave, but our kin told us it would be better to have a little patience. We were longing, however, for the hour when we would be back in Sololá, because it was more peaceful there and we were protected by the lawyers. Here, on this night, we were totally helpless.

Sunday dawned, and it was the same thing. We did not go anywhere. They told us the news that in a little while or so the *policía judicial* would come. I regretted having returned to my town, and now we were not able to leave. In a little while they could imprison us in San Martín, and then the situation would be much worse because we would be unable to communicate with our families, and they could send us to dark tortures.

We were praying to God to allow us to leave the town for Sololá. During the day, nothing happened. We had agreed with the lawyers that Monday we would return to Sololá. In the night some friends came to visit us, and at the same time they told us that they would accompany us to Sololá. I said thanks a lot. I do not know how it happened, but we were preparing for our exit about 11:00 P.M. and hundreds of persons arrived, men and women. The whole yard of my brother-in-law's house was full of people. Many were drinking their *tragos* because they felt that we were in a delicate situation. We were very scared, but the people were ready to defend us, and for sure no one wanted us imprisoned.

About midnight we left the house and went to the church to offer a prayer to the saint, San Juan Bautista. Many people accompanied us. Those who organized this visit were the señores of Catholic Action. At midnight sharp the town prayed for our liberation.

When we returned from church, the people did not want us to go to Sololá. They wanted us to stay another day with them to talk because there were a lot of people and it was impossible for us to talk to everyone. But we were ready to leave at 1:15 A.M. A lot of people went with us to Panasajar, where they bid us farewell. Many women and their families were weeping.

Thus it was. Little by little we left town, and we passed through San Jorge uneventfully. We went through San Benito until we reached Tzancuil. When we arrived in Tzancuil, owing to much trouble, weariness, and the *tragos* we had drunk, we were unable to walk any further. Thus we asked a person to row us in his canoe over the lake to a place called Jaibal near Panajachel. From Jaibal we took the road to San Pablo. On the road we drank some cups of *atol* of corn meal, and this is what sustained us a little.

When we arrived in San Pablo, we visited the church and asked God to free us from such a dark persecution. From San Pablo a pickup took us to Sololá. At noon we arrived in this town. Then we returned to the same house where we had been hiding. Later I told my friends to go tell our lawyers that we were present again.

We ate a little lunch, but still we were very worried. It was the first time in my life that I was hiding from the authorities, and only then it was because of such a false accusation. I have never behaved poorly with the people of San Martín or with the people of any other places. I did not know why they accused me of being a criminal. It was very puzzling.

During the same afternoon at 3:00 P.M., *licenciado* Emilio came to visit. I told him that he could go to the courthouse to inquire about the situation. When he returned, he informed me that the *indagatoria* would be Tuesday, 6 March, and that the witnesses needed to be present. However, the witnesses were unaware [of this], so I had to send a telegram calling them. A friend signed it.

In the afternoon of this day, Monday, my heart ached very much. I was very sick the whole night until Tuesday dawned. My heart did not quit aching until 7:00 A.M. I was not hungry. I just worried about my liberty because for certain I did not want to go to jail; it is better to be free.

At 10:00 A.M. the lawyers were to present us before the judge. They escorted us in their cars. When we arrived in the courtroom, they sat me down in a chair before the official.

Was the official the secretary or the judge? What were his instructions?

He was the secretary of the court, in charge of taking statements of the persons. He has the power to examine and to cajole, depending on how one supports his declarations. He represents the judge and reports to him. The judge just reads, certifies, and signs. If the secretary says that the defendant gave a poor declaration, the judge sends the accused to jail; or, if the official says that the declaration was acceptable, the judge signs the defendant's release and sets him free. If the secretary recommends jail, he gets it. If he recommends freedom, he gets it.

Then the judge is in another room?

Yes, it is private. The judge is not in the same room with the defendant. They do this because the people sometimes have a lot of fear before a judge, and they do not declare their matters. With a secretary, they have more confidence. They talk better because the secretary is not a judge. But also it is easy for a person to be condemned if he does not feel like talking or if he does not pay attention because here in Sololá or in Guatemala [City] the officials are like psychologists. If the accused is frightened, shakes, shuffles his papers, finds the proceedings difficult with a trembling face or foot, becomes pale while testifying, does not answer the third question, or does not help himself with the fourth question, he is guilty. It is a very delicate situation.

Delicate?

Yes. One should be normal and not think about other things. He needs to think about the situation in which he finds himself. This is somewhat difficult for a person who has committed a crime because of his own conscience, his own nervousness. Then it is easy to blame him. But if a person has done nothing wrong there is no problem.

What were the official's instructions to you when you were ready to talk?

"Sit down. Do not be afraid here. You are in the courtroom. The law will not kill you, but you have to tell the truth. If you tell the truth, the law will help you. If you tell a lie, the law will condemn you. Approach please. Answer all of the questions that I am going to ask you right now."

These were his words at the opening of the *indagatoria*. One is not able to lie, true. One must conform to his conscience. We began, but first he advised me to use my head and not think of other things— to concentrate on what he was going to ask me.

Most of the dialogue with the secretary of the court of the first instance comes from my taping the account that Ignacio had paraphrased in nearly the same detail in his written account.

First the official asked, "What is your name?"

"Ignacio Bizarro Ujpán," I answered. But the accused is listed only as Ignacio Ujpán. That was the first error.

"What is the name of your wife?"

"My wife is named Josefa Ramos."

"How many children do you have?"

"I have five children."

"What are their names?"

"My children are called José Juan Bizarro Ramos, María Bizarro R., Ramón Antonio Bizarro R., Susana Bizarro R., and Erasmo Ignacito Bizarro R."

"Are these children of wedlock?"

"Yes."

"How many times have you been sentenced for other crimes?"

"Never!"

"Have you ever participated in bellicose acts?"

"No; moreover, I have not ever been detained by the authorities for infractions."

"Where were you at 5:00 P.M. Sunday?"

"At 5:00 P.M. Sunday I was at a place called Xesucut watering onions. I was seen by particular persons—Abraham Novales Bizarro, and José Horacio Temó Morales. Also, two other persons saw me when I was returning from Xesucut, when I passed through a place called Chuachoj. I said, 'Adios,' to Señores Ignacio Ramos García and Bernardino Ujpán Flores. Those were the persons who saw me on that afternoon."

"Where were you at 6:00 P.M. of the same day?"

"At that hour I was in the tienda of the cooperative where the president declared an open session for all the members to examine the funds spent in the month of January to the month of February, and this meeting lasted four hours because many things were covered. We did not leave until a record was signed."

"Did you go to San Martín?"

"No!"

"Did you know the deceased, Julio Padilla Puzul?"

"No, I did not know him."

"Did you have problems with some of his kin?"

"Certainly not, before God and country, we never had problems with any *Martinero*."

This is what I declared before the señor official. Only then did I learn of the accusation made against me by the mother of the deceased. She says that I killed her son for a five-dollar debt. She says that five days before the death of her son I had said that if he did not pay me back in money, he would pay with his life. This was the *calumnia* that the *Martineros* made against me. But I was ignorant of these things, because never in my life have I threatened a person with death. Truthfully, before God, the man who died never worked in my crews, nor have I ever had working relations with members of his family. It is a great slander that my enemies have made up against me. I never dreamed that anyone was making up falsehoods against me.

And that was how the *indagatoria* ended at 11:30 A.M. Andrés was not there [since he was waiting his turn in the house of sanctuary]. After the *indagatoria* I was placed in the hands of my defenders. Again we went to the house from whence we came. There I chatted with my witnesses about the matter. By the grace of God, my *notificación* [notification; notice; information] went well. It is certain that I was somewhat scared because I never had to make declarations as delicate as this. But there were no problems, and I answered everything they asked me. My serenity served me well because I had no lapse of memory.

At 3:00 P.M. my friend Andrés left with the lawyers for the courthouse for the *indagatoria* while I waited in the house. As he marched to the courthouse, I prayed to God to free us from such a dark situation, and I began to read the Evangelist of San Mateo, Chapter 10, verses 16 to 20. This was all my hope. Later, at 5:00 P.M., I was still asking with all my heart, with all my mind, for God to free us of this evil. After my prayers to God, I felt a marvelous thing, as if nothing had ever happened, as if I had bathed. I felt fresh in my whole body.

Later, at 5:45 P.M., the lawyer arrived to fetch me in his car again to return to the courthouse. I thought he was allowing me to go to jail.

When I entered the courtroom, I first entrusted myself to God. Then I saw my friend, Andrés, seated in a chair, very sad. We entered the office of the judge. That is where the secretary told us that the judge of the court of the first instance ordered us freed under *caución juratoria* [juratory caution, or parole given by a person in custody but not yet tried and sentenced], with the condition to take extreme care to avoid problems with my enemies. The officials told us that our enemies could cause us other problems by indicting us again.

When they ordered our freedom, deep within I began to thank God, because it is certain we found ourselves in a difficult situation. When they gave us our freedom, the suffering I had gone through because of this *calumnia* was forgotten. The only thing was that it was not possible to notify the witnesses because it was too late, and they were worried. For now there were no problems for us.

At 6:00 P.M. we walked through the street, but I do not know why I was feeling afraid to walk. Also, I was greatly saddened thinking about what had happened. I was thankful to my companions who gave me much encouragement. They are honorable men. Some of those who accompanied me were members of Catholic Action, and some of them were members of Alcoholics Anonymous. But most of them were members of the cooperative.

When we left the courthouse, we walked to the park, where my friends began to eat a little because they had not eaten lunch since they felt very sad for us. Andrés and I had not eaten anything either. As it was now too late, we could not catch a bus for Panajachel. It was difficult to reach this town.

We wanted to enter a *comedor*, but we did not have money for dinner. But to my friends it was not important to eat. They wished to arrive home during the same night to calm all of the families in our town. It was impossible, however, to contract a launch. The owner said he would make a trip for us but not until early morning of the following day.

When my companions heard that the trip would not be until the next day, they began to drink shots of liquor and have a joyous party on the sand. When it was all finished, we got inside the launch to sleep. Everyone else slept, but I did not sleep at all because everyone was drunk and I was worried about being on the boat. I thought someone might want to go outside and that he might fall into the lake. To avoid serious problems, it was more important that I stay awake watching until our departure. And thus it dawned with everything okay.

It was very pleasant when 4:00 A.M. came. Wednesday began very calm when the launch carried us toward San José. At 5:00 A.M. we arrived. The people of my town were still sleeping when we entered. I was suddenly pained because I thought something else might happen to me because the suffering that I have endured due to the *Martineros*. I do not know why they conducted themselves badly and accused me of murder. I am a person who has done the most favors for the people of San Martín. Their thanks is to pay me with an unjust accusation. I do not understand these things very well. Could this just be my destiny? Or have they wronged me just because I tried to organize and promote an agricultural cooperative? We have almost withdrawn from the *Martineros* in favor of the cooperative. We have our own corn, fertilizer, and other beneficial things, and we do not much need their business anymore in San José. Whatever the case, I have to bear it. But indeed I am proud to say that I am an honorable person because I have a clean conscience that has never been blemished with evil things. What I must do is bear these difficult things in my life.

On this day, Wednesday, when the people of my town realized that we were in our own houses, many women came to my house to visit me. Many of them began to weep with joy because we were free. Moreover, all of the people know that we are working men. Many of them share my ideas. For that reason, the women came when they saw my physical state, which was very emaciated. I did not eat or drink or talk because I felt sick. Some of the women brought fruit juices, others beer, and yet others food. The house was full of visitors. Also women went to call their husbands who were working, telling them that we now were in town.

At 11:00 A.M., the men began to arrive to visit us. All of them came in and threw a little fiesta. They bought some chickens, and the women fixed some lunch. Also, the men bought a lot of bottles of liquor.

We began to eat lunch at 1:00 P.M., but the house was not big enough for everyone. We had to take turns for lunch. Some ate on the porch. The lunch did not end until 3:00 P.M. Many were happy; many were very drunk. They offered me drinks, but it was impossible for me to drink because my health was very delicate. And also the lawyers told me that I should take much care because of my enemies.

This Wednesday turned out to be a little fiesta for the people of

San José. When it was over, everyone was very content. A lot of them left for their houses, but many stayed with me and continued drinking.

While we were celebrating, suddenly a national police car arrived in town. All the people were alarmed because they feared the police had come to capture us. The townspeople tried to hide us from the police, but I did not want to hide anymore because Andrés and I understood very well what had happened at the *juzgado de primera instancia* in Sololá. They ordered our freedom. That is to say, the order to capture us was already canceled. Although I did not want to hide anymore from the police, I was curious as to what they were looking for; finally, I paid it no mind. However, many of those who were with me felt afraid and ran to their houses because they thought they might end up imprisoned with us. This was very strange because no one knew why the police were there.

The only thing that is known comes from a *Martinero* whose wife lives in San José. His name is Eduardo, but he asked me not to tell anyone because they could accuse him of something.

According to Eduardo on Friday, 2 March, a group of men who claimed to be policemen accompanied Señor Ignacio Puzul Robles, brother of Señora Olga Puzul. They said they were looking for us. It was discovered that this man paid some evil persons to execute us, but they were not of the law—they were just paid to kill us. Señor Ignacio Puzul arrived in San José at 3:00 P.M., and they entered a lot of houses asking for us. But on this day we were in Sololá.

These men of particular dress arrived together with Señor Ignacio Puzul. This señor and the contracted [killers] forced a youngster to open [the door to] her house, and they entered it. She was alone because her parents were working. They made her let them in on the threat of death. When she opened the door, these evil men tried to rape her, but the young girl screamed a lot and attracted two women who came to her defense. Then the men got into their car and headed toward San Martín. The only one who was recognized was the *Martinero*, Ignacio Puzul.

When the girl's parents arrived, they went carefully to the authorities to see who these men were. Unfortunately, the mayor had gone to Sololá. When he arrived in the afternoon, the offended parents presented their complaint against Señor Puzul, accusing him of the crimes of breaking and entering and the intent to rape.

On Saturday, Señor Puzul presented himself before the justice of peace and denied that a crime had been committed the previous day. In his declaration he said that it was true that on Friday he was in San José, but for the obligation of pointing out the house of some *Joseños*, Ignacio Ujpán and Andrés Bizarro. He said that he did not know whether these men were policemen. He said it was true that they entered the house but it was only to see whether Ignacio and Andrés were inside, and he said that he did not see whether these men wanted to rape this girl. He did confess, however, that he accompanied these men, and then the plaintiff asked that an inquiry for penal procedures be enforced. But the *Martinero* saw that the complainant was a girl of humble circumstances, and he did not give it any importance.

Later this man gave a sum of money to the señor justice of peace to set him free. He left content after having bribed the señor justice of peace. Already they did not take seriously the accuser's complaint, and the judge wanted the accuser to retract the presented accusation. They did not want the claim to go forth. But the plaintiff was aware of the bribe, and she demanded that the judge conform to the law.

On Tuesday, 5 March, the *Martinero*, Ignacio Puzul, did not appear before the justice of peace. According to him, he had already settled it with the judge, because this was supposed to be the day of the *diligencias* [proceedings]. Acting as if nothing had happened, the *Martinero* did not appear.

Now it was clear to the parents of the girl that the judge was in favor of the defendant. They could do nothing. Then the accuser, along with other *Joseños* who were frightened of these evil men, took other measures. Seeing that the justice of peace did not do anything for his people, they got the idea of sending three telegrams to three high functionaries of the government—one for the departmental governor of Sololá, one for the minister of government, and one for the judge of the court of the first instance of Sololá. They asked them for protection for the people because the strange men had entered the town and committed the crime of entering the homes of persons of humble circumstances.

Then the police came in this afternoon of Wednesday to investigate, or, better said, to bring action against [the perpetrators of] the attempted rape. They asked a lot of questions, but the witnesses answered that they knew Señor Ignacio Puzul only because he is a man of San Martín. They said that they saw the others but that they were *desconocidos*. But the women said indeed they had seen Señor Ignacio Puzul accompanied by *desconocidos*. Also, the women said that it was certain that they helped the said girl, named Elena.

After the investigation, the chief of police agreed that the crime had taken place, and then they went to San Martín. When they arrived in this town, they went to the house of Ignacio Puzul, captured him, and conducted him to jail in Sololá. From San Martín they left at 8:00 P.M., but it was impossible for some of his close kin to accompany him because the car was too small.

On this night there was much alarm among the people of that town when they saw the police taking away their countryman. But the greatest alarm was when the car of the policemen passed by the soccer field, and the police discharged their firearms. The *Martineros* thought that perhaps they had sentenced their countryman, but this was not the case. The police had fired their weapons to kill an animal. In the town there was a big uproar, and the women began to cry. However, when they went to look in this place, they found nothing [no body].

In this account [by Eduardo] nothing was faulty because on the same night of the same day some residents came to tell me what had happened in that town. How true, how certain is the proverb, "*El que mal hace, mal espera* [Evil awaits he who evil makes, or he who commits evil will meet evil]." God never abandons his children when their enemies try to cause them difficulties, but only if they have a clean conscience. My countrymen became content when they heard the news that Ignacio Puzul was imprisoned. However, I told them that such things should never be and that we should never cheer the adversity of our fellow man and only then would they understand how we would ever be free of such problems ourselves.

I do not understand how this all happened because the señores of San Martín wished evil for us, but thanks to God Almighty for having freed me from my enemies. Everything turned out to the contrary—Señor Puzul wanted to imprison me unjustly, and in the end it was he whom they carried to prison in Sololá.

The power of God is great because when we were in a delicate situation, a lot of people of different churches sent their prayers to God for our liberation. Mainly the Catholic church demonstrated their charitable work with my family. The organization of the mothers of families were helping my wife with prayers and also with some centavos for my children. I am deeply thankful for these favors that my family received during these times of suffering.

The people of San Martín said that for sure they were going to shoot us for this false felony. The mother of the deceased and some others collected 200 signatures of her neighbors asking the authorities to sentence Andrés and me to death. When the church became aware of San Martín's desires for us, everyone prayed to God. It is certain that God received the prayers of his children because we have a clean conscience.

On Thursday, 8 March, I got up a little sad, more sad than content because about 11:00 P.M. of the previous day, the señor municipal mayor came to visit. Instead of offering more protection, he only wanted to scare me more by telling me that I should sleep among the coffee groves because he had noticed that my enemies were searching for another *calumnia* so that they could justify killing me in my own house. I told him only thanks a lot, but before this señor left, I concluded that he was just lying because I know very well that we do not get along together well. Still, this news that he brought bothered me, and I was not able to sleep peacefully.

On this day a group of *principales* [elders] visited and gave me some advice. They told me that some of them had suffered false accusations of different kinds but never of murder. These señores also told me that in life there is always suffering of various kinds; they told me to be more patient and that if I could bear these things I would later be victorious. This was the advice these *principales* gave me.

After the *principales* left, some evangelists arrived. That is, the pastor of the Assembly of God came to console me also. He gave me the good advice of not taking out some kind of vengeance on my enemies. But truly I never thought about taking vengeance on my enemies because I always read the Bible and extract good ideas from it. Nevertheless, I thanked these señores for their sound advice.

On this day I did not go anywhere because I felt very sick at heart and afraid because, as I have said many times, I am a person of humble circumstances. For certain, I am not accustomed to living with such bitter things that make life very unpleasant.

During the day I was not without visitors in the house, but when night fell the visitors retired to their houses. Only then did I feel bothered, because they left me alone. I practically did not sleep the whole night. Thus it was until Friday dawned, and I gave thanks to God.

At 4:00 A.M. I went to get my two witnesses to go to present themselves in the court of the first instance in Sololá. When we arrived at the shore of the lake, there was a lot of wind, and the launch did not dock in San José. This obliged us to go to San Martín to catch the launch [which is the next port and has a better docking pier]. However, I went with much fear, because this is the town where my enemies are. Out of pure necessity we had to go there.

When we arrived in this town, we had problems because the

launch was of the Selta line [the tourist line, not the regular mail line]. They say that the Rosales line had problems with the passengers the previous week, and for that reason the mayor of San Martín solicited the Selta line. Two years earlier the Selta line solicited a route in San José, but the municipal secretary, Marcos Erasmo Ramos, was involved in a lawsuit with the line, and for that reason it did not want to carry people from San José. At the port in San Martín, they stopped us from boarding the launch, but we told the conductor that we urgently needed to go to Sololá. This man did not want to let us board until we told him that this secretary had already left San José.

When we arrived in Sololá, we then went to a *comedor* for breakfast with my friends. But I did not feel hungry. After breakfast we headed for the courthouse in order that my witnesses could present testimony in my favor. They had seen me on the day the crime was committed, Sunday, 18 February. When we entered the courthouse, we did not know the hour of the *notificaciones*, and when they told us it was not until 11:00 A.M., we had to wait. My friends then went walking to the market, leaving me alone. My lawyers, however, warned me not to walk by myself because my enemies would be able to provoke a great problem. During this short while when they left me alone, I felt very grieved because it is certain that many *Martineros* travel in these parts. When my companions returned, I felt reassured.

Later the hour of the *notificación* arrived for the first witness, and they called José Horacio Temó Morales. It took him until noon to make his declaration. After the first witness testified, the official told me that the *notificación* of the other witness would be at 3:00 P.M. We left the courthouse and went to eat lunch. Afterwards, the witness who testified left for Panajachel to catch the launch to San José to notify my close kin, because otherwise they might think I had remained in prison. Meanwhile I waited with the other witnesses for the indicated hour, but we were unable to testify. Not until 3:00 P.M. did they take the *notificación* of Señor Abraham Novales Bizarro.

Well, this señor declared everything that he had seen, or, that is to say, all that they asked him. However, the *notificación* did not end until 6:00 P.M. It was very late when we left the courthouse, and it was impossible for us to travel to our town. Neither of us had brought bedding and we were short of money because we carried only enough for expenses for one day. Finally I thought of going down to Panajachel, and that is what we did.

We were able to eat at the Comedor Ramírez, but we had money only for dinner and travel to San José. We did not have money for a pension because accommodations in Panajachel are expensive. My worry was for the witness because he is a *principal* of the town. But the honorable *principal* told me it was no bother to spend the night in the street, which was better than spending many nights in jail. This man gave me much encouragement.

Immediately we walked in the streets without knowing what time it was. As we were walking through the streets, we met a great friend of mine, *licenciado* Jorge Carlos Morales Marroquín. He told me to wait in front of the Hotel Casa Contenta. When we arrived, we waited until 10:00 P.M., but he did not appear. Thanks to God, the caretaker of the hotel is my great friend Jaime.

I told him that we had no shelter for the night. This friend was moved to ask us to come into the waiting room because certainly it was very cold. We sat there waiting until my friend, the *licenciado*, showed up. I told him that we were traveling without money to pay for a pension. This friend, the *licenciado*, paid for a room for us. The *principal* was very surprised because instead of remaining in the street, we were put up in a hotel.

We arrived home at 1:30 P.M. [the next day] when the sun was hot. My close kin were waiting for me, and they were joyous. I was exhausted from walking hard and hunger. The rest of the afternoon visitors arrived to be informed of the problem. But I told them no one knows yet how it will all turn out.

In the afternoon of this day there was another serious problem that was very complicated. It all was caused by the señor municipal mayor. His father gathered some firewood [about 10 to 12 *tercios*, or backloads] on a piece of property belonging to the Tuc brothers of the village of Pachichaj. When the owners realized that the firewood was gathered on their property without permission, they arranged to bring it on their mules to the town to sell it. The *mozos* [workers] brought the firewood as they had been told by the owners of the land. However, the father of the mayor saw that they were selling the firewood [he had gathered], and he captured them. These two men then told him that they were only workers of the Tucs. Then the mayor took the opportunity to capture the Tucs when they arrived in town for a mass, or a sacrifice, that they had commissioned as a gesture of thanks to God.

At 5:00 P.M. the priest began the mass. They were celebrating the Holy Mass when the guards arrived to capture Señor Eduardo Tuc Pérez. But he asked them to wait until the mass was over. The guards and the *alguaciles* were sympathetic. When the mass was over, Eduardo was carried off to jail accused of being a big thief.

These things happened in my presence because I too participated in the mass. To many of us it was a blow to the heart because
there had been no sure crime. The mayor made a *calumnia*, and in
the afternoon Eduardo was imprisoned.

The mayor ordered two of his employees, one an official of the
justice of the peace and the other the municipal secretary, to Patzunoj,
where the *mozos* had picked up the firewood. He wanted them to
conduct an investigation because they were saying that Señor Eduardo Tuc had been threatening a boy with a rifle. They said he
wanted to kill him. But all of this was a lie, because first they said
Eduardo threatened him with a .22 rifle, and then, when the mayor
sent them to check for evidence for the accusation, they said that they
found 20-gauge shotgun shells. But this is something the mayor did to
these men because all the people know that the firewood was gathered
by the mayor's father. Because these men know how to benefit from
false accusations, they were able to send poor Eduardo to prison in
Sololá. Later, when the court of Sololá summoned the accuser, José,
the father of the mayor, for clarification, he did not wish to present
himself to confirm the accusation. He went around saying that he was
not guilty because he was only advised by the mayor. He thought the
Tucs had stolen his firewood. He did not want to present himself because he was afraid of going to jail. All of this was caused by the bad
advice they gave him in the municipality.

The mayor approved sending one of the Tuc brothers to jail because he now had been mayor for some time, and he was a declared
enemy of them because he claimed that this place called Patzunoj was
a section of land belonging to the municipality, and with much pleasure he would divide it among the poor people. When the people
heard he was going to give them *cuerdas* of land, they gave him
money in return. Each time this was the way it was. The poor simply
gave their money for what he offered them. However, the property
has owners, and for sure the mayor cannot divide it. Because they had
committed their money, these townsfolk say that the mayor is a man
good and clean. To wash his hands before the townspeople, he sent
one of the owners of this land to jail. This was funny because the
people of the town knew what the mayor had done for his followers.

On 13 March, my friend Andrés went to Sololá with his two
witnesses to testify in the court of Sololá. All day long I was sad for
him because the people went around saying many things against us.
Thanks to God, everything turned out well. Andrés returned on the
same day, along with his two witnesses. He had luck because his two
witnesses testified on the same day.

On Friday, 6 March, I got up at 4:00 A.M. for a trip to Sololá to present two more witnesses for my defense. They were Ignacio Ramos García and Bernardino Ujpán Flores. These honorable men saw me on that Sunday, 19 February, from 5:00–5:30 P.M., when I passed a place called Chuachoj as I was returning from Xesucut. The *Martineros* have fabricated the lie that I was in San Martín on this Sunday afternoon sipping liquor with other friends and later killed the boy. But truly on this day I did not go to San Martín, and I have sufficient proof.

Unfortunately, this morning the launch did not dock below San José because of so much wind. We had to walk to San Martín. I was very afraid, because my enemies are from this town. By the grace of God, 15 other *Joseños* walked with me. This gave me courage. When we arrived in this town, there were a lot of people boarding, and the officer of the launch did not want to take us. My countrymen became forceful when they realized we were being discriminated against. Because I was full of fear of lawsuits, I told them to be calm.

When we arrived in Sololá, we went to eat breakfast. Then we went to the courtroom of the first instance. When we entered the office, I presented my two witnesses. The official told me that the *notificación* would not be until 10:30 A.M. We waited.

When the indicated hour arrived, they called Señor Ignacio Ramos García. Later they called Bernardino Ujpán Flores. The declarations ended. As we were leaving the courthouse, we met two close kin, Jaime and Juanito, who are honorable workers. They told me that the police were looking for them to put them in jail. I went to a friend who works for the national police and asked him if it was true that the police were looking for two *Joseños*, and he told me it was true. But he did not tell me why. Thanks to God, none of these policemen know these two kinsmen. Then we went to the market but with much grief. Together we ate lunch. As we were returning to our town, I told them it was better not to go down to Panajachel because some *Martinero* might turn them over to the hands of the police. On this day I forgot my great problems. What was more important to me was the defense of these kinsmen.

In order not to return via Panajachel, we caught a long-distance bus for Santa Ana, arriving at 4:00 P.M. There we ate a little food and continued walking until we arrived in our town. When we arrived, we went to the office of the justice of the peace to find out why there was an order to capture these two *Joseños*. They told us it was all a lie. Judicially there is nothing against anyone in San José. Only then did these two friends go to their houses peacefully.

Three days later they investigated the meaning of the *pesquiza* [inquiry] about these two boys. I learned that the *Martineros* had paid some person again to fabricate some crime, but first they wanted to put my two friends in prison for a few days. These enemies were looking for a way to pester my close kin. They would claim they were big drug offenders. This was the *Martineros'* plan. But it was all futile because, when these two boys realized that they were facing a difficult situation, they acted in order not to fall into the hands of their enemies. They sent a telegram to all the justices of the peace in the whole republic asking if it was true that there is an order to capture Jaime and Juan. In two days the courts answered the telegrams telling them that there is no complaint against them nor any order to capture them. Thus, this falsehood was dismissed. The *Martineros* were totally embarrassed for a second time.

They try to imprison us, but they are not able because we have a clean conscience. We never think badly about them. They always cause much damage, but they are very wrong because the majority of them live on earnings from land in San José, the best land in the town. Still they are thinking the worst for us instead of wanting us as brothers. They are slandering us before the authorities. I ask God that the people of San José not also be slanderous because *la calumnia es peor que la muerte* [slander is worse than death].

Finally, news reached us that the *Martinero* whom I was accused of murdering was the head of a band of thieves. A day came when he was not able to escape, and he was killed for stealing.

∿ Checking the Sales of the Cooperative
16 MARCH 1979

On 22 February the cooperative was almost destroyed. I am thankful to the good hearts of my companions who expressed faith in me. It is certainly correct that I had been with them until late in the night on the day the boy in San Martín was murdered. My companions were my best witnesses. For the rest of February, I was unaware [of what was happening] in the cooperative.

When I arrived in the tienda on 16 March, it was to check the sales for the past month. When we finished the accounts, my companions were very content, but I was full of fear because it was night and the persecution I had suffered made me tremble. The earnings were good, but we still were not able to hire an employee so we had to continue with our turns at selling.

❧ The Day of San José
19 MARCH 1979

I woke up sick because during the night I drank *aguardiente*. I was drinking with my friends Antonio Cholotio Canajay and Juan Sicay Bizarro and two others. I do not know what hour I arrived home.

There was a mass scheduled for the afternoon because today is the day of San José. I was going to go to the mass to console my heart a little because I felt very shattered. But on this day I committed a great fault because I was not able to go to the mass. My wife and children went and took alms to the mass [$12 for the priest]. After mass some people from the church arrived to visit me, and I drank *tragos* with them. When they left, others came, and so went the afternoon. This day, Tuesday, was very peaceful.

Today my work companion, Andrés, went to Sololá to present two other witnesses to testify in his favor. By the grace of God, this friend returned on the same day without incident. In Sololá they told him that we would have to present ourselves to our lawyers for a very important matter with the the other friends who were fighting for us.

❧ Manuel Colom Argueta Is Murdered
22 MARCH 1979

At 9:00 A.M. we arrived [in Sololá] and went to see our friends. We told them we should eat together because we carried with us fish and crabs. Then they found the wife of one of our friends, and she prepared a soup. While she was preparing the lunch, we went to the lawyers to ask about the matter. They told us everything was going fine, but they needed money. Then we went back to the house of our friends.

Before arriving, we heard the news of the death of *licenciado* Manuel Colom Argueta, founder of the Partido Frente Unido de la Revolución. We lamented the death of this illustrious *licenciado*. Neither we nor our friends of Sololá ate lunch. The man we were mourning was famous. A lot of people were weeping for him. Certainly one could see an affliction in the whole city.

Personally, I did not know *licenciado* Colom Argueta; I knew him only from his photograph and his speeches on the radio, Nuevo Mundo. We heard him many times. His words were very sentimental, always addressing the well-being of the poor. What a pity they took his life and did not allow him to work! The soul of the exterminated

Manuel Colom Argueta is with God. God forgive those who assassinated him. In this world there are always those who are doing good and those who are doing bad.

On this day, Thursday, we all passed the whole afternoon very sad. We did not arrange anything relating to our problem. The trip turned out worthless, because our friends did not attend to us because of the death of Colom Argueta.

Was Manuel Colom Argueta's party, Frente Unido de la Revolución, a leftist party?

Yes, it was of the opposition. He was against the oppression of the government. He had a lot of dealings with socialistic people. He was not a Communist, but a socialist. It was a pity that they were afraid of him because, indeed, if he had become a candidate, it is certain that he would have become president. He had a large following and much influence over the majority of voters. At his meetings he always presented well the situation of the campesinos and the poor who do not have jobs. A lot of people supported him. For that reason, his enemies did not allow him to become a candidate because they felt that if he did, for sure the government in power would lose— Lucas would lose. This was their motive for killing Colom.

They assassinated him.

Yes, he was assassinated pitifully. He was traveling in a Mercedes-Benz, a car belonging to his wife. He was machine-gunned on a street.

Perhaps it was the policía judicial?

Without doubt. They are responsible for all of it. This is a criticism, true, but in reality they have done a lot of wickedness. In the news, a lot are suffering; a lot of children face hunger because the *policía judicial* apply their justice without proving their cases are true. Or they perform their justice for some money. Three great counselors of this party have died.

Who were the others?

First they killed Alberto Fuentes Mohr, who also wanted to form a party said to be of the left. And Fuentes Mohr was of one of the socialist parties, not Communists . . . or, I'm not certain, does the word Communist mean the same as socialist?

No, they are different.

Well, then the ideology that he had was socialistic ideology. They killed Alberto Fuentes Mohr. Later they killed the Quetzalteco lawyer, Jorge Jímenez Cajos. After they killed him, they killed Manuel Colom Argueta, who was the third of the three great lawyers—three persons of prestige! They eliminated the good who had abandoned the bad.[18]

❧An Ungrateful Companion Accompanies Us to Guatemala City
3 APRIL 1979

In the afternoon we went down to Panajachel to eat in the Comedor Ramírez. Immediately afterwards we went to sleep on the sand of the beach. There we spent the whole night. At 3:00 A.M. we boarded the launch for our town.

On Monday, 3 April, Andrés and I went to Sololá to ask the lawyers if they were resolving our case, because we have been very upset since the time our enemies falsely accused us. We can't work or eat peacefully because our enemies are going around saying that with their money they are going to put us in prison for a long time. I already have said many times that we are not guilty of this dark crime.

On this day the lawyers told us that we are certain to gain our liberty but that they needed money for their professional fees. However, we are already out of money. We do not have more with which to solve this bitter controversy. Thus went our trip.

As we returned home we thought about [how to raise] money. In the afternoon when we arrived home, Andrés and I arranged to go to the Ipala farm on the coast (where we work) to ask for a loan.

On Thursday, 5 April, at 5:00 A.M., we were ready to leave for Ipala, but there was no transport. It must have gone down to meet the launch to take the people to the fiesta of Sololá. We considered going alone, but then we decided it would be better to ask a friend to accompany us.

At 6:00 A.M. we reached the house of Señor Julián Chorol, our friend, and then we asked if he wanted to go with us to the coast. He said yes.

When we arrived at the farm, we talked with the administrator about a loan of $500. But this señor told us that for the moment he did not have the authority of the patron to give loans to the contractors.

However, this señor knows us well because we have been working on this farm for years. Always we have tried to work honorably. For that reason, the señor conceded us a loan of $300 in the form of an authorized check. At the same time he ordered a chauffeur to take us to the capital.

After looking for a pension, we went to eat in a *comedor*, but the *comedor* that we entered was very simple, and our traveling companion was very delicate and did not want to eat. He told us that when one is in the capital one has to look for a good *comedor*. Also he said that after eating one needs a good *trago* to make the food go down well. Well, this friend saw that we carried a check, and it is for this reason he acted very pretentiously. We had to take him to a bar to give him his *trago*. Andrés also drank a shot, but I did not want to drink. We bought them two-eighths of liquor.

After the *tragos* we went to eat. Then we went to a pension, but our companion did not want to sleep. He said that he needed a drink but not one of less value. I answered okay, and we went to a cantina where I asked for another two-eighths and a Coca-Cola for me. After the *trago* that I bought, Andrés asked for another two-eighths. But I was getting weary waiting for them because I continued to think about our situation. I told them we should go to sleep. Andrés helped make this point, and we left the cantina and went to the pension to sleep.

As Andrés and I were sleeping, Señor Julián Chorol told me he needed another *trago*. I gave him a dollar but with the stipulation that he return afterwards.

This señor tricked us and went to engage in a big drunk. I did not sleep. I just waited for him. By 5:00 A.M. this friend had not shown up. Then Andrés and I considered looking for him.

We looked in all the restaurants of Zone 1, but it was impossible to find him. Then we took a street bus to the second *cuerpo* [corps] of the national police to see if our friend had been detained. We asked for the name of Julián Chorol, and they told us that he had not been arrested. At this *cuerpo* they told us to go to the first *cuerpo* of national police because that body of police patrols Zone 1. Very distressed, we boarded another bus for the first *cuerpo*. When we arrived at this institution, we began to look for Señor Julián Chorol by his name, but this señor did not appear.

Andrés and I were very troubled for having brought such a bad companion. We thought that this señor had been killed. We also thought that for this man we could be put in prison because we took him away from his family. Moreover, he is close kin to my wife. Already we were in a delicate situation.

The police told us to look in the hospitals, but we were very tired. What we did was go to the Banco Agrícola to cash the check they gave us on the farm. When we arrived at this bank, Señor Luis was waiting for us, but he was quite drunk.

We cashed the check and went to a Rebuli bus. Only then did we calm our thirst and hunger. During the hours that we were searching for this wicked companion, we suffered a lot. When we arrived in Sololá, I asked this companion what had happened, and he told me he went to sleep with a woman whom he met in a restaurant. We had tried to be careful, but everything was to the contrary. God forgive me, but when we were eating in Guatemala [City], we did not give any to this ungrateful companion for having conducted himself so poorly.

Tuesday, 10 April, Andrés and I went to Sololá to pay our lawyers. We gave them $250 of the money they had lent us on the farm. We spent the day visiting some friends who had helped us a lot in the situation that we suffered.

❧ Losses in the Cooperative
APRIL 1979

In April the income of the tienda of the cooperative increased a little because the associates contributed another little sum of money to cover their [pledged] contribution [of $15]. But the debt also increased, because one of our companions bought some of our products on credit and delayed paying for them for some time. This affected our functioning, but gradually the money was recovered.

When we did our books in mid-April, the committee of administration discovered that the past three months were actually worse than we had thought, due to poor accounting. Because of incorrect arithmetic, a false increase of nearly $100 had been recorded.

Our business was normal for April, but we had little capital with which to operate. Days later we discovered that our problem had been the loss of some empty bottles. We lost nearly three cases. Also, there were rumors that some of the workers were giving back too much money when making change, due to their illiteracy. Hardly anyone was really to blame. We decided that the solution would be to have an employee in the tienda to avoid the losses of so much money and so many bottles. Thus, the board of directors began looking for a person to hire as a salesman in the tienda.

During the month of April, I was planting my *tablones* of onions in Xesucut. Until now I was preoccupied more with solving my situation than with my work. Now I could concentrate again on the land I had rented for planting onions. I planted 30,000 sprigs, part of it bought and the other part lent to me by my father-in-law. We irrigated them daily, but it nearly killed us. We struggled to buy chemical fertilizer, and we cleaned the field right away. During the month of April my family and I suffered much. We were short of corn, and we passed the month in pure pain.

❦ The Sad Case of Don Ramón, Who Burned Images of San Miguel and San Antonio
6 MAY 1979

Don Ramón was born in Santa Bárbara. His parents were *Catolicos Antiguos* [folk Catholics, as compared to Catholic Actionists, or reformed Catholics]. In his house he had three images. When his parents died, he kept the images, always respecting them and taking care of them with much devotion. Ramón always made [private] fiestas celebrating the days of San Miguel and San Antonio. His life was always Catholic, and he was a man whose mind was always clear, but he fell into the claws of alcohol.

Ramón was a very clever Tzutuhil. In this town they carefully paid him respect because of his intelligence. A little later he was named mayor of the town. Then Ramón realized the worthiness of being mayor, and he understood he was in a bad situation because he liked alcohol. Then he took the measure of changing his religion. He was Catholic when he took possession of the office of mayor, but some months later he changed his religion, joining the evangelist church (Central American Church). He thought that changing his religion would change his attitude. But it was not to be, because this man changed his religion and sank to drinking [more] *aguardiente*. Worse, he became very arrogant, justifying himself and never pardoning anyone. He was a bitter mayor.

The town regretted having named him mayor, but it had to bear him until his year was finished. When he left office, he continued to be a Protestant. In his house, however, he still had the images of the saints, but he abandoned them as if they were trash. One day this señor was annoyed at seeing the images taking up space in his house. It was a day when this man wanted to bathe in the *temascal* [sweat house], but he did not have firewood to heat it. He took the two images, chopped them up with a hatchet, and threw them into the fire to heat the *temascal*. His wife warned him not to do such damage, but he paid her no mind.

When the hour arrived to enter the *temascal*, his wife did not want to join him; she was afraid because her husband had burned the two saints to heat the *temascal*. But Ramón said that they were just sticks and did not contain the spirits and that the saints did not exist. For that reason, they would serve as firewood for the good purpose of bathing in the *temascal*. Still, his family insisted that he not bathe, but this man did not obey.

Finally, he entered the *temascal*, taking with him everything necessary for a good bath. He went inside when it was very hot. But once inside, his appearance changed—his face twisted. When he came out he could not speak. His family began to shout with fright, because when the man went in he was in good health, but when he came out he was totally disfigured. There was a great alarm in the town.

The following day his family wanted to ask him what had happened, but he was not able to speak at all. Ramón remained thus the rest of his life, only able to speak one word, "Jun . . . jun . . . jun." When a person wanted to greet him with "Buenos días," he answered, "Jun." When someone gave him a little something, he answered, "Jun." The rest of his life he had a twisted face, twisted hand, and twisted foot. He spent many years asking for alms in the market of Santa Ana, but many people did not want to give him charity. They hated him for having burned the two images.

Don Ramón said "Jun" in Spanish when he wanted to say "uno [one]." The people said it was the image of San Miguel, one of the most powerful saints, who punished him, and now he can say only "Jun." That is to say, just one of the saints punished him. Although the reader may not believe such a thing, it really happened.

I was aware of all these things because my adoptive father, Señor Martín, was brother to Ramón. For that reason, I know very well what happened in the life of this person.

In the month of May, I continued to work on the onions. My children helped me when they got out of school. During this month, a good friend from San Jorge named Gregorio, who is the owner of a truck, helped me somewhat by giving me hundreds of pounds of corn on credit while I sold it by the *arroba* [a 25-pound measure]. I would run out at the end of the week, and then he would lend me more *quintales*. That is the way it was during May. With the centavos I earned I was able to buy corn and other things to sustain my family.

◕ The Cooperative Hires Salesmen
15 MAY 1979

On 14 May Señores Abraham and Roberto Mendoza accepted the position of salesmen for the cooperative. The day before was when we called everyone to let them know that we had split the post in the tienda between the two men—each one working every other day. That is, they could spend one day in the tienda and the next day in their fields. One person alone could not do it. We agreed that the pay of these two employees would be $80, with each one earning $40 for working 15 days a month, with the condition that they sleep in the tienda overnight to protect the products. The majority of the associates saw the need for hiring two employees [to share the work].

A big problem emerged, however, because a group of three men and three women did not want to hire the employees because they felt we could lose more money in the tienda. They wanted to develop other ideas, but the board of directors had already arranged the hirings. There was much debate, but the committee of administration and the committee of control won. There were 25 votes in favor and 6 against. Thus, we finished taking our turns selling in the tienda on 16 May.

On 17 May the employees took possession of the sales. But there was a disturbance among the members because [two of] those who earlier had agreed to hiring the employees changed their minds and joined the group in opposition. The vice-president of the committee of administration joined the opposition, leaving only the president, secretary, and treasurer. And a little later the president and vice-president of the committee of control joined the opposition—the latter because he owed the cooperative. Thus, both the committee of administration and the committee of control were affected [by the factionalism]. I just encouraged the board of directors not to fall into the hands of the opposition. We fought intensely for a month, which demoralized the rest of the members. During that month the majority of the associates did not come to the meetings.

The president realized that the hiring of the two employees was splintering the group, but everything had been decided and nothing could be done. Then I got the idea of having one employee with less than the salary of the two combined. Because $80 is a somewhat large salary and the cooperative has very little capital, the tienda was not earning what the employees were receiving in pay. Thus, the committee began to consider paying a salary of $60 so that the cooperative could realize a little profit.

On 16 June we spent the whole night going over our accounts. Finally, we concluded that the sales were equivalent to previous months but that we earned only $19 compared to $100 in previous months. We realized the salaries of the employees were reducing the profits. Although the salesmen had behaved very well, their salaries were nearly equal to the sales.

ꙮ Our Employees Do Not Want to Work
22–28 JUNE 1979

On 22 June both employees asked to go to Sololá on the following day. The president of the committee of administration wanted only one of them to go, but they both insisted, claiming their trip was urgent. Then the president ordered the tienda closed but without informing the committee of control. When I hurried to the president of the committee of administration to ask him why the tienda was closed, he told me what had happened. Then I asked him to authorize me to sell in the tienda in place of the two employees. He did.

I opened the tienda at 9:00 A.M. When night fell, neither employee showed up.

When it dawned Saturday, 23 June, it was the same thing. At 6:00 A.M. I opened the shop. It was the day of the eve of the fiesta. The employees were more interested in it than in working in the tienda.

On the main day of the fiesta, 24 June, with the help of señores Jorge Flores Pérez and Julio Flores Ramos, both of whom are enthusiastic but illiterate, I opened the shop. The two literates stayed away.

Our cooperative is named, "La Voz que Clama en El Desierto [The Voice that Cries in the Wilderness]." We took this name from the Bible. These are the words of Juan the Baptist when he was in the wilderness. We looked for this name because all the other organizations have the name Juan Bautista and we wanted ours to be distinctive.

A few days before the fiesta, a sacred mass was offered in honor of San Juan Bautista. Everything was pleasant, and they lit the *bombas* [bombs, fireworks shot from mortars]. But not everyone attended.

When 24 June, the main day of the fiesta, arrives we always take out the image of San Juan Bautista in a procession through all the main streets of the town. On this day when San Juan visits the town, the persons who live near the streets receive him with great honor and worship him as he passes in front of their houses.

As is the custom, we of the cooperative received San Juan when he passed in front of the tienda of the cooperative. We adorned the street where the image passed, and we lit *bombas*. Conserving something of the history and customs of our fathers was very pleasant. But the priest wants to abolish them. However, with our organization, we will never allow him to oppress us.

On 26 June, it was the same. I went to open the shop at 6:00 A.M. On this day the treasurer told me that if I wanted to work in the tienda, it would be better to start working by the month. But I told him that I was doing this just to maintain the sales of the tienda. He asked me how much I charged for my days of work, and to set an example I charged only $2, which would be $60 monthly. On 27 June another associate, Ignacio Carlos Ovalle, sold for a day, and on 28 June the associate Fernando Jorge Méndez sold.

Two days after the fiesta of the town, I sold my *tablones* of onions for $120, only $4 a thousand, which was very cheap. With this money I bought a little clothing for my children, but it was not possible for us to enjoy the fiesta because we did not have much money. True, I had sold some onions, but I still owed the lawyers. For that reason, I was afraid to spend the money because I do not want problems with these señores.

❧ A Trip to Sololá to Pay the Lawyers
29 JUNE 1979

On this day no one wanted to work in the tienda, and it remained closed. Everyone was curious about the fiesta in San Martín. I too considered going to the fiesta, but finally I decided to go to Sololá to cancel a debt of $90 from last month for which I had been notified by telegram to pay.

When I arrived in Sololá, the *licenciado* Emilio Falla Jiménez had gone to Quezaltenango. His wife attended to me and looked for the contracts. She wrote me a provisional receipt stating that everything was paid. All of my commitments were cleared, and also I made a $7 payment for my friend Andrés. The lawyer's wife told me that the *proceso* [file of papers in the action] is already archived in the court of the first instance [and that we were acquitted]. She also told me that I ought to be careful not to go much to San Martín because my enemies could accuse me falsely again.

When I arrived home, my family was very content because we had disposed of the accusations of the tongues of my enemies. For lunch we ate beef. Unfortunately we were not able to spend a little time at the fiesta in San Martín.

❧ Milling Problems in the Town and Incorporating the Cooperative
1 JULY 1979

Since January of this year, there has been a serious problem for the women of San José. In the town there are four *molinos* (mills) of *nixtamal* (corn kernels). Three years ago there were only two that charged 3–5 centavos [a batch], depending on the number in the family. When they bought a motor and mill, Benjamín Coché Sandoval and Mario Ovalle Tuc raised their price of grinding to 15 centavos for what used to cost 5 centavos. This was all instigated by Señor Mario Ovalle Tuc, who told the other three to elevate the price. They agreed.

The women appealed the higher price, but the ungrateful millers shut down their business when the women came with their *nixtamal*. The owners of the mill claimed that they could not grind the corn because they did not have any water.

Then, out of pure necessity, the poor women carried the necessary water for grinding, but then the owners claimed they did not have any fuel. Finally, the women had to agree to the higher price. Only then would the millers grind the *nixtamal*, and then they did so with inferior service.

Since we poor people would never be able individually to buy a motor and mill because of the high price of $2,000, I suggested the idea of [collectively] buying our own. Nearly all our wives in the town have been suffering.

On 1 July we had a general assembly for *gestionar la personería jurídica* [taking steps to acquire legal status, or capacity]. The secretary of the committee of control told the association what had been happening in the tienda in recent days. Fernando Jorge Méndez had been selling in the tienda since 30 June in place of the two employees. When these problems were aired, many of the associates reproached us, but little by little things calmed down. We decided a solution would be to name an employee at the salary of $60 per month instead of $80. And finally we convinced Fernando Jorge to stay in the tienda for a month as the salesman. He accepted, with the condition that he would be able to work half the day in his fields and leave his wife in charge of the sales in the tienda while he was gone.

When all this was settled, I asked for a little more time from everyone, and they gave me their attention. I recounted all the suffering we were facing because of the millers, and I told them that we needed to have a mill in the cooperative to save us from the claws of the millers because they have us very oppressed. When we finished talking, everyone was pleased, especially the women. Everyone said if possible he was going to give a little additional contribution of $10. But a month would be allowed to pass to give everyone time to come up with the money.

The discussion ended and everyone was content. We threw a little fiesta with some sodas and sweet bread. One can see a little activity, but still I do not know if we will see it work out. Everyone said he would meditate a little and ask God to help us progress toward our goal.

On 2 July the new employee, Fernando Jorge, took over his job in the tienda. Then the members began to arrive again to take their parts as incorporated associates. Only the president was not participating as before. I do not know if there were problems in his family or whether we had committed some fault against him.

❧ I Am Named to the *Junta de Vigilancia*
TUESDAY, 10 JULY 1979

At 6:00 P.M. I went to my cooperative to check what the employee had sold during the day, because I have been named to the *junta de vigilancia* [committee of control]. The employee had $197.73 for the treasurer.

What is the responsibility of the junta de vigilancia?

Here [Ignacio reads a copy of the statutes] in this statute, Article 58 says that the *comisión de vigilancia* [committee of control] is the organ responsible for controlling the fiscal aspects of the cooperative, and it is comprised of three members elected for a year in an an ordinary general assembly. [Ignacio read several other technical regulations which I have excluded.]

In the night my wife bathed in a *temascal* because she is sick with a chill. For us Indians the best treatment for a chill is the *temascal*.

Can you explain how the temascal *is prepared and what happens when a person is inside it?*

Inside the *temascal* there is an *hornillo* [small oven or stove] of small stones. One carefully arranges these stones and makes a fire with *jocote* [American plum] and firewood, but not with any kind of firewood. The *temascal* is heated with firewood of *tasiscó*, in *lengua* [native tongue, Tzutuhil Maya] called *tzaj*, or, say, with cane of milpa. The *temascal* is heated with firewood that does not burn hot, because if one puts in firewood of *encina* [holm oak] or [some] other [tree], the *temascal* becomes too intense with heat, and it is easy for the person to suffocate.

The *temascal* is very important to us Indians for strengthening our muscles against the cold. It is very medicinal. When a person feels cold or has an ache in his body, the *temascal* is necessary. But he needs to take great care to cover himself when leaving the *temascal* because, if the air penetrates, it is certain he will die. This has happened to many persons.

Also, the *temascal* is necessary for pregnant women. Midwives recommend using the *temascal*. When a woman is 6 to 7 months pregnant, they recommend using the *temascal* for sure. It is most recommended when only a few days remain before giving birth. The woman's body is weaker, and the *temascal* allows a faster exit of the baby.

Also, the *temascal* is used as a method to treat persons who suffer from rheumatism. Many who suffer from rheumatism go to doctors, but they see no results until they use the *temascal*. Only after using it do they get relief. This is true, because among our close kin there are persons who suffer from rheumatism, and they are treated with the *temascal*.

It is true that there are not as many *temascales* in our town as there used to be. Families who do not own a *temascal* have to borrow those in other *sitios*.

When the Mayas use the temascal, *do they vomit to clean inside their bodies?*

For bathing in the *temascal*, we do not vomit. Moreover, what we need to do before entering the *temascal* is not to eat, because if one eats it is easy to vomit due to the hot temperature. When we leave the *temascal*, we are able to eat, but we avoid chili because if one eats chili, the mouth will suffer.

The mouth?

Yes, because chili is very strong and causes much inflammation. It serrates the mouth like a fire.

Is the use of the temascal *a religious act?*

Yes, for the indigenous people of my town, it is very sacred. Each woman who gives birth to her baby always bathes in the *temascal*. In respect the *temascal* is called *abuelita* [grandma]. In *lengua* it is called *katit*, which means *abuela* [grandmother] in Spanish.

There is a *secreto* [sacred or magical act] when one constructs a *temascal*. When one is finished constructing the *hornillo*, where one makes the fire, the eldest person in the owner's family has to buy a little tobacco or a cigar and smoke inside the *temascal*. This is to insure that the *temascal* will get hot with just a little firewood. Afterwards, the women are careful not to put in too much firewood so the *temascal* will not get too hot. Otherwise, it is easy to become dizzy and die if the *temascal* is too strong. This is what our dear old people say, true, but I do not know whether this *secreto* is worthwhile. But indeed they do it.

When you recently constructed a temascal, *did you perform a* secreto?

In this case it was my grandma who performed the *secreto*, because she had nearly recovered her health. She had to smoke either a cigar or pure tobacco in a *pipa*. You know what a *pipa* is. It was smoked by the ancient people of my town. Only a few *pipas* still exist among the old people. While the rest of us watched outside, my grandma entered the *temascal*. We covered the door, and she began to smoke. When she felt it was good and full, she asked that the warmth of the *temascal* not leave. Then one will not have to throw on much firewood. My grandma says that, if one does not perform this *secreto*, one can put in a lot of firewood, and the *temascal* will not get hot. It will not absorb the heat—just smoke. Thus, she told us that the *temascal* needs its *secreto*.

Is this what your old folks say?

This is what our ancestors and our grandparents who are still living say. My grandma also recommends [*costumbres*] when the first rains fall.

When the first rains fall, we give thanks to God, burning incense and candles. We have a lot of respect for something superior to man who makes these marvelous works. Thus, we have done this tradition, and we will continue to do so. They are customs of my parents that I must continue because it shows respect to give thanks to God for everything, because they say that when God wants [it] to rain over the face of the earth, he sends his angels to irrigate. I do not know for sure because we have not seen them, but we still give thanks that there is something superior that changes the seasons, because the seasons alone are not able to change themselves. Indeed what we have observed is that there is something superior to nature. So we continue to do these customs because they are recommendations of our parents, who say that one must give thanks to God, burn a candle, and burn a little incense to offer its smoke to the creators so that God will bless the earth.

❧ My First Cousin's Daughter Dies of Malnutrition
12–13 JULY 1979

In the night I went to the cooperative until 9:30 P.M. I did not go to sleep until 11:00 P.M. because I was listening to the news about Nicaragua.

At 5:30 P.M., 13 July, it rained and hailed very heavily. Such a great quantity of hail I have never seen before. My children were very frightened. Hail in ingots fell in the door of the house. It was very strange.

Together with my wife I lit a *velador* [candle in a glass], and we burned incense. It is a tradition of my grandparents to give thanks to God for having sent his angel to irrigate the earth.

On this same afternoon, the daughter of my first cousin, Ignacio, died because of malnutrition and many parasites and also lack of a doctor. Well, there are doctors in Panajachel and San Luis, but for the poor they are expensive. My cousin tried to cure her with *curanderos* [curers], but it was not possible.

❧ The First Catechist Is Dismissed
14 JULY 1979

At 4:00 P.M. I wrote a few pages on the typewriter [that he bought from an anthropologist], but they were not coming out well because I am not able to type. I am just practicing.

At 3:00 P.M. Sunday I went to a meeting in the parochial assembly hall. They tried to replace the president of the association of families. This organization is is scarcely a year old. They also talked about changing the first catechist. The president of Catholic Action said that the first catechist, who is Señor Santiago García Cruz, is very *bravo* [churlish]. He wants to send people to work, but he does not want to work himself. They say that now there are 90 catechist men, but only 5 to 7 of them are active. The rest feel offended. The president and the others named another person [as first catechist].

What is the association of families?

It is an association of Catholics who have organized to help someone who falls sick or has hard times. They go to the house to investigate and console the afflicted. But in this case, I was witnessing some bad things. The association is worthwhile, but the leaders were not doing what was necessary. The association is very important because we Indians do not have information or money. I wanted to help them organize well and to collect some centavos on behalf of others to counter sickness, to buy medicine, or to send the sick to a doctor or a hospital. But they do not understand. They think this organization is only for going to pray with a sick person. I do not think this alone is worthwhile. I do not know what they are thinking, but they say they are a group that just goes to pray. Do you understand what it means to pray with a sick person? They spend an hour praying with the sick. I told them to organize this group well, but no. It has been impossible until now. They have their few centavos, but I do not know what the money is for. About two months ago I had a meeting with them. They had about $18 to $20 in their treasury. They had contributed their 5 to 10 centavos, but they want to keep the money, not use it for the sick. It is better to help those who are sick, but they do not want to do this. I do not know what they are thinking. On the contrary, their custom is not to arrive until a person dies. But what can you do for a dead person? The organization for me is worth the effort. It is valued in gold because we could be able to help ourselves. If one is poor or without money this organization could help to buy corn for his family. But he would have to be positively sick, not just lazy and trying to swindle the organization. Why should we give food to the lazy? But if he is justifiably sick, he should be helped in whatever manner possible! But the leaders are not serving the community. They are not using their heads because, if the function of this group is just to console with prayer, it is not useful. This is not all the help that is needed.

For me, praying is useful, just as it was useful to my fathers, my past grandfathers, and my ancestors. But we also need to help and work a little for the community.

ᕈᐧ An Agronomist from Caritas Visits the Cooperative
TUESDAY, 17–18 JULY 1979

In the morning I got up and gave thanks to God, and my family and I ate. Then I went to Panasajar to fumigate a little milpa and beans, finishing at 10:00 A.M. Then my wife and I went to a meeting in the parochial assembly hall on behalf of an agronomist invited by Caritas of Guatemala. The meeting was very pleasant. I thanked God that the agronomist spoke very clearly of the situation in which we are living. At this session, 25 men and 20 women attended. The señor agronomist will support the organization of the cooperative. We left this meeting at 1:30 P.M.

After dinner at 7:00 P.M. I went to the tienda for a meeting of the committee of administration to summarize last month's business. The cooperative has granted $151.65 worth of loans to members. We did not finish until 1:00 A.M.

At 3:30 P.M. I began to write a little history of the cooperative with the typewriter. I worked until 7:00 P.M. It is difficult and takes much patience.

At night I went to the tienda to try to persuade the associates to buy a motor and mill by the month of August. I arrived home at 11:00 P.M., and then a señora asked for two *arrobas* of corn on credit, which is worth more than $12. She finds herself in a very needy situation. By the grace of God, I do have corn and more than $12 worth. I did not deny her. She left the house very happy.

In the night it was impossible for me to sleep because of the uproar. At 2:00 A.M. a little horse was born at our neighbor's house. The señora gave us hot coffee with bread, and we ate. It was very pleasant because the señora who owned the horse had a little party.

ᕈᐧThe 4-S Club Is Organized
20 JULY 1979

I woke up with much insomnia. We did not get up until 7:00 A.M. We ate a little bread and some bits of fish in *chirmol* [mixture of chili and ground corn flavored with tomatoes, onions, parsley or coriander, and salt] with tortillas. I did not go to work in the fields.

I worked on the history of the cooperative with the typewriter. I have to be patient.

At 1:00 P.M. I went to a meeting in the cooperative. On this day the 4-S Club was organized. It is composed of 33 boys [who are sons of members] of the cooperative. Also some boys whose fathers are not members were included. Two are 20 years old. It is a project of DIGESA [Dirección General de Servicios Agrícolas, or Directorate General of Agricultural Services] that is directed by the agronomist, Máximo Mario Yax, and Señor Luciano Rojas, who is an advisor. This project is to organize the children so that they can learn how to work better and so that they will not be induced to do evil things. The promoter said that within a few days he is going to give each child $35, which will total to $1,155, for buying onion seeds and for raising fowl. All of this was very nice. We are enjoying moving ahead with the cooperative. Our efforts are producing results.

Until 8:00 P.M. I was writing on the typewriter a history of the club for the children. Later when they are bigger they will be able to read it. Giving thanks to God, I went to bed.

A Political Meeting
24 JULY 1979

In the night I went to a political meeting of the Partido Revolucionario (PR), which is looking for a candidate for mayor. But these men already have arranged everything. Julián [Choral, who is secretary-general of the PR], said that he is going to be the candidate. But I am sure he will lose the election. At 11:00 P.M. Julián and others came to my house to share their thoughts. I had to buy four-eighths liter of liquor to find out which persons they are preparing to run as candidates. For me everything was okay. I did not go to sleep until 1:00 A.M., but I did not sleep peacefully.

Why did you think Julián was going to lose the election?

I did not tell him personally, "You are going to lose the election." But my thoughts were that he was going to lose because of his attitude with the townsfolk. The townspeople are aware of how he has behaved. I just studied the situation and concluded he was going to lose. One time the Partido Revolucionario gave *láminas* [pieces of sheet metal for roofing] to persons who had suffered damage by the earthquakes. This man received a quantity of *lámina*, but he did not give it to the poor people. He sold it for himself. Then I thought, "Is this person going to be mayor? No, better not."

That is to say, they wanted your support?

Yes, and I said no, because this man is going to lose. No, it is better not to get mixed up in these things. After I invited them over for drinks to find out what was going on, they told me that Julián wanted to be mayor for sure. And I said, "It is okay. If you think he is going to be the candidate, it is all right." I did not say anymore [because they had already arranged it]. But I predicted he would not win the election because the people know him too well.

❧ Santiago's Day and a Bull Escapes
THURSDAY, 25 JULY 1979

This is the day of the fiesta of the apostle Santiago. Thanks to God, dawn came peacefully.

In the morning I lit a *velador* in respect for the image of Santiago (an engraving given to me by my deceased mother). As is always our custom, we also burned incense. Thus it was for half the day. During the morning, I also sunned a few planks for Chico [Peralta] because they are wet. [He is making a new bed for my wife, who is expecting.]

I did not eat dinner, and at 6:00 P.M. I left the house to go to a meeting to choose the person to run for mayor. It lasted half the night, but it was all negative. [They could not decide on a candidate.]

My son Erasmo became sick to his stomach with vomiting and indigestion. It was a lot of bother. At 1:00 A.M. I left to look for medicine in the tiendas. He was grave, but by the grace of God, he improved.

During this fiesta the procession was very solemn, but the bullfight was also very pleasant [the bullfighter does not kill the bull]. However, it seems that they had not secured the gate tightly, and the bull escaped and began to chase all the people. He struck many people. Among the people the bull became more crazy, and it arrived where the procession was taking place. He struck those who were in procession, and the *mayordomos* [rank-and-file members of the brotherhood] who were carrying the saint had to put it down.

They say that everyone in the procession abandoned the saint and disappeared. But Santiago was well-dressed in a red velvet cape.

When the bull saw Santiago, it thought he was a bullfighter and jolted him to the ground. However, no one plucked up the courage to help the saint. When the bull saw that the image was not moving, he perhaps thought that Santiago had already died, and he continued chasing people in the streets. No one was able to confront this furious bull until he arrived at a narrow street. There the captain, chief of the national police, was able to kill him with his revolver.

This animal caused serious damage, and thus the owner of the business [of the bullfighting] had serious problems with the town. They sent the image of Santiago to Guatemala [City] for repairs, and the owner of the business had to pay $500. But it was necessary to prosecute him.

❧ More Problems with the Mayor
26 JULY 1979

In my town there are a lot of people who do not have a place to construct their *ranchos* [rustic houses with straw roofs and adobe or cane walls]. In 1964–1965, when the mayor was Señor Sebastian López G., they moved the soccer field because its former location was distant from the town. The señor fought to obtain a piece of property near the town where it actually is now. But when they laid out the field, it covered more than three *cuerdas*.

In 1978 the people who were poorer asked that they be given a little *sitio* for constructing small houses. The mayor, Señor Juan Mendoza, gave it to them, but it was not a whole *sitio*, just half. He gave more to those who gave him more money and just a little to those who gave him little money. It was a nice business for the mayor. However, he gave these places to the people without making it legal.

On this day, 26 July, the mayor told them that he was not able to legalize their rights because some of the councilmen do not agree to do so. He said he needed more money and that if they gave him more money he would go to Sololá to a lawyer for the legal documents. The people came back to give money to the mayor because they were concerned about their security. But everything was futile. The mayor did not go to Sololá.

Also, there are two families which were not able to give money to the mayor. He took back their piece of *sitio* and gave it to a family of San Martín which bought it for more than it was worth. Then the poor people came to me for ideas. But I told them that I did not want any more problems with the mayor.

How could the mayor legalize the holdings of the people?

He was just trying to swindle more money. He could have legalized their property at the tribunal with just the secretary and the syndic. He needed only to have the secretary draw up the papers stating that the municipality of San José authorizes Señor Such-and-Such to be the legitimate owner of a *sitio* donated on behalf of the municipality and that it cannot be encroached upon by another person. The syndic signs these documents as a witness and representative of the Public Ministry. He signs with the mayor. But they did not do this. It was just a business going to the poor people asking for more money to legalize the papers, or execute the deeds of the *sitios*, and telling them that if they do not give more they will lose their *ranchos*.

☙ My Wife Has a New Baby
27–28 JULY 1979

I got up early at 4:30 A.M. and bathed in the *sitio*. I considered going to Sololá on an errand, but I decided not to go. I decided to wait until another day. I was afraid to leave my wife alone because she still was expecting to give birth.

At 8:30 A.M. I went to San Martín with Chico Peralta to buy some things for the bed he is making for me. We arrived back at 10:30 A.M.

I was cleaning my house, shaking the dust off things since a lot of dirt falls in the house because I do not have a loft.

I intended to go to the beach to inspect my fields, but my wife told me not to leave. I had to obey her. I just went to the house of Chico Peralta to help him a little while.

At 2:00 P.M. I was called home to lunch. We ate meat and hot tortillas that my wife made. My wife did all the kitchen work also. Afterwards, she began her pains. Luckily, the midwife, Virginia Ramos H. (Carlota), arrived at this moment. At 3:00 P.M. sharp, my wife gave birth to the baby.

And that is the way it was. I was working to prepare the necessary things for the delivery. My wife's parents were very angry because they did not get to participate. But this was not due to lack of respect; my wife was just fortunate to have her baby [quickly]. Before lunch, I was very sad, but when my wife gave birth to a baby girl, I was very happy. Many kin arrived to celebrate with us. It is always the custom to drink some *traguitos* when a boy or girl is born.

All night long until it dawned 28 July I did not sleep at all. I was taking care of my wife because she is very delicate and should not be left alone after recently giving birth.

When a little infant is born, a custom of us Indians is for its mother not to breastfeed it until two days have passed. If the mother is weak, she does not give it milk until four days later. During this time, the father or another member of the family has to go to ask the favor of another woman to give her breast to the little baby girl or boy who was just born. Also, it is the custom that, when this woman bears another baby, the other woman who just had a baby must reciprocate by breastfeeding her baby. During the night I had to go to ask two women. One of them denied me: she told me that she felt very cold. The other, Señora Elena, however, said, "With much pleasure."

Not until 5:00 A.M. was I able to sleep two hours. I got up at 7:00 A.M. and prepared some little things for breakfast. We ate meat and the same for lunch, but it was just a little for each of us, as I have several [to feed] in my family. All day I stayed home, and I was a little sick with insomnia.

On this day, Chico Peralta brought the bed of *canoj* [a durable wood from the mountains]. I gave him all the material, and it cost me a favorable price of $49. I thought that he was going to bring the bed sooner so we would have it when my wife gave birth, but it was not to be. Such is life. *El hombre pone pero Dios dispone* [Man proposes but God disposes].

At 8:00 P.M. I went to the tienda of the cooperative just to visit. All night long the baby did not sleep. She just cried.

María wanted to cook lunch, but she was unable. It was a niece of Anica who prepared our lunch of tortillas.

During the night I went to a meeting at the cooperative. We did not finish until 11:00 at night. They told me that the mayor wants to expel the poor people who are constructing their *ranchos* near the soccer field. It is a big problem because the councilmen know that the mayor took money from them. For that reason, they want to conduct an investigation.

❧ A Visit with a Curer
TUESDAY, 31 JULY 1979

At 6:00 A.M. I went to a *curandero* of bones for my finger. When I was planting coffee in June, I received a small blow to my finger, but little by little the pain became worse. I had to go to a *curandero*.

How did he cure you?

Each day my finger hurt more. Each time that I worked, it bothered me and the ache became worse. Then I decided to go to the same
curandero who cured the hip of my grandma. His name is Ricardo
Tziac Sicay. I asked him to cure the little finger of my hand.

He took out his sacred bone for curing bones. Frankly I did not
see what kind of bone it was because it was inside a bag. But he told
me it was a bone. He grabbed my finger and rubbed material over the
affected part. It was painful, and I shouted a lot. After he had treated
my finger, he tied it tightly with a rag, a piece of material. But it began
to ache a lot.

Did he cure it?

He cured it, but I had to go three times for treatment. He
treated me in the morning, again in the afternoon, and again the following day. By the following day, it hardly hurt when he rubbed the
bone over it. Now I can move it and work with it. But it is defective
because, when I am tired from work, it still hurts a little. It is crip-
pled, but it does not stop me from working.

[There is] something else. He did not charge me for this service,
not a thing, nothing! It was free. I asked him if I owed him anything,
and he told me, "No, because I did not buy this knowledge. It is a gift
from God that I am able to help you." I asked again if he would allow
me to pay him $2 to $3. "Do not worry, your finger is not very serious,
and it is sinful for me to receive money because of my bone. I have
not bought it. It is a gift of God. You do not have to pay me anything
because it is my destiny." This is what he told me. This man did not
take my money!

❧ Santo Domingo's Day and a *Secreto* for the Baby
SATURDAY, 4 AUGUST 1979

This is the day of Santo Domingo in the *cofradía*, but they are
not going to celebrate until the fifth. This is very crazy.

Today makes eight days since my wife delivered the baby. It is
the custom of us Indians to have a little party when a baby completes
eight days of life. On this day one bathes the baby and puts it in a
hammock.

Also, we bought seven pounds of meat. My sister-in-law, Enri-queta, began to work from 4:00 in the morning. When everything was cooked, we gave a little to the neighbors and close kin.

At 10:00 A.M. the midwife arrived and washed the house, signaling that the sickness of the woman [giving birth] has to leave the house. Then she bathed the baby. After the bath she made a *secreto* with the hammock. Ignacito and Susana had to hold the hammock while the midwife hit them, not with a belt but with a young chicken. We allowed the midwife to strike the children hard until the chick died. Immediately we cooked and ate it. This signified to the children that they are not able to harm the baby girl. The midwife said that the two children now are a little bigger and have stronger blood than the baby. Because they have more strength, the baby can die easily. She also said that the baby needs a ceremony with a shaman so that the influences of the larger children will not capture it. I gave $7 to the midwife, but it was not a payment, just appreciation.

We ate lunch, but my wife did not want to eat. Her health is very delicate, and she ate only a little.

❧ Santiago Cojox: A Real Shaman
SUNDAY, 5 AUGUST 1979

In the afternoon I went to San Martín. But when I arrived, I got a little scared because there had been many people on the road and in the streets. I thought they would be able to make another *calumnia* against me. I asked God to give me strength.

My trip to San Martín was to buy a sombrero and to arrange a trip with the owner of a truck. On the trip I also took the opportunity to meet the real shaman of San Martín, named Santiago Cojox, to ask him the name of the day [that the baby was born] because *ajcumes* [shamans] count the 13 days of the gods of the earth, who are Aj, Ey, Ix, Batz, Ajpub, Quemel, Tziquin, Imox, Bakbal, Cauok, K'ik, Tijax, and Can. The shamans are able to tell the luck of the person according to the day on which he was born. The shaman told me that the baby was born Cauok, which is the day of the god of the lake and good luck, but only if one makes the necessary ceremonies. Later I am going to complete the history of the gods and their significance.

When I pointed out to Ignacio that he later says there are 20 days of the gods, he went to visit with Octavio Toc, a knowledge-

able shaman, who confirmed the names of the 13 gods he had listed and told him the names of seven more—Kjánel, Toj, Ajmac, Kat, Quej, Tzi, and Noj. Ignacio was unable to talk again to Santiago Cojox because of a delicate political situation in San Martín.

❧ The History of the Arrival of the Protestants
6 AUGUST 1979

On the road to Xesucut, I met Señor Hector Có Mirón. He told me a little of the history of the arrival of the Protestants in San José.

In 1920 there were only 20 houses in the town. He spent 14 years providing different services for the town, free. In 1929 the Protestant (Evangelist) religion arrived in San Martín la Laguna. In 1934 the first Protestants arrived in San José. [Other informants stated that Protestantism actually was introduced in the 1920s.] They came from Patzún, accompanied by some *Martineros*, and they intended to establish the religion in the town. But no one in the town wanted Protestantism because the people thought it was a religion contrary to their beliefs. The only person who was eager to receive the Protestants was Señor Don Esteban Gody, who provided his house for their worshiping of God. Some days later he was given a new life and at the same time accepted the word of God.

The second Protestant was Don Héctor Có Mirón. Then, at this time, there were two *Joseños* who were Protestants and who spread the knowledge of their visitors about the sacred word. A little later, Don Antonio Castro joined, and this made three Protestants.

When the members of the Catholic church noticed these three, they rose against them and looked for many kinds of misinformation to present before the authorities with the intent of getting these persons to abandon their religion. These three persons, however, made the utmost effort to stand firm. It was a grave situation for them when Señor Benjamín Peña Puzul was the mayor, Abraham Bizarro Ramos was syndic, and Don José Temó Toc was the first *regidor* [councilman]. These three were dedicated enemies of the evangelist religion. Many people in the town believed them because they were the functionaries of the local authorities. A little later the mayor, Benjamín Peña, and his council charged a *calumnia* against the first three believers and sent them to jail in Sololá. The mayor and the council

presented a legal charge against the three Protestants for having organized in a particular house and inciting the the people to abandon
their old religion. Moreover, they claimed the meetings took place
past the hour [late, around 10:00 P.M.].

Then Don Esteban Gody and Hector [Có Mirón] went to Sololá
very closely guarded as if they were big criminals. When they arrived
in Sololá, the political *jefe* understood the cause of these two men,
and he realized that the accusations against them were false. These
two señores stayed in Sololá for only two days while the political *jefe*
sent for the mayor of the town to clarify the charges. The mayor arrived with his councilmen. Everyone was present for the political *jefe*
to observe, and the political *jefe* concluded that the falsehoods were
those of the mayor. The mayor and the councilmen were nearly imprisoned, but this did not happen because Esteban Gody and Héctor
Có Mirón had compassion for them. There was a lot of suffering when
the Protestant religion arrived in the town.

Also, Don Hector told me some things about the town. Before
the Protestant religion arrived, the people suffered because there
were a lot of services and work in the town and on the farms because
of the *mandamientos* [forced labor migrations]. A time came when the
Joseños were not able to perform all the services. They depended totally on the ability of the people of San Martín, because it was a time
when there were few neighbors and when they found themselves indebted to the people of San Martín. This was caused when the government ordered the *Joseños* to work on the farms and gave them
money for expenses. But the money was not enough. It was exhausted
on sustenance, and for that reason they were obliged to ask the *Martineros* for money.

The *Joseños* were freed from these obligations a little when President Ubico entered office. Not until then were the *Joseños* gradually
able to return to their homes. Then they began to repay their debts.
But indeed many of the *Joseños* remained on the farms all of their
lives.

This is what Don Hector told me. It was very interesting because
we certainly had not realized how our parents suffered in those times.

Also Don Hector told me that at this time the *Martineros* were
gaining by buying the land of San José at very low prices. Many *Joseños* agreed to pledge their land for only *arrobas* [of corn]. But when
they left for the coast, they found it difficult to pay their debts. And
thus in those times the *Martineros* took advantage of the lands of the
people of San José. These things happened before the arrival of the

evangelist (Protestant) religion. I spent about three hours talking to him under the hot sun. I wished I could have bought some sodas, but it was impossible because we were chatting outside of town. Anyway it was very pleasant. I considered returning home, but finally I forced myself to go to Xesucut to inspect my fields.

A Bomb Explodes in Panajachel
9–11 AUGUST 1979

At midnight we arrived in Panajachel [from a trip to the coast], and we went to drink coffee in a restaurant. Immediately afterwards we went to the beach to spend the rest of the night.

We had just reached the shore of the lake when we heard a powerful bomb explode at the Cacique Inn, which was very near us. It gave us a great fright. We worried that the police and soldiers might come and blame us for it. Although I did not go to investigate because I wanted to avoid any more problems, it was certain that it was a strong blast. We hid below a launch that was being repaired, but, by the grace of God, nothing happened to us. We were thanking God when 3:00 A.M. came. Andrés caught the launch for San José, and I remained sleeping on the beach.

Already it was Friday, 10 August. I got up at 6:00 A.M., washed and went to Sololá.

At 7:00 A.M. I ate breakfast, and then I went to look for my friend, *licenciado* Emilio Jiménez, who was in Xela, Quezaltenango, when I was in Sololá in the month of June. When the lawyer saw me, he smiled and said that the case was totally won and that this *calumnia* is already in the archives of the court of Sololá. I had to pay the transport and cancel the debt for carrying the crew. I did not have time to go to the bank. Thus, I sold the check that they gave me on the farm to Señor José Morán, who charged me one percent to cash it.

When all of this was finished, I felt like having a beer because I was very pleased that the lawyer had told me the legal matter was all finished. But I had to summon the strength not to drink the beer because I was carrying money that was not mine. I thought hard about spending money that did not belong to me.

At 5:00 P.M. I arrived in my dear town very happy and gave thanks to God for having liberated me from the hands of my enemies. I felt as if it were a fiesta. We ate contentedly, although our food was very simple because we are poor people who cannot afford to eat more than greens.

At 7:00 P.M. I went to Andrés's house to tell him that everything was settled [regarding legal matters]. He became very happy. Then he ordered two drinks which we drank in his house. When we finished, we left to drink in a cantina. Andrés became inebriated and lost all consciousness. Meanwhile I saw him home. I was conscious when I returned home, but it was very late. My wife was very angry because I had been drinking. But it was certain that we had overcome a great obstacle that the *Martineros* had erected for us.

When I got up on Saturday, 11 August, I felt a big ache in my head and a great weakness. I was hardly able to get up until my wife sent for three beers, and this is what I drank so I could get up. During the day I did not go anywhere. I ate breakfast, lunch, and dinner very contentedly.

The Mayor Slanders Me
SUNDAY, 12 AUGUST 1979

I got up happily [but this day turned out to be one I won't soon forget]. José and Juana went to the fiesta of Santa Ana. We wanted to go too, but as we were short of money, it was not possible.

At 8:00 A.M. I left to visit a friend, my first cousin. But, before I arrived at his house, Juanito Mendoza, the mayor, attacked me in front of the municipality, leveling a slander against my character. He said that he does not want me to be a candidate for mayor because others have told him that, if I become mayor, I would cancel all kinds of taxes for the *Martineros*, and the town would fail. But this is an insult, because I had not said anything, nor do I have interest in filling the office of the tribunal because I do not want to live with any more problems. I do not want to apply justice. I have a very tender heart. True, the *principales* [town elders] have asked me many times to be a candidate for mayor, but I have not given them an affirmative answer. For that reason, Señor Juan Mendoza is the father of the lies because he would like to slander me. I know very well that this señor is afraid of me because I know all of the disgraces that he has committed in the municipality, including all the money that he asked from the people when he offered them land.

At the instance when the mayor attacked me, he was protecting himself because he was wearing a revolver. He thought that I was afraid, but by the grace of God, I did not feel afraid or very angry, just serene. But I told him everything he had committed. Also, I told him that first he would have to pay back what he owed the inhabitants of the town before he could talk to me. A lot of the people were aware of our confrontation because it took place in the atrium of the municipality. The guards and the *alguaciles* were prepared in case a misfortune occurred. But by God's grace, nothing happened.

At 1:00 P.M. a political commission from Guatemala [City] came to my house to organize feminine blocs. They stayed a long while chatting in my house. Juanito Mendoza sent a delegation to invite the politicians to his house. But these señores from Guatemala [City] also know that the mayor is a liar, and they did not accept his invitation.

Later in the afternoon some *principales* arrived at my house. Then we went to the mayor. When we arrived the elders asked the mayor why he wished to harm other persons. There the mayor confirmed that he is a liar because the *principales* could tell he was lying. When we left the mayor, we went to a tienda to drink some beers. We parted very happily.

☙ History of the Dance of the Flying Monkey
12 AUGUST 1979

The people of these towns believe in the *Baile del Mico Volador* [Dance of the Flying Monkey]. It is a dance that is very sacred because it deals with great animals of the forest such as the jaguar, the puma, and the monkey. It is a very old dance that in these times the men are not lively enough to perform; the dancers must fly from a long pole that measures 40 meters high by means of great lassos more than 50 meters long.

The dancers have to fly by means of a lasso until they reach the ground. Before beginning the dance, they have to make great sacrifices to look for a tree in the forest. When they look for a tree, a shaman goes also and carries candles, myrrh, incense, and a lot of sugarcane liquor. Also, they take a lot of meat that they eat below the tree where they make the sacrifice. This serves to protect the tree from breaking when they cut it. Before felling the tree they have to make three kinds of ceremonies, and the fourth time is when they are ready to cut. On the last night of the ritual all the dancers have to offer presents under the tree to ask pardon of the god of the forest [for cutting down the tree]. At dawn they begin to chop down the tree.

After the tree is felled, they begin to strip off the bark or shell, and on the same day they carry it out. Not just the dancers, but the entire town helps because the pole is green and heavy.

In the morning the people have to walk three to five days to arrive at the point where they are going to perform this dance. When they reach the place, they allow the pole some time to dry. While it is drying, they guard it day and night against witches or other shamans. When it is time to plant the pole, they have to make other rituals to avoid danger to the flyers. The first dancer (monkey) is the main shaman of the group and in charge of laying the foundation where they plant the pole. When he is finished laying the foundation, they begin to burn candles, myrrh incense, and offer a lot of rum. But before planting the pole, they first have to throw four living roosters inside the hole. The pole kills them when it falls inside the hole. Along with the four roosters they bury a liter of cane liquor. This serves as a sacrifice for the deity of the pole so that on the main day of the fiesta there will be no danger for the dancers.

When the pole is planted, they have to do four more rituals, and the pole always has to be guarded by the authorities of the town, who are collaborating with the dancers. Furthermore, they believe that it is dangerous for women to cross over the pole before it is planted, because the shaman says that, if a woman passes over the pole, it is possible that on the main day of the fiesta it will break. Also, when the pole is planted, they do not permit a woman to pass under it. This is the reason they guard it until the end of the fiesta.

This dance of the flying monkey they did in my town, but earlier, according to my grandma, who has lived in this world for 101 years! She said they did the dance of the monkey for the last time about 60 years ago when a son of hers, called Humberto Bizarro Temó, was a dancer. Also, she said that the first shaman of the dancers was called José Bizarro. Since Don José Bizarro died, no one has wanted to be in charge of the dance of the flying monkey.

Well, what I know is that in the year 1952, when I was 12 years old, they did the dance of the flying monkey in Santa Ana la Laguna. It was very beautiful, but at times one was afraid to look at the dancers. I went to watch the titular fiesta of this town, and what made me happy was the dance of the flying monkey. I noticed that, when the dancers erected the large pole, they gave it much respect. Before climbing they had to face and kiss the pole. Also, they had to pour good rum at the base of it, and each had to kneel at the foot of it. Around them were big candles that burned 24 hours.

During this time, the *jefe* of the monkeys was Señor Humberto Canajay, the main shaman who guarded the surroundings of the pole and the dances. The first shaman placed himself on the reel. He was in charge of untying and uncoiling the big lassos from which the monkeys flew to the earth. In this dance there were jaguars, pumas, monkeys, and also dancers with the names of angels, who wore a dress very different from that of the monkeys.

When I asked why, in a dance of animals, were some persons dancing in the form of angels, the response was that the angels come from heaven and fly with their wings and protect the dancers from falling from the pole. I noticed that the angels flew toward earth, and when they reached halfway down the pole they began to sing a very beautiful song. However, it was difficult to comprehend what they said because they were about 25 meters above the ground when they sang. When they reached the ground, they finished the song. Then they went to kneel down at the foot of the large pole and began to sing the song again. But it was impossible for me to learn this song in the year 1952.

Not until this year of 1979 did they perform again the dance of the flying monkey. Twenty-seven years have passed since they have done this dance because no one wanted to be the first monkey. I do not know why it was that Don Humberto Canajay wanted to do it again, because he is very advanced in age, about 85 years old. Still, he is an elder who is very strong with the muscles of a younger man. It is true that I did not go to see the fiesta of Santa Ana, but I am acquainted with Señor Humberto Canajay because he has worked in my crew on the coast.

I am certain that in the history of these towns it was in the year of 1979 that they said good-bye to the dance of the flying monkey, because in this fiesta of Santa Ana they performed the dance with fatal consequences. It happened on 11 August, the day before the fiesta. No one knows what happened to Don Humberto, the first shaman; that is, perhaps the first monkey failed with the rituals and was not able to control the reel that was on the point of the pole. They say that Don Humberto did not know why on this day a dancer released the lasso when he was still 25 meters from the ground and fell to his death. However, on this day, the eleventh, it was not as bad as what happened on the main day of the fiesta.

My close kin and my son José told me what they saw at about 1:00 P.M. on 12 August. They say that from the point of the pole, or from the reel, about 40 meters high, the dancer Pablo Sicay fell.

When the dancer fell to the earth he was totally disfigured and unrecognizable because the bones of his face were all broken. Also, when Don Humberto realized that one of his companions had fallen, he also allowed himself to plunge toward the ground with the lasso, but when he reached midpoint, about 17 meters from the ground, the lasso jammed and the reel of the wheel would not turn. Humberto lost control when the reel stuck, and he let go of the lasso and fell to the earth. However, this man with much luck did not die, but he broke his spinal column. The same car that carried the deceased also carried Don Humberto, who was in critical condition, to the hospital in Sololá.

Señor Don José García informed me that Don Humberto Canajay spent weeks in the hospital of Sololá. But he still lives. However, he lost all his strength, and he walks with a cane because he suffers with his vertebral column. Don José García was chatting with Don Humberto Canajay about the dance and what he had suffered in the past year and why two of his friends of the dance died. The answer that Don Humberto gave was that they were bewitched by some men of Santo Tomás Chichicastenango, who do the dance of the flying monkey but not as well as the Santanecos. The *brujos* of Chichicastenango are still young and able to make witchcraft to prevent him and his fellow Santanecos from performing a better dance. Don Humberto said that he had lost two of his companions of the dance but that now he is making rituals to bewitch these men of Chichicastenango. He knows very well that his companions suffered the mishap because of these *brujos*.

This information of Don Humberto was taken at the end of August of this year. Don José García arrived in Santa Ana soon after the fiesta to buy old things. When it was opportune, I recommended that he get the information from Don Humberto. When Don José got these facts, he told them to me. It is certain that it will be difficult for them to perform this kind of dance in the highlands again because it will be hard to find men strong enough.

❧ A Councilman Threatens to Kill Me
15 AUGUST 1979

When I left the cooperative, a *regidor* named Erasmo Coché Morales insulted me. First, he treated me like a thief because I am participating in the cooperative. I did not say anything bad back to him because it was just a matter of his drunkenness. He followed me, but I did not want to run because I thought he was going to throw stones. I stopped. Then the señor councilman hit me with his fist on the left side of my face. I did not want to hit him back. God will deal with him. He told me that if I become a candidate for mayor he is is going to kill me for sure with a knife. I did not give it any importance because I know that Señor Juan Mendoza advised the councilmen and I know well it is because of fear.

❧ A Ritual for the Baby
THURSDAY, 16 AUGUST 1979

After breakfast I left to work in Joyabah to stake out some land for planting coffee. But I was very sick to my stomach, and I suffered a lot. I ate lunch with my family and my friend Ignacio Cuéllar in my house. It was somewhat pleasant.

After lunch I stayed in bed and reflected about my sickness. I did not want to leave the house, but I needed to go to San Martín because, as a favor to the midwife, we needed to make a ritual for my baby girl. She said it should be done, and we felt obliged to do it. We sent for the first shaman, Señor Santiago Cojox, but he did not want to come with the person we sent to call him. Thus, I had to go bring him personally. We did not return together until 6:00 P.M.

We ate a dinner of beef, and then we waited until 9:00 P.M. What happened was more important for the baby than it was for me, but I wanted to know how the shamans do the rituals. Well, the shaman began to count the 20 days of the gods. It was true that when this man was making the ritual we were visited by some spirit, because we clearly heard a big noise in the yard of the house. For privacy the ritual was in the house of my grandma, which is farther away from the road than my house [his grandmother's house is in the same home-site]. To respect them [the gods], we had to drink some shots of liquor, but not many.

Señor Santiago Cojox remained in my house for the night. He talked of very pleasant things with my grandma. He told me that, if I was interested in learning to count the 20 days of the gods, he would teach me with much pleasure. I answered, "*Muchas gracias* [Many thanks]." Certainly it is very important, because in time we are not going to have shamans like him. It is a pity that I am not able to learn these things because I do not have the time. Thus, the stay of Señor Santiago Cojox was very interesting. We did not go to sleep until 1:00 A.M.

❧ Anica and I Bathe in the *Temascal*
MONDAY, 27 AUGUST 1979

I felt somewhat sick so I asked my wife to prepare the *temascal*. She did everything necessary to heat it. At 8:00 P.M. I entered the *temascal*, and my wife accompanied me. Although the heat was intense, we endured it. When we left the *temascal*, we drank a lot of water. Also, when we left it, I said good-bye to the aches of my muscles. I felt like a new man. For us Indians, the *temascal* is the best medicine when a chill or other illness attacks us. We do not take medicine unless the sickness is very serious. Then, if our medicine does not produce results, we seek help from a doctor. After the bath, I slept the whole night very peacefully.

❧ The New Motor at the Tienda Does Not Work
28 AUGUST 1979

I got up at 4:00 A.M. and went to grind corn at the cooperative just to see how the new motor [that we just got] was working. When I arrived, I asked the boy on the shift to bring the key to the room to start the motor. But he told me that the mill did not work because the plate was set in a bad direction. For the committee of administration, it was a serious problem. They had no patience, and they abandoned it.

I returned home and went back to sleep. I did not get up until 7:00 A.M. After eating breakfast, I went again to the cooperative. But no one on the committee of administration came to see how to arrange the plate of the mill. Then I went to others who have knowledge of bricklaying. They told me they were not able to help because they had a lot of work. Then I went to San Martín accompanied by Don Juan Sánchez, thanks to God [since I was still wary of going alone]. We talked to a lot of people looking for a professional mason. They all told us the same thing—that they have a lot of work. Finally, Señor Don Rudy Rivera told us he would go to see if he could fix the mill. We returned very happy. Don Juan is not a member of the cooperative. He accompanied me just as an honorable person.

When we arrived home, my wife had lunch prepared. We ate and then immediately went to the cooperative.

At 2:15 P.M. Don Rudy Rivera arrived in the rain with another bricklayer. He showed me what was wrong with the plate and told me that they could fix it in one day for $10. For me, patience solved this serious problem. My companions of the cooperative were extremely pleased because they saw the results of my work.

Here Ignacio relates an episode concerning the new fiesta of the beheading of Juan Bautista in which the majority of the townspeople celebrated despite an attempt of the priest of San Martín to suppress it. Ignacio speculates that the priest prohibits all kinds of activities such as having a marimba because he wants all the business for himself. In this episode Ignacio foils an attempt of the municipal secretary to start a political party under the guise of a soccer team.

❧ My Friend Picks My Pocket
FRIDAY, 31 AUGUST 1979

At 2:00 P.M. on this day, Andrés called to settle our accounts [from the earnings of our crew on the coast]. When all the debts had been paid, we had $80 left, which we split between us. After completing our accounting, Andrés sent for two-eighths liter of liquor. Since I had a hangover, I drank very little.

When we finished our drinks, we went to the cooperative to test the [new] mill. We spent this day mainly grinding *masa* [dough] for the women.

When we left the cooperative, Andrés took me to a tienda to drink more *tragos*. He got drunk and went home. I stayed drinking with some friends. I remember that one of my friends took $15 that was in a pocket in my trousers. Although he thought that I was good and drunk, it is certain that I felt this friend put his hand in my pocket and take the money. I thought he would return it the next day, but it was not so. He kept the $15. More than losing the money, it is important that I know the character of the people [with whom I interact]. I thank God that I have never behaved in such a manner with my friends. By the grace of God, this friend did not take all my money. In total I had $40, so I had $25 left. I did not wish to demand it back or tell my wife. For me it was just another lesson.

On Sunday, 2 September, I got up but I did not wish to eat breakfast or to drink another *trago*. Although it was raining, some female evangelists came to our house to pray. We ate together and passed a pleasant afternoon.

⌘ Flooding and Fatalities
9–12 SEPTEMBER 1979

We knew it was raining hard in the mountains because strong currents were running through the town. When I got home, I sent my wife to the telegraph office to send a telegram advising my assistants that there would not be any more trips with crews these days because the rains have made it very dangerous.

There was fear in the town because big landslides tumbled down in the hills nearby. Many *cuerdas* of corn and coffee of the *Joseños* were buried. It was very strange—we had never seen anything like this. By the grace of God, there had been no deaths in the town.

At 9:00 P.M. I went to the cooperative of the tienda. There we heard the news that in the village of Patzilín there was both material and personal damage. There were gushes of water from the downpour that flooded the rivers. Strong currents flowed from the junction of rivers that descended the hills, and they swept away Señor Mauricio Có along with horses and bulls and great quantities of crops. The inhabitants of the village looked for the señor but could not find him. When night fell, they gave up the search. The señor municipal mayor witnessed these things when he and other *Joseños* were returning from a judicial mission in Pachichaj. He almost died.

The dead body of Señor Mauricio Có Quiché was not found until Tuesday. It had been carried by the current five kilometers away to the Tolimán River. The residents asked the justice of peace to let them bury Mauricio without taking his cadaver to the hospital in Sololá. Thus, the justice of peace knew that they buried him in the village of Patzilín without an autopsy.

Tuesday at 5:00 A.M. Andrés and I went to tell our assistants that weeks would be needed to clean the roads and that we would not be taking *cuadrillas* to the coast until then. We arrived home at 9:00 A.M., and the rest of the day, I did not go anywhere else. I just stayed home reading and sleeping a little. At noon it rained lightly, but in the afternoon it rained very hard.

The rains of yesterday caused a lot of damage in the agricultural regions of the town. According to the information collected by the municipality, there had been about $2,500 worth of damage to coffee, corn, and onion fields. This amount did not include the village of Patzilín. We are sure that there was more damage in this village than there was in the town.

The rich were taking advantage of the situation, hoarding all the corn they had to sell. The times were not difficult for them. They were joyous! All day there was no corn to buy in the tiendas, and the rich raised their prices.

Also, news arrived of fatalities in Pamuyuc, which is between San José and Santa Ana. A house with a family inside was entirely swept away; it disappeared. At 10:00 A.M. the justice of peace went again to the Tolimán River to extract another body of a person who died because of Monday's rain. The corpse was one of seven who died in the jurisdiction of Santa Ana. They carried it to Santa Ana. It was impossible to take it to Sololá because it was putrefied.

On this same day, Wednesday, at 11:00 A.M., the mother of the wife of the deceased Mauricio Có Quiché arrived in my house. She was crying a lot because of the death of her son-in-law. She gave us the full information.

Mauricio lost his life only because he was helping a señora who was in her house on a slope. A slide fell from the road and swept him into the river. The señora told me that there was much fear in her village. The people do not sleep in their houses because there are hundreds of landslides. When night falls everyone gathers to sleep in the church. Also, she said that this torrential rain is destroying the land. All day long Wednesday it rained hard.

℘ Don Asturias Dies in His *Temascal*
13–14 SEPTEMBER 1979

Thursday, 13 September, dawned sad because the rain continued to cause death. On the radio we heard that they were finding bodies on the southern coast. These bodies were carried by the rivers from the west, and they did not appear until they reached the coast.

During the day I went to replant 38 sprigs of coffee, but with much fear because it was dangerous due to the slides. Because I was bored in the house, I also went to plant a little in Joyabah and Popoya, although it was difficult.

It was hard to cook breakfast because the firewood was wet and would not burn. My wife struggled to cook tamales. For dinner we ate roasted tomatoes and chili.

At 6:00 P.M. another very sad piece of news arrived—the death of Don Asturias. We did not find out how it happened until I went to the post office at 8:00 P.M. where they told me. They say that Señor Domingo Asturias, who does not have a family, was very cold and wanted to warm himself a little. He made a fire inside the *temascal* about 1:00 P.M. When it was hot, he entered. But the temperature was too hot, and Don Domingo died peacefully on top of a board. When his neighbors realized that he had not come out of the *temascal*, they went to investigate—but he was already dead.

During the night, the justice of peace went to Patzilín for the legal inquiry, but he did not enforce the law. He allowed all of the bodies to be buried without sending them to Sololá for an autopsy. This was because of the *mordida* [bite, or bribe]. For many it was sad, but for the señor justice of the peace—it was a nice business! However, he did suffer a little under the rain.

It dawned raining hard. There was much sadness, because where one would like to be working, land was sliding. Although it dawned somewhat calm, it continued to rain, and it was threatening. At 10:00 A.M. I went to Xesucut to bring *elotes* [ears of corn] to eat because corn is certainly expensive. When I arrived home, my wife cooked them, and we ate them at 1:00 P.M.

On this day, Friday, 14 September, the Red Cross of Guatemala came because Santa Ana sent word that they are suffering. They are isolated because of the landslides and bad roads. Also, inhabitants have died, and the people have lost many things. Santa Ana was thus the first to ask for help from the government.

The Red Cross of Guatemala brought many provisions such as corn, beans, rice, and more than 600 ponchos (*chamarras*, or serapes) made in Japan. Since it was impossible to travel in cars to Santa Ana, they left all of these things in San José for the municipality to take to Santa Ana. As the señor mayor is a little cunning, he immediately sent for a list of the families of the dead. Then he sent only a few things the government left. Most of it remained in the municipality of San José, but Santa Ana requested it. Always the mayor of the town likes to make a little profit.

❧ The Day of Independence of Our Homeland and a Dark History
15–16 SEPTEMBER 1979

In all parts of Central America, they celebrate Independence Day very much. Unfortunately, in this town, it was to the contrary. In previous years, the municipality celebrated and always gave gifts to the schoolchildren. This 15 September, however, was very sad.

The señor mayor declared a day of mourning because of the deaths of some of the inhabitants of the village of Patzilín. But it was deceiving. Certainly all of us *Joseños* are aware of what is happening in the municipality. They took the money budgeted for the celebration of Independence Day and prepared a good lunch with good drinks. Meanwhile, they abandoned the children by declaring a day of mourning. It was all just a lie because, if it indeed were a day of mourning, they should not have prepared themselves a good lunch. For the children they declared a day of mourning; for themselves they had a fiesta.

Also, this Independence Day was a nice business for the señor mayor. He distributed the provisions to the flood victims in the village of Patzilín. These poor people deserved this kind help because they truly suffered damages. The greatest disgrace, however, was that the mayor ordered his councilmen to call their close kin and friends to give them gifts of ponchos and provisions. The mayor gave these things to persons who were not harmed, and he gave them to his friends and to two of his concubines. He acted very badly because, instead of helping the people who needed it, he gave to his family and friends. Only a little was left, and this was sold to others. It was indeed a dark history in our town.

All day on 16 September I did not go anywhere because last night I drank a lot of *tragos* with my best friends Benjamín Bizarro Temó, Damián Juárez, José Canajay, and Carlos Velasco Velásquez. We talked incessantly about the dark history of the municipal corporation.

On this day, Sunday, the day passed very sadly because of what happened in my town. It was raining slowly all day.

In the afternoon, I needed a drink because I felt sick. My friend Chico Peralta came and bought two bottles. We drank them. Then this friend went to get more bottles. But when he returned, he was quite drunk, and I did not want to open the door. So he went home to sleep.

> *Here Ignacio describes another trip to the coast with crews for the cotton farms. He made the return trip during a cold, rainy night. The lights of the truck failed so he had to hold his arm out the window to illuminate the road with a flashlight. His arm nearly froze. Several times they had to dig the truck out of the mud and carry sand for the tires. When he reached home, he was cold and wet. He caught a cold and had a high temperature. Then he became so sick with malaria that he was unable to go outside to relieve himself (his house has no indoor plumbing).*

ᕱ What Happens Among Us Humans
13 OCTOBER 1979

Although a husband and wife think each other is faithful, things may turn out to the contrary. As the proverb says, *"Cara vemos pero corazón no vemos* [We see the face but not the heart]."

My wife's sister is called Catalina Cristina, and her husband is called Fernando Jorge. It happened that Catalina has a secret husband. One night Fernando Jorge discovered his woman in the arms of another man in his own bed. This caused a big problem in this family. These two men nearly killed each other.

They called my wife to witness these things, but she did not give them any importance. I believe that each family has to look out for itself in such matters, because we are not worthy of judging the behavior of another person.

This family continued to have problems. The saying, *"En la casa uno tiene su propio enemigo* [One finds his own enemy in his own house]," is true. It is certainly the case of poor Fernando Jorge. His female enemy is in his own house, and the second "husband" of his wife is his very good friend. They helped one another, they worked together, and they ate together without Fernando knowing of the clandestine relations.

ᕱ A Rabid Dog Bites a Fat Pig
SATURDAY, 20 OCTOBER 1979

Now María is seriously ill with a temperature. Almost the whole family is sick. Not just my family is sick, however. Nearly the whole town has been hit with a strong outbreak of flu.

We ate a good lunch of beef. In the afternoon I rested in the house. An evangelist pastor came to visit. It was very pleasant.

There are a lot of rabid dogs throughout the town. At 5:00 P.M. I started to go for a walk, but as I was leaving, a dog with rabies entered the house, which frightened my family very much. My wife trembled with fear, but the youngsters thought it was funny. They do not realize that a rabid dog is dangerous.

This dog bit a fat pig in our homesite. I went to advise the owner of the rabid dog, but this señora swore to earth that she did not own the dog. But one of her sons agreed with me and confirmed in front of his mother that the dog was theirs. The señora agreed that, if the pig dies, she will pay me without malice. If the pig dies, however, I will find that [what she said] is a big lie.

ᕍ Two Big Earthquakes
SATURDAY, 27 OCTOBER 1979

I left to work in Panasajar, but only for a half day because there was much fear in the town. Two big quakes hit, and nearly the whole town was alarmed. The men who were working in the hills went running back to their houses thinking that something had happened to their families. Also, the families of those working in the fields thought they had suffered some misfortune. But by the grace of God, nothing happened.

ᕍ All Saints' Day
1 NOVEMBER 1979

In the morning I went to irrigate onion seeds for half the day on the shore of the lake. After lunch I went to the tienda of the cooperative.

In the afternoon I intended to go to the cemetery to visit the tombs of my close kin who are dead, but I did not have time.

It is the custom in all the houses of the town to eat *elotes*, *guisquiles* [a climbing plant whose fruit is the size of an orange], pumpkins, sweet potatoes, and yuccas. And some families make *atol de elotes* and other things to offer to the spirits of their deceased kin. Our belief is that our parents, grandparents, and brothers worked the earth and cultivated different kinds of fields when they were living. The spirits remember all that they did in their natural life, and it is for that reason on these days one prepares something to please them. The whole town practices this custom.

In the night we held a political meeting in my house with a group of citizens. When we gathered, they asked me for *elotes*, but I told them we did not have any. Then Don Bonifacio said we should go to his house to get some. I agreed to go with him, and we brought back a sack of them, which all of us ate. These friends gave one another their traditional *tragos*, and thus we terminated the meeting. But my friends continued to drink until 1:00 A.M. When they left my house, I do not know whether they went home or to the cantinas. I went to sleep.

ᕳ All Souls' Day
2 NOVEMBER 1979

We arose very content and went to the cemetery. My family and I went to the cemetery to visit deceased close kin. We carried candles and incense to burn over their tombs.

As we were returning from the cemetery, we met my wife's grandfather, whom we bought a shot of liquor. This señor is more than 80 years old. He gave us good advice on how to endure poverty and other obstacles of life. His words were meaningful because he told us that in these times the suffering is little compared to what was suffered earlier. We thanked our grandpa a lot [for his recommendations].

During the day, I was cleaning my typewriter and writing a few pages. I thought about organizing a *cuadrilla* for the coast, but I decided it would be better not to compete with the other contractors. I decided to wait until another day.

ᕳ I Bring Home Bad Shrimp
3–9 NOVEMBER 1979

When I arrived home [from the coast], my wife made a tasty broth [with shrimp I brought]. We ate it for dinner, but an hour later the entire family became sick. We are accustomed to eating animals from the lake, and we did not know why the shrimp made my family sick. The afternoon turned out somewhat comical and somewhat sad. My wife nearly died from eating the shrimp, and the children were serious. Only to me nothing happened. The food did not make me feel bad. Because of the shrimp, there was a problem in the house. My wife declared that she would never cook it again.

After arriving from the coast, we heard a big noise on the loudspeaker calling all the residents to a meeting at 8:00 P.M. in the municipality because the engineers had arrived to delineate the landmarks [boundary markers] of the seven neighboring towns—San Martín, San Luis, Sibinal, Santa Apolonia, Carcha, Santa Ana, and San Jorge. Although my wife was in serious condition, I thought it important to go.

In this meeting, they collected a dollar from each resident to cover the expense; that is, to buy the food for the engineers and their helpers. But there was a problem because the residents had already given much money. They say none of them knows where this money is now. Thus, a lot of people did not want to give any more money, but the mayor threatened to sentence those who did not.

Also, an official who spoke on behalf of San Martín said that this town is not in agreement with the currently measured landmarks. I talked four times in this meeting because the committee in favor of delineating the landmarks is not legalized. It has not been legalized because the townspeople know well that the committee is working clandestinely. For this reason, the citizens do not want to make another contribution. This is the fault of the mayor. The committee hardly knows how much money has already been collected. I told the mayor in this meeting the trouble he is causing and that the works have no merit. A group of people are on my side, but the majority are with him, because these poor folks believe there are surplus lands [that they may get]. But we know very well that all the lands were divided in 1914 with the same indicated title. The mayor is doing this only to gain a little money. Certainly he is not interested in improving our town. The mayor was unable to manipulate the people at this meeting.

After we left at 11:00 P.M., a group of good neighbors and I went to a tienda to drink some beers. We continued drinking and almost got drunk until I realized it was already Thursday, 8 November. I arrived home nearly good and drunk although my wife was very ill from eating the shrimp the day before. By the grace of God, I did not continue drinking.

In the afternoon, my wife's condition with her stomach deteriorated. I did not think about drinking anymore. I was more preoccupied with buying medicine for my wife. Not until then did she feel better. In the night my friend Chico arrived offering more *tragos*, but I accepted just one more drink, and then I went to sleep.

On 9 November I got up somewhat sick and drank some coffee. Then I went to Panasajar to irrigate my cultivations. On this same day some of the citizens left with the mayor and the engineers toward Chuisuc, which is between San Martín and San José.

They say that San José and San Martín could not prove their boundaries. San José tried to plant landmarks indicated by the engineer, but they penetrated into the jurisdiction of San Martín. They just planted a cement marker, but they were uncertain so they did not continue. At 11:00 A.M. they stopped working.

In the afternoon of this same day there was much talk of *Joseños* threatening *Martineros* and likewise *Martineros* threatening *Joseños*. The news spread throughout both towns. The *Martineros* say they will win because they have money and it will be no bother to pay for a number of lives of *Joseños*, and that they will indeed do it if necessary. The *Joseños* say that they do not have money, but, if the *Martineros* live on land of San José, it is on this land that they will die.

These two towns are somewhat loco; they should not kill one another because they are brother towns. San José needs San Martín just as much as San Martín needs San José. They like these suits, but for sure there are no lands worth fighting for, certainly not two big stone markers. If only one of these towns considered how much these two big stones cost! I am certain that what is wanted is not worth one's life. I do not understand what is happening between these towns, but the mayor is clearly at fault.

❧ A Meeting in the Cooperative
24–28 NOVEMBER 1979

In the afternoon there was a meeting in the cooperative concerning the reception of the technicians who are coming to make a demonstration for all the members. We decided to take a special collection of 50 centavos from each person to buy dinner and refreshments for them. We all agreed on these matters and retired at 11:00 P.M. This training is supposed to be tomorrow at 3:30 P.M., and everyone was asked to be punctual. Also, they asked me to stop milling *masa* for the women to prevent the others from being delayed.

On 26 November I got up and went to the mill. María brought me coffee, and I finished milling about 7:30 A.M. I worked very well and earned $3, but it belongs to the cooperative. I just ate breakfast and went to the shore to irrigate.

I ate lunch with my family, but I almost felt sick in my heart. I felt a big pain in my back. I do not know why I am aching so much. Perhaps it is from so much work, but if I do not work, I do not eat!

At 1:30 P.M. I opened the mill to make *masa* for the women. I closed it at 3:30 P.M. The tienda did the same.

At 4:00 P.M. the technicians began to raise our consciousness about the duties and responsibilities of a cooperative member. All the members who were in the town were present. Four who were on the coast, naturally, could not attend. Everything was very tranquil, and everyone paid close attention because it was the first time in history for such a meeting. The training ended at 7:30 P.M. They said that tomorrow they will draw up the *acta de constitución* [incorporation papers] according to the new general law of cooperatives, number 82-78. This night was very nice, almost like a little party. The *consejo de administración provisional* [provisional board of directors] had a meeting to collect another 25 centavos from each associate for tomorrow's expenses.

We assembled again early on 28 November to prepare what we were going to eat for the lunch. We have a committee of social works, which was in charge of buying chickens and additional things.

At 9:00 A.M. we began to draw up an *acta de constitución*. The act was drawn up by the expert agronomist, Joel Ambrosio Valle. At 11:00 A.M. the act was finished, and we all signed it. This meeting was conducted in the parochial assembly hall.

Is this how you legalized your cooperative?

Yes, the memorandum drawn up had the list of all the persons who wanted to be members with their exact surnames and numbers that correspond to each person's *cédula de vencidad* [national identification card]. The list also included their occupations. After all the members signed their names, the copy was certified at the Instituto Nacional de Cooperatives of Guatemala (INACOP). This institute then authorized the legalization of the cooperative. It also authorized a ledger, book of inventory and balance sheets, cash book, and an auxiliary book for bookkeeping. Frankly, it was not I who did all of this. We organized together, but another person did this paperwork. However, I have all the statutes.

Then up to this point the group was really a pre-cooperative.

Yes.

When everything was finished, we went to Chuitinamit for lunch. Our wives had gone ahead of us to prepare the food. Each person sought his own group with whom to eat. It was very peaceful.

After lunch we had rested a while when an evangelist pastor approached us. He gave us good advice on how to enjoy the good life—both material and spiritual. I respected his words, but others thought they were a joke. I observed, however, that all of us needed his counsel.

At 3:30 P.M., the technicians left very happily for Panajachel. They took a lot of photographs. An associate, Diego José Ramos, gave them some first-class onions, and they were very appreciative.

☙ Insecticide Affects My Heart
30 NOVEMBER 1979

Because of the two days of meetings with the technicians, I was unable to irrigate my tomatoes in Panasajar. I began yesterday, and I

am doing it today, but it is very difficult. One has to irrigate continu-
ously. At 8:30 A.M. I went to Tamalaj to spread fertilizer, spray the
plants with insecticide, and cover them with leaves to protect them
during the summer [dry season, from November through April in
most of the region; actually winter in terms of the sun]. At 11:00 A.M.
I arrived home somewhat sick because the poison of the spray affected
my heart, which is weak due to the great suffering I have endured
that was caused by enemies in February and March.

❧ A Landslide and Dryness Make Irrigating Difficult
3 DECEMBER 1979

My wife, José, and I got up at 5:00 A.M. to go irrigate in Panasajar. Again we irrigated four *tablones* of onion seeds. We finished at
7:30 and went home. While my wife heated tortillas, I wrote a little.

After lunch, I went to Xesucut to clean below the river with
three other *Joseños* and three *Martineros*. It was difficult because the
river that we use for irrigation no longer runs below the *tablones* because of a landslide and much summer [dryness]. All of us worked
hard, and each of us ate near our plots of onions.

I collected the dry *monte* [scrubs] and covered the *tablones* with
them and then burned them. Then I irrigated the *tablones* just to
soften them a little because they were very dry due to the summer.
In the late afternoon I cut off the points of the plants [so that the roots
will grow more]. The sun was very hot, and I was very tired.

At 5:00 P.M. I arrived home. Later, Felipe arrived to offer me
some land cultivated with coffee. We went to inspect it. I offered him
only $400, but I do not know whether we will make the agreement
because I do not have all the money.

❧ A Shooting, and Students Riot in San Martín
23–24 DECEMBER 1979

While we were eating dinner, Ramoncito told me that in San
Martín a man who was the owner of a lottery was killed. The death
was cause by an agent of the national police. I thought this information
was false, but later all the people were saying that it indeed was true.

They say it was in the middle of the afternoon. Many had gathered for the lottery in the municipal atrium. It was full of people.
Because it was almost Christmas, there was a lot of activity. The agent

of the national police was drunk in the door of the substation of the police. He began to play with his revolver, and suddenly it discharged. The bullet struck the front of the owner of the lottery, who was about 40 meters away, and lodged in his body. This was a dark history for the *Martineros*.

When the students saw the owner of the lottery dying, they immediately united with most of the townspeople to attack the police. There was much savagery in San Martín.

Led by the students, the majority of the townspeople penetrated the headquarters of the police and destroyed the transmitting radio used to communicate with different branches of the institution. They disarmed and beat the captain and did the same to the other policemen. They destroyed the objects in the headquarters. Not just that, they also beat the mayor and his members. It was a big disturbance.

With considerable difficulty the captain managed to communicate with the departmental *jefe*, and within an hour the launch of the national police from Panajachel arrived to help them. But their efforts were in vain because the people were armed with sticks and stones, and the reinforcements were not able to penetrate the town. But the policemen from Panajachel sent a message to the police of San Martín who were in the town center. The *Martinero* policemen managed to join the *Panajacheleño* policemen, but the former received many blows. The captain lost his visor cap and nearly fainted.

The policeman who committed the crime remained in jail but was badly beaten. Also, many of the *Martineros* were injured, but they had done it to themselves.

This was an opportunity [for the students] because for some time they have not gotten along with the police for the simple reason that the police are policing the town well. They are preventing the use of drugs and other evil in the streets at night. That is to say, the students in this town do not want order—they are very anarchistic. So they took advantage of the situation when one of the policemen committed a crime.

On Monday at 5:00 A.M. many *Martineros* woke me up because they were in the streets of San José. It was very strange for me because, when I opened the door of my house, there were many *alguaciles* [municipal policemen from San Martín] near my house. I asked them what they were looking for, and they said they were looking for a policeman. They jailed the policeman who committed the crime. Because of much fear, the guards and the *alguaciles* did not lock the jail; they just closed the bars. When the *alguaciles* were sleeping, the policeman escaped. When the *alguaciles* realized that the policeman

had taken the road for San José, the guards and the *alguaciles* penetrated the jurisdiction of San José without informing the local authority. But the authority [the mayor] did not actually conform to the law,
because he knew where the *Martineros* were looking for the prisoner.

About 7:00 A.M. they found the prisoner hiding in a coffee grove
three *cuadras* from my house. I saw clearly when they caught the poor
prisoner. They abused him as if he were a snake. It pained me to see
the poor man. Almost all of his body was purple and blue, and his face
was disfigured. I told them that it was a disgrace to mistreat a person
in such a manner, and they threatened to strike me too just for telling
them not to be so brutal.

When they passed my house, they stripped the prisoner, and I
saw that his whole body had sustained many blows. What I saw this
morning disheartened me, and I will never forget it! The *Martineros*
truly acted shamefully. It is not the duty of some guards to beat a
prisoner. There are laws for such cases. If a person is guilty, he can be
judged by the law and jailed for his crime. I do not know what is
happening to the *Martineros*, who claim to be intelligent men. It is
just the opposite.

A few days later the authorities investigated, but very confidentially. That is to say, none of the *Martineros* went to jail. All that we
know is that they made a list of 40 persons who instigated the great
disturbance that was seen in all of San Martín.

The crime [shooting] happened at 3:00 P.M. on Sunday, 23 December. Many *Joseños* witnessed it, including one of my brothers-
in-law.

The Year Ends
31 DECEMBER 1979

Andrés and I went to the coast with a crew of just 50 persons.
By the grace of God, nothing unusual happened. This is all I am able
to write for the year of 1979. I ask whoever reads these pages to excuse
all of my errors. The fault is my lack of study. I am just a sad campesino. I am doing this with the help of Dr. James D. Sexton, who has
been helping me financially. I am sure that without his help I could
not do any of it. Thanks to God and to Señor Sexton for his effort. God
willing, we will continue to write more pages. Here I am pausing to
ask God to help me write what little I can for the year 1980.

❧ The New Year Begins
4 JANUARY 1980

On Friday, 4 January, we took a crew to the Ipalita farm. I was somewhat sick because on the first of January we drank some *tragos*, which made me feel bad. For two days I did not eat.

After breakfast we went to clean *tablones* of onions in Xesucut.

We ate greens for lunch and continued working until 5:00 P.M. My family left to go home, but José and I stayed to kill *zompopos*, which destroy the onions. These animals are very clever because they work only at night. They know they will be killed in the daytime.

What are zompopos?

A *zompopo* is an insect [a very large, macrocephalic ant] that lives inside the earth. It has its nest three to four meters deep in the earth. It is very clever because, when there is not much insecticide, the *zompopo* eats the plant in the daytime. But when we apply insecticide, it does not come out by day. It realizes it should come out at night to eat the plant. It is a very intelligent and destructive insect which eats onions, tomatoes, beans, and corn.

❧ San Martín Kills a Man from Tzancuil
MONDAY, 14 JANUARY 1980

While I was planting onions, a señora came to tell me that San Martín had killed a man from Tzancuil named José Rosales, who was an Indian who had worked many times in my crews on the coast. According to the señora, some drunk *Martineros* killed the poor man with stones and a machete because they thought he had money on him. But it was not so. San Martín is turning into a slaughterhouse that kills a lot of people. When the señora told me this, I felt a profound sadness. But what can one do about death? May the spirit of the fallen José Rosales be with God, and God is the one who will pardon or punish those who committed this brutal crime.

While my wife returned, José and I remained until 7:00 P.M. to irrigate onions and to poison the insects that are eating them. At night I ate a little, but I was not very hungry because of the weariness.

We Indians are never able to stop working 12 hours a day, sometimes 14 to 15 hours daily. It is certain that we suffer a lot. This is because we do not have a real profession. But we have to bear it. Our only refuge is our faith in God, owner of the universe, who helps us daily in our work.

✷ Helping My Father-in-Law in the Municipality
MONDAY, 21 JANUARY 1980

Today my wife picked the first tomatoes of the year—the first of the harvest. At 1:00 P.M. we arrived home. My wife cooked a pumpkin for lunch.

At 2:00 P.M. I went to the municipality to pay the tax of the *ornato* [a $2 mandatory tax paid each year to the municipality] that all citizens must pay. I took the opportunity to investigate the record of the birth of Ramoncito, my wife's nephew. My father-in-law says that Ramoncito's grandfather went to the registry to get a certificate of birth, but that they looked for two days and could not find the record. The name Ramón appeared in the registry, but the person was already dead. But Ramón's father was Felipe, who is deceased. Felipe had a son named Ramón, but this son lived only three days and died. His name appeared in the registry, but he had already died. Some ten months later, another son was born whom they gave the same name of Ramón. It is this son who is living, but in the registry they could not find his name.

A brother of my wife's father wanted $200 to affirm in writing Ramón's date of birth in an appropriate court. For me it was amusing because, when I arrived at the registry, I asked them to give me the book. In a matter of 15 minutes of searching, I found the name of Ramón Pablo Bizarro R. It cost me just 60 centavos—10 centavos for the value of the paper and 50 centavos for the value of certification. *Para el hombre listo hay otro más listo* [For every clever man there is someone more clever].

When I took the birth certificate to my father-in-law, he became very happy. It is certain they were facing much grief because they did not have the $200 that one of his brothers wanted for doing the job. The señor who asked for the $200 became very angry with me because I prevented a good business deal for him. But this is what has to be done when a person does not work legally.

❧ Robbery and the Question of Witchcraft
25 JANUARY 1980

At 4:00 A.M. on 25 January in San Jorge, Señor Teodoro Yax Muñoz drowned in a pot of boiling broth. Teodoro Yax was the full brother
of Ignacio Yax, but Ignacio was more clever, and he has a cantina and
property. Teodoro was poorer and just lived in the streets drinking
with his friends and surrendering to vices.

On the night of 24 January, Teodoro sipped drinks with his
friends and then went to his brother's cantina. There they told him to
go to sleep. Teodoro left the cantina, but he did not go to bed. He
went to the kitchen. When he entered the kitchen, his brother's
woman was cooking some 25 pounds of meat in a large pot. The meat
was to be given to their guests during the fiesta.

When Teodoro entered the kitchen, he grabbed a chair and sat
down to warm himself by the fire. Since he was very drunk, the
warmth of the fire made him sleepy, and he began to nod his head.
Suddenly, his head fell into the great pot of stew that was boiling. Poor
Teodoro's head was cooked with the beef. A few minutes later, the
woman entered the kitchen and discovered that the head of her husband's brother was boiling with the meat. Since they were clever, they
took him out without making a fuss. They told the authorities when it
was 8:00 A.M., but since it was the main day of the fiesta, the authorities did not investigate the death of Señor Teodoro. They then buried
him without a major problem. The news spread days later among the
neighbors.

Still, they say, the broth was served to the guests coming to the
fiesta without their knowing the meat was mixed with the head of
Señor Teodoro. The death of Señor Teodoro Yax was caused by a witch
who earlier had performed witchcraft for Teodoro Yax's brother in the
cofradía of Maximón in San Luis, but Señor Ignacio did not know that
it would affect his brother.

In the cantina of Ignacio Yax a tape-recording radio (radio and
tape recorder) was lost, or better said, was stolen, but they did not
know by whom. Some days later Ignacio and his wife went by canoe
to San Luis, where they consulted with a sorcerer. Then they went to
the brotherhood of Maximón to make the witchcraft.

The *brujo* told them that although they did not know who had
stolen the radio, whoever did it was going to die during a fiesta. After
they returned from San Luis, they forgot all about it. But Ignacio
remembered it when his brother died. Only then did Señor Ignacio

say that he had made witchcraft, but without knowing that his brother had stolen the recording radio.

Days later, when the apparatus appeared, it [was discovered that] Teodoro Yax had sold it to a drinking friend who lived in the same town. Poor Ignacio, however, had everything turn out expensive for him. He lost his recording radio, he was out the expense of the witchcraft, and it cost him to bury his brother whom he himself had bewitched. But the strangest thing was that the poor guests drank broth made with pieces of human flesh. I have written these things with the help of my friend Abundio Yax, who furnished the information and who is a neighbor of Señor Ignacio Yax.

❧ Our Baby Anica Catana Is Baptized
1–4 FEBRUARY 1980

We arose at 5:00 A.M., and my wife began to prepare food for the baptism. Fortunately, my sister-in-law, María, arrived and took charge of the cooking.

I was very hungry but not able to eat because I was attending to other friends. Nine o'clock in the morning came, but the *compadres* [godparents from the point of view of the real parents] had not shown up. The mass began, but still the *padrinos* [godparents from the point of view of the child] did not appear. My wife was waiting in the church with the baby, but the baby had no *padrinos*. I went to look for them at the house of my friend Diego José, but he had already departed for his fields. Finally I decided that, when the mass was finished, I was going to ask anyone to stand as godfather to the baby, Anica Catana.

As the mass was ending, however, the car of my *compadre*, Julián, appeared. Only then did my nerves calm.

After the baptism, we went home to eat breakfast. I sent for some beers, and my *compadre* bought more until we got drunk. In the afternoon my friends Miguel and David arrived. We drank so much that we lost control of ourselves.

During the night I went to the registry to get a replacement for a *cédula* of a *Joseño*. My *compadre*, Julián, left for San Luis almost drunk.

On Monday, 4 February, we got up very late because my wife and I went to bed a little drunk. Last night, we talked to Juanito Mendoza, the mayor, who told us he was a sincere man. But I am not able to believe him because I know his character.

ᕙ Desperados Paint the Town
FRIDAY, 8 FEBRUARY 1980

In the morning there was much alarm in the town because from 1:00–2:00 A.M. some desperados painted the walls of many houses, including mine. For the first time in history, these subversives wanted to tarnish our town. Although we *Joseños* do not have much knowledge [formal education], we indeed respect other people's property and the laws. There was surveillance during the night, but the road patrol did not have the courage to confront the subversives, because the patrol thought these wretched persons carried firearms. Possibly these persons wanted to sow terror in the town, but this would be difficult. All of us are religious, almost 97 percent, and that means we have respect for the law of God, the law of the country, and we have respect for the human being.

ᕙ A Trip to the Hospital Dr. Rodolfo Robles
19–20 FEBRUARY 1980

After helping my wife cook dinner, I had to write a letter to a good friend. After finishing the letter, I could not sleep because I felt nervous due to a problem with my eyes. Also, I was thinking that it had been a year since the *Martineros* had accused me falsely. I did not lie down until midnight, but sleep did not come. I considered catching the bus in San Martín or Santa Ana to Guatemala [City]. It was already Wednesday, 1:00 A.M. I asked God to lead me down a good path.

At this same hour a friend arrived who works in Guatemala [City] and who was my school companion. When I opened the door, we recognized each other. Then I decided to go to San Martín to catch the bus, and I asked him to wait for me.

We arrived at the Trébol [major cloverleaf conjunction in Guatemala City, where one can take buses or hire taxies]. I got off the bus and waited to connect to the Hospital de Ojos Dr. Rodolfo Robles.

At 9:00 A.M. I presented myself but without having breakfast. I waited my turn, but there were a lot of people. At 11:00 A.M. I asked permission to eat a little, and only then then did I leave to eat some tortillas and a little meat in the street, which cost me $1.

They did not examine my eyes until 2:00 P.M. The doctor told me that on 26 March they would operate on my right eye. After the the examination, I went to the city center to find a pension.

I asked for a room in the Pensión San Judas, but they charged me $2 and gave me a dirty room. I did not want to stay, and I asked for my money back. The owner was very unruly, but with good words I convinced him to refund my $2. Immediately I went to the Pensión Sánchez. He charged me the same, but it was sanitary.

❦ A Strike on the Farms
23–28 FEBRUARY 1980

All this week in San José there have been no classes for the third grade. The teacher says he is sick, but this is a lie. He just does not want to work. This is always what happens after he has spent a little time in town.

At noon we returned home thirsty and hungry from watering onions. José Toc was waiting with 15 workers. My wife rushed to prepare a little food, but I did not have time to eat because the bus was already waiting for the passengers to leave.

On the Flor de Mi Tierra bus line, we arrived in Ipalita. After chatting with some friends, we went to bed in a shed.

When Monday dawned, we could see that there was a little cotton to be picked. We gave the list of 15 workers to the administrators. They gave us the sacks which we gave to the workers, who went to work. After the crew went to work, they told us that there is a workers' strike because the salary is very low. They told me at noon the strikers would arrive on this farm, but I did not pay much attention to what they told me.

We went to draw the rations for the *cuadrilla*, but when we arrived on the farm, those in the office were very frightened. There was a notice that within a moment the strikers would arrive to sentence the administrators of the farm to death.

We had just received the provisions and were returning in a tractor toward Ipalita when we met three pickups full of people in the road. They told us to return to the office, but I told them that I had some sick people in the shed, and only then did they set me free. I thought these were frivolous things, but at 11:30 A.M., after we had arrived at the Ipalita farm and were resting a little, three truckloads of *gente desconocidos* [unknown people] arrived with machetes and cudgels shouting, "Strike, strike, we want higher salaries, death to the farm owners!" They asked us to applaud, and with much fear we had to clap. When they first arrived, I felt like running to hide in the cotton field, but I managed to stay and observe what was happening.

The *jefe* got out of the cabin of his truck and asked the person in charge of combustibles for the key. With a faint face, the poor manager gave it to him. Then the *jefe* entered and filled up three trucks with gasoline at the gasoline pump. While he was doing this, four other trucks full of men and women arrived. Then they went to the cotton field to round up all of those who were picking cotton to complete the stoppage of labor. The poor, needy people did not want to leave. They wanted to continue picking cotton. But the strikers hit them, burned the cotton they had picked, and forced them to the trucks. They captured many, but others escaped. For a while they took me, but I acted as if I were one of them. When the *jefe* was not noticing, I went to get a drink of water, and then I slipped into a house of a señora.

I returned when the trucks were leaving the farm. The *caporal* [leader of the crew] told me that they had carried off some of the workers of Tzancuil in the trucks.

For us it was very painful. The leaders of the strike said that, if they returned and found someone picking cotton, they would burn the person alive for not supporting the strike.

What happened to the people of Tzancuil whom they carried away?

In the afternoon the leaders of the strike left for La Gómera, and they took the poor workers far from the farm. They did not come back until the next day.

On foot?

On foot, because the strikers had left them lost. There was no car or truck that they could ride in. They had to walk. But I do not know whether they slept in the cotton field. They did not carry a thing with them [no bedclothes], just their bodies.

Then they didn't kill them.

No, but the guerrillas said that, if they continued working, they would return and kill them. They said, "First time, we are only going to burn the cotton and the sacks. If tomorrow you return to work, we are going to kill you for sure."

Why did the guerrillas think you were one of them?

They were confused. They carried away all of the contractors who were opposed to the strike. I was there, and I was scared because

I did not want to go with them. Thus, I walked among them acting as if I were one of their companions. I was scared to stay with the workers because the guerrillas might discover me. For that reason, I stayed among them just to dissimilate . . . to hide.

Then there were a lot of guerrillas?

A lot . . . a lot, first four truckloads arrived, and then later more trucks came, perhaps 70 to 80 in each truck.

Were all of them guerrillas?

I do not think all of them were guerrillas; perhaps they forced some of the workers to participate. The poor people do not have any reason to say no because they want to keep living. If they do not respect the guerrillas, they kill them.

How many guerrillas do you think there were among the strikers?

Perhaps 30 or 40, the heads, the leaders.

Did they have arms?

Revolvers. I did not see any arms like machine guns, but they might have had them in the sacks. For certain they had pistols. On other farms they killed some administrators with revolvers. Where the administrators had conducted themselves badly with the campesinos, they killed them for sure. But on this farm where we were, they just stole gasoline and diesel and burnt cotton and tractors. These are some of the more serious things that we have witnessed them do in recent years. They burned a lot of cotton, but it seems the biggest loss was in cars, tractors, and trucks. They told me that the losses on the farm where we were amounted to $95,000.[19]

All Monday afternoon passed very sadly, and the workers were very frightened. Many left to parts unknown. Indeed, they abandoned the farm.

Tuesday, 26 February, dawned. The workers did not do anything, and the employees of the farm did not work and did not go to their offices. It was a lot of pain for me to return home whatever way possible. Also, I was worried about the crew we had brought and another crew that had begun to work on 6 February. They told me they preferred to abandon their work and go home. But I did not have money for their transportation. I told them to be calm while I went to San José to get money to take them home.

At 7:00 A.M. I left the farm and headed toward Santa Lucía, but before we reached the village of Cerro Cristalinas [near San Luis], we met hundreds of truckloads of people who had met the same fate of being thrown out of work in the strike. When we arrived in Santa Lucía, there were thousands of people armed with cudgels, machetes, stones, and revolvers. But also there was a greater number of security forces (army and police) keeping order.

When we reached San Luis, I gave thanks to God because I was now close to my town. When I arrived, I went to tell Andrés the situation. At the same time, we got travel money and arranged for Andrés to go and bring back the *cuadrilla*.

The next day two workers that I had left last Sunday arrived. Without doubt, they had not waited for Andrés. They told me that the situation on the coast continues to get worse. I hardly wanted to hear this because I did not want to make myself sick worrying about these things. It is certain that I have lost money, about $400. In short, only God will know what is good for us.

On Thursday I got up a little sad because I did not know what Andrés had faced yesterday when he went to the coast. We ate breakfast, and then we went to Xesucut to water onions. My wife prepared a lunch of tamales and herbs. We took our children because they are losing time for the pleasure of their teachers, who are not giving classes.

At 4:00 P.M. we quit working, and on the street we met the boys who had remained on the coast. They told me that Andrés had brought them back on the San Martín bus.

After a late dinner of fish and hot tortillas, I went to Andrés's house. He told me that the situation is bitter; we did not stop talking until 10:00 P.M.

What did he tell you?

Andrés said that the situation was worse, because they would not let them work and that there was much hunger because they would not let the women make tortillas for the workers. All of this is an oppression of the guerrillas. They said to the women, "Be careful not to make tortillas for the workers." The same thing they said to the *flonque*, "Be careful that you do not cook beans for the workers. If you cook beans, if you make tortillas, we are going to kill you." Then with much hunger the poor people had to go to wherever they could get food. There was no way to work or eat.

❧ Summoned to Work with the Engineers
WEDNESDAY, 5 MARCH 1980

I was writing a while in the evening when news arrived that the engineers had come to continue demarcating the landmarks. The news does not say when they will begin their work.

After a lunch of crabs and good, hot tamales, I went to irrigate onions in Xesucut. For the first time they gave me a *citación* [writ of summons, citation] on behalf of the municipality to work with the engineers on the landmarks. In the night the mayor invited all residents for a meeting, but the town paid little attention.

At 8:00 P.M. I arrived in the assembly hall to see what they were going to discuss. But it was not useful because only 16 persons showed up, including everyone on the corporation and the committee.

After the poorly attended meeting, I brought up the matter of the summons I had received. I asked the mayor and the committee if they would allow me to work with engineers when I was more caught up with my work. They agreed.

❧ I Buy Lunch for Two Destitute Salvadoreños
MONDAY, 10 MARCH 1980

[While we were on the coast,] we went to a small *comedor* to eat dinner. As we were eating, two señores arrived and asked for some tortillas and beans. They did not have money to pay for dinner; when the woman who owned the *comedor* heard that they had no money, she became very angry. She did not want to give them any tortillas. Because there have been times when I was in the same situation, I had compassion for these men. I told them to ask for a complete dinner and I would pay for it. Later these men told me they were from San Salvador.

❧ The Mayor Summons Me and Cites Eduardo Coj Cordón
THURSDAY, 13 MARCH 1980

About five minutes after I arrived home, an *alguacil* arrived to give me a *citación*. Without being able to rest a little, I had to go to the municipality. When I arrived, the mayor was waiting for me. The mayor told me that I had to go with the engineers to the mountains to help them demarcate the landmarks. I told him that this week I was not able to go because of so much work and that I could not go until next week. The mayor, since he is a hypocrite, told me that some of the committee had said that if I was not going to work he should sentence me a fine. I know very well, however, that it is he who wants to fine me. The reason is that I take a number of *Joseños* to the coast to pick cotton. They are poor people who wish to go to the coast out of necessity. They do not gain a single centavo by working in the mountains to demarcate the landmarks.

On this day Señor Coj Cordón was sentenced a fine of $50. The mayor was behind this. They sentenced this poor man just because he did not obey the mayor to go to the mountains with the engineers. We are this poor man's witnesses. He did not go to work because he is a poor person who does not have land and moreover is not a native of San José. He and his family sell firewood. But the mayor is an oppressor who gave a sentence of $50 to a man who does not earn $2 a day. These days to have to pay a $50 penalty is a great sin. The mayor earns by sentencing him. Señor Cordón is also a man who is not able to speak or read Spanish. For this reason the mayor agreed to sentence him. Moreover they severely punished this poor man by making him relieve himself in the same jail where they serve his food. It's a sad story for a mayor to behave in such a manner with his town.

❧ Pressed to Work on the Landmarks
15–16 MARCH 1980

I got up at 6:00 A.M. after sleeping peacefully all night long. After breakfast I went to irrigate onions, finishing at noon. Then I bathed in the lake for an hour.

After a lunch of meat, I wrote a little. Then I arranged things to carry with me to the mountains because I have to go to work with the engineers on the landmarks. Then I worked for my father-in-law a little.

Later I had to go borrow an axe with which to fell trees. I talked with a friend a lot [about the mayor] until 11:00 P.M. I did not go to bed until midnight.

On Sunday, 16 March, I got up at 6:00 A.M. and prepared my traveling bag. After bathing at home, I left at 10:00 A.M. for the coast toward the La Sirena farm. At noon we passed through Patzilín. At 1:30 P.M. we passed through Pachichaj. Near the house of my friend, Hugo Zamora, we rested awhile. At 6:00 P.M. we ate.

When we finally arrived at the La Sirena farm, we imposed upon the administrator's hospitality and asked him for the use of a pack animal to carry our travel bags. He provided one, and he gave us a large shed in which to sleep.

During the night, the majority of the 80 persons who were working with the engineers arrived. I chatted with some friends whom I knew a number of years ago when I was selling [merchandise] on the farms. One of the persons whom I talked with and whom I had known earlier is Señor Don Juan Quiché. He told me that he began working on this farm when he was 12 years old. They gave him the work of an adult, and they paid him only 10 centavos a day. Gradually they raised his pay to 50 centavos a day until he reached his limit in pay. He told me his sad situation. When he retired from this farm, they gave him a paltry, discriminatory pension that not even a dog deserved. The farm gives him each 15 days 25 pounds of corn and 5 pounds of beans. This is what he and his wife get for a fortnight. The farm does not give him a single dollar to buy other things.

We began to think about these things. It is better to die than to suffer in such a manner. It is certain that the farm owner only wants a helper who is in good physical condition, but when the poor person gets old, the owner does not even want him on the farm. Don Juan told me that he worked 50 years on this farm as a bricklayer. Nearly everything that one sees on this farm he constructed. Now all that he is getting as recompense is less than a pound of corn and two ounces of beans daily. He would like to leave the farm, but he is not able to do anything—no one will give him work because he is like an invalid due to his age.

❧ The Story of Mariano the Buzzard
17–20 MARCH

On Monday I got up at 5:00 A.M. Then I went to the house of Señor Juan, where we warmed our tortillas and cooked our coffee and ate breakfast. Yesterday, they told us the work would begin at 6:00 A.M., but it was all a lie. They gathered all of us workers in front of the office of the farm to wait for orders. They said we had to wait for the residents of Santa Apolonia Carcha to show us where the landmarks are. Also, they told us we had to wait for the mayor of San José.

At 9:45 A.M. the mayor arrived with some residents, and they entered the house of the engineer without talking to the rest of the people. At 10:20 the mayor from Sibinal arrived. The mayor of Carcha did not arrive, and the other two mayors were not able to do anything because the administrator of the farm left for San Miguel Cotz. The two mayors of San José and Sibinal went walking around, and who could say what they were trying to conceal? We lost a lot of time.

At 11:00 A.M. we ate lunch on the porch of the office in groups, commenting on the lies of the mayor. At 3:00 P.M. we went to the coffee groves to look for firewood, and then we prepared food for the afternoon. At 4:00 P.M. we ate dinner. I had meat.

At 5:00 P.M. we went to the Tolimán River, which is very near the farm, to look for the landmark, but it was all useless. We did not find anything. When we returned, the mayor told us that a *mozo* [farmhand] would be in charge of showing us the landmarks tomorrow. Still we had doubts because we were not seeing any real landmarks. Very happily we told *cuentos viejitos* [folktales]. At 10:00 P.M. we went to bed.

What kind of cuentos viejitos *did you tell?*

These are stories told by the old people, who mostly did not know Spanish. In the past there weren't many kinds of things like comics, but the old folks had their pastimes of telling stories that were fascinating to their grandchildren. They told stories like the one of the coyote and rabbit, which is very long but amusing. Although the rabbit is smaller, he excels in all things and dominates the coyote, who is larger. What a pleasant story it is!

We still tell these stories. My aunt and my grandma have told them to me. When we do not have anything to do, these are the stories we tell. Stories like the one of the jaguar-man who went to marry pigs in the forest and the one of the idler who turned into a buzzard. There are a lot of them, some very long.

What about the story of the idler and the buzzard?

This story my grandma told me along with other grandchildren when we were little. It is one of the funny stories that grandfathers and grandmothers tell the children.

Little children, there is a man who is called Mariano— Mariano is a lazy person. They say that when Mariano was a child, his parents sent him to cut firewood. Instead of looking for firewood, however, he looked for shade and went to sleep. When he arrived home that night, they did not give him food.

As Mariano grew up, so did his laziness. When he became a man, he thought about looking for a woman. After all his travels, he was able to find a woman by the name of Pascuala.

Then Mariano and Pascuala joined (married) and intended to make a home. But the two were the same—neither wanted to work. Mariano would leave early in the morning to bring firewood, but he would not get back until late in the afternoon. He lost his jobs with the people. He delayed 10 to 15 days for each *cuerda* of work. He suffered much poverty and sickness. Also, his woman went to houses to ask for work as a weaver, and when they gave her weavings to do, poor Pascuala took 15 to 20 days for each piece. Thus it was. The unfortunate couple were two lazy persons.

For poor Mariano, dreaming was his major occupation. Then a day came when they gave him work by the day. As poor Mariano did not want to work, he lifted his face upward looking at the birds. Finally, he lay down over a large stone, gazing at some buzzards flying around. The buzzards thought that some dead person was lying on the stone, and they began to fly near him. Suddenly Mariano said happily, "The birds just pass their lives flying, and I work every day and do not earn a living. I would like to be happy like these buzzards, who do not have to worry about building a house or planting or working; they pass their lives resting."

Mariano said these things without realizing that a buzzard was listening. Suddenly the buzzard lit above the stone where he found Mariano and greeted him.

The buzzard said to this man, "*Compadre* [Friend], what is it that you are thinking and saying? I was just listening to you from above."

Mariano answered, "I am very sad. Every day I have to work, and, if there is no work, there is no food."

"*Compadre*," said the buzzard, "we also are suffering a lot. We eat when someone like a chicken dies, and when we do not find dead animals, from much hunger we eat dung. Your life is very nice because you work and you are able to eat a lot of good things. We buzzards like to work, but God was harsh to us, only giving us wings to fly."

"Friend," said Mariano, "eating dead animals or eating dung when necessary is not a problem but happiness because you do not work, but my life is a disgrace."

The buzzard saw that Mariano was worse than a dead person, and to give him the solution [to his troubles], the buzzard told him, "If you want to be happy, I will lend you my jacket so that you will be able to fly free in the air and see all that you wish, but you also have to give me your clothing to cover my body, and then I will have to work."

The story says that Mariano thought he was in heaven when the buzzard told him these things. Then he took off his clothing and gave it to the buzzard. The buzzard did the same thing, taking off his jacket and giving it to the man. Then they said good-bye. Mariano went flying, and the buzzard began to work.

When the afternoon passed, the buzzard carried a backload of firewood, but he did not know which house to take it to. Luckily, Mariano passed by flying, and the buzzard said, "*Compadre*, I have problems; I am not familiar with your house."

"Friend," said Mariano, "I am going to guide you. Enter the house where I light. My woman is called Pascuala."

The buzzard-man carried the firewood on the road, and Mariano flew nearby. When the buzzard-man was about to arrive, Mariano lit on the house. The buzzard untied the wood and went inside the house.

Mariano had hardly gathered firewood, but the buzzard, who had converted into a person, had done a little.

"What a miracle you have brought firewood," said Pascuala. "You have hardly ever brought it."

"Ah, yes, I have brought firewood because now I am changing a lot, " he said.

"But why have you come with your face black and very dirty and stinking?" Pascuala asked Mariano, although it was not Mariano.

Then he answered, "Yes, it is because the sun burned me a lot, and I worked hard today."

"My poor husband," said Pascuala, "if you would like, we can prepare the *temascal* so that we can bathe tonight."

"Very well, if you want to do it," the man said.

Then Pascuala heated the *temascal* very hot to take off the dirt. When it was ready, the buzzard-man and Pascuala entered the *temascal*. But when he felt the intense heat, he shouted, "I am not Mariano! I am a buzzard! Your husband lent me his clothing, and I lent him my jacket. Thanks, but I have another jacket." He put on new wings and flew away.

Poor Pascuala was left surprised inside the *temascal*. When she left she made the townsfolk realize that Mariano turned into a buzzard because of laziness.

Days later, poor Mariano, who was converted into a buzzard, wanted to talk to his woman, but he was not able to speak. All he was able to do was to say, "Utz, utz, utz," in the yard of the house. Pascuala became very angry and grabbed a piece of firewood and killed Mariano, the buzzard.

My grandma told me this story, which is very old. It served as an example for us to do work when our parents gave it to us without laziness. If they ordered us to work, we should work and not go to sleep. In our life it is always difficult to earn a living. If a person works well, he is able to eat. The buzzard, who eats only dead animals and waste, is the laziest of all the animals.

My grandmother told us, "Children, this will serve you when you are adults. To be lazy is undesirable—it is better to die than to be lazy. So that you will not turn into buzzards, work and obey your parents."

These are the words that my grandma, Catarina, told me. In addition to the stories of the idler and the buzzard and the coyote and the rabbit, there is the story of a woman so lazy that she obliged dogs to help her work. One day the female dog was helping her prepare her food while the woman went to wash clothing. The dog cooked her baby for broth. This example teaches women not to talk to the animals. There is also the story of the witch who is in the Hill of Chuitinamit. They are amusing stories that we should sometime write about.

On Tuesday, 18 March, we warmed tortillas and ate. Then we presented ourselves at the point of rendezvous. I asked the señor administrator if he had talked with the mayor about giving us a guide to show us the landmarks. In front of a number of *Joseños*, the administrator said that he had not arranged anything with the mayor. Then we realized that the mayor was telling us lies. Many said that the landmark of San José was 100 meters from the church of the said farm. The mayor and some residents were certain that in this region there was communal land of San José. But the engineer had trouble measuring with his equipment because of poor visibility. He placed it 100 meters from the church, but he could not place it in the Tolimán River because the water was rough and there was lack of visibility. The title indicates this, but I do not know what is happening to these señores. They are fools. We examined the map and walked to the indicated place. We worked a lot, but it was impossible to find the landmark because it has been 66 years since it was put there.

In the afternoon we were very tired and about eight kilometers from the farm. But a member of the false committee told us that we could not quit until 6:00 P.M. However, for such weariness, I stopped working at 4:00 P.M. When the rest of the men saw me, they stopped, too. I was the first to take the sharply sloping road back to the farm, and the rest followed.

In the afternoon we cooked our food and ate dinner. We and our friends got our bags and began the journey back to San José. Bonifacio and I walked very slowly. Not until 9:00 P.M. did we arrived in Pachichaj. When we arrived in this village, some friends gave us a good dinner. We slept in the house of my friend Eduardo. Bonifacio slept inside the house, but I slept on the porch. Eduardo and I discussed the mayor, who is causing much damage to the town.

Wednesday, 19 March, dawned. During the breakfast that they gave us, we discussed politics a lot. Then very slowly we headed home, and we passed through Patzilín at 1:00 P.M. On this day they celebrated the fiesta of their village, and some of our friends stopped us to talk. From this village we left at 6:00 P.M., but on the road darkness caught us, and it was difficult to reach San José. By the time we got to the Hill of Choperal, we were nearly walking on our hands because of the stones and darkness.

At 10:00 P.M. we reached San José, and then we went to Bonifacio's house. He bought two beers, which we drank. Afterwards we both retired.

On Thursday I did not get up until 7:00 A.M. because I was very tired. I ate a late breakfast at 10:00 A.M., and then I went to Xesucut to irrigate onions. When we arrived, the river was full of people, and it was impossible for us to irrigate. At 1:30 P.M. we returned home very hungry.

I had to wait for my wife to make a lunch of fish broth. Afterwards, I wanted to return to Xesucut, but I could not because my uncle José arrived and drank some *tragos* of liquor and got drunk. I had to stay and take care of him. During the night I took my uncle home, and then I went to sleep.

❧ A Team from the Army's Office of Civic Action [*Acción Cívica Militar*] Arrives
FRIDAY, 21 MARCH 1980

I wanted to go to irrigate very early, but it was impossible because of the cold. I waited until dawn.

We met some boys who buy and sell onions. I sold 15,000 for the price of $20, which is very cheap, but we have to bear it because we are selling onions at a time when the price is very low.

On this date, the civic body of the Army of Guatemala arrived in San Martín to attend to patients who have decaying teeth. To each patient whom they attended they gave nutritious supplements—milk, *mosh* [grain of oats served in soups and *atoles*], *incaparina* [a mixture developed by the Institute of Nutrition of Central America and Panama (INCAP) that consists of cottonseed meal, corn, sorghum, calcium carbonate, yeast, and vitamin A, all locally available products that are ground to the consistency of flour and are soluble in water and may be used to make *atoles*], and a lot of vitamins. This took place not just in the town of San Martín, but also in the towns of San José, San Jorge, San Benito, Santa Ana, and Santa Rosa la Laguna.

My two youngsters, José and María, left for San Martín for an evangelistic fiesta along with other *Joseños*. They did not return until 11:00 P.M.

My Family Has Teeth Extracted
SATURDAY, 22 MARCH 1980

It was a very cold morning. I did not get up until 7:00 A.M. My wife heated the tortillas while José went to buy meat. We had to make a broth for breakfast.

At 9:00 A.M. my wife and the youngsters left San Martín to visit the military doctors. The only one who stayed with me was Susana Julia. At 3:00 P.M. I heated the tortillas and roasted a little meat and ate with her.

At 5:00 P.M. my wife returned from San Martín. They pulled three of her infected molars, three from Ramón, and three from Erasmo Ignacio.

All day Sunday I stayed home. We did not eat breakfast, lunch, or dinner peacefully because my family had much pain in their mouths, from extraction of their teeth.

On this date I sold a *cuerda* of onions (50,000 onions) in Xesucut for the low price of $80. I sold them because I have much need for money. On this harvest we lost a lot of money, but we have to bear it.

Operation on My Eyes
24–31 MARCH 1980

For dinner we had a little meat, but very small portions because we are a large family. In the night I entrusted myself to God because tomorrow I am going to Guatemala [City] for an operation on my eyes. I became a little sad because I do not know how the operation will turn out.

Tuesday, 25 March, dawned. I got up at 4:00 A.M. and entrusted myself to God. Then I went to the shore of the lake to catch the launch to Panajachel. At 10:30 A.M. I arrived in Guatemala [City]. I ate a little breakfast, but not contentedly because I was thinking about my health.

I then went to the Congress of the Republic to talk with *licenciado* Morales because I will have to remain some days in the capital. I wanted some support or some economic help. But this señor gave me no comfort. I fought a lot for him when he was a candidate for representative, but now that he has earned a good reputation and other prerogatives, he does not remember a poor person who fought hard for him.

For lunch, I did not enter a *comedor* because I am short of money. Rather, I bought a few tortillas and *chicharrones* [cracklings] in the street and ate them. Then I went to get a room. They charged me $2 for a night in the Sánchez Inn. At 7:00 P.M. I ate dinner on the street, and then I returned to the room and went to bed.

When Wednesday dawned, I gave thanks to the Creator of the Universe. I got up at 5:00 A.M. and paid a taxi $4 to take me to the Hospital Rodolfo Robles, which is very distant from the center of town. My appointment was for 7:00 A.M., but they did not receive me until 8:00 A.M. By the grace of God and the good hearts of the doctors, they performed a special operation on me. I hardly felt a thing the moment they took the bad [small growth] out of my eye.

After the operation they discharged me and told me to come back tomorrow. I left with little pain, and I went to the central part of the town to send a letter to Dr. Sexton, but scarcely had I arrived at the post office when my eye began to ache. I returned to the pension where I had rented a room. The pain grew stronger by the hour. I wanted to call the *bomberos* [firemen; rescuers] to take me back to the hospital, but there was no one to help me. I was nearly forsaken. I managed to arrive at the pension, which was somewhat distant from the post office, and I did not go out for anything else because I could not bear to move my head. It felt as if my eyes would fall out. I endured much thirst and hunger; the pain was very intense. All night I remained in one position with my face held up.

Well, the operation turned out favorable, and they charged me only $20. But in addition to the expenses of room and board, I had to pay an extra $50 for miscellaneous items.

Thursday dawned, but it was difficult to begin the day because the pain punished me very much. I did not eat breakfast; I just drank water to calm my thirst. I wanted medical attention, but my appointment was not until 2:00 P.M. What is worse, they did not see me until 3:00 P.M. After the treatment I ate a little, and again I set out for the pension in the city center, but constantly in much pain. I was not able to sleep.

It was much worse for me because I was by myself. I saw others who also were operated on, but they were accompanied by their families. Well, I have kin, but I do not have the money to give them for travel and food.

The rest of this day I spent lying in bed with much pain. I bought some pills, but they did not help.

On Friday, I got up giving thanks to God the Creator, who sees all, both the visible and invisible. During this night, I was able to sleep a little. I left to drink some coffee, but I did not eat anything.

My appointment was for 8:00 A.M., but I waited for the doctor until 11:00 A.M. Then he took off the bandage and told me that the incision was very inflamed. After bandaging my eye again, he told me not to come back until Monday, because there is only emergency care in the hospital on Saturdays and Sundays. Since I was short of money, I intended to go back to San José to get some.

At 3:00 P.M. I left Guatemala [City] and arrived in Cocales at 5:00 P.M. I waited for a ride in a truck, but I could not get one. I had to stay on the porch of a tienda, although I preferred not to be in this place because they were making a lot of racket. Since I had no place else to go, I had to put up with it.

I was lying on this same porch at 10:00 P.M. when I heard the noise of a bus. Then I got up and saw it was the bus of San Martín. Without doubt, it had had a breakdown on the road, and for that reason had not arrived in the afternoon. It carried me to San José, but I did not get home until 3:00 A.M. on Saturday, 29 March. Because the movement of the bus had made the pain in my eye worse, I did not sleep at all when I arrived home. All day long I lay in a hammock with ice on my face.

On Sunday, 30 March, the pain continued. My eyes felt as if they were going to fall out. Many tears flowed from beneath my bandage. I thought about the money that I needed in order to go back to Guatemala [City] tomorrow. I was lying in the hammock when my friend Andrés came to tell me that he had gone to the coast and they had given him $250 as an advance for the work. He gave me $50. Only then did my nerves calm. On this same afternoon I went on the launch to go to the house of my friend, Raimundo Ramírez Ralon, in Sololá. He gave me a bed, and I was able to sleep well.

On Monday I got up at 4:00 A.M. I wanted to take the bus in order to arrive early, but it was impossible. There were a lot of people

traveling, and not until 5:30 A.M. was I able to travel with Rutas Ig-
ueras line. While I was traveling, the pain began. By the time I
reached the hospital, I was in total pain. But there were many who
were sick with their eyes, and I had to wait until 1:00 P.M. for the
doctor to take off the bandage and take out the stitches. Only then
was I able to see, but still with great pain. They told me that it would
be like this until the next appointment. On this day I had not eaten
a thing because the pain was too intense. I felt better with the bandage off, and quickly I ate some tortillas in the street because it was
already late.

Luckily I was able to rest a little on the bus to San Martín. I
arrived home at 8:00 P.M. I was happy to be home because I was
worried that I was going to have to spend Holy Week in Guatemala
[City]. But by the grace of God, they set me free. Two of my companions, however, remained under treatment during the most important
week.

❧ Alfredo Bonifacio's Daughter's Body Is Lost
1–7 APRIL 1980

Because the doctor recommended that I not go out in the sun or
work very hard, I did not go anywhere. He also told me not to read.
It was easy for me to do what he said because I felt very sick. But I
have faith in God that my eyes will heal in a little while. I just rested
at home in a hammock.

In the afternoon my great friend Alfredo Bonifacio came to visit.
He was a little drunk because he was feeling sad about his daughter,
who had been in the hospital in Sololá for eight days. She had had a
baby, but the midwife had not delivered it well. Also, Bonifacio says
that his daughter's husband is very uncivilized and hits her a lot. He
told me his daughter is now going to die, and suddenly he began to
cry a lot. Although I told him to calm himself, he could not. He said
that tomorrow he is going to visit his daughter. He stayed with me for
two hours.

Sunday dawned, but for me it was not very peaceful. Nevertheless, one has to make out because in this world no one is free [from
problems]. Again I stayed home, but now the pain was less.

My family went to the church, but not I. I ate lunch almost
normally.

When the launch arrived in the afternoon, it brought the news that the daughter of Alfredo Bonifacio had died in the hospital. The news said that, when Señor Alfredo saw that the body of his daughter was not in the hospital, he tried to go to Quezaltenango to get it. When his kin became aware of what had happened, they mobilized and left on the same launch.

I got up and did not pay much attention to my being sick. I had to do something for this friend. Some boys and I contracted a pickup, and we went to Sololá. We took the route to Santa Ana, but at the point of San Jorge the car was not able to climb the road. We had to work to clear the road, and little by little the car made it over the mountain.

At 10:30 P.M. we arrived in Sololá. When we entered the hospital, they told us that they had already returned the cadaver from Quezaltenango and taken it to Panajachel. When we arrived in this town, we found Señor Alfredo with the remains of his daughter. He was trying to arrange for a launch, but it was nighttime and no one wished to make the trip. When he saw us he felt solace.

For us it was a little difficult to obtain gasoline because all the stations were closed. Thanks [go] to the "good" heart of the chief of the national police, who sold us five gallons for the price of $15. Even though we beseeched him [to charge a lower price, telling him] that we faced a lot of pain, this "good" señor had the noble heart to charge us $3 a gallon for gas.

We returned in the pickup with the corpse of Angelica Gloria. We suffered a lot on the road because it was terribly cold, and we had to pass through the mountains where they say there are a lot of guerrillas. Although it was bothersome, by the grace of God, nothing happened on the road.

We arrived home at 3:00 A.M., and a lot of people were waiting for us—nearly the whole town. Many of them were drunk, especially the kin. Also, I am witness that when we left for Sololá the Blue and White team remained to construct a *panteón* [aboveground vault or tomb]. When the town realized that the boys were working, many women and children helped. They informed us that in a very few hours the said *panteón* was completed.

When Tuesday dawned, 7 April, the whole town was feeling sad because the woman who died was charitable and religious, but her destiny obliged her to leave this world. The whole town attended her funeral. Throughout the night there was the most profound sadness. About 200 persons were drinking their shots of liquor as a sign of mourning.

The March 1980 Election and Political Problems
MARCH 1980

During the month of March there was the election for the tribunals of the towns [surrounding the lake]. Alfredo Bonifacio Temó was the candidate for mayor running for the Partido Institucional Democrático (PID). Owing to the great blow he suffered from the death in his family, he did not pay any attention to his candidacy, and his opponent took advantage. Alfredo lost the election to his enemy, Abraham Có, but we did not give this much importance.

Didn't Juanito want to be mayor? Didn't he run again for mayor?

Yes, he wanted to be mayor again in 1980. He wanted to be reelected, but we did not want him.

In your party?

Yes, and the other parties told him they did not want him either. They told him nothing could be a worse disgrace for our town than for him to be mayor again.

Then he was not a candidate?

No, he was not a candidate. He wanted to be, but we in the parties knew what he had done to the people, and each party said, "Juanito no, Juanito no, Juanito no." None of the parties wanted him.

Can you explain a little more about the election and why your party lost?

[As I have said] the PR wanted Julián Chorol as candidate for mayor. But we in the PID did not want him. [In addition to selling *lámina* donated by the PR to victims of the earthquake,] he also sold in the villages some of the notebooks and pencils that the high officials of his party gave for the schoolchildren. They gave these to him to give to the teachers. But it was not so. The same thing he did with some balls.

Then Señor Abraham Có Bizarro declared that he wanted to be candidate for mayor but with the party Frente Unido de la Revolución (FUR). That is when we of the Partido Institucional Democrático (PID) selected Señor Alfredo Bonifacio Temó for our candidate. Then when these two groups saw that we had found a man who was somewhat prudent, they began to grumble. But we were just completing a requirement; we did not have ambition to gain something. But in this time FUR still was not legalized. Then Abraham Có was not able to become a candidate for mayor because his party was illegal.[20] It was certain that he had part of the people because they wanted to get acquainted with another party. Also, the Democracia Cristiana had a problem because they were not able to choose their person for the mayoral candidate. That is where Abraham benefited, because he gave a sum of money to the secretary-general of the Partido Democracia Cristiana. They say that the secretary-general received $100 to list Abraham as their candidate for mayor. Later they went to the electoral registry of Sololá, and there Abraham was allowed to remain the candidate. Since Abraham was an official when Juan Mendoza O. was mayor, he realized that mayors receive large gifts (bribes), and for that reason he fought a lot to be elected. Also, the ex-mayor helped Abraham so that we would not win the election.

We had the majority of the people, but money makes everything. Abraham's grandfather has money, and two days before the election Abraham sent a commission to the villages to give $2 to each citizen to vote for him. The people of the villages were very happy because $2 is a lot of money to them; they have to walk three *leguas* (12 kilometers) [to vote], and they needed spending money. One day before the election the said commission went to the houses of the *Joseños* and gave each one $1 to vote for Abraham. Also, the *Joseños* felt happy because for the first time a candidate for mayor gave money. Thus, they thought that when he took office, he would give them more money since he had already demonstrated his generosity. That is why the majority of the people voted for him. When the votes were counted, it was revealed that only 96 persons were honest. Abraham received more than 366 votes (I am not sure of the exact number). We lost because we did not give money to the people. Another reason was that when Alfredo's daughter died just before the election, it was a great blow. We did not go out and campaign. Ultimately, the people regretted having made Abraham mayor because he conducted himself very poorly with the people. He was very paternalistic and autocratic.

What happened to Juanito Mendoza when he was no longer mayor?

He spent some months in town and then he left to join the police again.

During the months of March, April, and May a great problem developed for me because of the election. Certainly I had not imagined that the people had created a falsehood against me. It happens that Abraham Có, who was elected mayor, is close kin [Ignacio's cousin]. Since he is mayor, I also have respect for him. Moreover, we are friends, and together we founded the cooperative in this town. He was the provisional president of the cooperative. However, he became candidate for mayor, and our candidate was another person. Abraham won with the Partido Frente Unido de la Revolución, which is a new party of the left. They knew that this party is something of an enemy of the government, and after the election they felt intimidated. They made up the lie that the elected mayor was going to be kidnapped by the party of the right. They began to spread false notices throughout the town, and the whole town knows that I am the one who runs an official party [in the town]. But I am not a person who likes to harm or wrong anyone. I do not know whether he was my enemy or whether he considered me an enemy. It was certain that we were distant to each other, and Abraham was afraid to talk to me because they told him that within a few days he would be abducted. But I too was pained because it was possible that another person could perform the kidnapping, and the townspeople would blame me. The majority of the people sympathized with the señor, and already they suspected me. They thought that within a few days something would happen, but they did not know when. These were lies, because my companions and I know that there is nothing against this friend. What the people were going around saying was pure wickedness.

In April the falsehoods of the *Joseños* multiplied. At first I thought it was no more than a comedy and I did not pay much attention. But finally they were able to upset me completely because some went around saying they were going to kill me although it would cost them money. If necessary, they would sell their land to pay for my death.

I do not know how the news got out that already there were 16 *Joseños* who were going to be kidnapped. Many of the boys then would not speak to me. I do not know why these things happened. Well, I always entrust myself to God, but Abraham and the other 15 were doing the same thing. Constantly the news came that they were trying to work out a way to abduct me from my home and kill me. Already there was a large number of them, but I stood alone; my companions of the police were afraid to speak to me because they were afraid they also would be persecuted.

But my conscience was clean because I do not like to get involved with things that are not worthwhile. In a few days, however, the malicious gossip intensified, especially with the women. This is when my weakness grew. There were nights when I was unable to sleep just thinking about these things. There were also days when I did not eat anything because of such pain. I wanted to arrange a meeting with Abraham in the Catholic Church, but the director, who is Abraham's grandfather, was completely obstinate. He did not do a thing for us. I appealed to the cooperative, but the members simply said that we were obsessed with these matters and did nothing. I wanted the hand of Alcoholics Anonymous to help us achieve a better understanding, but never did these friends do anything for us. I saw that no one would extend his hand, even though mine was clean. Finally, since no one wanted to intervene for us, I became angry, as the word of God says, "*Sed manso como paloma pero listo como serpiente* [Be calm like a dove but ready like a snake]." This was my motto because it made it possible for me to remain quiet.

There were people murmuring, and seeing that nothing was going to be done to stop it, I got the idea to go to the proper authorities. I was able to raise $200 to initiate an investigation conducted by the national army to calm this negative situation that the people were formulating. I wanted to pay a commission on behalf of the authority of war for an inquiry about the lies. I wanted to go forward with this plan since my conscience was clean for not having done anything bad against my fellow man. I was ready to travel to Guatemala [City] to ask for a commission of the government, but my wife was worried. She told me to have more patience, because calling a commission would mean a number of *Joseños* would go to jail, since the whole town knows that there are about 25 persons behind this injurious, false accusation. My wife asked me, "If these men go to jail, who will look after their families? Their children will suffer." These were the words my wife told me, and only then did she convince me.

I thought hard about the children of these liars. Also, the evangelist church (Central American Church) gave me its hand and supported me a lot because they told me not to take such measures. These persons of the evangelist church were very much in my favor.

The same thing happened to Abraham that happened to me. He was very much afraid and now was unable to sleep in his house. He left to work early and returned late at night because he was afraid of being abducted. But this was a lie of the people. When he took office as mayor, he would not talk to us because they told him we were his enemies. Usually he dresses like a Ladino, but to confuse abductors he dressed like an Indian. But this was funny because no one was planning to kidnap him.

❧ Detained by Guerrillas While Returning Home
16 MAY 1980

Ignacio omitted this episode from his written account, but he told me about it on tape in August of 1980 and added some details on tape in August of 1982.

It happened on 16 May 1980. I was not there because I was in Guatemala [City] on that day. But according to all the information of the *Joseños*, the guerrillas arrived at 3:00 P.M. They took away the mayor's pistol and other arms because they said that they had heard an accusation on behalf of the townspeople that the mayor had been conducting himself poorly with the inhabitants. (But they later gave back the mayor's pistol.)

There was then a meeting in San José for almost the entire town, because there were many guerrillas dressed in *overols* [overalls; fatigues] like the army and well armed. Afterwards, the guerrillas went to San Martín.

Since I had gone to Guatemala [City] on this day, I arrived in San Martín at 8:00 P.M. with two other *Joseños*, Ruiz and *profesora* Isabel. We left the bus and headed to our town on foot. But just outside the town of San Martín we met the guerrillas. We wanted to pass in front of them, but they stopped us and told us we could go no further. Then I told them, "I have much need to go home because I have not eaten lunch."

Then the *jefe* of the guerrillas approached me and said, "Do you value life or death?"

Then I told him, "It is that I have a great need."

Then he told me I could not leave because I had to stay for a moment for an orientation [talk, or armed propaganda]. And thus we three had to stay with them on the road. They told me not to walk in front because we might suddenly meet soldiers; to avoid a confrontation I should walk in the middle. Then we headed for San José with the three of us walking in the middle of them.

As we were walking I asked what alternative they were seeking. Then they told me that they were looking for the alternative of equality, because here in Guatemala only the rich have money and we poor people do not. They said that they wanted a new structure, a new government, so that there will be no more hunger, no more sickness, no more rich, and no more poor—a structure of equality. The rich in Guatemala dominate the whole country. Also they told me that they are going to fight a struggle that will last not just a week but from one to ten years until they succeed, and that they are certainly going to overthrow the government of General Lucas and that many campesinos will have to die to achieve the peace that Guatemala needs so much. But they are going around offering these things, and I am not sure they will do anything if they gain power.

I asked them, "Where are you going to stay? Are you going to San José?" They told me no, that they were leaving for the countryside to sleep under the trees because they suddenly could encounter enemies who could kill them. Then I asked them how they learned to handle their firearms. They told me that they have had their practices [training] in the mountains. They also told me that the people have to take up arms, even the women and children, for them to win the war.

Thus, we continued to walk. When we arrived near the town of San José, they took the road leading to Tamalaj, and we entered the town.

I was not afraid because I know something about military maneuvers. But the teacher walking with us was trembling. She thought they might kill us on the road, but nothing happened.

When I arrived in the town, it was something else. I was surprised that all the people were frightened. For the first time in the history of the town of San José, guerrillas had taken over. The people were saying that the guerrillas were looking for me because I was with the government, but this was not true, because, when I had chatted with them, they had not said anything bad. When I arrived home, my family was worried because they thought the guerrillas were looking for me, although they did not know if they wanted to kill me or to tell me something. But I had talked to them, and they had said nothing against me.

This is what happened that night. Frankly, although many say that in San José there are guerrillas, we are witnesses and we know the town very well. The town is too small and too poor, and I cannot believe there are guerrillas here because we all work in our fields. To be committed to this organization, it is necessary to give up time for the [military] exercises, but we poor people have to struggle each day; if we do not, we have no recourse for the following day. Naturally, we have to work and cannot undertake such grave action because we have no money; we are very poor. Thus, I know very well that in San José there are no guerrillas, despite rumors that there are four. In any case, the majority of the people ignore them because, as I have said, we are poor.

But afterwards the guerrillas announced in a bulletin that the whole town was with them. Although many men, women, and children went to look and listen, it was not because they have a commitment with the guerrillas—it was just a curiosity. Never before had they seen such people. It was not because they have an obligation to them. Thus, the guerrillas' claims were not true. Still, some say that it was bad [for the townspeople to go to see them]. Others say that it did not matter because the people hardly know what a guerrilla is. For them it was like going to watch a fire.

What kind of arms did they have?

Frankly, I did not see the make of the arms because I was talking to them at night, and I did not ask what kind of weapons they had. But indeed they carried very powerful arms like those of the army, such as 30-30 carbines and the Thompson [machine gun].

Automatic arms?

Well, yes, automatic arms—that I realized. Pity, I carried a flashlight, but since the batteries were nearly spent, it was not possible for me to see well. But I was able to see that they carried powerful arms with plenty of ammunition. Also, they carried a transmitting radio, although I do not know whether it was for communicating with their companions.

And what was the organization?

The organization is called ORPA, which is to say, Organización del Pueblo en Armas [Organization of the People in Arms]. But their appearance is confusing because they are dressed in the uniform of the army. The only way one can tell [the difference] well is by their hair. In the army, all have crew cuts, or short hair, but in ORPA they have fashionable hair because they want to keep it long. Thus, one can identify them as guerrillas. But their clothing and commands are like those of the army. For instance, when I was talking to them, the *jefe* commanded a front guard and a rear guard just as it would have been done in the army.[21]

These were the things I was able to see on this night. It was the first time I experienced talking to them. People had said that there is this organization, ORPA, but I never had been able to speak to them until this night. It was not that I wanted to talk to them; it was just that I met them on the road.

❧ My Wife Is Worried That I Will Join the Protestants
24 JUNE 1980

During the months of May and June, I was attending the Central American Church as a friend because I know it is possible to visit all churches. But when these friends saw that I was attending regularly, they wanted to oblige me to be baptized. However, I was not looking for a permanent religion; I was only doing it because they were my friends.

On 24 June, the day of the main fiesta of the town, I am not very happy because my wife thinks that I am going to stay in the Central American Church. But I am not planning to change my religion. It is true that I have not been drinking liquor because I have been able to bear everything that is happening to me. However, on the 24th I do not know why I had the desire to drink, but I did with some friends until dawn.

❧ Reconcilation with Abraham
JULY 1980

In the middle of my problem with Abraham, I wanted to resign from the cooperative. I did not continue with those of the *consejo de administración*, although we had been trying to better our society. Everything was negative. Finally, I pondered a lot our having fought to establish this cooperative, and I asked for a meeting with the board of directors, committee of control, and the committee of education in order to arrange a reconciliatory meeting with my companion Abraham and for a clarification of how this false injury was started. Those señores agreed to what I asked, and they set a date for the meeting. It was my friend Manuel who went to call my friend Abraham, who was afraid of being kidnapped.

At 8:00 P.M. we all gathered, with Abraham coming last. Only then did I extend the hand of friendship to this friend, who clarified all that had happened. He says that an anonymous letter had arrived that said within a few days he would be kidnapped. Moreover, the mouths of others had said that we who were with the government were ready to abduct him. Then he became frightened because of all that the people were saying. Also, he said a brother-in-law told him to take special care because he had heard we were planning an abduction. And that is how this *calumnia* amassed. In front of everyone Abraham said that he no longer slept at night in his house. For many weeks he had abandoned it. Also, he said that he was extremely scared of me because in his political campaign he had criticized the government on this [very] subject—[kidnapping]. Moreover, he declared the injury he felt because of the statements of his kin [Ignacio].

I also declared that there was nothing that I held against him and that I had not gossiped or spoken badly of him, and that I did not think badly of any of his companions. On this night we provided a reconciliatory explanation that neither of us was guilty of these things and that they were just lies of the people. When everything was arranged, we drank coffee with bread as an indication of our new friendship. Also, I believe the people suspected that I was arranging for something bad to happen to someone when I had to go to Guatemala [City] a lot because of my eyes. But this was not true because I am in a lot of pain with my eyes. God forgive these persons who are gossiping, because I have said many times that I am a man of a clear conscience.

Here Ignacio relates another lengthy episode of a trip to the coast on 14 July 1980 while he was sick. A policeman wanted to put shackles on him and take him to prison for illegally transporting crews, but a bribe set him free. A hurricane attacked the travelers en route to the farm. The hurricane uprooted trees and forced the bus driver to park on the side of the road until it calmed. When Ignacio returned home he was quite sick, and the racket of the children made things worse. He said that his wife went to look for a doctor but could not find one. "When we are sick, we hardly ever take medicine because we have no money, and when we have money we are not able to find a doctor," he states. He was so ill that he was unable to make entries in his diary.

❧ The First Failure of the New Tribunal
THURSDAY, 24 JULY 1980

The first failure of the new municipal corporation, which had been in power for 39 days, is almost funny. This news circulated in the entire town. It happens that the municipality has some land in Patzam, where there are three groves of avocado trees. Each year the municipality is in charge of selling the harvest. The *regidores* [councilmen] negotiate the business of selling the avocadoes. Since they are the councilmen, they do not sell the avocadoes themselves. First they ask the mayor, who tells them to do it.

Since the avocado groves are somewhat distant and on a slope, they took [enough] companions with them to carry only one load.

According to the news, after these señores picked the avocadoes and packed them into bundles, they went to a piece of neighboring land where José Carlos has planted *malanga*. This plant provides a fruit beneath the earth like yucca, which is nourishing for us Indians. Thinking that this small plantation had no owner because it was on the bank of the river, or, better said, thinking that the owner had abandoned the plantation, they began to uproot the plants. They took out about 1,500 pounds. They discovered that they had dug up so many that they could not carry them all. They brought their loads of avocadoes in the afternoon, and then they returned to bring the *malangas*.

Well, they were not sentenced because they are the corporation, but indeed they paid for the *quintales* of *malanga* they robbed. There was much shame and much criticism for these men in the town.

❧ Soldiers Come to San José
1–4 AUGUST 1980

I taped an account of this episode on Friday, 8 August 1980, when I saw Ignacio in Panajachel for the first time since 1976. After I returned home, he sent to me in the mail a written version with less detail but still covering the main points. What follows is primarily from the taped version.

On this day a company of soldiers arrived in San José, but we did not know what they were doing or what they were looking for or if something bad had caused them to come. They formed an encampment very near the town in a place called Xeynup, where the river flows below the Hill of Chuitinamit near the path toward Santa Ana.

Although I felt sick, José and I went to Tamalaj to throw fertilizer on a little grove of coffee. At noon we went back home for lunch.

On Saturday, 2 August, I was feeling a little better. José and I went to spread fertilizer on two *cuerdas* of corn, but we could not finish because we ran out of fertilizer and I was somewhat sick. We worked only until 2:00 P.M. Then I told my youngster, "Let's go by the soldiers because people have said that soldiers hit and mistreat [others]." So I told my youngster, "Let's go by the soldiers and see what it is that the people are talking about." But, no, [nothing happened]. When we passed, they were eating lunch. Very content I said, "*Buenas tardes* [Good afternoon]." And they said, "*Que le vaya bien* [Good day, or may it go well for you]." Then this was the way it was on Saturday.

On Sunday, 3 August, another group arrived—about 40 to 50 *guardias de hacienda* [semimilitary border patrol who are uniformed and armed treasury officers] and additional soldiers. There were plenty—more than 200!

On this Sunday there was a wedding, and a lot of people went to mass. Although I did not go, I saw them going to the church. About 1:00 P.M. the army wanted a meeting in front of the Catholic Church for a declaration on communism. A captain or colonel (I could not tell very well because they were not wearing their insignia) held a meeting while all the people were inside the church for the mass. When they came out, they were surrounded by soldiers who told them to tell the people that there was a meeting that everyone had to attend.

The *caporal*, or leader, spoke with a loudspeaker. Well, for us it was very well because he said they are not persecuting the working people, the honest people. They were just against the Communists. He also said that they did not want Guatemala to suffer like Cuba, Russia, Angola, and Afghanistan.

The colonel spoke in Spanish, and my dear friend Julián Chorol translated into *lengua* [Tzutuhil]. But it was a pity that the military person said one thing and the translator said something else. It was almost dishonest. The people did not understand well what the military man was saying because he would say one thing and the translator another. For a while it was nearly amusing.

On Sunday afternoon a hard rain fell. I was home because, as I told you, I was sick. My wife and others went to the place where the soldiers were. As I said, for us it was a thing of curiosity. We did not think it was for a war. My people did not know. My people did not realize that we were living in a very delicate situation. So they went there, including my señora.

My señora said that, when they arrived, the soldiers were trying to cook, but since it was raining hard and their firewood was very green, their fires would not light. Then about 5:00 P.M. my señora arrived to tell me, "Look Ignacio, those poor men are suffering a lot. The firewood they have is very green and does not burn. It is impossible for them to eat because they are not able to cook."

Then I said to myself that I do not have a hard heart and I have plenty of dry firewood. Also, I had suffered the same in the army. Thus, my friend Felipe and my two youngsters, José and Ramón, and I each carried a *tercio* [the amount of firewood one can carry on one's back]. We reached their encampment, but since it was raining and the river in front of them was rising, we could not take the firewood close to them. However, a few of them were on our side of the river, so we left the dry firewood with them. Only then were they able to cook their dinner. Also, I was able to chat with them a little and ask why they were here. They told me that the guerrillas had said that Sunday night or early Monday there was going to be a confrontation—if not Monday, then Tuesday. Then they told me that at 8:00 P.M. no one would be able to walk near them because if they saw someone approaching them, they would shoot them with their rifles. Then I said, "Very well."

There was nothing more than this to my errand. I just wanted to leave a little firewood. It was not because I was obliged to help them. It was just that I had compassion for them because they were not able to cook their food, and moreover I have suffered similar circumstances in the army.

About 7:00 P.M. a squad of soldiers left for the location of the municipality [to announce a curfew]. Then there was a public announcement in all the streets of the town that no one could go out between 8:00 P.M. and 6:00 A.M., and that anyone walking along the shore of the lake would be shot on the order of a higher authority.

Monday dawned, and, by the grace of God, nothing happened. Indeed, nearly the whole town was scared because there were a lot of soldiers. Most of the townspeople did not leave to work. Mainly they stayed close to home.

On this day, the military was still there, and another force arrived. But by the grace of God, nothing happened. No soldiers or guerrillas were killed. They say that they were asking only for the *cédulas de vecindad* and the *cédulas de ciudadanía* [identification papers] of those who passed in the area. And this was all that happened.

On this day, Monday, they celebrated the fiesta of Santo Domingo Guzmán. José and I went to spread fertilizer on a little coffee.

We arrived back at 11:30 A.M. Still I was sick, but I was struggling to work. When I arrived home, my wife gave me a telegram from my great friend James D. Sexton. It made me very happy. Although we ate only greens, we ate very happily. The rest of the day I worked [on some pages of my diary].

❧ An Abduction
5–7 AUGUST 1980

I intended to go to Panajachel to visit my great friend James D. Sexton, but because I was sick, I did not get up early. All day I was working [on my pages] at home. At 3:00 P.M. I prepared my papers to visit Panajachel. Because of the little time it took me to change my clothing, the launch left without me. It was only 100 meters away, but I could not reach it. All afternoon I was a little angry because I had prepared for the trip. Finally, I had to accept missing the launch, and I continued working. For dinner we ate fish broth.

About 7:00 P.M. the first kidnappings took place in the history of San José. It was a very serious thing for us. Two bricklayers were abducted. They were not *Joseños*, but men of Santa Elena who were staying and working in San José on a private construction. I do not know whether they were abducted in their house or in the street, but they were abducted very near my house. When I opened the door of my house next to the street, these señores were seated on the sidewalk nearby eating Tor-Trix [corn chips packaged in small bags]. They said, "*Buenas noches*," and I answered the same. They were kidnapped not more than a *cuadra* [275 feet] away.

I thought it was just as well to work at home, and I began to write a little. I do not know if I was writing or eating when they were kidnapped because about 8:00 P.M. my wife called me to come eat because she had the tortillas ready. But no one heard anything. All was quiet.

Without realizing anything was happening, I continued writing after dinner because it had been a week since I had been able to write. At 9:00 P.M. I lay down, and about 15 minutes later a platoon of soldiers came. They stopped at the corner of my house. There were a lot of them, about 50 to 60.

"*Púchica*! [My goodness!]" I said, "What is happening?" I was scared. "*Púchica*!" because they were on the corner, and they were talking harshly. "*Púchica*!" I said, "Are they going to come inside?"

Well, frankly, I do not have any kind of weapon, not a thing. But I was worried about my pages. They would not serve them for anything, but I was thinking that it had taken me a long time to write them, and to remember everything again would be difficult. They might tear them up, and I was concerned.

Well, they did not come into my house. I thought that they were looking for something, but nothing happened. I did not know that they were looking for the persons who had been abducted.

Then I went into the street and asked some boys, "What is happening with the soldiers? Where are they going?"

"Well, who knows what they are looking for," one answered.

About a half hour later a boy named Pancho arrived. "Did you see the military?" I asked. "They came and left again for the municipality."

"Perhaps it is for the boys," Pancho answered.

What boys?" I asked.

"The two boys who were abducted near your house."

Well, this gave me a great fright and a case of the nerves. I felt bothered because my house is on a major street. I thought that the army would cause no harm because at the very least they would be contradicting an order. But I thought the guerrillas could return. The army was on one side of the town, and the abductors [who were thought at that time to be guerrillas] came from the other side of town. They might think we had been accused of something and return to abduct us. Thus, I got the children up at 11:00 P.M. and went to sleep in my mother's house which is more inside the *sitio*. This Tuesday night I hardly slept. Never before have we witnessed a kidnapping, and I felt very sad. We were realizing that the situation continued to be difficult. But I did not know how it was going to be resolved.

On Wednesday, 6 August, I went to the coast with Agustín María. In San Martín we had to wait for the driver. At 8:30 we left San Martín. While we were waiting for the chauffeur, a platoon of soldiers arrived in town. When we passed the place called Chocal, part of San Martín, we met two truckloads of soldiers, but it all went well.

In Santa Lucía we ate lunch, but the bus broke down. The same thing happened when we arrived at the La Noria farm. At 4:00 P.M. we arrived on the farm, but we had only gone to bring back the crew, so we immediately began the return trip. In Santa Lucía we ate dinner.

At 11:00 P.M. we passed through San Luis. We waited until 1:00 A.M. out of much fear. At 3:00 A.M. we arrived in San José. We arranged for the crew of Tzancuil to stay in San Luis. They were going to cross the lake by launch.

When we arrived in San José, Agustín María and I settled the accounts. Each of us earned $70, and our helper earned $50.

When we were waiting to pass the hours of the night in San Luis, the driver of the bus began to drink a lot of beer. He became inebriated. It was another person who drove the bus to San Martín. When we arrived in San Martín, we carried him out of the bus as live weight but fast asleep and unaware that he had any responsibilities.

They say that I was called by the justice of the peace to clarify whether I had seen the abduction or whether I had heard anything. But since I was not home, I could not present myself to the justice of the peace. I do not know whether they will call me again. Frankly, I did not hear or see anything.

On Thursday, 7 August, I was resting in my house but feeling cranky for lack of sleep. In the morning of this day, they told me that the soldiers had left on their return trip.

A lot of people have criticized the army. For instance, people of Santa Ana and of Santa Bárbara have been saying that members of the military enter houses, steal a person's things, and rape the women. This is the uproar in Santa Ana. But we do not much believe them now. Furthermore, I know the army, and I was a soldier who did not have the heart to do such things. Then I said [if this is true] the whole situation of the army has changed. Before, the military had a lot of respect. But we saw in San José that the military did nothing bad to the town. When they left, they were grateful for all the services the townspeople had given them. They walked through the town, but they did not enter the houses. They walked through the streets, but they did not do anything to the people.

When I arrived in Panajachel in August of 1982, I asked Ignacio what had happened to the two men who were kidnapped. He provided the following details that subsequently emerged in San José.

The truth was that during this night I did not much know what happened, myself. What I knew was that the two masons had disappeared. Later the news emerged that the same men were kidnapped by the right because they had been accused of being guerrillas. When they were abducted, they took them to the place where we were the day before yesterday [where the soldiers had been encamped].

According to this news, they put them in some *tuneles* [gasoline barrels for the military trucks] and took them away, but no one knows where. Who knows?

According to this information, the real reason that these two men were kidnapped was not because they were guerrillas. It was only because one of the masons had committed an accident. He was riding a motorcycle in Santa Elena when he ran over a boy. In the inquiry of the court, he did not want to pay for the doctor for treating the child. Later the father of the boy told the military that the culprit was a guerrilla, which was a *calumnia*. I do not believe the masons were guerrillas. Just because one of them had an accident and did not want to pay he was accused of being a guerrilla. The other mason had done nothing at all.

And no one knows what happened to them?

Not one person knows. The only thing that is known is that they were carried away in *tuneles*. That is certain, but no one knows where they were taken.

First, there was a group of soldiers near your house?

Yes, and they earlier were the kidnappers. The second time they just took a different road. When the person for whom the masons were working realized that they had been kidnapped, he went to the municipality to tell them that the two men were lost. Then the mayor ran to the place where we were yesterday [the military encampment] to tell them, "Please come, two men were kidnapped!"

"Yes," they said, and another commission left, but they knew that they were there before. I believe you understand.

Eight days later the wives of the masons came to San José seeking information. They asked if anyone knew of their whereabouts, and they collected all of their belongings, such as their shoes and masonry tools. So these men indeed disappeared. About a month later their wives returned again seeking information, but no one knew anything to tell them.[22]

Working with Jaime Sexton
8–9 AUGUST 1980

I got up at 4:00 A.M. and arranged my papers for the trip to Panajachel. At 7:00 A.M. I arrived, and then I went to the house of my great friend. We went to drop off my papers at his house, and then we went to have breakfast at the Casa de Pays [House of Pies, which went out of business in 1982 for lack of tourists]. After breakfast, we recorded a little interviewing.

We ate lunch at the same hotel. In the afternoon I told him that tomorrow I had to make a trip to the coast. We ate a dinner of giant hamburgers in the Hotel Galindo. In the night my great friend gave me $15 and told me that it was better for me to sleep in a hotel [I had not yet bought extra bedding and thought he might rest more comfortably in a hotel], but I told him it was better to sleep in his house so as not to pay a lot. Moreover on this day we chatted a lot about our work [and *Son of Tecún Umán*, which was about ready to go to print].

On 9 August I got up at 5:00 A.M. and bathed [showered] with hot water. Then I said good-bye to this friend because I had to take a bus for the coast at 6:00 A.M. The guardian had not gotten up [to unlock the gate], and I was worried because it was already time for the bus. I had to look for a place to jump over the wall to the street. I boarded the bus of the Masheña line, which let me off in San Diego. With the money that Dr. Sexton gave me, I bought a sombrero for $5. I felt sick to my stomach.

When I arrived at the house of my sister [in San Diego], she offered me breakfast. I ate a little but not very happily. She gave me some pills for my stomach.

At 11:00 A.M. I caught the Méndez bus. On the La Palmira farm we met the military. We had to get off the bus with our personal documents in our hands. By the grace of God, it all went well. I stayed in Patulul. I did not want to eat lunch because of the heat.

When we arrived, the crew already had been paid. When we were returning, we encountered the military above La Gomera. We all had to unload, but everything went without incident. When we arrived in San José, I arranged the accounts with Agustín M., and each of us got $50. I drank a beer and went to sleep.

Ignacito Is Gravely Ill, and Military Airplanes Strafe Nearby Hills
10–12 AUGUST 1980

All day long I was resting in the house. I was caring for Ignacito because he is sick with a fever and vomiting. We bought some pills in the shops to give to him, but they did not help.

In the afternoon of this day we bought 16,000 seedlings of onions for transplanting in the *tablones* of Xesucut. Felipe and José are in charge of planting them tomorrow.

In August of 1980 I asked Ignacio to explain his mentioning of two airplanes strafing the hills near San José.

It was last Sunday [10 August] when two [propeller-driven] airplanes came. Perhaps they were looking for guerrillas in the Cave of Chuitinamit. They flew over Chuitinamit and places called Chulac and Chocaman. The latter pertains to Santa Ana and Santa Bárbara, and the former to San José and Chuitinamit. It was a very annoying situation, to say the least. The people of Santa Ana were very disturbed because of what happened—the airplanes fired a lot rounds!

With machine guns?

Monday it was with machine guns. Sunday there were bombs of mortars, if I am not mistaken. About 40 to 50 mortars were heard Sunday.

Near San José?

Yes, but not really close, a distance of 5 to 6 kilometers. We were somewhat nervous because even 6 kilometers is not very far. It was in the village of Tzarayá, where there are military encampments. Chuitinamit, which is very near San José [less than a mile away], was machine-gunned by airplane because they say that it is a cave of the guerrillas. But I do not think that anything is there, just animals. The mortars were farther away in Tzarayá by the mountain of Chixal.

But you were able to hear them.

Very well, because Tzarayá is a village of San José. The destruction of the bombs we heard on Sunday. Most of the townsfolk did not go out anywhere Sunday, and they did not go to their fields because they were afraid a bomb might fall on them. It was very near, and they could lose their lives.

On 11 August I did not go to plant onions because I was working on my diary. All day I was working in the house.

All night long I did not sleep because my son, Erasmo Ignacio, is very sick with fever and vomiting. He has been sick for days, but this night was worse. There was a lot of grief in the family. But with faith in God, I had to leave this child, and go to Panajachel.

When I arrived in Panajachel, I chatted with some women and then went to the house of my great friend James D. Sexton. When I arrived, this friend was already leaving for breakfast, so the two of us went together to eat breakfast at the Casa de Pays Hotel. For me it was a joy to be with such an honorable person and to be in a hotel, because we poor people never go to a hotel because our means do not permit it. That is to say, we are not able to afford the cost of meals in a hotel.

All day long we were working; the doctor in other work, and I on the pages of my diary. We ate lunch and dinner in the Casa de Pays Hotel. At 8:00 P.M. we went to sleep fairly tired from working all day.

❧ My Birthday
WEDNESDAY, 13 AUGUST 1980

On this day I was in Panajachel with my great friend James D. Sexton. It was my birthday, and I had completed 39 years of existence on this earth. I am very positive that during my years of being in this world I have had more suffering than joy. We ate breakfast in the same hotel.

Afterwards, we continued working on our pages. For lunch we ate in the Hotel Galindo. We each had two hamburgers. It was very pleasant, but I continued to worry about the health of my son, Erasmo Ignacio. We ate dinner again in the Casa de Pays. I wanted very much to drink a beer, but I did not want to abuse the hospitality of my great friend. [I thought Ignacio was still on the wagon, so I made a special effort not to offer him drinks.] We went to sleep at 9:00 P.M., and I entrusted the health of my son to God.

❧ Sexton Leaves
14–15 AUGUST 1980

This was the day that my great friend James D. Sexton left to return to the United States. It was somewhat sad because he had only come for some days here in Guatemala [two weeks]. But the friendship that we have is a lasting one.

We got up at 5:00 A.M., and my friend Sexton showered. Afterwards, he arranged his objects to carry. He told me that I should shower with hot water, but I thought it better to bathe in the lake.

This friend gave me remembrances [gifts]—so many that I could not carry them all in one trip. I had to return for them. He gave me an aluminum kettle, large white sheets, a blanket, two towels, four bottles of typewriter correction fluid, and two glasses—all new. I was very happy because, as I have said many times previously, we poor people are very thankful for gifts, although we are never able to give something of value in return because our condition does not permit it. For this reason my friend gave me these things, and I was very appreciative because they are a demonstration of affection.

Yesterday after dinner we went to the office of Rutas Lima to ask about the hour of departure, which they told us was 7:00 A.M. It is for this reason my friend had to arrange his luggage, but when we left for the street we had to wait on Rutas Lima until 8:00 A.M. Then I said good-bye to this great friend, who caught the bus to Los Encuentros.

I returned to the house that we left just to collect my things. Then I left for the market to eat breakfast. Afterwards, I went to Sololá to buy two small trousers for Ramoncito and Erasmo Ignacio. In Sololá I chatted with my friend Isabel, who told me that yesterday the wife of my friend Benjamín died, which made me feel very sad.

After buying the few things, I returned to Panajachel. When I arrived on the edge of the lake, I bathed. Afterwards, I sat in the shade of a cypress to write and record in my diary my stay with my great friend in this beautiful town of Panajachel, where I learned my first words in Castellano [Castilian] when I was a boy. God bless the persons who brought me to this sacred place and who taught me to speak Spanish when I was a boy. I will carry these things engraved in my soul until the day I die. All of these things I wrote under the great cypress tree of remembrance.

On 15 August my wife and I went to bathe after breakfast. All day long I rested in my house.

❧ A Teacher Dies
30–31 AUGUST 1980

At 5:00 P.M. I was lying down on my hammock when suddenly they told us of the death of the Indian *profesor* Jaime Sosa Leal, a native of San Luis, whose corpse they found in Chijom, part of San Luis. But his death was very negative; some say he died by accident, and others say they killed him. It is certain that it caused much sadness in the entire town because he was a teacher who was a real friend. Many children cried a lot, including José and María, because he was their teacher.

Can you explain the death of the teacher more? You told me it was over a woman? Was it his wife?

Yes, they say this, but he is not a native of San José. We knew him because he was teaching the children in San José. They say that he was killed by another man. They say that Jaime's woman had first joined [married] another man. She later left this man and joined Jaime. Then the first husband took revenge by killing Jaime, according to a critic. But another critic said they killed him because he was participating in the radio station. Thus there are two critics. Moreover, they say two men went to jail for killing Jaime, but no one saw this. Jaime's father and father-in-law also told me these things when they arrived in San José. I gave them some soda pop, and they told me the whole situation—that Jaime had an enemy who was the former husband of his wife. These two still suspect that he is the one who killed the teacher.

Does the one critic say that the cause was that the radio was communistic?

They said that the radio broadcasts communistic doctrine.

On Sunday, 31 August, nearly everyone was talking about the death of *profesor* Jaime Sosa Leal. In the morning of this day my assistant came to tell me that a crew is ready to leave for the coast. I told him very well, and that we would arrange it for tomorrow.

At 10:00 A.M. I went with my family to watch a little soccer. The *Joseño* team lost to the workers of Panajachel.

We wanted to hear about the burial of *profesor* Jaime on the radio, but it was impossible because the broadcasting station, La Voz de San Luis, suspended its ordinary program and just played sad music.

❧ Gerardo Is Adulterous with His Brother's Wife
MONDAY, 1 SEPTEMBER 1980

On this day I was very tired, but still at night I had to go to the cooperative with Agustín M. to count some money. We stayed until 11:00 P.M.

I did not witness it, but my wife saw what happened to Gerardo Mendoza. He has a brother named Domingo with the same surname. They are brothers of the same mother and father from a poor family but ready to do bad. Although these brothers both are poor, Gerardo is a little more clever than Domingo.

Domingo goes to work on the coast on cotton plantations and in the milpa to earn a living to sustain his family. Each time that Domingo goes to the coast, he asks his brother to do him the favor of taking care of his family. They have lived this way for some years. There is no room for doubt that Gerardo stays and takes care of the family. He is enamored of his brother's woman, and they therefore began giving each other sexual pleasure without anyone else realizing it.

But they say that Gerardo carelessly told another person (who in turn told Domingo) that when his brother left in a crew he had sexual relations with his woman. Domingo did not make a fuss or protest to his wife. He had the virtue of enduring these things. One day he decided to look for work on the coast, and again he asked his brother to care for his family. But all was to the contrary. Domingo returned within three days, but he did not enter his house, which is between the coffee groves and the exit to San Martín. Instead, he stayed near it, and when night fell he was watching until the hour when his brother would arrived to receive sexual favors from his woman.

About 10:00 P.M., Gerardo got up and left his house and headed for his brother's house without realizing his brother was vigilant. When Domingo saw his brother begin to have sex with his wife, he went to the municipal commissary to ask them to capture his brother. When the guards and *alguaciles* drew near, Gerardo was naked and enjoying the best moment of his life. But they entered the house and dragged him to jail nude. They did not permit him [to get] his clothing—they took him as he was. They carried the woman off to jail with him. The hour was already late, and the children had already been sleeping. It was indeed savagery.

Gerardo's wife took her husband some clothing, and then she met with my wife and told us the story of her marriage. Gerardo's brother had a lot of compassion for him and did not ask for justice against his brother. But indeed the law punished him with 60 days in jail.

Why did you say this was savagery?

I say this is savagery because it was unconscionable of him to commit such immoral acts. Since he did not have the good conscience of being a brother or a kinsman, it is savagery. Do you understand the word "savagery"?

Yes, I understand the word "savagery," but I wanted to know whether you thought it was because the guards took him to jail naked or because of his attitude.

All of this pertains to attitude, because if he had a good attitude they would not have taken him to jail, and if he had a better attitude he would not have been deprived of his clothing. To me all of this was savagery. From the point when he began to commit the crime of entering into immoral acts with his sister-in-law until he was deprived of his clothing.

Did they put the woman in jail naked, too?

No, she had clothing. But the man had abandoned his clothing in his own house.

I understand; he did not carry his own clothing to her house.

No, no, no. He left them in his house and went naked to do this act, and when the police arrived he did not have any clothing, so they took him to jail without any.

And the police threw them both in jail?

Yes, one with clothing and the other without clothing.

In the same cell?

No, no, no, they were different. It was not possible for them to be content because the man was in one jail and the woman in another.

Did the woman stay in jail?

She paid a fine, but it was very little.

The man paid more?

It was more for the man, but he also was exempted because Domingo was conscientious and did not ask for the maximum sentence (18 months) allowed under the law—just 60 days. Gerardo's brother is a good person.

❧ Careless on the Coast
TUESDAY, 2 SEPTEMBER 1980

In Patulul a heavy rain caught us. We lost time when the truck broke down in Cocales, but I was able to eat my breakfast at 3:00 P.M.

When we arrived in La Goma, the tires went flat. We went to a garage to have them repaired. We were suffering but we were not regretful.

One way or another when one believes he is clever he does the most stupid things. I entered a shop to drink a Pepsi-Cola with my friend Bernardo. When we entered the tienda, an enjoyable comedy on television attracted our attention. We did not realize when the bus pulled out. We ran for it, but we were not able to catch up with it. And now night had come.

With much fear we took the road at night, walking through very strange places. By the grace of God, the rain had stopped. Neither of us had *sombras* [plastic sheets used as rain capes]. All of our things were in the bus.

We walked five hours on foot, but we walked lightly and very scared.

At midnight we arrived on the Ipalita farm. All of the boys were sad thinking about what might have happened to us. We did not talk much until we reached them. For certain it grieved me very much because, if we had met members of the military, they would have thought that we were bad persons. By the great will of God, nothing happened.

When the following day dawned, my whole body ached for having walked so much. I was scarcely able to walk.

❧ Soldiers Arrive for a Declaration
7–8 SEPTEMBER 1980

Before breakfast I received a card inviting me to celebrate a mass for the soul of the missing teacher. When they brought me the card, I felt very sad.

At 6:00 A.M. a squad of soldiers arrived in town for a declaration. The people were alarmed, but it all turned out tranquil.

On this same day the government appealed for the people of all the towns of the department of Sololá to go to the capital of Sololá. Eighteen *Joseños* and 42 people from the villages of San José went to Sololá. The declaration was made not just in the towns of the department of Sololá but also in the whole Republic of Guatemala.

The residents did not return until 8:00 P.M. When they came back, the soldiers were also in the town. It was like a fiesta, because those who went to Sololá gave in to the pleasure of drinking their *tragos* with the soldiers. Also, the cooperative prepared a dinner for the soldiers, but just bread and coffee.

Can you explain the appeal of the government?

This activity was in all the towns. They came in launches, trucks, and buses to carry the people to Sololá just to applaud the army and to say, "We are with Lucas!" This was the reason for the summons.

Were they obliged by the colonel in Sololá?

First there was an oppression: "He who does not go to Sololá is a Communist." Thus the people were afraid, so many of them went.

I understand, but who said this?

The military commissioners.

In the towns?

Yes: "If tomorrow the people do not go, they are Communists." And the poor people got up very early [to go].

How many arrived in Sololá?

Oh, I believe thousands of persons.

Just to say they were with Lucas?

Yes! Just to say this, "Applauding Lucas, we are with him!"

Was he there?

No, he was in Guatemala [City].

On Monday, 8 September, they celebrated the mass for the soul of the deceased teacher. Teachers from San Martín and San Luis came, as well as the family of the deceased.

For lunch we ate meat. On this day I canceled a loan of $190 from Alfonso García.

❧ Checking a Birth, and a Guerrilla Ambush
12–14 SEPTEMBER 1980

We got up a little late. While my wife made breakfast, I shaved. After a breakfast of tortillas and eggs, I went to the civil registry to investigate the listing of the birth of a boy from the village of Pachichaj.

I was just helping the boy, but when I arrived at the civil registry they told me the same thing they had told him—that they had already looked for his name and could not find it. It could not be found because the boy's father was tremendously ignorant and had entered the boy's name incorrectly. But the most culpable was the ex-registrar, Mario Rodríguez Gález, who did very poor work in this town. Many people have their names incorrectly entered.

The same thing happened to Señora Elena Pérez Pinto. She wanted proof of her true age and discovered that her name did not appear in the registry. She could not contract a civil marriage. She had to initiate an *juicio civil* [civil suit] with a lawyer before the court of the first instance to settle her name. It cost her money, but she was very poor and unable to finish her suit. From so much worrying, she fell sick and died without winning a suit for her birth certificate. What she won was her death. But this was caused by the ex-secretary, who nearly always was drunk and paid no attention to his work.

In this afternoon José and Ramón went to cut firewood while I went to San Martín to get a loan of $50 from Señor Alfonso García. This money was for a trip to the coast to take the crews their *recomendaciones*.

What are recomendaciones?

They are sacks of food from the homes of the workers that their families send to them while they are on the coast. They may contain oranges, avocadoes, meat, or fish.

Then they are things to sustain the workers.

Yes, because there [on the farms] they eat just beans—just beans! So their families send them fish, oranges, avocadoes, or other things. They put them in sacks, and then we bundle them up into bundles of 200 to 250 pounds each and take them to the workers.

When I arrived home, the youngsters had not yet returned with the firewood. When they arrived, they were very frightened because they had heard bursts of machine-gun fire that lasted almost an hour. It was not confirmed until 6:00 P.M. that the bullets were nearby in the jurisdiction of San José and San Martín, where there had been a confrontation of the National Army and guerrillas of ORPA. The news says that, in the places called Chinimayá and Pancoy, soldiers were wounded and their companions carried them to the road that goes to San Martín. They carried them in some trucks that had come from Guatemala [City] for the business of onions.

When the wounded arrived in this town, they were given first aid in the parochial pharmacy. Then they left on the launch for Sololá. According to the news, there were 50 other soldiers in the area, but it was a mystery whether they were alive or dead. At 8:00 P.M. more concrete information arrived saying that the guerrillas had ambushed the army, but when the army returned the fire, the guerrillas scattered. Then the army discovered the nest of the guerrillas, where they found provisions, arms, munitions, and more.

During the night, radio patrols passed through the town of San José. The whole town was scared and did not sleep peacefully.

When the sun came up on 14 September, I gave thanks to God that we all woke up healthy. At 7:00 A.M. my friend Agustín arrived to tell me a piece of gossip about Andrés, but I did not pay any attention to it. Then we ate breakfast, and immediately my wife went to wash clothing in the lake while I stayed to take care of the baby. About 10:30 A.M. Señor Gilberto arrived to ask if I would help to get a birth certificate for his son. I said, "With much pleasure!"

As we were leaving, we discussed the situation we were in. He told me that the soldiers were sleeping in the village of Pachichaj when it dawned yesterday. We were talking about these things when soldiers arrived in town. I did not pay much attention to them, but some neighbors said it was certain that they carried shotguns, provisions, and other objects of the guerrillas. These soldiers were eating refreshments near the house of my wife's father. Later they left for Santa Ana. This is how I got the news.

❧ A Letter from Jaime Sexton
20–22 SEPTEMBER 1980

I was in my house thinking about what I could do to earn some money. Times are very expensive. Everything has a high price. The children asked me to buy meat, but I do not have any money. Breakfast was just *guisquiles*, and lunch was tamalitos with a broth of *chipilín* [wild greens].

While we were eating lunch, Benjamín arrived drinking. He offered me a *trago*, but I did not accept it because I was thinking about working.

A little later Lucas, the mailman, arrived with a registered letter [containing a check] from Dr. Sexton. For me it was a blessing from God, because I was certainly in a difficult situation. I have cultivations, but they are not ready for harvest. A friend [Francisco] had lent me 50 pounds of corn for 15 days. Thus, we were trying to endure.

While I was sleeping during the night, my cousin Domingo awoke me. He was somewhat drunk. It was warm in the house, and when I opened the door for him, the cold air hit me. This is why I woke up sick at dawn. During the day, we went to Tamalaj to pick *guisquiles* and avocadoes.

On 22 September, after my children left for school, my wife, who carried the baby on her back, and her mother accompanied me to Xesucut to water onions. Afterwards we picked the first ears of corn for the season. When we got home, my family and I happily ate the fresh ears.

Military Commissioners Persecute My Brother-in-Law
TUESDAY, 23 SEPTEMBER 1980

I left, a little happy and a little sad, to cash the check Dr. Sexton sent me. I did not have a single centavo on me, so I told Don Francisco that I would pay him in the afternoon.

When I arrived in Panajachel, I was very hungry and very thirsty, but since I had no money I could not eat in a *comedor*. Señora Rosa, the owner of a tienda, gave me some coffee and bread that I said I would pay for later.

I was relieved when I cashed the check. After paying the señora, I went to Sololá to certify some pages for Dr. Sexton. At noon I ate in a *comedor*, and then I bought a few groceries.

When I arrived back in Panajachel, I paid for the launch. Then I rested under a cypress while waiting for the launch.

When I arrived home, my wife was very sad because there was bad news that my brother-in-law, Bernardo, was being persecuted by the army. They say that, when the guerrillas took over the town four months ago, he welcomed them. It seems that these are false rumors because, when the guerrillas came, he did not talk to them. According to the news, they were looking for Bernardo's house, but he was in the capital selling onions.

I went to Bernardo's house and talked to my sister. She was sad and crying because people were saying that in a little while or so, Bernardo would disappear.

I consoled my sister for nearly two hours. At 8:00 P.M. Bernardo arrived, unaware that people were talking about him. When he saw so many people he wanted to abandon his house and family immediately. I told him, however, to have more patience, and gradually I was able to calm his nerves.

Still, Bernardo did not sleep in his house during the night. Instead, he slept in a coffee grove. He told me that he has been continually threatened with anonymous letters asking for a sum of money. Later, some friends, who have confidence in me because I am secretary-general of the official party, told me that the military commissioners sent the letters to Bernardo just because he has land and a little money. They wanted to swindle him. I did not tell my brother-in-law because they [the military commissioners] could provoke an incident. I just gave him some clues to calm his nerves.

How much money did they want, and what kind of clues did you give him?

They wanted $1,000. I told him, "Do not worry. Perhaps they are not guerrillas. Perhaps you have enemies because of your business or your land, because you have a little money. Nothing will happen."

I know very well the commissioners wanted to scare him by claiming that he welcomed the guerrillas. They also claim that there are five other men and two women who welcomed them.

I hardly slept the whole night. I could think only about my brother-in-law's situation. Evil men wanted to kill him just because he is dedicated to his work. Everyone knows that Bernardo is a working man. These thoughts made my heart ache so much I stayed in bed nearly the whole day. At times my heart felt as if it did not want to beat. All day I felt drained.

∾ Mayan Culture Dying with the Aged
25–26 SEPTEMBER 1980

I cleaned coffee all day in Chuanup. In the afternoon a very great sadness permeated the whole town. While I was chatting with my brother-in-law, Bernardo, we heard the news that Señora Rosa Angelica had died. She was wife of my uncle Jorge Bizarro, who died a year ago. I was feeling sad for Doña Rosa when we also heard that Señora Josefina Monroy had died. Both of these women were about 75 years old and both were originally from San Martín la Laguna, but they had lived a long time in this town. However, these two women had conserved the traditional dress of their natal town with their typical blouses, mantles and skirts. These days such clothing is disappearing with the old people of San Martín. Although the *Martineros* speak Tzutuhil gutturally, these two deceased women left children, grandchildren, and great-grandchildren who are pure *Joseños* and who speak Tzutuhil as we speak it.

When the town heard the news, it was very touched. Many people went to the wake to console surviving members of both families. Since drinking is traditional when someone dies, throughout the night and at dawn there were many drunks.

I got up with a calm heart. After breakfast, the children went to school, and I went to Xesucut to inspect my cultivations.

When I returned, my wife and I went to accompany the bodies of the two women to the church. First we carried the body of Doña Rosa to the church and then the body of Doña Josefina. Then many religious acts were celebrated. Finally, we took them together out of the church to the cemetery. The entire town of San José and many from San Martín participated in the religious acts.

The burial ended at 3:00 P.M. I worked very hard digging and covering the graves. Afterwards we ate lunch, and I did not go anywhere else.

❧ Trying to Get a Good Price for Coffee
28–29 SEPTEMBER 1980

I got up giving thanks to God, although I was still in a precarious financial situation because I have a large family. But since I am working, I am happy. I hope some day I will be able to have a good time; perhaps it will never be possible.

After breakfast I went to Chimucuní and Chisibel to plant coffee. While I was there, I picked greens to have for lunch.

At 3:00 P.M. Ramón and I went to kill *zompopos*, and we did not return until 6:00 P.M. At 8:00 P.M. I went to the cooperative to tell the board of directors about negotiating a good price for coffee, but these men did not give me their attention, so I returned home.

On the night of 29 September we discussed in the cooperative a trip next Sunday to the coast to Santo Tomás la Unión. The cooperative also gave me 300 pounds of fertilizer on credit, which Uncle José and I spread on three of my fields.

❧ The Bishop Jesús Orellana Orantes Arrives for a Good Business
SUNDAY, 5 OCTOBER 1980

San José and San Martín had a big fiesta for the reception of Jesús Orellana Orantes, Bishop of Sololá. In San José, Catholic Action helped a lot to prepare [for his arrival], and the cooperative made a carpet of flowers.

The Señor Jesús had a nice business because beforehand he sent word that if no one wanted confirmation he would not visit the town. A week later the catechist held a meeting and made a list of names of 400 persons who wished confirmation. When the bishop arrived, in the period of 90 minutes in the church he confirmed 400 Catholics. Each one paid $1. That is to say, in 90 minutes, the bishop earned $400 in San José.

In San Martín the catechists made a list of 700 names for confirmation. Thus in that town Señor Jesús made $700, acting as if he had come to bless those of the town. But that was not so. On the contrary, it was more like a business because in one day he earned $1,100. Why are such things? They say it is true that he collected a dollar from each person—a dollar! Instead of helping the poor, he took their precious dollars. Furthermore, the señor bishop stated that, without confirmation, one would not be able to see God in the next life. But I believe this is a lie. Why must all of the most humble pay to know the word of God? The sacred scripture says that one cannot buy the word of God with gold or silver. With this new deed I see a lot of faults in the religion because the bishop sent word that, if there was not a large number of confirmations, he would not visit the towns. Thus, they responded that there would be thousands, and then he confirmed his coming. One can conclude that this señor came to make money and not to preach the word of God.

My two children José and María went to receive confirmation, but only so they could observe all that was happening. Frankly, I did not go, but indeed I have faith in God, who is the omnipotent King and Savior. On this day my family, friends, and I had lunch, and we discussed these matters.

❧ Looking for a *Beneficio de Café*
6–7 OCTOBER 1980

Without breakfast I left for the coast with a friend, Antonio Cholotio, as a commission of the cooperative to look for a *beneficio de café* [processing plant where coffee is dried, processed, and made ready for shipping], because we in the cooperative want to sell our product at a good price [which would be $75 to $80 per 100 pounds]. In past years the *Martineros*, who like to make a profit off San José, have bought our coffee but at unfairly low prices. Since the *Joseños* have had no one with which to negotiate better prices, they have had to sell their coffee to the *Martineros* at the low prices. For that reason, we in the cooperative wish to help our dear *Joseños* [by negotiating a higher price].

We first went to Mazatenango, where they told us that they offer a price only when the coffee is harvested, not beforehand. Then we went to San Pablo Jocopilas, where they told us that for the moment they are not offering prices because they are just beginning their work. When we reached Santo Tomás la Union, we went to three different *beneficios*, but all offered low prices ($40 to $45 per 100 pounds). Finally, we went to Señor Homero Ordoñez, who received us well. He promised to help us negotiate the coffee in November at a price of $60 per 100 pounds. Although this was still somewhat low, we were somewhat happy.

In the afternoon we continued to talk to this man in his house, and later we went to eat in the market. During the night, we slept in a shed where there is a machine that dries coffee. We slept fairly well.

At daybreak Señor Homero gave us some bananas, and then we took the bus for Mazatenango where we ate breakfast. In Mazatenango we bought some fruit, and then we caught the bus for San Luis.

When we reached El Transito, we had to stop for a half hour. A lot of cars were stopped because of an accident. A Rutas Lima bus had hit a truck and another car. Three persons had died. Because they had already carried the injured away, we did not see them. But we saw the dead because the justice of peace had not yet investigated the accident, and the bodies had not yet been taken away. When we arrived in San Luis, we ate lunch there and then went to San Martín.

> *Here, on 15 October, Ignacio told of another trip to the coast to take care of matters concerning his cotton-picking crews. He decided to look for work on the Esquipul farm because the farm where he had his crews did not pay attention to needs such as medicine.*

❧ The Governor Acts Loco
FRIDAY, 7 NOVEMBER 1980

My friend Antonio talked to me about making a trip to consult with the governor. Antonio has served three times as *alguacil*. He says he is very tired, he does not have a house in which to live, and he does not want to serve as *alguacil* anymore. For these reasons, he needed to consult with the governor to ask if he would spare him from serving as *alguacil* in the year of 1981. He said he wanted to petition the governor to be freed from this service because he has more power than the municipality.

We went to Sololá, and after eating breakfast there we went to the colonel's office, where we were not well received. He nearly had us imprisoned, but we were ignorant as to why he wanted to send us to jail, which caused us much anguish. He told us that no one was allowed to look into his office. We asked his pardon, and only then did he let us leave. But I think this man might have become mentally ill, because he said no one could look into his office. When he did this I cursed him as a disgrace—as a crazy person!

What did the colonel, the governor of Sololá, say?

It was very strange. We were asking for his help, but he did not want to receive us in his office. He told us that they were not going to attend to anyone. "We do not want a person in the office. Right now I am going to call the police to take you away to jail," he told me.

"My colonel," I told him, "but we have a request. We do not have anything unusual, just a petition."

"No, I do not want a petition. I do not want anything. For sure you had better leave, or I am going to throw you in prison."

"My colonel, excuse us. We did not want to bother you. Allow us to leave."

"Get the fuck out! I do not want to talk to anyone!"

"Very well," I said. And to myself I thought this man must be suffering from mental illness—he is loco. Or perhaps he has a premonition of death. We had no bad intentions, and we were using proper deportment. We were just asking a favor, but the favor he was offering was jail. For this reason, it seemed to me he had a presentiment of death. And in October [1981] they killed him.

The guerrillas?

Yes.[23]

After we left the governor's office, we went to the notary, Tomás Ricardo Galindo, to get a written statement to present to the mayor of San José. The lawyer drew up the memorandum according to law. After all of this we went to eat in a *comedor*. Then we went to Panajachel, where we rested under a tree waiting for the launch to San José.

What happened when you presented the memorandum to the mayor?

The mayor accepted the petition, and Antonio didn't have to serve the office.

❧Discussing a Business Venture for Tzancuil
20–31 OCTOBER 1980

Today Señor José Toc Sicay of Tzancuil came to talk about a business venture for the first of November. He said that in Tzancuil they celebrate All Saints' Day in a big way and that we could sponsor a *zarabanda* [dance] and sell liquor. But he did not have the money to set up the business.

I agreed to join his business plans, and we called Agustín María to discuss the proposition. He also agreed to take part. We decided to buy cases of liquor, beer, and soft drinks, and cigarettes. We agreed that José would be in charge of getting the license for the *zarabanda* and hiring the marimba and that all of us would be responsible for obtaining a license for selling liquor.

On 21 October, Agustín María and I went to get a loan for the business. It was a shame that they did not give us all the money we needed. Thus, we went to the president of the cooperative to ask for a loan of $200 with interest for eight days. He conceded. José and I both contributed $100, but this still was not enough, so we asked my wife's father, who owns a cantina, to give us part of the liquor on credit and part paid in advance. He accepted our proposition with the provision that we give him part of the profit. In this manner we obtained everything we would need for 1 November.

On 29 October my father-in-law and Agustín María went to San Luis for the beer. At 8:00 P.M. they returned to San José with 40 cases of beer and 10 cases each of soft drinks and cigarettes. Part was paid with a deposit, and the rest was to be paid when the business was over.

On 30 October my father-in-law went to San Luis to get 10 cases of liquor. Since we had only $400, he again paid only for part, and the rest was to be paid when the business was finished. He had to pay with just a deposit because we also needed money for transportation and assistants to help us carry our loads.

In the night Agustín María told me that he did not have time to go to Tzancuil because he is the *juez* [vice-head] of the *cofradía* of Santo Domingo Guzmán. The brotherhood would not give him permission to go, and therefore I was obliged to look for a helper. I went to Carlos's house, and he agreed to go with me if I would give $5 to his family. Only when all of this was taken care of was the trip confirmed for the next day.

On 31 October I got up very early. At 7:00 A.M. José came in his canoe from Tzancuil to tell me that everything was ready for the business, but he said that it was unnecessary to go today. He also said that he could carry some of the drinks back with him but that his canoe was too small to carry all of them.

In the afternoon we went to the cemetery to clean the tombs of our deceased ancestors. We carried flowers and pine needles to adorn the graves a little. At night my wife cooked ears of corn, *guisquiles*, pumpkins, and sweet potatoes, and we ate.

❧ A Business Trip to Tzancuil
1–2 NOVEMBER 1980

On this day there was such a strong wind that launches were not able to cross over the lake. Since it is a tradition of our parents to celebrate on each fiesta, my wife cooked meat in the morning, but very little because we are poor. Lunch was leftovers from breakfast.

At 3:00 P.M. the launch came from Tzancuil to take us for the business. Since it was a holiday and the wind was up, my wife cautioned, "Do not go, Ignacio." But we were in much need of money, and I wanted to earn a few centavos for my family. Furthermore, I already had committed myself to the trip, so I felt I must go.

My son José and I left on the launch, and we stopped in San Martín to buy some more things. But by now the lake had become more stormy. The wind became stronger, and a lot of water splashed inside the launch, nearly filling it up with water. We struggled to bail out the water, and we got soaked. We were close to the point of perishing, and we paid little attention to the merchandise we were carrying. But there was nothing we could do to help ourselves. We could not go back to San José, and we were stranded in the middle of the lake with the wind very strong. There was no place in the lake where we could take refuge. Although the *launchero* [pilot] was very experienced, at this moment he regretted having agreed to make the trip. Since it seemed that this moment was going to be our last, we prayed to God.

At this moment when we were close to death, I thought it was okay for me because it was my whim to make the trip even though my family had warned me not to. But I was distressed that my son José was with me. To be in such an unfortunate predicament was not his fault. When we could throw no more water out of the launch, I said, "*Dios Mío* [My God], we are going to die!" And each of us entrusted ourselves to God. I believe that there is a superior being, because, at the instant we entrusted ourselves to God, we witnessed a great mercy—the wind calmed. Only then were we able to head for the shore and dock. We all lay down on the beach and pondered what had happened. The owner of the launch and his helper asked for a half-liter of *aguardiente*, and I gave it to them gladly. They drank it as if they were drinking pure water.

At 7:00 P.M. we reached our place of business, but our clothing was very wet. Then we began to sell our goods. It was very strange. The place that they prepared for the dance was full of stones, but the people were dancing among them. We sold our liquor in the open air without a roof. The air dried our clothing, but it was very cold, and we suffered a lot. However, we sold a lot of sugarcane liquor.

It is a pity that I did not have a camera with which to take pictures, because we saw very strange things, and, as they say, there was much savagery. During the night a lot of people drank, but the old people drank very much apart from the young people. There were groups of young boys from 10 to 12 years of age and groups of poor little girls from 10 to 12 years old drinking. When these children were not able to walk, they collapsed among the thickets. They were not able to get back to their homes, which, if I am not mistaken, were 2 to 4 kilometers away. It was very strange that the parents of the families came with their provisions to dance and get drunk. They brought their bags, sleeping mats, and serapes and placed them around the location of the marimba, but when they got drunk they forgot their bags and slept among the stones with their children somewhere else. When the sun came up, in every direction there were drunks, adults and children of both sexes—what a sight! It bothered me very much because it was the first time I had seen such things. Only when it was very hot in the sun did the drunks get up, but when the children rejoined their parents, they began to drink again.

The marimba began again at noon and continued until 3:00 A.M. on 3 November. We finished selling everything we had brought.

Also, I observed other things concerning children from five months to a year of age, or perhaps a little older. Their mothers gave them swigs of liquor from mouth to mouth. I asked one of the mothers why they were giving firewater to the babies, and she responded that it was a tradition of their ancestors, so that when the babies become adults they will not forget they also have to drink their shots of liquor. Furthermore, she told me that the best thing about the fiesta is to get drunk. Also, she told me that giving a swig to a child is a *secreto* because, when the parents are dancing, there are evil spirits, that is, spirits of the dead who much earlier had drunk their shots and danced. These spirits come to the marimba, and it is easy for them to tempt the baby and make it die. But, if this person has made a *secreto*, or if the baby has been given its little drink, nothing will happen. If they do not give little swigs to the babies, it is easier for them to die because they will have no defense.

I also made some other observations. I asked a señor who was sober and collecting money at the marimba, "Which is the most important custom in the village?"

He answered in a mixed dialect of Cakchiquel and Quiché that was very confusing, "Drinking during the two fiestas of May and and November is the most important. People save their money for 5 to 6 months to buy rum on 3–5 May to celebrate the day of Santa Cruz, and afterwards they save another 6 months to buy cane liquor on 1–2 November, which is All Saints' Day and All Souls' Day. We eat greens, chili, tortillas and salt, but not meat. We prefer tortillas and salt so that all the women and men can save their money to spend on *guaro* during the fiestas."

Then I asked him, "Isn't it a custom for you to buy meat and invite your kin to come eat with you?"

"No, this isn't a good custom," he told me. "The good custom is to get drunk. Honor and respect is shown when one gets drunk. If one gives a drink to one's father or to one's mother, it shows respect. If one does not receive a drink, there is no honor."

To me this was very strange. Tzancuil is not more than 10 to 12 kilometers from my town, but it has different customs during the fiestas. Also, I asked him if he thought we were the only ones selling *aguardiente*.

"No," he told me, "what you are selling is very little. They have a lot of *cusha*, or clandestine sugarcane liquor, hidden. Perhaps they have some 30 to 40 gallons more; some families have 2 to 3 gallons of rotgut rum. For that reason, not all of them are going to buy from you. If all of them did, you would run out of *aguardiente* in an hour. But they have a lot hidden there in their bundles. When they finish a bottle, they go back and fill it up again. Watch!"

And the truth was about 1:00 P.M. a señora brought a bottle of bootleg liquor, and when she finished, she went again to her bundle and returned with her bottle full of contraband rum. So it was true that they were not just drinking what we were selling. They were also drinking a lot of *cusha*.

We indeed suffered a lot to get acquainted with these customs, and it was difficult for us to buy a meal. José Toc Sicay, who had suggested the business, did not sell us a meal. His wife told me that she had no food to cook. I asked a señora to sell me a meal just one time, and finally I persuaded her. When she arrived, she brought me a cooked chicken, but we had a lot of meat without any tortillas. Also, they did not bring us any salt. This lunch was very funny, but, thanks to God, Agustín María arrived with tortillas from my house. And that is what we ate.

When the marimba finished, José Toc wanted to pay them, but he was too irresponsible. All the money he earned the first night, he lost. He nearly went to jail because the owner of the marimba was very mad since $80 was missing. To avoid problems, I had to pay this sum.

What was the problem with José Toc Sicay?

I knew from previous experience that I had to be careful with borrowed money. I thought he would do the same. When the marimba began to play, I asked him, "Do you know these boys who are helping you?"

"Ah," he told me, "they work with me. They are my good friends."

"Very well, what I am telling you is to be very careful. They are your friends, but you do not know their hearts."

"Yes," he told me, "do not worry."

Then I told him, "Be careful with the money." And then they began the business with the marimba, and I began the business with the *tragos*. He was negligent. I do not know whether it was weariness or whether they began to drink with the earnings, but they began to drink at about 3:00 A.M. I still told him to be careful. He asked me for a drink, and I said no, because we had an obligation. Without doubt he got drunk on clandestine *aguardiente*, because we did not give him anything to drink at our cantina. When I saw that he was drunk, I did not say anything because I thought he had taken his money to his house for safekeeping. I knew that the money from the *aguardiente* that we had sold I had safely on my own body.

At daybreak I asked him, "How much did you earn? Let's see your money. Let's count how much money you have."

"I don't have it," he told me.

"And where is your money?"

"It is lost!"

"You do not have your money. Look!"

Then he began to cry because he had no money. Then I told him, "Ask your helpers! If you lost it, they have it. Why have you lost the money? It belongs to someone else. We still have not paid the marimba players!"

"Yes," he told me. I sent him to his helpers, and they told him, "We do not know where the money is." Without doubt José gave drinks to his assistants. I am certain that they stole the money. The $80 was lost on the first night. All the time I was questioning José, he was crying a lot. This is the reason I had to pay the $80. It was better that we not earn anything than José go to jail. Thus, nearly all that we had earned in the sale of liquor went to make up the $225 for the marimba. We had only $40 left. We had to pay $10 for a launch to take us back to San José with the empty bottles, which we had to carry to the beach and which were a lot of trouble. We even had to give the *launchero* a beer because he too was drinking.

At 10:00 P.M. we arrived at my house, but we had to carry the bottles. It was almost noon when we finished and counted the receipts. Since we had lost everything we had earned from the sale of the drinks, Agustín María and I each earned $15, but of this money we each had to give Carlos $5. In total we both therefore earned $10.

It was a bad business deal for me, to be sure, but the experience I had was worth more than the money. However, I swear to God that I am not going to do this dark business again, because I saw a certain wickedness of the people. Also, under oath, I declare that I will not sell alcoholic beverages again, because it is a curse to induce the poor people to drink and do these intolerable things. I believe whoever sells these things is responsible for what he sells. Well, this is apart from people who can drink with moderation. But for this class of people it is very dangerous. A lot of people injured themselves when they smashed against the rocks. I do not want to see such disgraces again.

Isn't Tzancuil an aldea?

Yes, it is an *aldea* of Santa Rosa la Laguna. These people live very, very poorly. They are very, very backward without education or civilization, and they give too much importance to drunkenness. I am an Indian of the Tzutuhil race, but we are not accustomed to giving a *trago* to a child. My youngster, José, who is 16 years old, does not drink. But he saw how calamitous drinking is in Tzancuil. And strangest of all was the mother giving her child swigs of *aguardiente* from mouth to mouth. I observed as a person drinking only a can of juice or soda rather than *aguardiente*, beer, or wine. I am just a campesino, not an anthropologist, but I know it is very important to observe and analyze why these people do such things. Do these customs have an origin, or are they just a mental illness? I do not understand, and for sure I do not have much book learning, but I believe it is important to eventually study these things. When I was witnessing these events, I was thinking about you anthropologists.

❧ Guerrilla Threats on the Coast
5 NOVEMBER 1980

At 7:00 A.M. Agustín María and I took the launch from San Martín to San Luis, where we caught a bus to Tiquisate. After a bad lunch in Tiquisate, we went to La Colonia del Prado to look for the house of the administrator of the Esquipul farm. We asked at a lot of houses, but no one would tell us where his house was located. We had to board another bus to Pacaya.

We crossed the river by launch, and then we passed through Moyuta, where we headed for the farm. We arrived at 5:00 P.M., but no one would tend to us; they told us to wait until tomorrow.

We ate some tortillas, and then we went to the sheds, where we slept with some people we did not know. There was much fear because the guerrillas did not want us to work on the farms. Also, they say that they want to finish off the farm owners as well as the contractors. This night we spent with much fear.

On Thursday, 6 November, at 6:00 A.M., the Spaniard, Enrique Girón Godoy, confirmed the work and gave me all the conditions. After all of this we bought a few tortillas and ate them walking because we were in a hurry to get back to San José. We did not eat lunch until we reached Tiquisate.

During the night, we spread the news that we were going to work on the Esquipul farm. We told the people that the work is very good.

❧Guerrillas Confront My Crew
8–15 NOVEMBER 1980

Today I went to confess all my sins to the priest. I do not think I have [committed] great crimes, but I had to comply with Catholic Action so that no one will think badly of me. I went to mass, and afterwards I drank some beers with some catechists. Everything was pleasant.

From Saturday until Monday Agustín María, Carlos, and I worked hard to organize a crew. We gathered 135 in San José alone.

On Monday night Agustín María and Carlos went over the list of people to determine the amount of an advance. The cooperative agreed to give me a loan of $1,000, Señor Alfonso García lent me $400, Gerardo Vásquez lent me $50, and Carlos obtained a loan of $100. All of this money we gave to the crew. For the trip tomorrow we had to look for three trucks and a bus for transportation. Also a crew from Tzancuil left for San Luis by launch to be taken from there by truck.

All night until dawn I did not sleep at all; I just thought about the trip to the coast. In the morning we prepared the people for the trucks. Agustín María then went ahead with Jesús's truck, while I waited with José for the bus and Carlos went to Tzancuil to take the crew by launch to San Luis. I was the last one left.

When we arrived in Cocales, they told me that in San Luis four workers from Tzancuil were detained as prisoners because they did not have their personal documents. They remained in a military detachment that searched all of us and asked for our identification papers. But we all had our *cédulas* [national identification papers], and there were hardly any problems.

At 2:00 P.M. we arrived at the river, but all the other companions had already crossed it. They left my name for the payment of their passage across the river. Those of us in the last truck crossed the river, and then we ate lunch and went on foot to the farm. However, when we were walking through Moyuta, we were told to take much care, because there were a lot of guerrillas roaming around killing peasant people. Although this scared me, I had to muster the effort to continue.

When we arrived on the farm, the rest of the workers were waiting for me because, as I have said, there are no employees to receive the crews. We had to wait until the next day, and we slept under some large trees.

In total we numbered 180 persons. Many were too frightened to sleep in the open, but by the grace of God, dawn came without incident.

We got up at 5:00 A.M. and arranged our traveling bags again, group by group. We made our fires to make coffee and warm our tortillas. Then we ate.

At 7:00 A.M. they received us on the farm. When we gave them our list of workers, they told us that we all could stay at the Limones farm. Then the workers left in carts. Agustín María, Carlos, José, and I stayed at the farm with the *flonques* and millers waiting for the provisions and to take the list of the workers to the office. But we were very afraid that, sooner or later, evil might arrive.

The crew bosses conducted the workers to the the sheds. They left their traveling bags and then went to pick cotton. They say that, before the workers reached the fields, a group of 15 to 20 men blocked the road to prevent the crew from going to work. But the crew was large, and among the *Joseños* there were five men who are not natives, including a *Salvadoreño*, who threatened the men blocking the street with their machetes and led the crew past them. But we spent all day extremely worried because something could happen to the workers. By the grace of God, when they finished weighing the cotton, nothing had happened. Then we all went to the sheds.

When we arrived, our dinner still was not ready. We had to wait until 7:00 P.M. Then they took us to the sheds to sleep. We four contractors slept apart from the rest of the crew because the evil men might look for us in the night, and we are the ones they would most prefer to harm.

On Thursday, 13 November, we were still on the coast taking care of the people, but with much grief because the *flonque* told me that, when he was washing *nixtamal*, some *desconocidos* came and asked for the contractor [Ignacio]. [Pretending not to know], the *flonque* simply said that the contractor lives in his house. At the same time, the men looking for us painted a shed with the initials of ORPA and PGT (Partido Guatemalteco de Trabajo) [both guerrilla groups]. They told me these things at 4:00 P.M. When we went to look, we indeed saw the inscriptions that they had left. All the rest of the day I hid. I did the same thing the next day, 14 November.

I waited on the coast for them to give me the money for the advancement and travel for the crew, but they told me I had to wait until tomorrow. When they paid me, they warned me to be very careful because near Moyuta some men were intercepting the contractors and stealing their money. In this village there is not much security, and for that reason there are a lot of thieves and bullies.

On Saturday I was still with the workers. At 5:00 A.M. we left but walked inside the cotton field so as not to be on the road and thus avoid the guerrillas. At 7:00 A.M. we reached the office of Esquipul.

When we went inside, the administrator gave $1,400 for the advance that we had given the workers and $600 for travel. But they gave me $1,000 in cash and $1,000 in a check. I was very nervous because they say that the administrators have been sentenced to death by guerrillas. When all of this was settled, we had to look for another road back for the sake of our security. Instead of traveling up to Moyuta, we went down through the Santa Ana farm to pretend that we were persons looking for work rather than contractors returning with money. We acted as if we were looking for work until we crossed the river and reached the Xebacu farm. From Xebacu we walked back up until we reached the paved road, where we caught a bus for Tiquisate. Not until Tiquisate did we eat in a *comedor*, which charged us $3 for the four of us. After lunch we boarded the Tropicana bus to Cocales, where we tried to catch the Rebuli bus to San Martín. We waited for the bus, but it did not show up. Finally we rode in a car to Santa Alicia, where we waited for a truck to carry us to San José.

While we were waiting for the truck, we were told the very sad news that Carlos's father had died on 13 November. Carlos's father had been sick when we left for the coast, but Carlos did not think it was serious and left to take the crew to the coast. Without doubt he thought that his father would recover, but the sickness turned out to be fatal. When they told us this news, Carlos lost his composure and began to cry. It was very sad as we traveled in a truck to San Martín. When we arrived, Carlos could walk no further. I had to give him one-eighth liter of liquor to calm his bad feelings. Only then did we arrive home, but thanks to God we arrived with all the money.

In San José each of us went to his own house. My family was happy to see me. I ate dinner, and then I went to give Carlos's mother my condolences. I also gave her $10 for the expenses of the nine days of the wake.

❧ A Little Profit on the Coast
13–20 DECEMBER 1980

We left San José la Laguna for the coast to bring back the crews. At 5:00 A.M. we reached the river, and we crossed it by canoe. When we reached the office, not a person was there.

At 7:00 A.M. they opened the office, and then I went to bring the crew. When we all arrived at the farm, they paid the workers. Because the boys received good pay, they were very happy. After they paid the crew, they paid me my commission of $1,000 and $500 for travel. Certainly, this was the first time I had received so much money. When all of this was settled, we headed for the river. Those who were afraid to walk across went in a canoe.

At noon we arrived in Cocales, where we ate lunch. Then we boarded the trucks. At 5:00 P.M. we arrived home without incident, by the grace of God. My wife was waiting with dinner.

When we finished eating, I gave Agustín María $250, Carlos $200, and José T. $100. I paid each according to his contribution. I kept exactly $350 and $50 for various expenses. Fifty dollars was also spent to repay debt on the farm. For my companions and me, everything had worked out well.

❧Christmas
21–24 DECEMBER 1980

I stayed home to prepare to celebrate Christmas, but our celebration did not cost us much. We just bought what was needed for the kitchen and a few other things. I have saved my money because I am thinking about building an adobe house. If God allows it, I will do so in February of next year.

Christmas passed peacefully. For me there is no better time than Christmas. It is always peaceful. Sometimes lack of money creates problems, but my wife and I are happy because we never fight. When necessary, we correct the behavior of the children. But it would be a bad example if we fought in front of them.

❧Soldiers Appear
1–2 JANUARY 1981

The pages that follow are for the year of 1981. Because of work, I have not recorded every day of this year, but everything that I have written is true. Sometimes what happens to me is bitter; other times it is happy. But that is man's fate.

Today is New Year's Day, 1981. It was very pleasant for my family. Why not tell the whole world, "Happy New Year for 1981!" The 365 days of the year are good for working and for pondering whether we are treating our loved ones well. Indeed we are thinking about how to obtain peace. It must be cultivated. Peace is respect, and if we respect one another as human beings, we are obeying God.

During the morning a lot of friends came to visit me. We drank some beers.

Since 31 December 1980 a company of soldiers has been supervising the whole town. They were on every corner. But by the grace of God, we *Joseños* are all dedicated to our work. Perhaps some are dissident, but they find no support. The soldiers stayed in town very peacefully. The people were friendly with them, and both the soldiers and the people were drinking their traditional *tragos* and eating tamales.

I met some soldiers and asked them if they would like to go for some drinks. They responded that they would like to very much. I treated them to some shots of liquor in a cantina. For sure these men are suffering a lot because of the immense cold. To us *Joseños* it was unbearable to be outdoors, but they were obliged to be out. In total, seven truckloads of soldiers came, but everything was quiet. My family and I passed the day at home.

The day of 2 January 1981 began peacefully. I was ready to make a trip to the coast with a crew, but I did not go to the houses of the persons to organize them because competition with other contractors is intense. I said we should not make a trip, but some friends encouraged me, and finally I agreed to take a crew tomorrow. Then my companions went looking and found 45 persons who wanted to go.

❧ We Sell Our First Coffee of the Year
5 JANUARY 1981

My wife got up at 4:00 A.M. to wash *nixtamal* with water, and then she went to the mill to make dough. After breakfast my family and I went to pick coffee in Tamalaj. Together we picked 400 pounds. In the afternoon we returned very hungry because we had to carry the coffee to the house. When we reached home, I made some cool drinks while María went to a tienda to buy a little bread to satisfy our hunger. While she was gone, I sold the coffee at $11 per 100 pounds. We ate cold tortillas and *chirmol de tomate*, but we hardly washed our hands because we did not have enough water.

❧ Youngsters Fight Over an Avocado, and the Image of Jesús
6 JANUARY 1981

My wife got up at 4:00 A.M. to prepare breakfast, but I did not get up until it was ready at 6:00 A.M. Afterwards, we went to pick coffee again. With us went a son of my sister-in-law named Ramón.

We ate a cold lunch of tortillas and fish in chili, and we drank a lot of water because the sun was very hot. We quit working at 4:00

P.M. As we were weighing the coffee with the canisters, an avocado fell from a tree. Then the two Ramóns, our son and my sister-in-law's son, ran to fetch the avocado. One of the boys was faster than the other, and they began to fight. Both ended up crying, with many blows and a lot of dirt in their mouths and eyes. Curiously, neither one got the avocado because, when they began to fight, they forgot about it. Neither had the avocado, but they both had black-and-blue marks that they gave one another. My wife and I had to run to separate them. We punished them by making each carry a load of coffee. But, as they are children, when they arrived home with dirty and bruised faces, they began to play together again. Already they forgot what had happened at work.

We arrived home with 450 pounds of coffee, which we sold at $11 per 100 pounds. Then we ate a dinner of fish broth.

In the evening they called me to a meeting at the municipality. However, the meeting did not take place because there the electricity went off. At 8:00 P.M. I went to the post office to get a certified letter from Dr. Sexton. It contained a check as a Christmas present.

This day is very much celebrated in the town. All the members of the *cofradías* take out the image of Jesús and visit families, who receive them well and give them bread and coffee. Sometimes the families give them bottles of good rum. By late afternoon, some of the *cofrades* [members] are a little drunk. But they have to continue with the image until they finish visiting each house. Sometimes they do not finish until 11:00 P.M. The families give offerings to the *cofrades* for the church.

On this day they came to our house at 9:00 P.M. Since we did not have anything to give them, they just rested. It turned out very funny because my wife had left out some fish that we were going to eat for breakfast. But when the *cofrades* entered our house, a dog came in with them. Because of negligence, the dog ate the fish. More than anything else it embarrassed me, because the dog devoured the fish inside the house in front of a lot of people. They might believe that we are careless in our home. It is true that I was a little disgusted with my wife, but at the same time it made us laugh.

❧ Meeting Isabel Julia de Castillo on the Road
WEDNESDAY, 7 JANUARY 1981

I got up very tired yesterday from so much work. But José Juan and I still went to water tomatoes. We ate breakfast at 8:00 A.M., and then we went to Chixicay to pick coffee. We picked only 150 pounds. While we returning home at 12:30 P.M., we met *profesora* Isabel Julia de Castillo. We did not eat lunch until we got home.

At 4:00 P.M. my wife and I went to get a radio that we were having repaired. We got back home at 6:00 P.M. and made coffee, which, along with bread, was our dinner. During the night, I wrote a little and went to bed.

❧ The Army Murders Isabel and Mariano, Two Teachers
THURSDAY, 8 JANUARY 1981

I got up very late at 6:30 A.M. We ate breakfast at 8:00 A.M., and then my family agreed to go to Papayo to pick coffee while I went to fumigate tomatoes in Panasajar. As we were leaving the house, the death knell began to sound, which surprised us very much. We asked each other who had died. For sure we were unaware of anything happening yesterday. When we asked a neighbor, he told us that two teachers, Mariano Roberto Miranda Vargas and Isabel Julia de Castillo, had died.

The news that we received said that they had set out for San Luis on a motorcycle, but when they arrived on the farm in Chijom, they met soldiers of the army who had just finished having a confrontation with the guerrillas. Without doubt the soldiers were very angry when they encountered the teachers. And they gave them death.

But according to the news of witnesses who were hiding in the rocks, first these evil men tied up *profesor* Mariano and then raped *profesora* Isabel. When they were finished raping her, they took her watch and money. Then they shot her and *profesor* Mariano. What made it even more distressing was that *profesora* Isabel was three months pregnant.

There was much sadness in all the town because the two teachers had worked in San José. Many people of San José went to their funeral in San Luis.

The information regarding what happened is very clear. In San Luis there was much mourning because a lot of the residents who are Indians have died. The army had taken them for guerrillas, but the truth is that they were just workers who were picking coffee on the Chijom farm. Women and boys of 14 years of age died. The military claimed it had a confrontation with guerrillas, but that is all false. The true news is that a butcher of San Luis, who likes to hunt, took his rifle to kill some *gallaretas* [rare, long-legged lake birds which are swimmers but scarcely fly] among the tules. Unfortunately, when this man fired his rifle, the military thought that some guerrilla had shot at them. They opened fire with machine guns and abandoned the road they were traveling on and began to kill the *mozos* of the farm. In this massacre 18 humble peasants of the Tzutuhil race died. The pain was very greatly felt in all the towns of the lake.

Also, they took away many persons in army helicopters, including the man who carried the rifle. They did not kill him where he had shot his rifle. They took him up in a helicopter, and the next day his body appeared in Godínez, tortured and riddled with bullet holes.

On this day the bodies were taken in a file to the cemetery, accompanied by thousands of people of San Luis. They say that they were put under a lot of pressure not to say anything bad about these bullies.[24]

On Friday I got up at 4:00 A.M. to get ready to go to Sololá to certify some pages for Dr. Sexton and to cash a check that he had sent me. But I received notice that the municipality has already posted the *boleta de ornato* [an annual $2 tax for each household], but I still had not paid. For this reason, I could not make the trip. I kept sleeping until 6:00 A.M. Then José and I went to irrigate tomatoes. When we returned from irrigating, we ate breakfast, and then my family and I went to pick coffee. All of us picked a total of only 150 pounds. In the afternoon we rested.

❧ Rescuing a *Joseño* from a *Temascal*
SATURDAY, 10 JANUARY 1981

Ignacio first wrote out this version by hand. I also taped a more detailed version in 1982. What follows was culled from both but mainly draws on the taped version.

After breakfast we went to irrigate tomatoes on the beach. Then in the afternoon my wife and I went to make a corral for watering some pigs in the *sitio* of my wife's father. As we were finishing the corral, it was my luck to act as a *bombero*, but with much fear. I had to save a woman named Elisa Alvarado Pantzay, who [seemed] already dead in a *temascal*.

The woman, whose father is a Ladino and whose mother is a native of San José, had just given birth to her baby. As is the custom for women who have recently given birth, she wanted to use the *te-*

mascal. Since she did not have her own, she, like many other women, came to use my father-in-law's *temascal.*

Well, on this afternoon, Elisa's mother and aunt prepared my father-in-law's *temascal,* but they put in too much firewood. When the three women entered, it was undoubtedly extremely hot. Elisa fainted. I did not know that the women were using the *temascal,* because I was minding my own business, but while I was chatting with my mother-in-law, the other two women came out of the *temascal* shouting and crying. When the people heard the uproar, they hid and shut the doors to their houses. No one dared help them. I saw that their situation was serious, so I approached them and asked, "What happened?"

They implored earnestly, "Look, please help us. Elisa has died in the *temascal!*"

"What happened?" I asked, "Why haven't you taken her out?"

"We are not able to. Please help us!"

"But señoras," I answered, "how can I help you if she is inside the *temascal?* Isn't there someone who can go inside with me to take her out?"

"No, Ignacio, help this woman! She is dying, or she is already dead!" Because it is the custom for the women to take off their clothing while bathing in the *temascal,* Elisa's mother and aunt were pleading with me while wearing only their underwear. But they were not thinking about whether or not they were wearing clothing—they were thinking only about Elisa inside.

Then I told them, "If you will not hold me responsible for her death, I will go inside."

"Do not worry," they said, "go!"

When I entered the *temascal,* the temperature was nearly unbearable. Elisa's body was very hot, and she was not breathing. All her body was stiff. I tried to pick her up, but her body was slippery and greasy from much perspiration. I could hardly raise her. These women must have put in a lot of firewood, because she was nearly dead from so much heat. I took down the wool blanket that held in the heat, so that air could enter. Then I told Elisa's mother, "Please, call another person to come inside and help!" But there was no one who would help.

I did what I could to raise her. She was slippery, and although she had already given birth, she was, shall I say, a healthy woman who was large and heavy. "What am I doing here?" I said. "If I leave, and this woman dies, they are going to say that I screwed up." I was talking to myself in the *temascal* as if I were crazy. Elisa was not breathing, and she needed air. Her feet were totally white, white—they had no blood. She was stiff, or as one says, hard. I could not bend her feet—they were as if she were already dead. However, I could move the upper part of her body, but she was not breathing.

Then mainly I acted like a *bombero*. I began to give her mouth-to-mouth resuscitation. But she was not able to take the air. I had to tilt her head with her mouth up so that the air could reach her lungs. After 15 minutes she began to move and breathe. But she was unconscious. By this time I was bathing myself in my own sweat. My clothes were soaked.

Only when the people realized that I was inside the *temascal* did they approach to see what was happening. I told the other two women, who were crying a lot, to be quiet and call someone to help, because Elisa was beginning to breathe but I could not help her alone. When I told them she was breathing, they calmed down and called for someone else. But no one had the motivation to come inside and help me.

Finally, Andrés Ramos Toc approached, and I told him, "Andrés, help me here. The woman may die; I can't do it alone. She's reviving; she's breathing. Help me!"

Then he entered, and the two of us covered her with the blanket because it was true that we had found her completely nude. Then we carried her to the house of the same aunt who entered the *temascal* with her and which was nearby. We were embarrassed to carry her to her own house, which was about 2 to 3 *cuadras* away. So we laid her down on a bed in her aunt's house. All the time we kept resuscitating her. She was breathing and moving, but half her body was very stiff. For better ventilation in the house, we opened the doors and windows. In about 15 to 20 minutes, little by little, she breathed and looked at us. But she was still unconscious because she could not talk to anyone. Her eyes were open, but she did not recognize anyone. She was in a daze.

After working on her for about an hour, until 7:00 P.M., I told her mother and aunt, "Now, do not worry. She will regain consciousness. It seems that I should go home. We have already worked and helped her a lot. Do not worry."

Well, the poor women were very grateful, but I was not aware of what was going to happen next. About two minutes after she was breathing by herself, I thought she was nearly normal, although she was still pretty hot. As Andrés and I watched her, her kin began to arrive because they thought that she was alive and that it would not be dangerous to visit her. While she was near death, no one came near her. No one wanted to get close. I was the only one who had the courage to go inside with her.

Then I said, "We will see what happens." Andrés and I sat down to chat with the family and visitors. Then Elisa began to utter strange things, things of the other world. Imagine, she was there in the house saying many things, quarreling with her children, but no children were there. She was fighting with her husband [but he was not there]. She said she was washing in the lake, but she was in bed. She said that she was on the coast picking cotton, but she was not on the coast. She had been on the coast but not since she was 16, a long time ago. She said that the firewood would not light, and she told her children to bring dry firewood for the tortillas, but she was not making tortillas.

"*Púchica*," I said, "how is Elisa talking?"

"Yes," said Andrés, "a voice is talking."

Then everyone left. Well, I did not know what I was going to do. It scared me because I thought that now she was perhaps loco. "*Púchica!*" I said, "it will be worse if she goes crazy." It scared and worried me.

I told her mother and aunt, "Señoras, I am leaving. I have helped a lot. Perhaps she will gradually recover. Right now she is saying very strange things, and I do not know what is happening."

"Yes, Ignacio, we too are very worried. Right now it is uncertain whether Elisa will live or die, because she is saying very strange things." Then her husband, who is *regidor segundo* [second councilman] of the municipality, arrived. The house was full of people, who had brought canned juices and soft drinks and household remedies. I did not see everything that happened later, because I was very hungry and I went home.

I arrived home and ate, and I did not go anywhere else. I just stayed there. The things that Elisa said frightened me. I lay down, but I could not sleep. I began to think about a lot of things—all the suffering I had endured with her in the *temascal* and all the activity. I began to think about all that she had been saying. Her words seemed like some kind of foreboding.

"What will this be?" I said. "*Púchica*, who knows if she is going to live or die." But in my madness I do not know what caused me to think about these things. I asked myself, "What made me go to the *sitio*?" But the truth is that, if I had not gone, she would have died. Before God and my family, I was the only one who would help her. Later another man helped, and still later, visitors arrived, but only after she was breathing again.

What happened later? Did she recover?

It appears that she recovered, but I do not know why she hides from me when I meet her on the streets. She feels embarrassed around me, but I ignore it. When I get near her, she takes another street or goes into a *sitio*. Perhaps she is ashamed that I found her naked. However, she has nothing to be ashamed of, because when I found her she was at the point of dying.

I thought that perhaps later she would say, "Thanks, Ignacio, what happened to me?" or, "Thanks for helping me." But until this day [August 1982] she has said nothing.

❧ A Rumor that *Joseños* Have Died on the Coast
12–13 JANUARY 1981

I got up at 6:00 A.M. and went to San Martín to catch the launch on my way to the coast. When we left from San Martín, the wind was strong and it nearly capsized the boat. It scared us a lot. By the grace of God, all the men encouraged the *launchero* not to panic. Another launch that was loaded with a lot of men and women turned back because the women were so upset.

When we got to San Luis, we rode in a pickup to Tiquisate, where we bought some tortillas and then immediately went to the Esquipul farm. The reason for the trip was to inspect a crew that we had left on the third of last month.

This was an emergency trip because last night many women had arrived to say that several *Joseños* had died. They say that these women heard on the radio that guerrillas had killed them. Thus, Agustín María and I went to the coast heavyhearted.

When we arrived at the farm, we asked them what had happened, but they told us that the guerrillas had not come nor had anyone died. Only then did we relax a little. Then we went more slowly to where the boys were working. When we arrived, we asked them if anything had happened, and they said no and that they were happy with their work. They asked me whether the people at home had sent their *recomendaciones*, and I told them no because the news that we received said that most of them had died. The workers did not believe it and began to laugh because it is true that they were all well.

We spent the whole afternoon chatting with them. In late afternoon we ate a dinner of beans and plenty of tortillas that they gave us.

On 13 January I got up giving thanks to God for another day of life. We were happy when we left the farm, because all the workers were well. When we ate breakfast in Tiquisate, we bought some fruit for our families. At 6:30 P.M., when we arrived home, a lot of women were waiting for me to find out how their kin were. They were crying a lot because they had been told that everyone in the *cuadrilla* had been killed. But while I was on the coast, I had asked these men to send their wives letters, and when I showed them the letters that their husbands had sent, they calmed down. More than anything else, I believe that some other contractor had given the false news out of envy.

🖎Guerrillas Hit a Farm Where I Have a Crew
23 JANUARY 1981

At 5:00 A.M. I left with José headed toward the Esquipul farm to bring back a crew on the coast. We took a launch to San Luis, but it was not possible to get a car to take me to the coast. We ate lunch in a *comedor* where I met a driver, Señor Lucas, who told me that they would not able to make the trip tomorrow because the truck was broken down. Thus, we had no choice but to return to San José. In San Martín we met Señor Lucas again, who told me it was possible to make the trip but we would have to leave at 1:00 A.M. with the other truck because it had to go to Sibinal.

At 6:00 P.M. we arrived in our town. During the night I talked with Carlos and Agustín María about the trip. We did not sleep at all.

At 11:00 P.M. Agustín María, Carlos, José, and I left for San Martín. At midnight we left San Martín for Sibinal. We wanted to arrive early on the farm to oversee the paying of the crew, but we could not because the truck was heavily loaded and moved too slowly.

At 6:00 A.M. we arrived in Nahualate, where we met a policeman who asked us to take him to Sibinal where we were going to leave the cargo. The policeman did not want us to bring back the crew. We offered him $10, but he did not want to let us pass. We offered him $20, but he did not want that either. He told us that he needed more money. But we did not know why he had stopped us. We thought that perhaps some other person had accused us of something. The policeman did not let us go until 8:00 A.M. Though angry, we continued on to Tiquisate, where we bought some tortillas for breakfast and then continued on our journey.

We passed the Pacaya bridge, and a little distance from the river we met some people from Tzancuil who had traveled with another contractor. They told me I should go back and not continue to the farm because the guerrillas were there looking for contractors to kill them. These poor people began to cry because they had not been paid. When they said that the guerrillas had killed the paymaster of the farm and shot a *Joseño*, we became very frightened.

I told the driver that we would continue to the bank of the river. When we arrived, we found a *Joseño*, Alejandro Morales, whom they were carrying on a plank. He was not able to speak; he was almost dead. The bullet had hit his knee, and he had lost a lot of blood. When I talked to the *Joseños* who carried the wounded man, they told me not to go to the farm because the guerrillas were asking for me and wanted to know my name.

This scared me because I did not know how the rest of the crew were. Perhaps there were more who were wounded, and I had to muster the courage to go. When I crossed the river, the people of the village of Moyuta were very frightened because these things had happened within a kilometer from them. I took off my shoes and left them with the owner of the canoe. Then, barefoot, I proceeded without a sombrero but with a sack tied with a lasso, acting as if I were a wanderer looking for work.

Near the village, I found the *cuadrilla*. Both the men and women were crying and exclaiming about what had happened. They told me to leave because it was very dangerous to go to the farm. I asked whether anyone had been paid. When they said no, I told them to wait for me where the truck was. Then I continued down the road alone. Agustín María was too afraid to go and stayed with the crew.

When I was about to arrive at the office, I noticed a group of people who ran to hide in the cotton mill. They thought that I was one of the guerrillas. When I reached the farm, no one was in the office except the corpse of the noble Duarte Vallejo, bathed in his own blood. Then I went to the house of the payroll clerk. The poor man was crying because they had beaten him. He told me that the guerrillas had robbed the office $40,000 and had taken the machine gun of the murdered airplane pilot and acting paymaster, Duarte Vallejo. Also, they took the watches of the other employees and hit them. The pay clerk told me that I should go to Guatemala [City] to see what could be done about paying the workers of the *cuadrilla*.

Why did the guerrillas shoot Duarte?

Duarte, who I believe was a retired captain, was the aviator and chauffeur of Don Rolando, who brings money from the bank to the farm and who makes transactions on behalf of the bank and the farm. Duarte flew Don Rolando in a two-engine plane to pay the people. Duarte usually just drives and guards Don Rolando with his machine gun. Usually it is the administrator, Juan Federico Estrada, who pays the people, but probably he did not show up because he was afraid. Don Duarte had compassion for the people and took the place of the administrator. It was the first time he had acted as paymaster. When the guerrillas suddenly appeared, they immediately shot him because he was the only one with a weapon. They took the $40,000 from him and Don Rolando's watch, which was valued at $300. When I arrived, Rolando was still terrified.[25]

When I went back by the same road to the crew, there was total silence. Not a soul was on the road. I reached the river again and crossed it by canoe. When I reached the people, they were crying a lot over their money. I told them to have more patience and that I would be in charge of going to Guatemala [City] to get it. Only then did they climb aboard the truck. But there was not enough room for so many people. Two families had to stay behind—the family of the miller and helper and their son, and another family with children and a lot of suitcases. I had to remain with them. Unfortunately, there were no buses, and I had to hire an express car for $20 to take them to Tiquisate. Then I had to pay another $30 to get them to Cocales. Beforehand, however, I went to the hospital to inquire about the wounded *Joseño*. They told me that they had transferred him to Escuintla because his condition was very delicate.

When we got to Cocales, it was almost 6:00 P.M. We could not continue to San José, but by the grace of God, a person gave me the name of another person who makes express trips. When I found him, he agreed to make the trip for $70, which was very expensive because he had to drive at night. I said very well, but that I would not be able to pay him until we reached San José because I already had spent all my money.

When we arrived at midnight the town was in a great uproar. Many people were crying. The kin of the wounded thought he had died, and my family thought I had died, too, because people had come to tell them that I had been killed. Not until I arrived did the town quiet down.

When I got out of the car that had brought us to San José, the parents of the wounded man wanted to hit me and throw me in jail. They were very angry with me. But I told them, "Be more patient. I'm not to blame for anything. It wasn't I who inflicted the wound. It was the guerrillas." In their great ignorance, they wanted to strike me.

At this moment my wife came to advise me that she had heard the noise of the car getting ready to leave. Then I told her to go home and get the $70 to pay for the trip. When she returned, I paid the señor, and we went to my house.

A lot of friends came to see me. I told them everything that had happened. I also told them that the injured man was in very serious condition. These friends sent for beers, and we drank them. Also, many of the members of the crew came, but they were now drunk because of their frightening experience. Never did we think something so serious was going to happen to us.

Here I want to write that, when one's luck seems bad, God is still with him, because God was with me during everything that happened to me. We had left at 1:00 A.M. in order to arrive at 6:00 or 7:00 A.M. on the farm to oversee the paying of the crew. But one never knows about things that seem inconvenient at the time. At the same hour the crew was getting paid, we were being detained by the policeman. He did not let us go until 8:00 A.M., and it was 8:00 A.M. when they sentenced the paymaster. If the policeman had not detained us these hours on the road, I would have been killed. But God is great because when we left on the road from San Martín, I was meditating a lot, admiring God! I had a foreboding that something bad was going to happen. But I thought that perhaps I was going to lose money or that I was going to get sick. I did not anticipate what actually happened. Also, the people were very surprised about what happened to us. But indeed that is life. No one is free from problems. We must be patient for the persecutions to pass, little by little. We must always remember that Jesucristo is our friend wherever we are. He knows about our difficult situations and will help us. I say this because in each of my difficulties, God and my conscience have liberated me from many enemies.

❧ Trying to Get the Pay of My Crew
25–29 JANUARY 1981

I got up feeling very sad. My whole house was full of people who came to visit and ask if the farm is going to pay the crew because we are all poor people, and we need what we work for. However, the guerrillas say that they are in favor of the poor. But this is just a lie because these men say they support us, and they leave us without being paid. They stole $40,000; they killed the one who pays our salary; and moreover they shot one of our humble race. What I think is that these men are against society—they do not like the rich or the poor. More than anything else they are assassins. All day long I stayed home.

I also stayed home on 26 January. During the night, the crew came to my house again to ask me if I could go to the coast to demand payment. I told them I would go tomorrow. They wanted to know if it was necessary to select some men to go with me because of the delicate situation on the coast. I said yes, but I had to agree to pay for expenses for those who would accompany me. Roberto Mendoza Pérez, Ignacio Oliva y Oliva, Pedro Mejía, and Gerardo Bizarro Canajay were named, in addition to my two helpers, Agustín María and Carlos.

On 27 January at 2:00 A.M. we left San José for San Martín. In San Martín we took a bus for Cocales, where we arrived at 6:00 A.M. There we ate some tortillas and drank some coffee. One of our companions, Gerardo, went to Escuintla to check on the man in the hospital. Then we caught a bus for Tiquisate.

When we arrived at 7:00 A.M. on the Esquipul farm, we learned that the administrator had not come since the day they had killed the acting paymaster. He was too afraid. The pay clerk told us that we would have to wait a while for him to come. But in the afternoon it was impossible for us to find tortillas to sustain ourselves. We just ate radishes and two tortillas each that our companion Ignacio Oliva carried.

At 6:00 P.M. there were no people. Everything was quiet. We asked to be allowed to sleep with the pay clerk, but he was not sympathetic with us and said no. We had to sleep on the porch of the office where they had killed the acting paymaster only four days ago. We all were scared, but there was no other place to sleep, so we had to stay there. We thought the guerrillas might return to kill us. By the grace of God, nothing happened to us. But we certainly did not sleep well.

The next day it was the same. We stayed on the Esquipul farm. We got up at 5:00 A.M. to wait for the administrators. By 7:00 A.M. we were very hungry. A señora sold us tortillas and a few beans. This was our breakfast.

At 8:00 A.M. the administrator, Juan Federico Estrada, arrived— trembling with fright! Little by little he began to talk to us. I asked him for the money owed the crew since the Sunday of the accident. He said it was impossible to pay such a large amount of money, but he gave me a list with the name of each worker and the amount of work he had done along with an order to take with me to Guatemala [City]. When I told the boys, we took the road back toward San José. When people asked us where we were going, I told them that we had come looking for work but we could not find any and we were returning to our town. They warned us to be very careful because they had met members of the military who were looking for guerrillas. We thanked them.

Then we crossed the river and rode the bus to Tiquisate, where we bought some tortillas. At 11:00 A.M. we left Tiquisate. In Cocales, Roberto Mendoza, Ignacio Oliva, and Pedro Mejía stayed behind because we did not have enough money for the six of us to get to Guatemala [City]. Thus, these three companions returned to San José while the other three of us continued on the same bus to the capital.

We arrived at 3:00 P.M., but already it was impossible to get the pay from the Banco Granai & Townson S. A. because it was closed. But I told Señor Rolando Vega de Ochoa that we had no money with which to eat or pay for lodging. He is the representative of the farm owner, Lorenzo Orantes Martínez. Don Rolando was on the farm when they killed Duarte, and he knew our situation. He signed a check for $50 so that we could eat and sleep. He said he would subtract the money from what we would be paid tomorrow. Then we hurried to the after-hours window of the same bank and cashed the check.

Then we went to Zone 1 and asked for lodging. They charged us $3 per person. We ate dinner at the Pérez Comedor, where they charged us $1.50 each.

On 29 January I got up at 5:00 A.M., but my companions slept until 6:30 A.M. For breakfast we went to the same *comedor*. Then we went back to Zone 9. When we arrived, the bank was still closed. We had to wait until 9:00 A.M.

When it opened, we went up to the fifth floor to Don Rolando's office. Then we settled the account. In total, the pay of the workers and the commission was $4,000. But the señor did not want me to carry such a large check. He thought I might lose the money or someone might rob me. I said, "Do not worry. I will give you a legal receipt."

He answered, "No, Ignacio, it is not that I do not trust you. I say this because for this much money you could lose your life."

I answered, "Don Rolando, give me the check. I have faith in God that nothing is going to happen. The people are in great need."

Then Don Rolando took me to the bank. They gave me the money in a private office in the basement of the bank [for my protection], but it was already 11:00 A.M. My friends were anxious, but when they saw me coming out of the bank, they were relieved.

I carried the money in an old, dirty, agave bag. No one could tell that it was full of money. Calmly we walked to Zone 1. It took us nearly an hour to reach the office of Rebuli. The three of us took our seats on the bus, and I put the money below the seat where no one would notice it. We napped on the bus, and in Escuintla we ate lunch.

At 6:00 P.M. we arrived in San Martín, where the boys from San José were waiting for us. When they asked me if I had the money, I told them no. They did not notice that I was carrying it in my bag because it certainly looked like a bag used for trash. We chatted along the road, but they were very upset because they needed their money.

When we reached my house, I told them to go call everyone so that I could give them their money. When everyone arrived, I told them, "Here is the money and list. Please, I would like to have order and not a commotion." Then I paid them according to how much they had worked on the farm. By the grace of God, it all went well. I did not finish until 10:00 P.M. Paying them was slow because I was careful not to make a mistake that would cause me problems later. When all was finished, our commission came to $375, but most of this had already been spent on expenses from the 24th until today. We were left with $25 each. After the accounts were settled, Agustín María and Carlos sent for beers. We drank plenty. We were very tired from the hardships of the last six days.

The next two days I just stayed home resting.

❧ The Government Decrees That All Will Become Literate
1 FEBRUARY 1981

By the grace of God, dawn came without incident. After breakfast at 7:00 A.M. José and I went to water tomatoes in Panasajar.

Today Señor Bishop Jesús Orellana Orantes went to the village of Tzancuil again for the profitable business of confirming the people. I do not know how many were confirmed, but certainly a lot of people from San José went to meet the bishop.

They called a meeting in the parochial assembly hall to announce that the central government has decreed that all Guatemalans from 15 to 60 years of age must learn to read and write. Any citizen who does not comply will be fined from $5 to $100. In this meeting the director of the national school announced that the census he had taken with the rest of the teachers indicates that there are 562 children aged 7 to

14. But to date only 200 had enrolled. He said that anyone who does not enroll his child by the end of the next five days will be fined according to the law. About 60 persons attended this meeting.

℘ We Celebrate a Mass of Grace
2 FEBRUARY 1981

This was an unforgettable day. We celebrated a fiesta and at the same time a mass of grace. For all of our work, we earned only a little money. We suffered a lot, but that is life. Then we bought meat, and my wife prepared the food. After the mass, the board of directors of Catholic Action ate at my house. It all ended peacefully. The directors went home, but Agustín María and Carlos stayed until 7:00 P.M.

℘ Building a New Kitchen
5 FEBRUARY 1981

I got up at 5:00 A.M. I was very cold. My señora made a fire in the kitchen and prepared breakfast.

After eating together, we began to move things out of the kitchen. Then Felipe and I began to disassemble the roof. We took down the wood, and then we demolished the walls. All day long we worked very hard. We destroyed the kitchen because it is very small and fills up with smoke. For that reason, we want to build a larger one.

I pitied my poor wife. She had to cook lunch in the yard of the house under the heat of the sun because we do not have another place for her to work. In the afternoon we began to pick the first tomatoes of this year.

℘ A Meeting in Guatemala with FEDECCON
6–8 FEBRUARY 1981

Immediately after breakfast at 7:00 A.M. we went to irrigate tomatoes. We finished at 9:30 A.M., and then I began to work with three *mozos* digging out dirt to build a house [kitchen] in the *sitio*. For lunch we ate tamalitos with hot beans.

After lunch I ran to the house of Domingo Quic to ask for money I had lent him. But he did not give me anything. Then I went to work again until 3:00 P.M. While I soaked my feet, I arranged my papers for the 4:00 P.M. launch to Panajachel [because my friend Benjamín and I were about to leave for Guatemala City]. In this town we ate bread and drank soft drinks while we waited for the Higueros bus. At 6:30 P.M. we left Panajachel, but the trip was painful because it was fast, bumpy, and scary.

At 8:00 P.M. we ate dinner in a town called El Tejar. At 9:15 we arrived in the capital, where we looked for a pension named Río Jordan. While Benjamín slept in the bed, I slept on the floor. Before going to sleep, I had to write in my diary.

On Saturday, 7 February, we left the pension at 6:30 A.M. to eat breakfast in a *comedor*. Then we went to the Federación Guatemalteca de Cooperativas de Consumo (FEDECCON), where they received us very well. After a half hour they took us to a school named Don Bosco.

At 10:00 A.M. the meeting was called to order. There were [representatives of] 27 cooperatives present. This was the first time I had attended. Everything went well. They discussed many things, including cooperatives that are not functioning well.

At noon, they served us lunch. We had chicken, but it was a pity they gave us only bread [and not tortillas], which was not sufficient to satisfy our appetites.

After lunch the program continued. At 5:00 P.M. they gave us coffee, but we were very hungry. We had to endure our hunger until 9:00 P.M., when the meeting ended and they took us to the Santísima Trinidad Hotel. At 10:00 P.M. we ate tortillas. Doing without tortillas is difficult for us Indians.

I chatted a lot with a friend named José Pérez Méndez about the cooperatives, and we did not go to sleep until 11:45 P.M.

On 8 February we got up at 6:30 A.M. I then went to buy some soap with which to bathe. After bathing, I ate breakfast in the same hotel. They gave us a meager breakfast.

At 9:00 A.M. the general assembly began again. They told the 76 persons attending that there is going to be an election for the new directors of the federation, so we formed groups to elect the president. But those of Totonicapán already had a lot of support, and they did not want us to participate in their group. Since they gave us a half hour to form groups, I talked with other representatives of other cooperatives, two from the capital and some from San Diego, and we formed our own group.

In total eight candidates were nominated. Ours was *profesor* Conrado Tello. The vote was democratic and secret. When the ballots were counted, our group had won. We did the same thing for the treasurer and the *vocal* [the substitute for various offices]. Also, we voted for the *comisión de vigilancia*. There were six candidates, including me. But a woman named Lara Salazar y Salazar won. It was happy occasion because five men lost and a woman won.

Also, we voted for the secretary of the *comisión de vigilancia*. Five candidates, including myself, were written down. Three of us, two from Totonicapán and myself, tied with 13 votes each. We voted again, and again the vote was tied. Then the directors asked for another vote, but they said that if the next vote was tied, there would be a raffle to determine the winner. When the third vote was counted, the two others received only 13 votes each while I received 17. Thus, I was elected. For all those who voted for me it was a happy occasion but unusual because it was my first time at such a meeting and already 17 people were in my favor. Although no salary was involved, I valued their vote of confidence.

Later we took the oath of office and drew up a record of all that had happened at the meeting, signed by all the participants. Then we went to lunch and said good-bye to one another on behalf of each one's town.

Then Benjamín and I went by bus to San Luis. We arrived at 8:00 P.M. short of money, so we just ate tortillas and slept on the porch of the municipality.

❧ We Continue with My New Kitchen, and the Literacy Program Begins
9–13 FEBRUARY 1981

All night Benjamín and I did not sleep because it was very cold. We did not have more than a sheet with us. We went to the shore of the lake to wash. Since we had to wait for the launch, we did not leave San Luis until noon.

At 1:00 P.M. I arrived home. The mason and his two helpers were laying the cement for the new house [kitchen with separate walls and a separate roof].

In the afternoon there was a lot of activity in town. They wanted to begin registering the adults, including my wife, for the literacy program. However, my wife is not literate, and she does not wish to become literate. In her case, I am guilty. I can read and write, but because of all my jobs and work I did not teach her also. Not until now are we seeing a little light. Now she is able to sign her name and write the name of her town. For me and my family, it is okay to learn a little more. But others are becoming enemies of the school because they say that it robs them of their time and that they are too old for learning to read and write to do them any good. It is a big problem because they are ordered to attend school but are not able to because of their work.

When it was ordered that everyone had to learn to read and write, it was discovered that there are 563 adults (the majority) who do not know how—just in San José, not including the villages.

How many teachers are there?

There are nine in the school. Also, we got the idea to name two members of our cooperative as literacy teachers for about 70 persons who are illiterate.

Are they able to teach them how to read and write?

Yes. The two teachers in the cooperative are authorized by IN-ACOP. They are *Joseños*. Also, some nonmembers of the cooperative attend the literacy classes because there are a lot of illiterates and not many teachers. Also, there are two persons in the Catholic Church who are teaching reading and writing.

Then there are four extra teachers?

Yes. There are in total 13 teachers who are instructing the people. But not all the students come each day. Some go today, others tomorrow.

On 10 February we worked all day putting up the walls of the new kitchen. My wife continued to cook in the yard under the heat of the sun. But such is the life of us poor people.

In the evening I went to the cooperative. All the directors were delighted that I hold an office in the federation. On this same night they began to teach the adults to read and write.

From 4–6:00 P.M., two hours a day, the adults are attending because there was a decree that those who do not attend will be fined $50 to $500. Who can afford $500? It is better that they attend even if they do not understand. They go just to be able to say that they are present, but they are not interested in learning. This is a big problem.

On 11–12 February I was still working on the construction of the house [kitchen]. It was hard work, and in the afternoon I was very tired, but I still had to write in my diary.

On 13 February we had to suspend work on the house because we ran out of adobe. Five of us made 250 pieces, and José helped us a lot.

ᘒ Irma and Pascual Start A Fire
SUNDAY, 15 FEBRUARY 1981

I stayed home to make certified copies [on my typewriter] of the memorandums of the federation. At 9:00 A.M. the sawyers brought the wood that I will use to build the house [kitchen]. It cost $207.50, which is very expensive. I am not sure I will be able to complete it.

This afternoon, Don Pascual and Doña Irma, who are married, decided to go inspect a little coffee they have planted in Tuibuj. Irma was pregnant and did not want to work, but she needed some exercise, so they took a walk. There were a lot of chick-peas in the fields, and Irma asked her husband to toast a few to eat. Don Pascual complied and began to gather dry brush to toast them, but their luck was bad. They did not realize that the mountain was dry, and it caught fire. They burned a dry hill that was not worth anything. But since starting a fire is frowned upon, poor Pascual tried to put it out. It was futile. And poor Irma came running to town to tell the authorities and ask for help. Then the guards and *alguaciles* went to look for people to put the fire out.

The guards went down to the soccer field to order the people who were there to go put the fire out. But the boys did not pay any attention to what they were saying, and they just kept playing. There was even a *regidor* playing with them.

On Monday, 16 February, 22 residents were fined because they had not obeyed the order to put out the fire. This fire caused a lot of damage to their families. Included among those fined was the *regidor*. His fine was $5.

Today we resumed work on the house [kitchen]. Moreover, I had to work because the *mozos* were not much concerned with the work. By the afternoon I was very tired.

On Tuesday the problems over the fire continued. Pascual and Irma were fined $25 each. I do not know how the mayor is able to do such things to poor people because the land that burned did not have a single stick on it for firewood. It was just dry grass.

In the evening we went to the cooperative to approve the budget for the present year of 1981. The salary for the employee of the tienda will be $70 per month, and it will total $840 a year; the miller will be paid $35 a month for a total of $420; the rent for the house at $12 per month will be $144; electricity will cost about $48; water, $3; bookkeeping, $120; per diem travel expenses, legal matters, and the like will be $360; and unforeseen, miscellaneous expenses will be $150. In total the cooperative will spend $2,085 for the year. We finished approving the budget very late at night.

Last night they said that at school the children did not have places to sit because there were not enough desks. Today I went to see for myself, and sure enough many children were writing on the floor. It was a sad sight to see!

In previous years parents enrolled their children in school, but if they had two or three children of school age, they enrolled only one. They did not want to lose the money that the children could make working. Thus, the number of children of school age enrolled was 400 to 500. But when the government decreed that all children of school age had to go to school, they made a list, and it turned out that there are 700 children of school age. Now that the number of children of school age has doubled, there are not enough classrooms and teachers. Still, the government said that if the parents do not send their children to school, they will be fined $25 to $50, depending on the situation of each family.

In the afternoon of this same day I presented a proposition to the board of directors of the cooperative to see whether we could help buy some desks. But there are members of the cooperative who have hard hearts because they did not want to approve this motion. And the children remained without desks.

❦ Finishing the Kitchen
21 FEBRUARY 1981

All day long I worked hard to finish the house [kitchen]. We built the roof but not the doors because I do not have enough wood. At 6:30 P.M. we quit working. I bought some beers, but not everyone drank because among us were persons of different religions—the mason and his helpers were Protestants.

❦ Attending a FEDECCON Meeting
28 FEBRUARY 1981

Yesterday I went to Panajachel to the Banco Agrícola Mercantil to cash a check that Dr. Sexton sent me as a gift. This morning I took the Rebuli bus to Guatemala [City] to attend a meeting of the board of directors of FEDECCON. But it was a shame that the federation did not want to give us a little money for travel. Because we did not have money for expenses, we asked the agent, but he told us that the federation had no money. Like a beggar, I returned from the capital to Panajachel.

When I arrived in Panajachel, it was very late, and I went to buy some tortillas. Then I went to the beach to sleep on the sand, but I was very cold because I did not have any bedding.

❧A New Municipal Office Is Inaugurated
13 MARCH 1981

On Friday the new municipal office was inaugurated. It was very tranquil. The mayor invited different persons—members of the Catholic Church, members of the Protestant Church, the *principales*, the *cofradías*, and various residents, including me. I had to obey.

We waited half the day for the representative of the government, but he did not show up. The minister of the government was probably afraid to come because of the guerrillas. Since the lunch was getting cold, finally one of the masons inaugurated the municipality. Then they showed us the new offices, assembly hall, and jail. One group at a time went in because there were a lot of us.

We then witnessed the inaugurations of the new post office and telegraph office. But again the *jefes* of the government did not show up. The person who performed the inauguration was in charge of the post office in San Martín. Afterwards, they showed us the interior of these offices.

After the inaugurations we went to the assembly hall of the school to eat lunch. After lunch they brought liquor, but I did not drink because it was hot. The mayor very much appreciated our presence. About 3:30 P.M. each person went home.

❧Guerrillas Visit San José
15 MARCH 1981

Ignacio wrote out and told me this episode on tape in nearly the same detail.

I am going to explain what happened, but for me these are delicate matters because I am not obliged to any group [of guerrillas].

More than anything else I am a *campesino*. My duties are working in the fields and with my family. Other things are secondary to me. I am not interested in knowing who the guerrillas are or how they live in the mountains or what they do in the mountains. But the truth is that they came to our town, and I am going to say a little about what happened.

At 6:30 P.M. on the day in question, I was certifying copies of a memoradum for FEDECCON when Felipe came to warn me, "Ignacio, suspend your work. Do not make any noise with the typewriter because right now the guerrillas are in front of the municipality, and they are gathering some people for a meeting."

"Really, man!" I answered.

"Yes, really. Be careful! You had better shut your door," he told me.

"Very well," I told him. Then I stopped typing and put my papers, diary, and typewriter in a sack and hid them. They are very important to me. "If someone comes to search the house they will see there is nothing," I told my wife.

Then I told her, "I am going to see what they are doing." But I did not act as if I were looking for the guerrillas. Instead, I acted as if I had not heard that they were in town. I put on my sombrero and carried two avocadoes as if I were going to give them to a friend. I did not act as if I were looking for the guerrillas because someone else might accuse me of being their friend. Thus, with the avocadoes in hand I went to the house of my father-in-law. When I reached the corner, I could see what was happening in my town.

There were about 25 to 30 guerrillas, including two women, eating bread and drinking sodas in the street and dressed in green uniforms like the army but with different shoes and longer, styled hair. The guerrillas wanted to gather the poor who were here and there, and some people went up to them, but it was more out of curiosity. They do not know what a guerrilla is. The guerrillas were well-armed, but everything was very quiet, and there was no fear—nothing.

But they stopped Señor Roberto Cojbx, who was in his car. They told him, "You are not going to leave because we are here. You can go after we leave." The guerrillas thought that Roberto Cojbx might go tell the army, so they detained him. And Roberto Cojbx did as he was told.

While the guerrillas were eating and drinking, I managed to talk to Roberto Cojbx. I asked him, "What happened?"

"Look," he said, "these people will not let me go."

"Can't you go by the road near my house?" I asked him.

"No," he said, "the car sits very low, and the holes might break the springs. I must wait."

Thus Roberto and I talked, but I was watching what was happening although I was pretending I did not know what the guerrillas were doing. It just seemed to me that they were eating and drinking quietly and that they were taking a lot of bread with them to the mountains. When they finished eating, they returned the empty bottles and disappeared. They said that the oppressed people would one day be free, and they left for an unknown destination. Two youngsters, who did not worry that the guerrillas had come to kill people, were curious and followed them. They said the guerrillas took the road to Patzilín.

After the guerrillas left, what an uproar there was in the town with the people saying this, that, and the other thing! There was great alarm.

Then I went to the municipality to see a cloth banner that they had put up in place of the banner of the government that was already there. The banner of the government said, *Todo Guatemalteco será alfabetizado* [Every Guatemalan will be literate]. The banner of the guerrillas said, *Organización ORPA jamás será vencido, pueblo que lucha pueblo que vence* [The organization ORPA will never be defeated. People who fight are people who conquer]. They tied it with a rope and left. The banner was white with red letters and the symbol of a black hammer and sickle.

As I was reading the banner that the guerrillas left, I began to chat with the mayor. He told me that the guerrillas had asked for him because they wanted to kill him, but fortunately he was not in his office. He was in the assembly hall.

"Where is the mayor?" the guerrillas asked him.

"I do not know," he answered. "Who knows where he went? He left."

"And who are you?"

"I am an *alguacil*." If he had told them who he really was, they might have killed him.

"Where are the *chicotes*, the whips that the *alguaciles* use to capture drunks?"

"Here is one."

With this you punish the poor," they said. And they threw gasoline on it and burned it. Then they looked for firearms, to see whether there was a rifle or revolver or anything. But they found none.

"Are there any prisoners?" they asked.

"There is no one."

"Ah, good," they said, and they left.

This is what Abraham, the mayor, told me. He was still frightened when I talked to him, so I invited him to drink some beers at Bernardo's tienda.

When we arrived at this tienda, Señor Bernardo was trembling. He was afraid because he had been obliged to sell the guerrillas bread and sodas. I acted like a journalist, but I wanted the information just for myself.

"How is everything?" I asked the owner of the tienda.

"I tell you I am scared," Bernardo told me.

"Why?"

"Yes, man, I am afraid the military commissioners will accuse me because I sold sodas to the guerrillas."

"I do not believe so," I said. "Your sales were just to make money. They came to buy bread and sodas, and what wrong have you done?"

"Yes, but I was afraid and alone. I was not able to keep track of the sales." He also said that he had a companion in the tienda but that he was scared speechless. He could not move; he was like a dead person.

Then I asked Bernardo, "How much did you sell?"

"Thirty-eight dollars' worth," he told me.

"That's good!" I told him.

"But it seems that they did not pay me for all of it," he said, almost crying.

"Why?"

"Because I was not able to keep track of the sales; there were a lot of people. But they did pay $38," he told me.

"Is that so?" I said. "You should be satisfied."

No one knows whether the guerrillas, who might have been sleeping near the town, or someone else took down the banner that the guerrillas left hanging on the porch of the municipality. The *jefe* of the military commissioners ordered a patrol to guard the banner so that no one would take it down, while he sent for a military detachment to inspect it and take it down. But through negligence the patrol was not aware when someone took down the banner. This caused a problem because, when the military arrived, it began to suspect that there were one or more guerrillas in the town. But I do not believe there are any guerrillas in San José.

The mayor and the rest of the people were very nervous because they believed that the guerrillas could return. The mayor was especially worried because he thought that if they had not killed him the first time, they could the second time they came.

Can you explain the power of the military commissioners? Who are these men?

You see, the military commissioners are persons like me. They are not salaried; they do not have uniforms. They just have power. The military commissioners are persons who have been discharged from the military. They name them military commissioners. They are the low-level *jefes*. Whatever happens in a town they inform the military in San Luis or Sololá. This is their duty, true. But when they name them to this office, they grow a lot in importance. For them it is like becoming a god more than anything else. They do not respect humanity. They more than anything else are men who work in the countryside, who do not have salaries, who do not have uniforms, but who act as spies.

They go to where there are meetings. They look for people who have communistic doctrines; they look for people who criticize the government. Then they go to a *comandante* and say, "This person is bad; this person is part of a guerrilla system; this person is criticizing the government; this person is criticizing the army." That is the reason that there have been a lot of deaths in Guatemala. One may be friendly with a person, and later one is accused of doing something. Then come the higher-ups to kill the person because he is against the army or against the president—to kill him! And this is how all the massacres we are witnessing in these times have taken place. And this is happening a lot in San Martín.

More than anything else it seems that the [head] military commissioner in San José is a fine person. At times we quarrel in our meetings of the cooperative over policy, and he comes [to serve as mediator]. We tell him about our concerns so that our actions will not cause difficulties that the higher-ups will condemn. Only then does the commissioner meddle, and we have only been a little dominated. We ask his advice.

I was discharged from the army. I was a soldier. I am not against the army nor am I in favor of the Communists. The soldiers and the Communists will have their problems because they fight each other. Perhaps they are fighting for money or for high offices. I do not have to fight for anything because I have my hoe, my cans for irrigating, my corn for cooking. I do not depend on them for a job. I am not against [anyone].

The commissioners wanted me to be a special collaborator for them. They asked me to collect information about guerrillas. They wanted me to get special credentials signed by the *comandante* that I am a special collaborator of the army.

"Many thanks," I said, "but I do not have time. I am not in a position to tell you anything because I am just supporting myself in the countryside. I cannot inform this *comandante* because my milpa needs attention. It needs fertilizer. How can I do this for you? I cannot," I told them.

"But, man, we know that you are a person who has power in this town."

"Perhaps," I said, "but how can you believe I have power? I do not have money or other things. I am poor. I have a big family. I have to work on my land. Someone who has power is rich; such a person can collaborate with you. I am not able. I am sorry."

"But you are able to collaborate with us."

"What collaboration?" I answered.

"It is that we have a lot of commissions. You can help us with $2 to $3, or $1 when possible."

"Ah, yes," I told them, "when it is possible I will help. But I cannot give a piece of my hide to various people. We shall see."

So they struggled, trying to get me to be their helper. But I do not want to dirty my hands or my conscience. It would grieve me to say that a person is bad when perhaps he is not. And if a person is bad, his own bad punishment must stop it.

For this reason I know that the commissioners are persons. Some are conscientious, but not all of them. It seems that those who are not just want to live off the people. They do not want to work. Many times the government wants the good for us, but those who bother us are the commissioners. They are the lowest, vilest, and most disgraceful. They like to pester a town, and the government does not know what these men are doing. The government thinks that the commissioners are somewhat good elements. But they are the ones who do the evil things. We have realized that this is true for San Martín. The commissioners there are fat; they do not work; they just drink in the tiendas. This is one of the things that we are observing.

About how many commissioners are in San José?

About 17.

Plenty.

Yes, 17.

❧ Erasmo Ignacio Has the Measles
16–20 MARCH 1981

We wanted to stucco the new house [kitchen]. The mason began, but it was impossible to finish because my children were sick. We had to suspend the work again.

By the 18th it had been some days that Ignacito was sick. I thought he would be cured soon, but he was not. On this day I did not work.

On 19 March all night long I did not sleep. Instead I just cared for the child, who was in serious condition. There was much grief, and there was no doctor.

On Friday, 20 March, I left at 2:00 A.M. for Guatemala [City] for a meeting with my companions on the committee of control. Because of my commitments, I had to leave the child who was critically ill.

In Guatemala [City] everything went well, but it was impossible to return on the same day. I had to remain in the capital.

On Saturday, 21 March, I left the capital at 5:00 A.M. I thought I could reach the launch that left from San Luis, but I was unable. And there was no car leaving. I ate lunch in San Diego, and I did not arrive home until 7:00 P.M. They told me that my son Erasmo Ignacio has the measles.

On 23 March he continued to be gravely sick. On the 24th his temperature finally went down from the measles.

❧ Anica Catana Gets Sick
26 MARCH–10 APRIL 1981

The situation became worse. The baby Anica Catana fell sick. Now I was not able to attend to our work, and our money ran out. I had money for food, but we needed money for medicine.

During the next six days, from 26–31 March, the baby was the most ill. She nearly died. My wife cried a lot. What a terrible misfortune! There was no one who could cure her. I could not find the nurse. I went to a *curandera*, but I was told that she was sick. Then I ran like crazy for the house of Daniel Bizarro, but they told me that he was in Sololá to buy medicine.

Because of the heat of the sun, the baby's temperature increased. Finally, the launch arrived, and we ran to call Señor Daniel, who then gave her an injection. Not until midnight did the measles disappear. But this baby suffered a lot. Because of the sickness of the children, I stayed awake a lot. I hardly slept at all.

On 10 April all day long I felt depressed without any earnings from work. The children little by little were getting better, but I needed more money for the medicine, which costs a lot. Well, María now could make tortillas, and she helped her mother a lot because my wife also suffered from much weakness. But by the grace of God, her health was a little better. Gradually, I was curing them. I could buy a little medicine, and they gave me the rest at the health clinic.

∾ Bullets and Grenades and the Army
28 APRIL–3 MAY 1981

Today is when the señores of the army arrived again in the place called Telnic. A detachment walked through the town, but there were no problems. A lot of women went to sell them tortillas, *chuchitos* [small tamales with a small piece of meat and chili], tamales, and fruit, although earlier they had been afraid to because the other towns had gone around saying they are bad. However, they got along and coexisted with the civilians. They just gave us a little fright.

On 31 April at 8:00 P.M. my wife and I went to the house of a sister to get a loan of $15. We chatted and chatted until it was already 11:00 P.M. "Let's go," I said to my wife. And then we left the house.

We were just two *cuadras* from arriving home when we heard bursts of machine guns. We could hear the bullets in the air. But my wife and I had not reached the door to the house. And the bullets continued!

We barely arrived home, and it gave us a great fright. It was about a kilometer away, but the night is very quiet, and it sounded very near. When we got inside we wanted to abandon our house because it is next to the main road. We thought that perhaps there would be an engagement with the guerrillas. We also heard grenades. It was a great alarm. But when day broke, everything was very quiet. Nothing happened.

During the day of 1 May, the news spread that the señores had fired their arms to see whether the enemy was near. Moreover, they say that they were drinking their *cervecitas*. By the grace of God, however, nothing happened.

In the afternoon of 2 May, I met with the boys of the cooperative. They said that it was necessary to prepare a lunch for the señores of the army. We bought corn, and our wives cooked it. The reason was that they thought these men were suffering for the defense of the country. The army sent word that they did not need lunch on Saturday but that they would eat dinner on Sunday with many thanks.

The afternoon of Sunday, 3 May, was very pleasant. The men of the army played a game of soccer with the men of San José. The men of San José lost. A lot of people were in the countryside. When the game was over, the men of the cooperative carried tortillas and fish to the soldiers, who were very appreciative. The señores of the army asked for a list of all the associates so that nothing would happen to them [that is, so that they would not be falsely accused of supporting the guerrillas].

This afternoon was very peaceful. Already we had forgotten the great fright that the army had given us during the last two days.

❧ I Am Patron of the Dance of the Mexicans
2–29 JUNE 1981

Three of us planted five *cuerdas* of corn in three days in Quixal. Because of the rain, we were not able to work all day.

On 9 June the corn sprouted. On 10 June we began to weed and apply fertilizer. In four days we finished. We did not work again until Sunday because I had to lose time in the dance [of the Mexicans] celebrating the fiesta of San Juan Bautista.

Although I have not written about the Dance of the Mexicans, we already have been practicing it for months. But because there was no patron, the practice was failing. The patron is a very important dancer because he is the one who begins and ends the story of the dance. When they talked to me, I told them it was a pity that no one was collaborating with them, and I agreed to be the patron because the dance is a tradition of our ancestors. But I would have to go to Quezaltenango to rent a suit.

On this day I sold a *tablón* of onions for $50 to buy my shoes and rent the suit. On 17 June eight of us left San José at 1:00 A.M. [for Quezaltenango]. Because I allowed my son Erasmo Ignacio to come along, I suffered a lot. He walked until Santa Ana. We wanted to take a bus from this town, but it was night and raining hard, and the driver told us he was not going to make the trip to Quezaltenango because there was a lot of mud on the road.

Here in Santa Ana we ate our lunch at 3:00 P.M. After eating we took a bus which took us to the asphalt road, where we arrived at 7:30 P.M. There we boarded a bus to Quezaltenango.

Depending on the [financial] ability of each person, the suits were rented at different prices. I rented my suit, which had not been used much, for $13, a regular price, and the rest of the dancers rented their suits for about the same amount of money. At 11:30 A.M. they gave us the suits with the masks. I received two masks.

After eating lunch in Quezaltenango, we returned to Kamibal. Because I had to carry the baby [and could not keep up], the others went on ahead. The clothing weighed a bit and so did the child. My companions arrived at 7:00 P.M., but I did not arrive until 9:30 P.M., which was very late to be traveling on the road. I regretted having agreed to let Erasmo Ignacio go with me.

When I arrived home, the neighbors came to see the suits and masks. I did not go to bed until 11:00 P.M.

The following day, the child was gravely ill and not able to get out of bed. He had walked a lot in the cold and rain and had fallen sick, which for me was another problem.

All night until dawn we were in the house of the tutor for a ceremony. The shaman who performed the ceremony is from San Jorge. The men who were dancers lined up in their order of the dance with the patron, myself, at the head of one line and the patron's wife, a man dressed as a woman, at the head of another. The shaman called the names of the 20 gods and the name of the deceased spirits of other shamans so that none of the dancers would be tempted by some evil spirit, especially the patron. All of us bought candles and some eighths of a liter of *aguardiente* for the shaman.

The Dance of the Mexicans is the story of a farmer who has a woman, servants, livestock breeding area, and a lot of property. In the early morning, when they begin to dance, the patron and the Maruca [a comical name for his spouse, María, because it is the name for someone who cannot be trusted] dance three turns with each dancer until they finish with all 22, including the two bulls. The patron is at the head of one line followed by a *mayordomo* [administrator], a dancer dressed as a black, and the rest of the dancers with a bull at the end. In the other line the Maruca is at the head, followed by a *caporal* [leader], another dancer dressed as a black, and the rest as cowboys with another bull at the end. Twelve are in each line.

The two elderly persons—the patron, who really is old, and Maruca, who really is a young woman but who dances in the order of an older spouse and is thus called old—begin to dance with each person in each file until they complete both lines. This takes about two hours. When they are finished dancing with each dancer, two cowboys ask the patron to lend them the two bravest bulls to celebrate the fiesta. The patron responds, "With much pleasure," and he lends his large livestock. But beforehand the two cowboys have to erect a good restaurant and throw a good banquet so that the patron's wife can enjoy the fiesta.

Later, they have a bullfight. Then the first cowboy, who is called Penacho and who owns the cantina named Cantina Resbalón [Slipup] de Mexico, looks for the cowboys, who have gathered in his cantina to act as waiters.

When everything is prepared, the patron and the Maruca dance a lot on the corners of the square until they reach the cantina. When they arrive, they greet Don Penacho politely.

Then the patron asks, "What kinds of drinks are there in the cantina?"

Penacho responds, "Many different kinds of drinks."

Then Penacho gives two glasses to the patron and Maruca. As the patrons drink their drinks, Don Penacho leaves the cantina to guard them, making sure they do not fall down in the street because the tequila is very strong. When the patrons ask how much they owe for the drinks, Don Penacho answers that they do not owe anything because they own everything.

Then the patron and Maruca have to dance with each of the cowboys again until they arrive again at their posts at the head of the file, which takes some time. When they finish, Don Penacho goes to the two waiters and leaves, dancing with a bottle, because his business was bad with the Mexicans, who acted like thieves and who left him with just a bottle. Don Penacho had been serving the Mexicans drinks, but they had not paid him sufficiently because they were dancers who just left and returned to the marimba. He says that he had to taste what the owners had been drinking, and he leaves with his own bottle. (But the truth is that not everyone drank liquor. Mostly they had sodas in their bottles.) [There was actually a mock-up of a small cantina with a sign, La Cantina Resbalón de Mexico, with drinks of either liquor or soda pop, whichever a dancer wanted in reality, but the meaning of the dance was that they were all drinking beer or liquor and not paying for it because they were dancers.]

In this dance there are two persons with the masks of bulls. The cowboys set up a bullfight. They ask the patron to take out a tame bull so that the woman can fight, and Maruca is the first to fight the bull. Then the *mayordomo*, *caporal*, black, and the rest of the cowboys bullfight. The last is the old patron.

The cowboys say that the patron's woman is very young and that they want the patron to die. For that reason, they take out a very mean bull so that they can have the woman and all that she would inherit from the patron. The patron dies, but before expiring, he calls together all the cowboys and tells them that all his belongings are to go to them and to just take care of his wife. Then he dies. They put the mask of death (a mask with the face of a dead man) on him, and they put him in a casket and take him for the burial.

It was very nice when they put me in a casket and carried me to the church. It was 24 June, and many people saw them put me into the coffin. A lot of people cried, but many people laughed. I was well aware when they put me down in the coffin, but they waited about a half hour before they took me out. In about 20 minutes I lost consciousness. [I do not know whether it was from weariness or sleepiness.] I did not feel a thing when they opened the box. When I came to, I was on a bench, and my wife was guarding me. They told me I was in a deep sleep: I did not feel a thing when they took me out. I woke up about an hour later, and my wife asked me if I wanted a beer or an eighth of a liter [of *aguardiente*]. Gradually, I realized that I was in the convent [a room of the church], and I asked my wife to give me the eighth, and about five minutes later I felt good again. I do not know if some spirit captured my soul because when they put me in the casket, they began to sound the death knell. It could have been this, or it could have been the eyes of the people. [The climax of the dance is when the patron dies, and there were many people outside the church from all the different towns, including San Jorge and San Martín, who had come to watch the fiesta.]

Can you explain what you mean by the power of the eyes?

We believe in the captive eye and captive word. On certain occasions it has really happened. This was the case of a brother of mine, Jorge, who has the same mother as I. About eight years ago I told Jorge, who then was about 12 years old, "Jorge, take a bath and get a haircut, because your appearance is ugly! Clean yourself up a little!"

Jorge answered, "Who is going to obey you, Maximón?" [That is, he suggested Ignacio had contact with Maximón.]

I answered, "I am not Maximón, I tell you, but wait until night. Maximón will come to scare you." I told him these words, but only as a joke. But when Holy Wednesday dawned, Jorge woke up gravely ill. My mother came to tell me that I had bewitched him. She also told me that I was a witch and that I should not bewitch my own family. But for me it was just a laugh because I know I am not a witch. I admit that I told him that Maximón was coming to scare him, but I was just joking. But I do not know why the child became sick. I think that perhaps he was already sick or that he became frightened when I told him these things. For me it turned out to be a big problem because they accused me of being a witch. This boy paid a shaman to make a ceremony to cure him. The shaman said that I had told the boy these things when it was a dangerous hour. For these reasons I am very much afraid to say bad things to persons. I do not know why, but things that I say come true. Words and eyes have an ability or power of the blood.

On 29 June, the day of the Apostle San Pedro, we went to San Martín to present the dance for the people. It was strange for the people because when the patron died, they did not want to put him in the coffin because of much fear that he might actually die. For that reason, it was strange when they put me in the casket and took me out again without any problems. When I was inside the box, hundreds of people were around me. I participated without alcohol. I waited until I got back to San José to drink because I did not want to drink in San Martín. The people were pleased that a worthy function had been presented. In San Martín they gave us lunch and $50, but the tutor kept all of it. He did not even buy us some soft drinks. Perhaps he was too deep in debt to pay for the marimba.

A problem emerged with the religious persons. A group of catechists did not want to participate in the dance during the fiesta. They say that the dance is a great sin. They impeded our participation in the atrium of the church. But we had asked permission of the priest and the president of Catholic Action, and most of the townsfolk are in favor of conserving their traditions. Perhaps those who are against them say that we are not in accord with things of the world, that we are backward. These six men turned against the president of Catholic Action and his board of directors. The directors told us it was better that dancers not march in the procession. We understood well. These six persons hardly passed the fiesta peacefully. We indeed spent it well, by the grace of God.

But also there is a traditional custom that on the second day of the fiesta, or 25 June, the mayor has an obligation to call the *principales*, the *cofradías*, and Catholic Action for a lunch and some cherished drinks of liquor. After the lunch it is customary to dance to the better, ancient sounds of the marimba (that is, one that is not electric but may be accompanied by a saxophone). When the *principales* feel like drinking, they collect money among the group to pay for the drinks. They also begin to give liquor to those of the municipality. In the end the *principales* get drunk, but they are respected and the *alguaciles* and guards are in charge of conducting them to their houses. Thus the day of the 25th passed.

Also, the president of Catholic Action, Señor Jorge Sicay Tuc, was there drinking and dancing with the *principales*. Later the six persons [mentioned above] went to the priest to accuse the president of Catholic Action of being very drunk and of dancing. They said that he was a disgrace to the church. The priest began to believe all of the lies that they formulated. He sent a note to the president of Catholic

Action which said he was suspended from his office from 2 July to 2 August. The president wanted to clarify all of these things and to see who had seen that he was very drunk.

Also, they [the six persons] told the priest not to celebrate mass on 1 July, the last day of the fiesta, when they take San Juan Bautista to his new *cofradía*. The six men told him the gossip and that it would be better not to come celebrate the mass because it would just support these backward ways. Then the priest imposed an order that this day should not be celebrated. But the *principales*, *cofradías*, the association of women, and most of the catechists organized the procession to accompany San Juan Bautista to his new *cofradía*. To avoid problems, however, I told the dancers not to participate, and we did not. Señor Jorge Sicay remained suspended from his office. He wanted to have an investigation, but the priest also turned against him and lied; he said that he was not accused by *Joseños* but that some *Martineros* had seen him. The priest, as the head of the church, does not have reason to create falsehoods. There was discontent in the entire town. Because of this situation, a *principal*, the mayor, and five other families converted to Protestantism. They concluded that the Catholics did not want anything, neither the traditional customs nor anything else. Who knows what they want? And the mayor, who is the nephew of the main leader [of the six persons, Juan Bizarro Gómez], saw that the six men were making problems for others, and thus he went to the Assembly of God Church.

On 2 August Don Jorge Sicay again took possession of his office, but it happens that his enemies are very clever. Eventually they got rid of him after the death of a woman [to be discussed later].

Looking for Medical Help; How Things Are of This World
2 JULY 1981

We went to San Martín to look for a dentist because my wife is suffering a great pain with a tooth. Also, José is very sick with an infected throat. It was impossible to find a doctor, so we went to the pharmacy of a *Martinero*, Francisco Có. We asked for medicine for José, but Señor Có told me it would be better to have him examined. As we were returning, we bought a pound of meat and potatoes that we cooked and ate for lunch.

In the afternoon of the same day, at 5:30 P.M., we went with José to San Martín to have a medic examine him. They gave him medicine for $3. When we returned, it was already night.

Also, Erasmo Ignacio has been sick since 1 July [since the trip to rent suits for the dance of the Mexicans]. It is true that I sold three *tablones* of onions for $200, but because my family is large, I am nearly out of money. We are experiencing a lot of illness; I hope to God it will soon pass.

News arrived about Colonel Ignacio Cuc, who left San Martín for Guatemala [City]. In San Martín the medic, Miguel Rojas, left with him to visit his sick people in San Luis. There were also other persons riding in the pickup. It was not realized that one of these persons was a guerrilla. When they arrived at the La Providencia farm, the guerrilla jumped from the car with all of the luggage of the colonel [including his uniforms and a revolver]. Thinking that the luggage belonged to the guerrilla, the others did not advise the colonel. Miguel Rojas got off in San Luis, but the colonel later suspected he was the culprit (and a guerrilla) because he was the only one the colonel knew to accuse. [The others were unknown to the colonel even though he gave them a ride.] After the colonel stopped the car to let Miguel off, he continued his journey to Guatemala [City], where he discovered that his luggage, including his 45-caliber pistol and uniforms, was missing.

Then he returned to [San Martín] like a madman and demanded the luggage from the poor medic. Then he had this poor man thrown in jail in San Martín as if he were a dangerous guerrilla. Then the colonel brought soldiers from a detachment to take this man to jail in San Luis. But before they took him away, the townspeople of San Martín gathered and told the colonel that if this medic disappeared, they were going to kill him also. The townsfolk told him this in the presence of the soldiers who had come with the colonel. They told him this because Miguel had lived in San Martín and San José for 20 years, and they knew he was honorable.

Miguel remained in jail in San Luis for 10 days. After the ten days Miguel came to my house, and I asked about everything that had happened. He told me that during the night they took him out of San Luis to Guatemala [City] for interrogations, but he says that they did not find him guilty. At night they brought him back to the jail in San Luis and then they set him free. But the colonel continued his civil charges against Miguel Rojas. But it was all futile. The colonel did this because they say he is clever, but he was not clever when they stole his suitcase—a lot of embarrassment for a *jefe* to be robbed of his revolver. For us it was amusing, but for poor Miguel it was sad.

The Army Calls a Meeting
17 JULY 1981

After breakfast I went to clean some coffee in Chimucuní, where there are a lot of woods. At 1:00 P.M. I went home to eat a poor lunch. It is true that we are cooking bad things and that we have a lot of illness. Now there are three sick children, and I do not have money to buy medicine or to buy corn and things to eat. It is certain that I am working hard, but we will not have a harvest until November.

In the afternoon of this day the town officials announced publicly that tomorrow there will be a meeting on behalf of the national army from 9:00–11:00 A.M. They say that on this day there was a meeting also in San Jorge and San Benito, but in San Jorge not many residents attended. The army went to the countryside to call them to listen. But it was negative because the *Jorgeños* did not want to listen. They say that they were hit by soldiers, but these were only rumors because no one was beaten or wounded.

The Army Has a Town Meeting
18–24 JULY 1981

I got up at 6:00 A.M., and we drank coffee. Then José and my uncle José went with me to prepare some plots for planting beans. We finished at 9:00 A.M., but with much hunger.

When we arrived home, we ate breakfast very late, and then we went to the municipality to hear the captain, Angel de León, speak at the meeting he called. About 80 percent of the *Joseños* came to listen to him talk from about 10:00–11:00 A.M.

Everything was peaceful. The captain made a declaration in Spanish condemning terrorism, saying that the terrorists are the most responsible for the deaths of many families, and exhorting the people of San José to rise up against Communists and telling them to look in the vicinity of the town for Communists and when they see them to tell the military detachment where they are. Also, he spoke of all that is happening in Angola, Afghanistan, Russia, Cuba, Yugoslavia, and Czechoslovakia. He said that there was not any work and that there was a lot of hunger and that children were suffering.

We were there listening. The mayor translated in the Tzutuhil dialect. But he was not able to translate well. A lot he forgot [either because he was afraid there might be a guerrilla in the audience or because he did not know how to translate well].

My thoughts are that in Guatemala there is also a lot of sickness and hunger. But who will help the families? There is no medicine in the health clinic. In my family I have three sick children, and who knows how many families in Guatemala are sick? I believe that in all the Latin American countries there is sickness and much poverty, and it is because their governments think the money is only for them and not for everyone.[26]

In my family we continue with these grave things—a lot of sickness. On Sunday morning the children are sick. We have spent our last centavos on medicine. In the afternoon I went to fish because I was tired of eating greens. By the grace of God I caught two pounds of fish, and we ate them for dinner.

Monday was the same thing. I ate a little breakfast with my wife and María because the three sick children are not eating. We went to plant three *tablones* of onions, finishing at noon. When we arrived home we cooked wild greens and ate them for lunch. In the afternoon I had to work hard cleaning onions and coffee.

On Wednesday I got up with my wife, and we had breakfast together. Then we went to clean onions. María remained to take care of the sick ones. We thought we would soon finish, but we were unable. At 3:00 P.M. we arrived home very hungry, and we cooked and ate lunch.

On 24 July I went to work in Pakap to finish cleaning milpa and applying fertilizer. But the sun was very hot, and I got thirsty and ran out of water. When I arrived home, only the sick were there. My wife had thought a lot about the cultivations, and she had gone to clean beans in Xepanicuy with María. Then I went to join them, but I met them on the road as they were returning.

∿ Sickness Continues
25–27 JULY 1981

Dawn came with much grief because our son José was in very serious condition. He had a high fever all night. As I have said, we have fields, but not until summer [(the dry season) will they be ready for harvesting].

At 6:00 A.M. I left to ask Benjamín Coché for a loan of $50. This friend received me well, gave me breakfast, and then gave me the loan. Then I went to pay a debt of $10. Afterwards I ran to San Martín to look for a doctor, but they told me he had gone to Guatemala [City]. My wife and I felt much shame because our three children were very sick—José has a sickness in his throat, Ramón's entire body is swollen, and Erasmo is swollen. It took a long time to reach San Martín. We did not find a doctor, so we went to the pharmacy of Don Pancho Quic. He was very surprised that the three were very sick. He told me that he could indeed cure them but that I would have to spend some money to buy medicine—about $50. I told him that I could pay $30 right now and the other $20 later. He gave them injections and gave us medicine to take with us. Because the sick ones were not able to walk well, we arrived home very slowly. I picked up and carried Ramón for periods on my back. My wife did the same with Erasmo Ignacio.

On Sunday, 26 July, my wife and I got up at 5:00 A.M. We agreed that she would carry the sick ones to San Martín for injections. Meanwhile, I went to ask God's help. I felt weak at heart for everything that was happening with the children. I believe they are things that will pass, but still such things weaken a man. When I left the church, María gave me breakfast of potatoes. Then immediately I went to meet the sick ones.

My wife's parents and other residents told me that it was a bewitching that someone made against me. I asked them why. I had not done anything bad or stolen anything. My conscience is clean. They told me to look for a *brujo* to counter the witchcraft. But I did not want to. All of my ideas were good—to buy medicine.

On 27 July the children were still very sick. I was in great need, but I did not leave to go outside. I stayed to take care of the children. In the afternoon of this day we sent for the medic of the health clinic to see if there was any other kind of medicine to take. The medic said no and that we should wait until we finish giving the medicine of Don Pancho Quic.

Father Pablo Is Murdered
28 JULY 1981

This episode is a combination of Ignacio's written and taped accounts.

We received the news that at dawn on 27 July, when it was still night, enemies of the North American priest, Padre Pablo, opened the door with force of arms and killed him while he was sleeping in his dormitory on the second floor. But the truth surfaced from the Catholic Church. When the men were ascending, a nun saw that they had a distinctive dress and faces covered with black cloth. She saw that they were carrying machine guns of the kind that the army uses.

Father Pablo tried to better the town of San Luis. He founded a small hospital that benefited the rest of the lake [region]. He also had the charge of taking care of malnourished children. In general he helped the town a lot. Moreover, because of his steps, they established the radio station La Voz de San Luis. He was the first to try by radio to teach adults to read and write. Many groups of campesinos were helped by his small loans through Caritas of Guatemala, and he made scholarships available for the cooperative Quetzal of San Luis. Also, he succeeded in finding an outside market for commercialized, typical weavings.

With him worked Pedro Tzal as the director of the radio, who had as his secretary Domingo Portillo. The latter two worked a lot in the radio station. I do not know for sure, but they say that Pedro Tzal and Domingo Portillo and others of the town and three women of San José, named María Luisa Coché, Estela Temó Mérida, and Berta Guerra, practiced a lot of communism. And they say that doctors and lawyers of other countries have worked with them.

Much earlier, before the death of Padre Pablo, the radio station was destroyed. All the people of San Luis say that the army destroyed it for transmitting communistic ideas.

Also, the director of the radio station was persecuted. One day armed men arrived at the office to kidnap him. They asked for Pedro Tzal, and the same Pedro told them, "Pedro Tzal went to his house to eat dinner." Then the abductors went toward the house while Pedro closed the office and hid. Days later, Pedro, as he was a clever man, asked Father Pablo to relieve him from being director. And Pedro departed.

Then a young dynamic person by the name of Gerardo [Chacon] became the director. This man was in a seminary, and he completed all his studies as a priest. But at the presentation of his title they asked him whether he wanted to go to Honduras. He answered that he wanted to work in Guatemala to help his town. Here, they say, he erred, for they did not give him his title as priest.

Gerardo was without work, and for that reason he accepted being the director of the radio, but only for a few days. Then the radio was destroyed, and the director was persecuted. But the truth is that the one who worked a long time and solicited money in Communist countries was Pedro. It was well noted that he had connections with Communist countries because he obtained money and a lot of things, including a two-storied house. He had communistic beliefs.

Gerardo was totally innocent. One night [in October of 1981] they took him out of his house and shot him in the yard. According to his family, he bled a lot, but it is not known whether he is alive or dead. They took him away inside a car. His remains never appeared.

With much fear Pedro went to hide on the farms. A little later Domingo Quic, his cousin, told me that Pedro Tzal had enlisted in the army. But he said that Pedro stayed only a few months in the army and then left. While Pedro was hiding in the army, his countrymen and many others thought he was dead. But not now. He is alive and collaborating with the army. He is also a member of an agricultural cooperative, Talixjoy of San Luis. But although poor Pedro no longer has problems with the right, he has problems with the left because he is now persecuted by the guerrillas for collaborating with the army.

Why did they kill the priest?

They say that he had communication with the guerrillas, but more than anything else it was a lie. The priest helped the poor people a lot. He helped families who needed help the most. He constructed a house and paid many women and men to take care of the children; he planted a lot of vegetables because he was not able to buy a lot of meat for all the children who did not have food. He cultivated vegetables and all, and he looked for cooks to prepare all of these things. He did not buy the things that he needed for the children. This was all that he did. He did nothing bad. In reality this man they killed had no sentiment [to the left]. They killed him in total error. He was a priest, a priest! This was not a lie because in San Luis his work was miraculous.[27]

Did Señor Gerardo have connections with the Communists?

They say it was not Gerardo they were looking for. It was Pedro.

Then Gerardo was killed by accident.

Yes, this is clear because they did not want Gerardo at all; he did not have any connections. When they killed him, he had just become the new director.

The right thought that he was Pedro.

Yes, without doubt! They thought he was Pedro, but he was not Pedro. It was Gerardo, because Pedro had left slyly.

Perhaps they were enemies of Pedro, who knows?

Who knows? Now he has changed: he is a collaborator. Much earlier he was persecuted and [about] to lose his life. Now he has to accuse others. I think this is bad.

At one time he talked to you in your house.

Yes, he came to see me, but in reality we did not do anything communistic, nothing. We just asked how to organize a cooperative.

But he is not a good friend.

One could say that, one could say that. In this situation with Caritas and all, I told the army.

The army?

Yes, they know it all because I do not want to be accused of things. Later I could be punished or my family could suffer. Better, I told Domingo to please tell the army all that we had done in San José because I do not want to suffer the consequences. So the army realizes how things were earlier in San José.

Then the army knows that he was in San José earlier concerning the cooperative and that nothing else happened.

Just this, one time, two times, just to tell us how to begin a cooperative.

Then Domingo explained to the army.

Yes, because he has the office of promoter of Caritas for groups who have loans. Then I told Domingo, "Please tell the army that you came here to talk to us about a loan, that we do not have communistic relations. No, no, because we do not know anything about that. We work and we owe, but we do not owe a Communist. We are indebted to Caritas, and we have used this money for planting, but please take this news." And Domingo went there to clarify all that had happened in San José. And the army was thankful because if they had discovered these earlier actions in San José, there could have been problems for us.

❧ We Fear Owls Arriving Are an Omen of Death
FRIDAY, 31 JULY 1981

We are still in a bad situation with three sick children. I did not sleep the whole night. Our son Erasmo Ignacio is the gravest. He is at the point of dying. At 2:00 A.M. two owls arrived and made noise above the house. We thought the child was going to die [because when an owl arrives there is usually a death]. I thought hard about taking him to a hospital or some doctor in Sololá, but I could not because we could not get the money. I wanted to sell a *cuerda* of land, but there was no one to buy it. I put my faith only in God. I told my wife that if he dies we will just have to bear it and that we must have patience because we cannot do anything else.

We did not have anything, but we thought about tomorrow's market in Santa Ana. Then we went to pull up a *tablón* of onions. We cleaned and prepared them, not finishing until 10:00 P.M.

❧ Carrying a Load of Onions to Santa Ana
1–2 AUGUST 1981

At 5:00 A.M. I left the house with María with a backload of onions. She also carried onions for the market. We arrived there at 8:00 A.M. and asked for breakfast on credit to be paid when we sold the onions. We sold them at a regular price and earned $15.

Then we went to visit the church. Later we bought fruit for the sick ones. On this day I suffered a great deal. It had been nearly 12 years since I climbed the mountainous path up with a load on my back. But I had to do it again.

On Sunday, 2 August, I went to church, and then we went for the treatment of the children. At the same time, we paid the debt for the medicine. Still we bought two small flasks of reconstituents.

We are suffering a lot. Everything is consumed—corn, beans, and money. We are scarcely eating. But God willing, I am awaiting an answer from my great friend James D. Sexton.

❧ Erasmo Ignacio Loses His Teeth and Almost His Life
8–11 AUGUST 1981

My son Erasmo Ignacio spent the whole night crying. He could not lie down. We had to seat him on the bed because lying down caused him to cry a lot. What complicated matters even more is that he is sick to his stomach, his muscles ache, and his eyes hurt. My wife told me to go outside and call a *brujo*, but I do not have money for a witch either.

We have been suffering these things since June. It is true that I sold the onions and earned about $300, but I have spent all of this money because times are hard and very expensive. We had to leave the sick ones because we have much necessity to go to look for firewood.

At 1:00 P.M. María brought me a registered envelope containing a check for $100 sent by my great North American friend James D. Sexton. My wife and I felt the glory of God to whom we had prayed. For us it was much consolation. It is true that my wife's father has a little money, but he does not help. He wants it more for himself.

On Sunday, 9 August, I went to the church to give thanks to God for all the help I had received. At 10:00 A.M. we went to Popoya to pick *guisquiles*. When we arrived home, my wife cooked this for lunch. For dinner we ate tortillas with greens of *chipilín*. The sick ones continued the same although we are buying little things for them and not giving them greens [to eat]. We are very tired of so much illness.

On 10 August we had the same problems. I went to work in Xesucut for another person, but my own fields need attention. My wife went to clean onions for us. We ate lunch together. We are working very hard. I do not know if someday we will be able to rest.

I am thinking about going to Sololá or Panajachel tomorrow to cash the check, but I do not have money for travel. All night until dawn I slept only one hour. For the child, it is always the same gravity. I want to take him to Sololá to the doctor, but I do not have money. It is true that I have the check, but I have not cashed it.

At 4:00 A.M. I went to Agustín María's house to ask for $2 for the passage. This friend did not deny me. With these dollars, I went to catch the launch for Panajachel. From Doña Rosa I bought two glasses of coffee and 10 centavos' worth of bread. I waited until 9:00 A.M., and thanks to God, nothing unusual happened. Then I climbed the mountain to Sololá to certify 21 pages for Dr. Sexton in the mail. Then I went to the pharmacy to buy medicine, which cost me a total of $17.

When I arrived home, we began to give Erasmo Ignacio the medicine. In a few days the medic, Miguel Rojas, pulled two of his teeth, and all of his skin peeled off. It was difficult to look at this child because his skin was peeling.

Why did the medic pull his teeth? Were they infected?

No, they were good, permanent teeth that were not infected. The poor boy complained that his ears, his eyes, and especially his teeth hurt. He begged to have his teeth pulled, and we decided it was better to do so. But the medic did not have the proper equipment to do so. There was much blood, and the child nearly died of pain. He was already sick. When I later told the pharmacist that we pulled his teeth, he scolded me well, saying that I was crazy to pull the teeth of someone who was sick. It could kill him for sure! He really criticized me for doing this. But we looked for a doctor, and we could not find one. We had no one to advise us. We did it out of ignorance. I think now that it was probably his nerves that were hurting his teeth the most.

Didn't the medic know better?

Sometimes they do not know better, and sometimes they are more concerned with making a few dollars than with whether a child will die. Since they were permanent teeth, he has a gap in his mouth. I promised him that later we will buy him some more [false] molars. I have much respect for this child even now, because he has surely suffered with his illness. I have told you enough of our problems with him. There was actually more, however. For instance, we had to bathe him with leaves of grass.

What kind of leaves did you use?

Leaves of metaplo, jiote stick, avocado leaves, and white honey. We cooked all of these together and then bathed him with the leaves so that his skin would grow back. We did this once a day.

When the medic pulled his teeth, did he give him something for the pain?

Yes, he injected him in the mouth with anesthesia, but it did not help much.

❧ They Ask Me to Be Head of a Brotherhood on My Birthday
13 AUGUST 1981

This is my birthday. I gave thanks to God the Supreme [Being] for having given me my fortieth year. Because of lack of funds, we did not celebrate.

In the afternoon of this day the head of the *cofradía* of María de Concepción arrived to tell me that they are going to elect me head of the *cofradía*. I told him that I had to talk it over with my wife.

❧ Señora María Luisa Is Murdered
18–19 AUGUST 1981

This episode is combination of what Ignacio wrote and I taped.

In the afternoon they summoned me to the parochial assembly hall to find out whether to name me head of the brotherhood María de Concepción. Since I had talked to my wife, I told the directors of Catholic Action that I would accept.

At 7:00 P.M. they called me for a training session in the cooperative on behalf of the technicians of INACOP (Instituto Nacional de Cooperativas). We were very pleased. We stayed in the cooperative arranging one thing or another, and the time went by. We took a girl who is on the board of the cooperative to her house to prepare us a little coffee because we were hungry and thirsty. Then another man went with the woman to bring the coffee, and at 11:00 P.M. we ate two pieces of bread each with coffee. We paid about 25 centavos each— five for each piece of bread and more for two small glasses of coffee. We waited until about 11:30 P.M.

I said, "Let's hurry up and go because it is late. Soldiers or guerrillas could come. We are late! Let's go, let's go!" And each person left for his house. Then I accompanied the treasurer through the center of the town to his house for safety, because he was carrying money that belonged to the cooperative. After seeing my companion home, I went directly to my house.

When I arrived home, my family was already asleep. It was certain that the two pieces of bread had not satisfied my hunger, but since it was the middle of the night, my family had already eaten. Then I noticed that my señora had left me some tamalitos, good and hot and folded in three napkins. She had also left fish. I said, "Ah, I'm still going to eat." I went to the fire where there was hot coffee, and I began to eat.

Suddenly someone knocked three times. "*Púchica!*" it scared me. I quit eating and remained still. About two minutes later, thinking they had left, I began to eat again.

Again there were three knocks on my door, and a strange voice said, "Ignacio."

"But who is this?" I said to myself. "Who is saying my name? Who can it be? *Púchica*, should I try to eat again?" Man, it was a scare they gave me! "Are they going to tear down my door? Who knows? Is it some bully?" But nothing happened.

After about two minutes I opened the door, and since there is a streetlight near, I could see that there was no one there, neither above nor below the street. There was just total silence. Then I shut the door and continued eating. Since I was frightened while I was eating, I had to rest a little before going to sleep to avoid indigestion. I grabbed a book and began to read a little. After about 15 to 20 minutes of reading the book, I fell fast asleep because it was late and I was very sleepy. It must have been about 12:00 midnight or 12:15 when I fell asleep.

What ended my sleep was the bang of arms. I heard the noise of the machine gun—ta, ta, ta, ta, ta, ta, ta, ta, ta.

"*Púchica*! My God! What is happening!" I said as I was waking up. "Get up, hombre! Hombre, get up! Something is happening in the town!" But no one answered me, neither my children nor my señora. They were fast asleep. Then I heard a very loud shot, "Bong!" It was the *tiro de gracia* [finishing shot].

"Ah, Christ, someone died. Is it the army or the guerrillas? Which of the two groups? My God!" I said. The most I slept was about 20 minutes or a half hour. It is true that I did not have a watch, but I turned on the radio and they gave the hour, which was 12:45 A.M. I turned out the light and thought about many things. They could arrive at my house, and they could find us culpable if they saw my light on because we were late at the cooperative. I knelt before the image of Jesucristo and put myself in the hands of God for anything that might happen. I stayed in bed, but I did not sleep.

Ten minutes after the burst of machine gun fire, a launch left for San Martín making a lot of noise, but we did not hear or realize when it had come. But the launch belongs to the father-in-law of the military commissioner in San Martín because it is the only one with such a [distinctive] sound.

About a half hour later I heard people passing to wake Castillo, a brother of the woman [who was shot]. I thought that perhaps there might have been an illness. I did not know that they had killed her.

Then I put on my clothes. "I am going to investigate," I said to myself. But later I said that I did not want problems. And someone might be able to say that we were late in the cooperative. So I decided not to go out. I stayed in my house, although I did not sleep at all.

At 4:30 A.M. we heard the death knell [of the Catholic Church]. "*Púchica*, someone died," said my señora.

"Yes, I wanted to tell you, but you did not get up." The bells continued—bong, bong. And the president of Catholic Action began to say with a loudspeaker, "All Catholics, come console the husband of the señora who last night was killed by whichever group, whose body today is going to Sololá."

Well, then I put on my clothing and got up. But I did not go to console the husband. I went to the pier. When I arrived to investigate, I saw the blood and all. There were a lot of bullet holes—they were countless, perhaps a hundred. The authorities were resting at a house that was on the other side of the road, and they were still examining the projectiles. It was grave, it was grave. Her two legs were destroyed. I did not see it happen, but the official news says that she was shot 17 times. They say that there were two groups. One waited in front of the door in the street while the other entered from inside the *sitio*. When she ran into the street, they machine-gunned her. There were still bloodstains in the street where she fell. They also say that the men who came to kill her brought a guide dressed in the clothing of San Luis with typical trousers, no shoes, and a black *chupa* [tight-fitting waistcoat], purely of San Luis. But it is suspected that he was a *Joseño*, a commissioner.

At 5:00 A.M. they took the cadaver to Sololá in an express launch for a forensic autopsy. They brought her remains back on the same launch. A lot of people, including all the organizations of the church, were waiting, which is the usual respect they give when there is a death. From the launch her body went to her house, where it stayed for a half hour.

I also went to the burial. We took her body from her house to the church for the religious acts. The president of Catholic Action, Jorge Sicay, who had organized the funeral and who spoke on the microphone, was accused of being negligent by his enemies because the father of the deceased was able to grab the microphone and say:

> Thanks to all of you who are accompanying me during this pain that is so great and unbearable. Also, I am grateful to the army of Guatemala. Also, I am grateful to the *policía judicial*; I am grateful to the military commissioners; I am grateful to the persons who have accused my daughter of guerrilla activities. I do not have reason to bother any of those whom I mentioned. God has his justice for them. There is a saying, "*El que a espada mata a espada muere* [or *Quines matan con la espada por la espada morirán*; He who kills (lives) by the sword will die by the

sword]." Now that the funeral acts are completed, let us go to
the cemetery.

We all went to the cemetery to leave the remains of María Luisa.
But there were not many visitors in the house because they say that
the whole family is under surveillance by the right. Well, they say that
María Luisa was receiving communistic doctrines because she participated a lot with Pedro Tzal and Domingo Portillo, the directors of the
radio station La Voz de San Luis. They say that when they gave clandestine courses against the army with a doctrine on how to end pater-
nalism and imperialism, María Luisa was a valuable person. Later she
tried to sow this doctrine from those in San Luis in San José. Gradually she convinced two girls in her house, but for sure I did not see
her act as a guerrilla. More than anything else she, a sister, and a
cousin passed out bulletins stating that the government of Lucas was
not worth anything. Also, they say that, when they celebrated the
anniversary of the fall of Somoza in Nicaragua, she participated in fiestas in Quiriguá and Puerto Barrios. It is not known for sure that Luisa
did participate. What is known is that she took with her a woman by
the name of Berta Guerra, who later, thinking it was safe, told others
that they were paid $5 a day for lodging and given free food and drink.
But it happens that Berta's brother in San José is a military
commissioner.

This is what was discovered about María Luisa. María also said
that she was going again with Berta on 25 August for a meeting in
Antigua, Guatemala. But before she could go, they killed her.

The *Joseños* say that she was accused by the military commissioners because Berta's brother is a military commissioner. Well, it is
true that in her life María Luisa was always a woman without respect.
I am not God to judge because only God is God and has the most
marvelous knowledge. But it seems that María Luisa asked for what
they gave her. She was against the Catholics and her religion. She
spoke badly about the catechists and mistreated the images. She also
spoke badly about the *cofradías*, and she said that the Protestant religion was not worth anything. Also, she said that the cooperative and
the commissioners and the authorities were not worth anything. She
was like an anarchist or worse because I suppose an anarchist respects
something, but she respected nothing, not even her marriage. In 1972
she abandoned her husband, children, and parents and went away
with Juanito Mendoza. Perhaps we have talked a little about her in
the first book. After working in the Comedor Ramírez in Panajachel,
she went back to San José to live with her husband, a weak man, who

took her back. But she was an indomitable woman who did not respect her husband, and she went to work in San Luis on programs for the radio. She had many husbands and was responsible for breaking up many marriages. Because of her attitude, the townspeople believed that she was indeed a Communist.

It seems to me that the people of San José did not feel sad [about her death] because when she was alive she did not get along with anyone and she acted as if she were superior to all the other women in the town. For that reason, they did not feel that she was what is called an "unfortunate one." Thus, all of this was bound to happen. I am going to repeat the proverb that says, " *El que mal hace mal espera* [He who evil makes, evil awaits]." This is true.

At the cemetery her father said these words:

> María Luisa, this afternoon we came to leave you in this sacred place with a lot of suffering and sadness for your mother and me. But your disobedience was too much. You would never take the advice that your mother and I gave you. Many times we implored that you not go to San Luis and other places, but you answered us that you were 18 and that we did not have anything to do with your life.

As he spoke these words, Bartolomé Coché and Rosario Méndez had many tears in their eyes.

Some in the Catholic Church were critical of what María's father said. The priest went around saying that he did not want to celebrate mass in the church anymore, that he was going to close the church, that he was the superior authority, and that Catholics needing mass would have to go to San Martín. The father [of the church] was afraid he might die because the father of the woman they killed on 19 August had said on the microphone that elements of the government had killed his daughter. Without doubt some of the six persons already mentioned [who were enemies of the president of the church] went to visit the priest to tell the latter that the president had conceded the microphone to the father of the deceased. Thus, the president of the church, Jorge Sicay T., was removed from office.

When they killed María Luisa, the men entered her house and searched it. They carried away what they found—land deeds, $3.60, and documents concerning her participation in short courses on the radio, and a radio-phonograph valued at $150. They told her husband not to worry, that they wanted her, not him. A little later the other women mentioned above—Berta and Estela—were persecuted, which I am going to describe later.[28]

❧ The Results of Slander: A Kidnapping
25 AUGUST 1981

Humberto Rafael Bizarro Quic, son of Benjamín Bizarro Temó, studied at the institute of Santa Elena. The government gave him a scholarship and room and board. This boy is very intelligent, but in the end he lost out. When he was finishing his last year of study to graduate as a teacher, he had an accident. He had sexual relations with a student of the same school. Her name is Susana Lidia López C., a *Joseña* whose father is Cornelio Humberto López. When the teachers realized that Susana Lidia was pregnant, they took her to a doctor. He verified that she had had intercourse with Humberto Rafael. The teachers called the father of the boy and the father of the girl, who questioned their children. To prevent a suit by the father of the girl, both parents agreed that the boy and girl would get married. But since Humberto Rafael did not know how to work in the fields, it was a great problem for him to have a woman [to support], and still the baby had not been born.

Humberto abandoned his woman. He wanted to look for work, but it was impossible because he did not have papers that identified him as some official. He went to the farms to work as a *mozo*. Better said, he hid from his wife.

Then the father of the girl accused his son-in-law before the military commissioners of being an active guerrilla, and the military commissioners denounced these things.

Humberto Rafael came back when his child was born. He entered the name of Beltrán Benjamín Bizarro in the registry for his son, but he was unaware that he had been declared a guerrilla by his father-in-law.

Then Humberto obtained work in San Luis with his cousin in the tienda Foto Maya. He had just worked a little when he was kidnapped in the street on 25 August. I heard the news because he is my kin. Humberto Rafael's father came to my house to tell me that his son had been lost. I did not want to say anything because I knew very well that Humberto had been denounced by his own father-in-law, because on 26 June Cornelio Humberto López had told me that he had denounced his son-in-law as a guerrilla. Since it was unimportant to me, I had kept it to myself.

Humberto lives. He did not die. But the interrogations were very hard on him. He received many wounds, and he came out almost an invalid. In December of 1981 Humberto Rafael passed through San José in close custody of the army. They had him tied with ropes around the waist—one in front and one in back as if he were a dangerous animal. [There was a person at the front of him with a rope and one in the back, and he was lassoed like a horse.] They presented him in this manner in front of all the other *Joseños*.

They say that one of the residents ran to tell his father, but Don Benjamín was out cutting firewood. When Benjamín arrived, he wanted to see his son, but the soldiers had already disappeared. Benjamín continued on the road. They say that he asked some workers who told him that the soldiers had just passed a few moments earlier. Don Benjamín told me that he found them in the jurisdiction of San Martín on the road for San Luis, about six kilometers from San José. Benjamín asked permission to be able to speak with his son, and they gave him 15 minutes.

When he found his son, he was in an avocado grove. They both wept. Don Benjamín took off his shoes and gave them to his son because it was a pity that his son was walking barefoot and that he was tied like an angry bull.

The soldiers told Benjamín that they did not know anything about whether Humberto Rafael had been abducted. The only thing they knew was that they had found him almost dead on a mountain and had helped him. Then Benjamín asked, "And why have you tied him up if you are helping him?" Then the *jefe* told him to leave or perhaps he would end up like his son.

I was told this information from the mouth of my uncle. No one knows for sure the whereabouts of Humberto Rafael. What is more strange is that he sends letters to his father without a return address. Perhaps he is oppressed. [His father thinks he may now be deranged.]

❧ An Abduction
2 OCTOBER 1981

I returned from the coast with a *cuadrilla*. In Tiquisate we contracted a bus. The driver wanted to let us off in San Luis, but I asked him to take us to San José. He did not want to because of word that there are guerrillas on the slopes. We had to conform and slept on the porch of the municipality. Some of the boys drank their *tragos*, but the commissary told us to be very careful because a lot of abductions are taking place. I did not want to delay going home, but I could not help it.

On the following day, Saturday, 3 October, we arrived home. My wife was very worried because she thought something had happened to us on the road.

Then she began to tell me everything that had happened last night. She said that a number of men had arrived heavily armed in a pickup. My wife saw these men. She told me that she left the house about 8:00 P.M. with her two babies to visit one of her sisters. There they gave her coffee, and she stayed about 30 minutes. Then she left for home with her two babies and passed near the house of Estela Temó Mérida, where the men were ready to act. But my wife did not know anything. She told them, "Buenas noches." Their answer was for her to disappear if she did not want to suffer the consequences, because they were about to make a kidnapping. My wife told me that it scared her when they spoke of a kidnapping.

About an hour later they sounded the bells advising the townsfolk that two women had been kidnapped—Estela Ramos Mérida and Estela Say Temó.

Who were the kidnappers?

They were wearing leather motorcycle jackets. They were the military, but since they were not in uniform they would be called unknowns.

The kidnappers were confused. They kidnapped a woman who had a family and another woman who was very young who are neighbors and kin to Estela Temó Mérida. Without doubt they were taken to the mountains and interrogated. When the kidnappers realized that they had the wrong women to persecute, three hours later in the same night they released them.

All of this created a grave problem for Estela Ramos Mérida, because her husband, Diego Tecún, along with the rest of the town, thought that she had been raped. But the two women said that they had not been violated. Who knows, perhaps they were not. More than anything else at issue was the shame, but their families were more relieved that they had been released unharmed. The problem was with Estela Ramos's husband. He thought she had been raped by all the soldiers, and because of the shame he wanted to separate from her. But this was a bit crazy because it was not the woman's fault. She did not go around looking for the savages who kidnapped her.

The news surfaced that those who were sentenced for kidnapping were the two women who were connected closely to the radio station La Voz de San Luis and who had been companions to María Luisa. Without doubt when they murdered this woman, they took her papers, and on these papers appeared the names of Estela Temó Mérida and Berta Guerra. The former was hidden in the house of José

Carlos, who is *jefe* of the military commissioners. The commissioners themselves were bungling things. When the military was looking for these women, the main military commissioner had them hidden in his house, which the soldiers did not search, because Estela's father gave him money. [If the soldiers had found the two women that night, they would have shot them.]

On Thursday, 6 October, José Carlos, the military commissioner, took these two women to San Luis to tell the soldiers that these were the two women for whom they were looking. But it was daylight, and they had protection. In the military detachment, José Carlos interrogated the women, and they confessed that they had received courses on how to operate as guerrillas, but they said the guilty one was Pedro Tzal, who was their *jefe*. These two women also declared that others of San Luis and three boys of San José were involved. The following day these three men were taken to San Luis, where they stayed for 22 days.

What happened to them?

They agreed to collaborate with the army and returned to San José.

The army gave the women employment as cooks to give them better protection for having revealed all of the things about the left—its organization and its members. Also they discovered the book that is called *Pensemos Juntos* [Let Us Plan Together].

❧ Son of Tecún Umán Arrives and a Golden Dream Revealed
SATURDAY, 17 OCTOBER 1981

When I arrived home at 1:00 A.M. from a trip to the coast with a *cuadrilla*, my family was waiting for me. They offered me coffee and something to eat, but I responded that I was not hungry. When I asked why everyone, including the youngsters, was still awake, María very happily brought me a large envelope that had come in the mail from the United States. I opened it and saw two beautiful books [one paperback and one clothbound] entitled *Son of Tecún Umán*. It was a very happy occasion for us.

I almost doubted the book would become a reality. In his letters Dr. Sexton had told me that we would have to have patience. After the first three years, I thought the pages were useless. It is true that we had worked almost 10 years. At times I was tired and did not want to continue, but I would think about our oath to make the book a reality. Finally the day arrived when it was real, and when we actually saw it, my family and I were delighted.

Without the help of Señor Sexton, I would not have been able to do anything. With his financial help, I have been able to work on my pages. I must say that at times I did not have the will to continue writing because of work in the fields and on other jobs. But the checks that I received encouraged me, and I continued until I saw a happy result. This night for me was a wonderful surprise. Because I was so content, I did not sleep the rest of the night. Although I understand the dates and the meaning of each thing [subheading], it is a pity that neither I nor my family reads English.

It was 5:00 A.M. before we realized it, and my wife prepared breakfast. We bought some pounds of meat to celebrate this honored day because it was the most success I have had in my entire life. I began to think about a dream that I had six years ago that my wife, children, and I have taken as spiritual guidance.

This dream I did not write in my diary because we considered it a dream of gold. On a Thursday in January of 1976, at 2:00 A.M., I dreamed that three young North American señoras appeared who had blond hair and red skin. They began to talk to me, but, "Pity," I said to myself, "I do not understand English." They continued to speak in English, but I did not understand. Then they approached me. They were well-dressed, clean, and neat. I have seen women who look like hippies; but, no, these three women were pleasant, neat, and they had sparkling blond or red hair. They were saying a lot of things that I did not understand when a man appeared in North American dress who spoke good Spanish. Then I asked him, "Señor, please, these women are speaking to me, but I don't know what they are saying."

Then the man began to speak with the three women. What the women said to him he told to me. "They are greeting you and wish to praise you very much. They have a book for you, but do not pick it up until they leave."

The book [looked like] a magazine [with a soft cover], and it was in English. "Is it for me?" I asked. "But I do not know them—not one of these women do I know!"

Then the man turned and said, "You do not know them, but they know you."

Then the women began to talk to the man again in English, and the man began to talk to me again. He said that it was not yet time to open the book and that I should do so later but that it indeed was a gift for me.

"Very well," I told him. Then in my dream I called my wife. I remember clearly that I said, "Anica, come here. There are three women who have come to greet us and bring us a gift."

"Very well," my wife said, coming out of the house. My señora is not able to speak Spanish. What the man said to me in Spanish I said to my wife in *lengua*.

"Ah," she told me, "very well, they bring you a magazine for later. Have patience. And why don't you tell them to come inside and sit down? Why are you outside when you could be sociable with them? They are grand persons, so tell them to come in and sit down."

Then I turned to the man who speaks Spanish, "Please tell the three women to come in and sit down a little while. Excuse my not having received them well; my wife invites you in."

"Oh, now that it is 4:00 P.M. we can't come in," said the man. "We four are together, and we must leave immediately. Another day we will come to visit you inside your house. We just are bringing you this gift." Then the three women gave the man a very pretty gift [wrapped] in turquoise cellophane paper, and he gave it to me.

"Many thanks, Señor," I said. "Do you know what it is?"

"I know," he said, "but I will not tell you. I will just say that it is for you, but do not open it yet; not until we leave."

"Very well," I said, "with much pleasure. Tell the women to forgive me. It is not that I do not want to speak English. Tell them that I respect them very much and that I wish them well. Pity they do not want to come inside."

"Do not worry," he said, "we will come back to visit you."

I did not have the new house built yet, and these three women left happy and smiling through the *sitio*. Then in my dream I told my señora, "Let's open this thing, because they have left. What do we have here?"

"Very well," my wife said. We put it on a small, very old table that belonged to my grandparents. We began to take off the cellophane paper and look at the book. We wanted to read it, but it was not in Spanish. Then my dream ended. I woke up my wife and told her what I had dreamed about the three women who were very pretty and neat.

"Pray to God! Pray to God! It signifies something for you," she told me. "Pray! It means that you will have good fortune, something advantageous and worthwhile." Thus was the dream.

Also I dreamed that the person who served as the interpreter was my great friend James D. Sexton. He appeared as a blurred image like a negative of a photograph, but it was clearly Jaime D. Sexton.

When the dream ended, I told my señora, "I am not going to write this down in my diary because it is going to serve us. For me it is a dream of gold. It is a dream that is very significant." And each time I receive a check, we remember the dream. Each time I receive information about the book, I say to my wife, "Do you remember the dream of some years ago?"

"Yes," she says, "how beautiful!" And when I saw the two books that arrived while I was on the coast, I said, "Do you remember the dream?"

"Well, yes," she told me, "it became a reality."

This dream we will never forget. I will remember it until I die because it is like good luck—like a very beautiful power. And my youngsters know this, but no one else. It is like a family *secreto*.

Then the dream has significance for the book.

It had significance much earlier, but I did not mention it in the first book. [In the dream] they showed me that I would later have a book but that I would have to be patient. Also, I saw that it was a bound book. The dream that I had six years ago encouraged me, especially when you told me in your correspondence about the [quality] of the pages. Then I remembered the dream and felt the effort was worth it. Although discouraged by illness or much work, I would begin again. The dream is like a person who obliges me to work. And this unforgettable dream turned out to be true. Only when I die will I forget it.

There are some dreams so sacred and important that one cannot forget them. Although I dream things that do not come true, sometimes they do. And the ones that do may be variable [both positive and negative].

I also dreamed of Ignacito about 20 days before he fell sick. We were bathing in water that gradually turned [dirty] like charcoal. We continued bathing our bodies, but now the water was unclean. I told Ignacito that it was bothersome and that it would be difficult to get rid of the dirt. I grabbed a towel to wipe off all the mud that clung to our bodies, but it was difficult.

What was the meaning of this dream?

It was a negative dream that came true. Ignacito went with me to rent the Mexican suits and then became gravely ill and nearly died, as I have said in my diary.

❧Customs of the Virgin Mary
18 OCTOBER–8 DECEMBER 1981

Already I have said that I have been selected to receive the image of the Inmaculada María Concepción in my house. Since not many people are chosen for this office [of *alcalde*], my wife and I gave thanks to God. [We did everything according to custom.]

Thus, those of us elected to the offices of *alcalde* [head]; *juez* [vice-head]; *mayordomo* [steward, or rank-and-file member of the brotherhood]; and *texeles* [low-ranking female members] get together to discuss how we are going to prepare the house [for receiving the image]. A day before the meeting, the *alcalde* makes a list of the members and their wives to advise them of the meeting in his house.

Then the wife of the *alcalde* has to to prepare corn for the *atol*, which is not obligatory but which is the custom. During the night of the same day, the wife of the *alcalde* has to prepare the *masa* with her helpers, who are devotees of the *cofradía* for one year. Now there is a mill, but in the past the women spent the whole night grinding the corn with grinding stones [metates and manos]. It is still customary to grind at least some of the corn by hand, and it is customary to do it on the day of the fiesta of San Diego, which is 18 October.

Thus, according to custom, [after they prepared the *masa* during the night,] my wife and her helper cooked the *atol*, and by 4:00 A.M. it was ready. Then they began to make the tortillas for a breakfast of meat.

At 4:30 A.M. the *juez* arrives accompanied by the *mayordomos*. He presents himself and his *mayordomos* from the first *mayordomo* to the sixth and last. Also, they all sit down in this order. The *alcalde* sits in another chair and instructs them in soft words to obey his orders and to always be ready for a burial when someone dies in the town and to respect and venerate the image of María. Then the *juez* repeats his recommendations.

This meeting is like a personal inspection. When it is over, the first *mayordomo* leads the others to the kitchen, where the women give them two large *jícaras* [ritual, gourd jars] each. Then they present themselves again to the *alcalde*, who orders them to take the *atol* to the houses of the members of the brotherhood in the following manner: the first *mayordomo* goes to the house of the *juez*; the second *mayordomo* goes to the house of the first *mayordomo*; the third *mayordomo* goes to the house of the second *mayordomo*; and so on. When the first *mayordomo* returns to the house of the *alcalde*, he leaves again to take *atol* to the house of the sixth *mayordomo*. The wives of the members receive the *atol* and send their thanks to the future *alcalde*. Also, the *mayordomos* take two large jars to the *texeles*. If these unmarried girls do not want the office, they reject the *jícaras*. [The job of the *texeles* is to carry large candles in the processions and to throw out flowers. They also carry water to soften the dirt for the male members of the *cofradía* who dig the graves.]

The *mayordomos* carry the *atol* to the wives of the members of the brotherhood to familiarize themselves with their houses and to get acquainted with their families. Meanwhile, the *alcalde* and *juez* remain in the house discussing and arranging matters of the *cofradía* until 6:00 or 7:00 A.M. [when the *mayordomos* return]. Then the *alcalde* orders the *juez* to call the *mayordomos* to the kitchen, where they receive tamalitos and bowls of broth. Then everyone eats breakfast.

Afterwards they leave and do not come back until 7 November, when it is time to whitewash and paint the house [of the *alcalde* in preparation for receiving the image of María]. I felt ashamed that the house to be used for the image did not have a loft [ceiling]. Thus, I bought planks and put one up.

On 7 November my wife got up and made breakfast. At 7:00 A.M. the *juez* arrived at the head of the six *mayordomos*. After breakfast they began to wash the walls. The house is stuccoed, and I thought they were just going to apply lime [whitewash it]. But the *juez* ordered the first *mayordomo* to bring two gallons of paint, and they began to paint it.

They had not finished by noon. My wife gave them lunch, and afterwards they continued working. Not until 7:00 P.M. did they finish.

The reason for adorning the house was to make it suitable for service to the *cofradía*. The *juez* is in charge of paying for the cost of the materials, and the *alcalde* is responsible for buying food and other things.

On Sunday, 25 November, we arranged the altar where they are going to place the image. All day long we worked. Finally, everything was ready, and we just had to wait for the fiesta. I wanted to receive the *cofradía* with much reverence on 8 December. But it turned out not to be. On Saturday, 5 December, I worked very hard and became very tired. In the afternoon I bathed, and it made me very sick. In the night I had a fever.

When day broke, I was very ill. I was unable to get up or eat. My wife made the preparations for receiving the *cofradía*.

On 7 December the old *cofradía* finished [their year's service], and they carried the image [of María] to the church. Already the new *cofrades* were participating. Because I was sick, the *juez* went in my place with the *mayordomos*.

On this day the medic, Daniel Bizarro, took my temperature and told me that it was 42 degrees and 6 tenths [degrees centigrade, or 108.7 degrees Fahrenheit, which was probably incorrect since such a high temperature most likely would have damaged his brain]. Thus 8 December passed, which is the main day of the Virgen de Concepción. According to tradition, the *juez* and the *mayordomos* arrived at 5:00 A.M. At 6:00 A.M. they ate bread and drank coffee. Then all of them went to the kitchen, where they received little baskets of tamalitos and pots of meat in broth. They presented themselves [in the same order to my father-in-law, who was substituting for me as *alcalde*]. He ordered them to give the baskets of food to the wives of the members of the *cofradía* in the same manner as they had distributed the *atol* earlier, but in a different order [to get to know the houses and families better]. When this was done, they went to the church to receive the insignias [two staffs, one for the *alcalde* and one for the *juez*] and the oath of office. The old officers left, and the new ones remained.

In the afternoon on this same day about 2:00 P.M. they take out the [image of the] Virgen from the church and carry it to the new *cofradía* accompanied by various religious groups. When the image is near, the wife of the *alcalde* goes out with incense to receive it in her house. When everyone is inside, the *principales* [elders], members of the *cofradía*, and the invited guests receive *atol*. But before drinking it, the *alcalde* gives reverence with soft words appreciating the arrival of the image and thanking those participating. He kisses the hand of the first *principal* and drinks *atol*. The *mayordomos* pass out *atol* in small *jícaras* to everyone inside and outside the house. When this is done, the *alcalde* says good-bye to the first *principal*, and everyone but the old *cofrades* leaves. The old *cofrades* wait for the hour of bringing the ornaments and other things of the Virgen [chest with clothes, silver crown, and silver plate for offerings]. About 7:00 P.M. they [go and] take out the chest of the old *cofradía* accompanied by the [traditional] *tun* [drum] and *chirimía* [flute]. The last *mayordomo* is the one who has to carry the cargo. The wife of the outgoing *alcalde* signals the departure by making a revolution inside the house and yard with incense of the old *cofradía*. Then, while burning incense, she leads the procession through the street toward the house of the new *cofradía*. When the procession is near, the wife of the new *alcalde* goes to meet the chest while burning incense. She walks about a *cuadra* to her house. When they arrive, she also makes a revolution inside the house from left to right while burning incense as a sign of welcome. They make another turn inside the house with the chest while burning incense. Then they set the chest on new palm mats. Then they arrange the clothes of the image and hand them over. The first *mayordomo* is in charge of delivering and receiving the chest. If everything is in order, they begin to drink their traditional drinks. About two hours later, the past *cofrades* leave, sad and crying. They say good-bye and go home without further obligation. Then the new *alcalde* takes up his duties.

Las Posadas
10–25 DECEMBER 1981

On 10 December I already felt a little better. Then I went to be with the *juez* and *mayordomos* in the *cofradía*. I had to do whatever was possible. My wife prepared breakfast. As is customary, to show respect the *juez* sent for a dozen beers. For respect and for the custom, I had to drink a beer. But I just ate a *tamalito* because I still felt sick and had no appetite. After breakfast my companions went home.

Little by little I was recovering my health from December 14 to 15, when we were preparing to begin Las Posadas. The *cofrades* carry small images of the Virgen and San José that we get from the *alcalde* of the *cofradía* of San José. We take these to various houses for nine days asking for lodging. On the last day the house that accepts them is the house of the *alcalde*, which has the big image of the Virgen. Then on 24 December we take the Virgen to the church for the birth of Jesús. This signifies that, according to the Bible, María and San José could not find an inn [in Bethlehem, Judea].

In this custom there are two groups. One goes to the house where they are going to put María and José and shuts the door without a light. Meanwhile the other group goes to accompany María and San José until they arrive at the homesite. In song they begin to ask for lodging, but the group inside in song refuse it. Finally they convince the group inside the house to open the door, and the group outside carries in the images. This is done for nine days [beginning on 16 December] until 24 December.

> *When I asked Ignacio for the words to the song, he wrote them out and sang them in a remarkably good voice on tape.*

When San José and María arrive at a homesite, the group outside sings the following:

Here at your door, after a hard journey, we beg shelter for the love of God.

The group inside answers:

Here there is no inn. On your way, pilgrims from strange roads. Who knows who you are?

The group outside says:

We are pilgrims in all the houses, shelter we ask, you look at us like strangers.

The group inside answers:

Say who you are. Perhaps you are friends.

The group outside:

They are José and María, who come very tired from Nazareth.

Group inside receiving them:

Come in with us, pilgrims. Peace and happiness be with you tonight.

On 24 December they carry María and San José to their *cofradía*. At 11:00 at night they leave in a procession until they reach the church to celebrate the birth [of Jesús]. After the nativity enactment, there is a very old custom. The *juez* of the *cofradía* invites everyone inside the church to go to the *cofradía* to eat tamales and drink (for those who drink). The responsibility for this is the *cofradía* of María Concepción. But we did not do this custom because it costs a lot of money. When the activities of Christmas were over, we just went to the *cofradía* [alone, without inviting anyone else]. We ate tamales and each of us drank one beer. Then we went to sleep. All of this passed without problems, and we avoided a lot of expenses.

Can you explain who participates in Las Posadas?

During the nine nights, the visits to the houses are prearranged. The real owner of the house and the Daughters of María and anyone else who wants to participate comprise the first group inside the house. Always the *cofrades* comprise the second group outside the house because they are the *jefes* in charge of the procession. Finally, the *cofrades*, the other group of Daughters of María, and whoever else has joined them outside are all let into the house. Then they have a religious celebration, and the owner may offer coffee, tea, liquor, *atol* and refreshments. But there may be houses where nothing is offered if they do not have anything. Each night the procession begins from the church. The last procession is from the house of the *cofradía* to take the large image of the Virgen to the church on Christmas Eve where it stays for three days. Then the *cofrades* take it back to the *cofradía*.

Can you explain more what the cofrades *do during the fiestas?*

The three important *cofradías* are San Juan Bautista, Santo Domingo Guzmán, and María Concepción. The former two *cofradías* are more respected, but the *cofradía* of María [has considerable respect]. It is more respected and venerated by the women for the importance of the mother of the Savior Jesucristo. When their children are sick, the women appeal to the Virgen María for their health. And they see positive results.

The *cofradías* celebrate the fiesta on 24 June, but they carry images from the *cofradía* to the church on 23 June, which is the day before the nativity of San Juan Bautista. First they take out the image of María in a procession toward the *cofradía* of Santo Domingo Guzmán. Then the two images go in procession to the *cofradía* of San Juan Bautista. When this is finished, the three images go in procession to the church.

When the image of María is taken out first, the wife of the *alcalde* of María walks in front with incense. When the image of Santo Domingo Guzmán is taken out next, the wife of the *alcalde* of Santo Domingo Guzmán walks in front of it. And when the image of San Juan is taken out last, the wife of the *alcalde* of San Juan walks in front of it. Then all three images with all three wives of the *alcaldes* march in the procession with the rest of the *cofrades* to the church for the main day (birthday) of San Juan Bautista. This is to show respect when taking the images to the church.

Also, the three *cofradías* celebrate from 28–29 August to com-
memorate the beheading of San Juan Bautista [a celebration started
by Ignacio and the Blue and White Sports Club some 12 years ago].
On 28 August they take out the images of the *cofradías*, and they
serve *atol* to the *principales* and the rest of those who accompany the
procession.

The *cofrades* carry the images to the church on 31 October to
celebrate All Saints' Day on 1 November and the Day of the Dead on
2 November. On 8 December members of the *cofradía* of María celebrate the day of the Immaculate Conception. But on 24 December
they carry the images to the church to celebrate the nativity of the
child Jesús. Not until 3 January do they take the images back to their
cofradías. On Sunday, the day of the Kings, they also carry the three
images to the church to celebrate Holy Week, and they do not return
them until Easter Sunday. On 4 August they celebrate only in the
cofradía of Santo Domingo Guzmán, but they take the image from the
old *cofradía* to the church on 3 August. On 4 August they take it to
the new *cofradía*.

Five days before each of these big fiestas, they invite the *principales* of the town. The first *mayordomo* is in charge of making the
invitation, preferably in the morning when the *principales* are at
home. The kind of invitation depends on the *cofradía*. If it is of the
brotherhood of María Concepción, the first *mayordomo* says, "Señor
Principal, in the name of God and the Virgen María, have a good day."
Then he kisses the hand of the *principal*.

And the *principal* answers, "State your errand."

Then the *mayordomo* says:

> Señor *Principal*, you are the most important person in our
> town. In the name of the *alcalde* of María Concepción I come to
> invite you to participate in the procession accompanying the Vir-
> gen María. You deserve the invitation because of your age and
> respect from all your service to the town. You are the person who
> occupies the office of *principal*. As witness to these *costumbres*
> that are going to be performed within five days, be compassion-
> ate with us. At the same time we ask forgiveness for our faults.
> It is true that we are not worthy to perform these *costumbres*
> that you did earlier.

Then the *principal* answers:

> *Mayordomo* of the *cofradía*, many thanks for this invita-
> tion. We, the *principales* of this town, are of advanced age, and

our death is getting closer each day. But tell the *alcalde* that, if
God gives us life for the next five days, with much pleasure I will
go. And for the moment give my regards to the señor *alcalde*,
because he is very close to becoming a *principal*.

Then the first *mayordomo* kisses the hand of the *principal* and
leaves. Thus, this is what the *mayordomo* has to do with the *principales*. Each *cofradía* sends its first *mayordomo* to the *principales*.
[There are 48 *principales*. The first *principal* directs all the others.]
The first *mayordomos* have to go to the houses of each one with the
same invitation. If one should be absent on the day of the invitations,
the *mayordomo* must return the next day until he has invited each.

When the main day of the fiesta arrives, the catechists, Daughters of María, Association of Women, *principales*, and *cofrades* all
leave the church together to go to the *cofradía*. They sing religious
hymns and prayers, always with the *tun* and *chirimía* in front of the
procession. When they arrive at the *cofradía*, first the *principales* enter, then the *cofrades*, and then all those accompanying. When everyone is inside, the *alcalde* rises to give reverence to the first *principal*
[if present, if not, to the second and sometimes even to the third
principal]. "Señor First *Principal*, good afternoon," he says as he
kisses his hand, but remains standing with his head slightly bowed
and hands folded in front of him. Meanwhile the *mayordomos* enter
with the *jícaras* of *atol* and give them to each person present. But no
one is able to drink until the head *principal* gives the order. When
everyone has *atol* in his hand, the *alcalde* says these words as a reverence to the first *principal*:

> First *Principal*, good afternoon to you. Now we are all here
> in this *cofradía*, so poor and humble. I don't believe we are per-
> forming the customs exactly as you did in the past. But since it
> is the tradition of our ancestors, we are the first who believe in
> the *costumbres*. Also the *principales* who are present have done
> the same or perhaps better. But, like time, things change. We
> who have this *cofradía* cannot forget what our fathers have done,
> and we are continuing it as a tradition. Thus, First *Principal*,
> have the goodness of receiving this *atol* with all present in name
> of María, mother of our Savior Jesucristo.

Then the first *principal* answers:

> Señor *Alcalde* of María, thanks to God and María for all the
> words that you have spoken. We are *principales* of very ad-
> vanced age. But also we are fulfilling a tradition of the *princi-*

pales who lived earlier. Now we are here in the *cofradía* waiting
for you to become a *principal* of this town. In this life we who
are going to die are being replaced, and you will be the *compadres*. We do not want others to stop our *costumbres*. Many
thanks for the *atol* that I am going to drink. Señores *Principales*,
in the name of God and the Virgen María, let's drink this *atol*.

Then everyone drinks his *atol*. When everyone is finished, the
alcalde again rises to his feet in front of the first *principal* and says:

Thank you. Today this *costumbre* is finished, what little [of
it] we have been able to do. I believe that, when you served, the
costumbres were better, but so as not to forget the customs of
our ancestors who are resting in the cemetery, we are doing what
we can. Thank you for having honored our invitation.

The *principal* answers:

Señor *Alcalde*, may God and the Virgen María bless you for
dispensing this gift that we received today. Well, many thanks,
and may God and our patron saint bless you.

Then the *alcalde* kisses the hand of the *principal* and leaves.
Then the rest [of the participants] file out behind him.

❧ A Custom of Bathing in the Lake
1–2 JANUARY 1982

The first of the new year dawned. I was a little sleepy because I
had not slept at all. We were in the church from 9:00 P.M. to 1:30 A.M.
on 2 January. Everything was peaceful. There were hardly any drunks
in the town. When we left the church, we came to the *cofradía* to eat
some delicious tamales my wife had prepared. At 2:00 A.M. we went
to sleep.

I got up at 6:00 A.M., and we went to bathe in the lake because
it is the custom. If a person does not bathe on this day it is believed
that he will suffer many consequences, such as sickness, slander, and
poverty. This is the custom of our ancestors, although now there are a
lot of people not doing it.

I ate breakfast with my family. Immediately afterwards we went
to the church to celebrate the mass with the *cofrades*. When we left
the church, I went again to the *cofradía* with my companions to eat

lunch together. My wife prepared lunch for everyone. But before lunch we drank a glass of liquor. When we finished lunch, everyone went home. Because my health was very delicate, I stayed resting at home.

❧ A Death, and Guerrillas and Soldiers
2–3 JANUARY 1982

My companions and I agreed to meet every Saturday to pray a rosary and sing hymns to show respect to the sacred mother of Jesús. Today was the first Saturday that we finished the prayer.

As we were finishing the prayer, they arrived to tell us that a daughter of my sister-in-law had died. I said good-bye to my friends, and then my wife and I went to her sister's house to give our condolences. We spent the whole day consoling them. And other friends arrived. They served some glasses of liquor, but everything was under control and went well.

At 4:00 P.M. on 3 January I went to the house of my friend Damián Juárez to ask him to make the coffin for the deceased baby [who died at the age of about one year of a stomach illness and vomiting]. This friend agreed to do it. At 9:00 P.M. he finished making the coffin.

I put the body of Letona in the coffin and closed it. A lot of the family members were crying. Then the *cofrades* left to put her in the ground. I did not go with them. I asked their permission to stay to continue to console the mother and father, who did not wish to go to the cemetery because it was too painful for them.

When all of this was over, my wife and I went home. The rest of the afternoon I rested. At 6:00 P.M. I was asleep. They say that at this same hour the guerrillas were in the same place where a detachment of military had been. When the military commissioners realized what was happening, they went to the detachment in San Luis to bring back the army.

At midnight the military arrived in town and went to the place where the guerrillas had been seen. But when they arrived, no one was there. Then the soldiers discharged their weapons just to frighten them because it was certain that the guerrillas were very close. But the guerrillas are too clever because they knew now that the army was near, and they changed places. They went to the soccer field, which is near the town. Some of the residents said they saw the guerrillas drinking a lot of liquor at the soccer field. But by the grace of God, there were no problems.

❧ Visits with Jesús and the Three Kings
5–6 JANUARY 1982

We were picking coffee in the morning. In the afternoon we went to the church on the order of Catholic Action. We three *cofradías* had to offer a worship to God for an hour, which was nice. At first we prayed. Then we meditated for an hour, and then we prayed again. Then we went home. They say they want to do this each Tuesday, but for me it is going to be somewhat difficult because I do not have enough time to be in the church.

After visiting the church, we went to the assembly hall to arrange what we are going to do on the morning of the sixth. But we had problems with the catechists because they do not want to continue with the old customs. But it was all solved. We have the obligation to continue with the visits as in previous years.

On 6 January at 4:00 A.M. my companions of the *cofradía* and I gathered at the church, and then we took out in procession the images of the Baby Jesús and the three kings, Melchior, Gaspar, and Balthazar. The first *mayordomo* carried the image of the Baby Jesús. We went to visit all the Catholic houses, but since I needed to water my onions, I asked permission to go irrigate them until 7:00 A.M.

All of us were very tired, but since it is one of our obligations, we had to bear it. By the grace of God, they received us well in all the houses. In some houses they gave us *aguardiente*, beer, soft drinks, and wine. Our *cofradía* did not want to drink because we had the main responsibility of looking after the image. However, the *alcaldes* of San Juan Bautista and Santo Domingo Guzmán drank because they did not have much responsibility.

On this day we finished the procession at 7:00 P.M. When we entered the church, the *principales*, Catholic Action, and a group of catechists were waiting for us. We put away the image of the child and went to the parochial assembly hall to count the money the people had given us in alms. In total we received $121.37. We put it in the hands of the new president of Catholic Action, Alfredo Bonifacio Temó. This money serves for the expenses of the church. When everything was finished, they gave each of us a beer that we drank because we felt very tired. Afterwards we went home. For me it was a very pleasant experience. At 10:00 P.M. we went to sleep.

You told me that some Catholic Actionists did not want to continue with this custom.

They did not want to accept the procession that had been done in the past. In reality, however, the *cofrades* are obliged to do this *costumbre* because all of the money that the families give for this visit serves the church. So the *principales* sent us to complete the custom because in each house where Baby Jesús arrives, they give some 10–25 centavos, sometimes 50 centavos. And this money is taken to Catholic Action to defray expenses of the church. Thus it is a service for the church, and the *principales* do not want to end it because it is worthwhile. But a group of catechists [the same that succeeded in getting the former president relieved of office] said they did not wish to continue these *costumbres* to avoid drunken parties and other things.

Then I told them, "If tomorrow you see us in a drunken party, tell us. But you cannot say anything before you see it. Perhaps we are not going to drink. But if it turns out that we get drunk, you may say something about it."

And on 6 January, after the procession, we counted the money, and I told them, "Señores Catequistas, yesterday you talked a lot about us. Who here is drunk? Who is drunk? No one. Well, look, the money that we went to collect the whole day is not for me or for some other *cofrade*. No, it is for the church. If it seems that we are not good, God be with us and with you for your poor tolerance."

An Incredible Dream
FRIDAY, 8 JANUARY 1982

I was sleeping tranquilly when I awoke at 2:00 A.M. Thinking it had dawned already, I looked at my watch. I was considering going to Sololá to cash a check that my great friend Jaime Sexton had sent. I saw it was only 2:00 A.M. "Still it is early," I said. "The launch does not arrive until 4:00 A.M., the latest at 4:30 A.M. I am going to sleep a little more." I went back to sleep.

Suddenly in a dream I heard the voice of a woman, "Ignacio, Ignacio, suspend your trip to Sololá. I tell you not to go to Sololá. Suspend your trip because a person is going to die now." For sure I did not see who was talking to me. I only heard the voice that was at the door.

"And what are you telling me?" I asked her, "that someone is going to die?" I was a bit angry in my sleep, and I said, "A person is going to die? Why?"

"It is that you are of the *cofradía*. You are responsible for burying the dead and for this reason I tell you not to go to Sololá."

"Okay," I said in my dream. "All right, I will bury the person."

"Now, I tell you," said the voice, "if you go you will be whimsical."

I got up again and woke up my wife and my son José and my daughter María. "Look, I had this dream," I said.

"What?"

"I dreamed that a señora told me not to go to Sololá. I heard the voice of a woman, but I did not see her face. What is the meaning of this dream? It told me that someone is going to die, but it did not tell me whether it would be a man or a woman."

"It is your madness," they told me. "You are loco."

But then José told me, "You had better not go to Sololá. Do not go! If your dream told you not to go, it is better that you not go," my youngster said.

And my wife told me, "Ah, it is the madness of dreams."

Then I began to think. Since the town is small, we know who is sick. "Who is sick?" I asked. "There is no one sick. It is certain that this is the madness of dreams. I am going to Sololá." I arranged my bag and went to Sololá without knowing what would happen.

By the grace of God, all went well on the trip. I bought a few little things for the family. But it was very strange when I arrived home in the afternoon at 5:00 P.M. I saw two men drunk in the streets. "What happened?" I asked my wife.

"Today at 3:00 P.M. they buried Señora Rosa (the wife of a *principal*). They are already finished. The *juez* and the *mayordomos* came for you to help with the service, but since you were not here, you could not help. What you dreamed last night turned out to be true!"

Then José told me, "Papa, I told you not to go. What you did was irresponsible. You failed, you failed. Such things are true. I realized that someone was going to die, and you should not have gone because you are in the *cofradía*, and you have the responsibility of burying the dead."

I did not believe in the voice that had told me not to go to Sololá. I thought that it was a lie—just madness. But in the afternoon it became reality. A possible solution is that it was the spirit of the woman. Afterwards I agonized over the dream because it had told me clearly in the soft voice of a woman that someone was going to die. When I arrived home, I had to meditate because my dream advised me of reality, and I was irresponsible. I believe that there is something sacred about the *cofradía* that we do not understand.

Also, these days when I dream, I am a little scared. They turn out to be true. [Another example] was much earlier, when I dreamed I was chosen the *alcalde* of the *cofradía*. It was 25 August 1981 that I dreamed of a woman by the name of María, who is a daughter of my cousin, Daniel. In this dream I was in Guatemala [City] with her. She told me that she wanted to accompany me.

"Look, Love, why do you want to walk with me?"

"Ignacio, I want you a lot and I am thinking of living with you because that is the way I feel."

Then I answered, "María, why are you thinking of such things? I am a man with a family and a lot of responsibilities. I have nothing to give you."

"Forget it, Ignacio. Do not think such things. I do not want anything. On the contrary, I have much to give you, and you need me. I will teach you marvelous things."

"But look," I told her again, "your father and elders will get angry with me and with you, too. You are a señorita, and we cannot do these things."

"No, Ignacio, do not think of evil things," she told me. "What I want to do is to take you to a good road."

But I turned to say, "María, because we are here in the capital, people will say a lot of things about us. How can you take me to a good road?"

"Look, I am going to do this," she told me. "I will guide you through this street. Do not worry. Come!" And in the dream she grabbed my hand.

"Look," I told her, "you cannot take my hand. No, Love." She is only 14, and she is kin. "I know what is in the capital."

"No," she said, "I need to show you the street where you can go." Then she took my hand. Actually, I was not very interested. It was a laugh for me that the señorita wanted to show me a street, because I know the streets of Guatemala [City very well].

Then she took me to a strange street and told me that if I took it everything would turn out well. "Look at it!" she told me. "You must go and watch for what you will see ahead. Ahead there is something good, and I want you to take this road, not this other road nor that one. You must take this one."

"María," I told her, "many thanks. Now I am going." Although she is no more than a youngster, I said thank you. "And you, where are you going?" I asked.

"Well, I will remain here. I am awaiting the day that I am going to fly."

Then I felt in my dream that I left. Little by little I passed a somewhat narrow street that was not clean. It was as if I passed through iron [grates] and other things. Then I thought that the road that the woman had sent me down was worthless. I felt that when I passed through the lattice that it was something not so good, but ahead, as she had told me, I saw all the good things. "What is this?" I said, as I saw a garden and other things in the capital. Then my dream ended.

I began to think about the significance of my dream. I asked myself, "Does it mean something good or bad?" I concluded that I would be named head of the *cofradía* of María Concepción. In my dream it was the Virgen María. All of the things of the *cofradía* I am doing with determination because my dream told me to have a good attitude and follow this road. After my dream I was more interested in the *cofradía*. And what the dream told me is almost reality.

I am doing well in the *cofradía*. I have always been able to keep up with the expenses. I am hardly out big expenditures. All I ask for is a little control in the *cofradía*. We do not permit drunken parties. It is true that sometimes we drink, but we do so with moderation. We do not have a lot of money to lose. Many persons say that the *cofradías* are useless and that in them there is uncontrolled use of alcohol. For me all of it is a blessing. For sure I am not losing anything. On the contrary, I am receiving the blessings of María. My grandma tells me that the people of earlier times lost. Better said, they sold their land or incurred big debts. "They did not know how to think," she said. "Try to do these things without drinking a lot." She said that formerly the *cofrades* spent weeks drunk, but that it was the old *costumbres*. They celebrated all fiestas, and they gave into drinking—all of the *principales*, *mayordomos*, and *texeles*. But she says that the one who was most damaged was the *juez*, because he is in charge of all the expenses in each fiesta. But now it is not the same, because all of the expenses are shared with the *alcalde* so that neither of the two comes out ruined. If one has the will, he can do what he wants. Everything depends on one's will.

You told me your forefathers drank a lot in the cofradía *because of their ignorance.*

Really, it was ignorance because the founders obliged the *alcaldes* and *jueces* to drink. This was a *costumbre* that I do not think had much value. The *cofradía* is worthwhile, but they were unable to control their drinking. They drank a lot of firewater in all the fiestas.

The *cofradía* of María had to buy a lot of drinks during the days of Christmas and the days of the fiesta of Holy Week. And the *cofradía* of Santo Domingo Guzmán had to buy a lot of *guaro*. These were the two *cofradías* that gave a lot of sugarcane liquor to all the *principales* and to all the municipal workers because it was their obligation. They only drank. I think this was stupidity.

Also, the *cofrade* of San Juan had to provide for all the fiesta of 24 June. He had to buy a lot of *tragos* for the *principales*, the municipality, and others in addition. Then the expenses were very severe. Now the *alcalde* divides the expense, and if they drink a little it is for the members of the *cofradía*. Now each *cofradía* takes care of itself. It decides for itself whether to drink a beer or a cup of coffee. In my *cofradía* we are not against the use of liquor. Every fiesta we buy a little alcohol, but not to get drunk. We have a drink or a beer before eating. We eat, and afterwards there is no more drinking. Thus, there is not much expense.

❧Building a School, and Oppression
SATURDAY, 9 JANUARY 1982

I got up at 5:00 A.M. and arranged my load of onions. María and I went to Santa Ana to sell them in the market. It was very arduous, but if I do not work I am not going to obtain anything; already I am thinking of suspending my trips to the coast. I am, however, thinking of continuing my trips to sell onions. Although one earns little, he does not need a lot of capital for the business. But on this day the business went bad. We earned only $4. We spent it all because we had to buy a few things for the kitchen. We ate a lunch of *chipilín* at 3:00 P.M.

At 5:00 P.M. my companions of the *cofradía* and I went to attend a mass. When we left church, we went to the *cofradía* to venerate the Virgen María.

From 8:00–10:00 P.M. we attended a municipal meeting concerning a great problem of education. It is a pity that I did not write about an earlier municipal meeting on the subject which took place on 15 October 1981. There are a lot of children, but the rooms of the school are insufficient for so many students. For that reason, the townspeople saw the great necessity of buying a *sitio*. Thus, through the municipality they formed a committee to take measures to buy the homesite. The organization of the committee includes two representatives each from Catholic Action, the Central American Church, the

Assembly of God, Alcoholics Anonymous, the military commissioners, and the cooperative. The committee members are respected persons so that there will be cooperation. The municipality was in charge of looking for property, and the citizens were responsible for determining its value.

Fifteen days later the municipality was able to obtain a *sitio* for $2,000. Then the municipality called another town meeting to announce that the homesite had been found. Then the citizens said that they would make a list of all the persons from 18 to 60 years of age to contribute $5, which they did. Collectively they raised the amount for the price of the property.

Sixty persons in town were not able to pay, but they went to work in a *cuadrilla*. When the farm owner paid them, they gave me their $5, which I gave to the committee.

When the town bought the *sitio*, the committee went to the government to get money to complete the work. CONANCE [El Comité Nacional Construcción Pro Escuelas] gave money, but very little, just for the engineers. But for us it was too much because, after buying the *sitio*, we were obliged to pay the freight of the trucks carrying sand. The committee said that the residents had to give an additional $7 each and moreover contribute labor. Who was able to say no? We were disposed to build this school; we had to give this extra money. What is more, the poor people of my town could hardly obtain it.

Then in this current meeting the maestro of the work presented himself with the mayor, Abraham Có Bizarro, to oppress the townspeople. Our intent was to draw up a memorandum to agree to work according to our means, but it was in vain. Now the maestro of the work says that we have to work 12 hours daily. We told him it was better to work 8 hours a day in accordance with the law, but he told us that, if we were not going to obey him, he would have us arrested and sent to a military detachment. This man was supported by the military commissioners, who said that he who does not work 12 hours a day will be taken for a Communist and then be taken to the army for hard punishment. The same maestro [a Ladino from Escuintla] said that, when he was constructing a school in the *aldea* of Totonicapán, there were five men who did not want to work 12 hours a day. He said that they sent them to a military detachment for 30 days to punish them, and he says that, after the 30 days, they were obliged to work the 12 hours. For us it was very sad because we gave our money, and then they wanted to kill us [with work]. But the maestro said that he had the power with the army to do what he wanted. Then no one spoke. This man wants to finish the work because he is working by contract, and for that reason he brings on this oppression in the town.

❧ Fiesta of Cristo de Esquipulas, and a Burial
15–18 JANUARY 1982

On behalf of the village of Pachichaj we in the three *cofradías* were invited to celebrate the fiesta of Cristo de Esquipulas [The Black Christ of Esquipulas]. The *alcaldes* of San Juan and Santo Domingo Guzmán left to honor the invitation. Also, the *juez* and all but one *mayordomo* of María Concepción left. He and I waited for the body of a girl who had died in the hospital of Sololá.

[While we were waiting,] I invited my uncle Benjamín to drink a beer because the disappearance of his son, Humberto Rafael, gave me much pain. We were drinking when Señora Eduardo Maldonado Chavajay arrived, and we began to chat with him. He is an evangelist, and he did not want to drink with us. He said that he is going around looking for work as a mason. I asked him if he knew how to build an *horno* [large, outdoor oven] for a bakery. He told me yes.

Then I wrote up a contract. Benjamín served as a witness to take before the authorities if one of us did not fulfill the contract. But more than anything else it was the stimulus from the *tragos* we drank because, when the contract was all finished, I asked myself what money am I going to use. But in the end I still agreed.

At 4:00 P.M. the body arrived. Then we went to the cemetery to dig the grave. The burial did not end until 7:00 P.M. When we left the cemetery, the father of the girl told me that he suspects that she was poisoned by someone. But I believe this is a lie because in the hospital there are no bad persons. Moreover, the child was sick for about six months because of malnutrition. Since only two of us dug the grave, we suffered a lot. But it is our obligation.

❧ The Evil Spirit
18 JANUARY 1982

A lot of people say they do not believe in the evil spirit. But the truth, says Don Francisco Rodríguez, is that it exists. His son left at 3:00 in the afternoon to irrigate tomatoes. By 6:00 P.M. his son had not returned. Since it was late, he went to find him. However, his son had taken another path. Francisco continued until he arrived in Papayo, where night fell. About this time he heard a strong wind coming in front of him. He wanted to hide, but he could not. In a few minutes the wind was so strong that the señor fell to the ground. He said that he wanted to speak but that he was unable. He felt as if someone were holding him down by his back [he was lying face down]. He told us that he remained thrown on the ground for about an hour. When he got up he began to pray, and very near he heard a voice like that of a person crying. When he heard these things, he was frightened even more. He was scarcely able to get home. When we arrived about 9:00 P.M., this señor was in serious condition. [Earlier he was very healthy.]

The reason that we went to his house was to find out whether, as some people had been saying, he had been beaten by the guerrillas. [He is my kin.] Other people were now with him, and he told us he nearly died. When I asked him, he said that it was an evil spirit who hit him.

Don Francisco always has things happening to him. Now it is an evil spirit. In March of last year, it was something else. He has a debt in BANDESA [Banco Nacional de Servicios Agrícola]. The loan had been outstanding for some time, and they wanted to collect their money. But he had no money. Without doubt he was disgusted with his wife, and each of them went to sleep in separate beds. But who knows what Don Francisco was thinking? He did not tell his wife when he got up very early, put on clean clothes, left his dirty clothes next to the bed, and went to catch the launch.

When his wife got up at 4:00 A.M., she realized that her husband was not in bed. Then she and her children went to look for him, but it was impossible to find him. Later they advised the authority, telling him that he had been kidnapped by some group and saying that the saddest thing was that they had taken him away without his clothes. Since his wife did not see him put on fresh clothes, she thought he was taken away naked.

Well, the news went out in the whole town that Don Francisco Rodríguez had been kidnapped. Since he is a catechist, they advised the church. All the other catechists said that he had been abducted because of the word of God. That is, he was kidnapped for being religious, since guerrillas do not like catechism or believe in God.

A lot of catechists visited the church to ask God to allow him to appear. They stayed there praying the whole day with the family. Also, a lot of people, thinking that he had been killed, searched among the coffee groves. And a commission looked everywhere all day long for him. There was much sadness during the day.

At 4:00 P.M. the launch arrived with all the people who had gone to Sololá, including Francisco. He did not realize that everyone thought that he had been kidnapped. In a few minutes he was called before the authority and later put in jail. This poor man began to cry because of everything that had happened. On the other hand, his wife was very satisfied to see her husband in jail because nearly the whole day she had suffered a great sadness. Also, the catechists pestered him with pleasure because all day they had prayed for Don Francisco while he had been happy in Sololá. Now, this almost seems funny, but at the time it was not.

On this Monday there was another meeting to ask for more money for the school. We had to give $2.50 each for other things like sacks for carrying sand. The mayor did not help us. The town is totally regretful for having compromised itself for this work. Furthermore, they say that each inhabitant must lose 8 days of 12 hours each of work. We are living like slaves, worse than slaves, because 12 hours a day is a lot.

As of 10 August 1982 residents were still working 12 hours a day constructing a big school with six new rooms. Women were carrying stones, and men were building.

ᐟ I Try to Resign from the Official Party
22 JANUARY 1982

I went to Sololá for a political meeting with *licenciado* Donaldo Alvarez Ruiz. For certain I do not have the will to continue in politics. I feel tired because I have been the political leader for 16 years. Because of my work in the cooperative, I would like to resign.

At 10:00 A.M. we met *licenciado* Alvarez Ruiz in the municipality of the Indians [in Sololá there is a municipality for Indians and another for Ladinos] to tell us to fight more for the official party. He told us that he has confidence in us Indians because we have always been winners for sure. Then the rest of my companions told him, "With much pleasure we will fight to advance the party."

But since I had wanted to resign, I told him, "Excuse me, *Licenciado*, I am ready to resign from this office of the party. I feel tired because already I have lost much time, and for this reason I do not wish to continue working for the party. Perhaps you are able to find another person who can relieve me."

The answer of my great friend was, "Ignacio, why are you thinking of leaving the party? Those who leave the government are the Communists who are against the government. Now, the person who leaves the party is taken as a subversive and executed. If you do not want to die, you must remain in the party."

These were the words of gratitude that the *licenciado* told me for all the battles I have waged to help in the electoral campaigns. This is a good lesson for me and for my children. It is better not to be in a political party. One does not earn anything. And later, when the person wishes to leave, they offer him death.

❧ I Take my Turn on Civilian Patrols
24 JANUARY 1982

On 20 January we began civilian patrols by order of the army to guard against the intrusion of guerrillas. [It had not yet been called *autodefensa civil*.] On this day, 24 January, when it was my turn along with four others to guard the town but without arms, I had second thoughts. What would we be able to do against such well-armed guerrillas? For me it was just a ceremony. During this night my companions and I agreed that if we saw a group of guerrillas, we would hide. But by the grace of God, nothing happened. Everything was peaceful.

❧ Is Thursday a Lucky Day?
28 JANUARY 1982

A lot of people say that Thursdays are better days, but I believe that all days always have bad hours. After dark the two youngsters were playing and dancing inside the house. I do not know why they left to go outside. My wife and I were very content when suddenly we heard Erasmo Ignacio shout, "Susana Julia has died!"

Then we ran out of the house, and when we reached the road we saw that a large rock was on top of Susana. By the grace of God, it was not on her head. When we got her home where we could examine her in the light, we saw that the tip of her right index finger was ground to the bone. This caused us much sadness.

We went to wake up the medic, and I wanted to take her to the hospital. But the medic told us to have patience. Only then did we think more clearly.

On this night I did not sleep at all. I took care of the child because she was almost unconscious and she cried nearly all night. Also, my wife cried all night, and neighbors arrived to see what had happened. For two months the child suffered with her injured finger. It is still maimed.

❧ Guerrillas Burn Buses and Murder Drivers and Their Assistants
5 FEBRUARY 1982

Ignacio typed out this episode, and I also recorded a version on tape. I supplemented some parts of the written version with details from the tapes, especially the dialogue.

The news on the radio said that in the afternoon the guerrillas arrived between Panajachel and San Jorge and between Sololá and Los Encuentros and that they burned two Rebuli buses and killed three drivers and two assistants. My companions of the Partido Institucional Democrático and I were planning to make a trip on Saturday to receive a short course in politics. But when my companions heard the news, they became very scared and did not want to go. Nevertheless, Erasmo Ignacio, my friends Benjamín and Felipe, and I decided to go.

At 6:00 A.M. on Saturday we boarded the launch, but when we arrived in San Martín the people were talking about what happened yesterday. [At first] I thought they were just telling lies. However, when we arrived in Panajachel, everyone was frightened. There was no activity in the town.

An owner of a cantina told me to be careful because the guerrillas were nearby. I replied to this señor how we had heard this on the news yesterday but that we thought it was a lie. Then the señor told me that yesterday the most unfortunate things happened. Above [on the ascent to Sololá just before the Catarata Fall] they killed Don Missael and his helper. I asked him how this happened, and he told me that the guerrillas took out the driver and shot him in front of his wife and children. Then they asked his assistant for the money, but he said he did not want to give it to them. After killing the driver, they poured gasoline on the bus and set it afire. Then they grabbed the helper by the hands and feet and threw him into the fire alive—in front of all the passengers. This is what the man said, and it scared me.

But finally we boarded a [small shuttle] bus for Sololá. When we passed the place where they had killed the two men, the bus was still there burning. I am sure that many people did not get to take their belongings because there were many burnt items like suitcases, trousers and shirts, and other things. Without doubt a lot of people were not able to take down their bags because the situation was serious. The wind of the fire blew away pieces of clothing. It was a grave burning, and it was frightening just to look at it. One could smell the foul odor of burnt flesh.

The driver, who was a witness to the killing of Don Missael, the driver of the Rebuli bus, confirmed the news. He said that he was ascending to Sololá in his [small] bus and Don Missael was descending in the [larger] Rebuli bus, which had begun the trip in Guatemala [City]. One group of guerrillas stopped Don Missael, and another group stopped him before the two buses met. They made him get down from his vehicle.

"I was trembling," he said, "but they took only my money, the day's earnings—$64." In front of him they machine-gunned Don Missael. Then the guerrillas asked Missael's helper for the money [he had collected from the passengers], but he said, "I am not going to give it to you." He was afraid of the owner of the money [his boss]. The bus was now burning. They threw gasoline on it, and it was very hot and flaming. They grabbed the helper by his hands and feet and threw him onto the fire alive, and it flared up. This man [our bus driver] told us that they did not recover the remains of the helper's body. It was totally consumed by the fire. However, they did not burn Don Missael's body. This man told us that the guerrillas obliged him to return [to Panajachel] if he did not want to die. He said that he did not eat or sleep after what he had seen. He asked his boss to let him off work until Tuesday, but his boss said that, if he did not wish to work, he would hire someone else to be the driver.

When we arrived in Sololá, they told us the same thing had happened on the road to Los Encuentros—the guerrillas had burned another bus. Also, they said that they had killed the driver and his helper. Also, they said that the guerrillas wanted to burn a third bus, but after they threw gasoline on it, it did not catch fire. When they saw it was not going to burn, they broke the windows with [machine-gun] bullets. We saw this bus towed by another vehicle. When we arrived in Panajachel, it was in front of the police station for a while.

It was totally sad when we were in Sololá. There was no activity. All the people were scared, including the señor who was going to give us a short course. Our trip to Sololá was hardly important. [There was no short course.]

We could not return to San José on the same day because there was no launch. Thus, we wanted to return via Los Encuentros, but they told us that there was still a confrontation between the guerrillas and the soldiers. In front of us arrived a vehicle of the *bomberos* with 16 bodies stacked in it like firewood. We saw them unload three of the bodies of people who had died in the confrontation in Los Encuentros. A lot of the indigenous people, who were with the dead bodies of their kin, were crying. It scared all of us very much. We wanted to return through San Diego, but the news said that in every direction there were guerrillas. We had to bear staying in Panajachel, but it was a pity that not one of us carried bedclothes. Only the boy, Erasmo Ignacio, carried a sack.

Because the news said that no one was able to walk after 6:00 P.M., we went to eat dinner at 4:00 P.M. By 7:00 P.M. the residents had already deserted the streets. There were a lot of police, soldiers, and detectives (judicial police). It was a pain to walk. We did not go anywhere because of the great fear. When night fell, I did not hear a single car pass in the street.

During this night we suffered a lot because we did not have bed-clothes and we tried to sleep on the sand. Later it got very cold. I put my son Erasmo Ignacio inside the sack he carried, but it was still too cold. Then I asked the conductor of the launch, who is a very good person named Nicolás, to let us go inside. Only when we were inside did we feel a little relieved. We slept a little, but it was not like sleep-ing at home. The pilot of the launch told us to take special care be-cause the guerrillas had said that they have marked the launches for burning within a few days. It scared us!

How many guerrillas were there, and what were they wearing?

According to the driver of the small bus, there were about 50 to 60 guerrillas who stopped the buses between Panajachel and Sololá. They were all young boys, but they were dressed in uniforms like the army. And they were well-armed.

How were the bodies dressed that you saw in Sololá?

They were all humble Indians dressed in the *traje* of Sololá. None was a soldier or dressed like a guerrilla. The bodies included women and children.

Were there soldiers in the area when this happened?

When all this happened, there were soldiers in Sololá, San Luis, and Godínez.[29]

❧ Building an Oven and Expecting My Grandma to Die
SUNDAY, 7 FEBRUARY 1982

Sunday dawned. When I arrived home my grandma was gravely ill [with aches and fever], but we were not able to do anything because she is very advanced in age. Then my mother and my wife told me to prepare a coffin so that when she dies we will not have to bother the people. I told them, "Let's wait another day."

All night long we did not sleep at all. We just took care of the sick one. During the day we worked in the *sitio*, but we were cranky from lack of sleep.

On this day we stayed at home making adobes for the oven, but we did not work all day. We stopped at 2:00 P.M. because my grandma became more critical. We stopped to clean the house to wait for the kin [because we were expecting her to die]. José left for San Martín to buy a can of black paint to paint the coffin so that everything would be ready. At the same time I sent a telegram to my sister, who lives in San Diego.

In her illness, my grandma said certain names of persons who have been dead for some time and whom we had never seen. She said that her father, Marco, and her mother, Amanda, were present. However, when my grandma was was healthy she told us that her mother had died when my grandma was only eight days old and that her father was about 55 years old when he died. I do not know why my grandma told us to light candles and incense. We did what she asked because she also said that other deceased kin were present.

The catechists arrived at night to pray in the house, but we said we were not going to do anything for my grandma because she is very advanced in age.

Three days later, when my brother-in-law, who is a medic, came to see my grandma, he examined her and said that our grandma was not going to die because she has good lungs, a good heart, and good blood circulation. Then he gave her an injection and left her some reconstituent pills. [This was the first time she had ever taken medicine, and she had never visited a doctor. It was her custom after 80 years to just take a drink when she felt sick.]

Little by little he gave the pills to her, and she regained her health. It did not cost us any money. It was very strange that a person who is more than 100 years old still has a good heart. We had thought that she was too old to be given medicine, but when she received this injection, she recovered.

❧ Making Adobes for an Oven and House
SATURDAY, 27 MARCH 1982

We have been working very hard with the youngsters preparing a place to make a small house and making adobes for the house and oven. Because we do not have the money, we did not hire any helpers. In all we made 400 small adobes and 200 large ones to form the base of the oven. Also we made 400 large adobes for the small house. All of this we had prepared for 16 March, when the mason, Eduardo Maldonado, and his two sons came to begin the construction of the oven. At $2.50 per day the price the señor charged me was a favorable one. His two assistants and I worked very hard carrying stones and sand. And I had to buy lime. I did not have the money, but since I had the obligation, I had to struggle to obtain it.

We were halfway through the construction of the oven when Don Eduardo told me it was necessary to build a house because, when one works with the oven, he needs a place to work [preparing the dough] and to store materials. It was a big problem for me because I did not have any more money with which to begin the house or buy *lámina* for the roof. Well, I did not have an obligation to build the house, but I decided to try.

I went to Cornelio Humberto, because he knows a little masonry. This señor told me that he was going to build the house with much pleasure. The value of his work day is $2, which is very cheap, because other masons charge $5 daily. Then my wife and I agreed that we would begin the other work. But, as I said, I did not have *lámina* for the roof. However, a friend lent me the sheets for nine months. Thus, we began to construct the house while the others were building the oven.

Now, we are two groups working in the homesite. Also, my wife is working hard because we do not have money to pay helpers.

I did not buy the wood for the house because I have a *cuerda* of land where I have cypress trees, which served for the construction. Also, we had expenses for the kitchen because all of us are in the homesite and we are giving everyone lunch. In all I found myself greatly compromised. Every day I asked God and the Virgen María to give me more intelligence to find a solution to these problems.

Gradually I obtained money. I sold some *tablones* of onions and some *quintales* of coffee. Also, with the help of my great friend James D. Sexton, I was solvent.

❧ Building a New House
27–31 MARCH 1982

The mason and his two helpers finished constructing the oven, and I was able to pay them. We continued working to finish the house. Because I do not have money to hire helpers, I worked very hard. Also, my son José helped.

On 29 March we finished the house, but I was scarcely able to pay Señor Cornelio Humberto López for his days of work. I thought about many things, like selling a *cuerda* of land where I have cypress trees, because Señor Eduardo [of Tzarayá] is making other things that will serve the bakery—a trough where one puts the flour, a board for mixing, and racks for stacking bread. It will all cost $53.50, but I do not have any more money.

Wednesday, 31 March, I went to the board of directors of the cooperative to ask for a $50 loan to be paid back in two months. They said they would lend me the money with much pleasure, but not until Saturday, 3 April, because they must have a meeting to see how much money there is. Only then then did I feel a little relieved about my situation. But also I am thinking that I will have some expenses for the fiesta of Holy Week because I am head of the *cofradía*. There is a *costumbre* for Palm Sunday, Holy Thursday, Holy Friday, and Easter Sunday, and I do not have money. Also, my family needs money. True, I have a little corn, but we do not eat just maize. We have coffee, but we need sugar and other things. Always we need money.

I thought, "What am I going to do?" What I did was to have more patience. I was meditating, "My Lord, you know how to go forward with these matters. Give me more intelligence to be able to work out something that will get me through these days."

❧ Getting the Materials for the Oven in Tzarayá
1–5 APRIL 1982

After irrigating onions, we ate breakfast. Then Julián Domingo, a boy from San Benito, and I went to Tzarayá to bring the materials for the oven. I did not have money to pay for the things we went to get. "Come Saturday to collect the money because right now I do not have it," I told Don Eduardo.

"Very well," he responded. Then I signed a receipt, and he brought me a trough for soaking the ingredients, a mixing board, some racks on which to set the dough formed into bread, and two [long wooden] shovels [for putting the dough in the oven and taking out the hot bread]. We were unable to carry everything he gave us in one trip. We arranged for his son to bring the rest of the items on Saturday, when we will cancel the debt. On this day the youngsters and I arrived home very tired. Then we ate lunch.

On Friday we were leveling the [floor] of the house because it was not finished. Also, we have not made a place for the door. Still we put the accessories for the oven inside the house. On Saturday, 3 April, Moisés, the son of Señor Eduardo, brought the rest of the items we had left in Tzarayá. Also, Señor Eduardo arrived to arrange the things in their proper place because I do not know anything about a bakery. I just watched them. When they were finished, I gave them $53.50, which the cooperative had lent me for two months. I gave all the money I had to the señor who had made the items for me. But I did not mind because I thought that some day I will be able to make a little bread when I get the money to buy flour and other things.

"Ah, poor Ignacio," Don Eduardo told me, "I am very grieved."

"Do not worry," I said.

"And when do you think you will make the bread?" he asked.

"Look," I answered, "all the work is ready, and we have firewood. But we do not have money to buy the ingredients."

"So," he replied, "would you like to try?" Don Eduardo is also a baker.

"I am thinking that when I have about $25 to $30 I would like to try it."

"Would you like to try it now?"

"Yes, I have the desire but not the money."

"Ah, very well," he told me. "But you are ready?"

"Sure, the tools are there, but I do not have money [for the ingredients]. But I put my faith in God and the Virgen María that I will be able to do it."

"Ah, very well," he told me. This is all he said, and he went to San Martín. I had given him only the money that I promised for the accessories.

When he came back from San Martín, he carried 100 pounds of flour, yeast, lard, and other things for the production of bread. I thought these were for himself and that he was taking them to Tzarayá.

"Good, Eduardito," I told him, "now you have returned from San Martín."

"Yes, Ignacio," he replied, "now I have returned. I bought these things."

"Well, you have reason because you are a baker," I told him.

"No," he said, "let's try to make the bread."

"What?" I said, very surprised.

"Let's try to make the bread together," he said.

"And the money I gave you, you used for this?"

"This money we will get back if I work a little here," he replied. "I just want to begin to work."

"Don Eduardito," I told him, "I am grieved because we may not get back your money. I do not know how to make bread, and we may lose out."

"Don't worry. If you wish I will work the bread."

"Very well, very well, if it is okay [with you], with much pleasure."

"God willing, maybe you will sell a little bread," he said.

I wondered why this man was going to do these things. I thought it was a blessing from God and the Virgen María. I told Don Eduardo, "It's all right. Tomorrow we are going to try to make a little bread."

It was an unforgettable day, Palm Sunday, 4 April, when Señor Eduardo made bread. At 3:00 P.M. he took out the bread from the oven. It had been difficult for sure because it took a lot of wood to heat the oven because it is new. But when the neighbors saw that fresh bread was baked, they bought all of it in the same afternoon. With this money José went to San Martín to buy more flour and other ingredients.

Holy Monday begins Holy Week. Again we worked with Eduardo. The same thing happened as yesterday. When we finished making the bread, we sold out on the same day. With this money I sent José again to San Martín for more supplies.

❧ We Continue Selling Bread During Holy Week
6–23 APRIL

On Holy Tuesday we began at 3:00 A.M., which was very early. At 11:00 A.M. we took the bread out of the oven. Still we sent to buy more supplies to bake more bread. We made two batches of bread in one day. All night we were working until Holy Wednesday dawned.

Don Eduardo and José made bread while I went to church to fulfill my obligations with the *cofradía* with my companions. This day was a little crazy. A little while I was working with the *cofrades*, and then a little while I was working with Eduardo making bread. I worked off and on with each.

All of the bread we made was sold on the same day. Again it was necessary for José to go to San Martín to buy more ingredients. They did not finish until 9:00 P.M., and still they sold bread.

Earlier I said that I did not have money to keep up with the expenses of the *cofradía*, but by the grace of God, with the little money we were able to earn selling bread my señora was able to buy meat and other things for Holy Week.

Holy Thursday we served the companions of the *cofradía*. We performed the traditional custom. We gave them bread, but truly it was a blessing. We did not know how we were going to get the money to cover the expenses, but it all turned out well. There was food in the house for the youngsters, and my wife also gave breakfast to others.

After serving breakfast to my companions of the *cofradía*, I settled the bill with Don Eduardo. I gave him the money [$53.50] that he had used to buy the ingredients.

"Here's your money, Don Eduardito, many thanks," I told him.

"Don't mention it, Ignacio," he replied.

"Now, I am going to pay your salary," I said. "How much do I owe you for your daily wages?"

"You owe me $1.50 daily because you gave me food and all," he said.

Because I realized how much we had earned and that it would be sinful to behave poorly with him, I said, "No, Don Eduardo. It's better that I pay you $2.50 daily because you did me the favor of helping me. I could not have made a single piece of bread [alone], and you lent me the material. Gradually we were able to earn a few centavos. Look, I am going to pay you fairly. I was able to get bread, give it to the *cofrades*, and still buy meat and all. I want to pay you this. For the meals, there is no bother."

"Very well," he told me, "thanks very much."

Then I paid him for the days that he worked. He left for Tzarayá very happy. And likewise I was very happy for all the favors this man had done for me. I will never forget it. It is true that for me it was a blessing because some kin of mine never says, "How are you, Ignacio, do you need something? Perhaps I can lend you $10." No. But, imagine, this man lives in Tzarayá about 6–8 kilometers from San José. And together we worked well. Many times I have said this was a blessing from the Virgen María. For that reason, I say that the *cofradía* signifies something sacred to me. When one works with will and devotion, he can accomplish wondrous things.

In the afternoon of Holy Thursday we were in the church waiting for the hour of mass. At 4:00 P.M. the priest began it. He did the memorial of Jesús, who washed the feet of the apostles and then sat down with them to eat the dinner of passover. Those who represented the apostles were some *principales* of the same names of the apostles who were with Jesús. It was a very pleasant *costumbre*.

When this was finished, the *cofradías* prepared the procession of the image of Jesús of Nazareth. This procession left the church at 9:00 P.M. and finished at midnight. A lot of respect and devotion was paid to the Holy Image. There was no liquor. All of it is a very sacred act with much respect demonstrated by the *cofradías*, catechists, association of women, and *principales*. The image of Jesús of Nazareth is raised by the men who are organized in groups. Also, the women organize to carry the image of the Virgen María, mother of Jesús. In the procession there are two kinds of veneration of Jesús: at the head of the procession all the men venerate Jesús, while a group of women revere the pains that María suffered. The prayers and songs are different in each group. When the procession ends, everyone leaves for his own house except we *cofrades*, who go to our respective *cofradías* to drink coffee and eat bread or sometimes to drink *tragos*. This time, however, we did not drink because for sure we had a lot of responsibility.

Holy Friday we were also in the church but just to guard the images—to make everyone respect them, being sure that no one entered who was drinking liquor. That was almost all we did.

[For those] in the Catholic religion on Holy Fridays, there is an obligation to fast. They say that only by fasting can one's sins be forgiven. Many people do this kind of *costumbre*. But we in my family are not able to bear the hunger. Never in my life have I fasted. At times I have endured hunger, but it was because I did not have money or I arrived home late.

At 12:00 noon on Holy Friday they perform the act of crucifying the image of Jesucristo on a very large cross. Then they adorn it with great candles and a lot of incense. Many who do not go much to church indeed show up on Holy Friday to deposit their alms at the cross to erase their sins.

At 5:00 P.M. the body of Jesucristo is taken down from the cross, and then the true Catholics take off their shoes to kiss it and leave an offering. In general, all the men, women, and children do this. When everyone is finished kissing the image of Jesucristo, it is put in a place like a coffin, which is put on a portable platform to take out in a procession. This procession is called the Procession of the Señor Entombed. It leaves at 7:00 P.M. and lasts until midnight or 1:00 A.M. The people of the town adorn their streets with carpets of natural flowers, and they deposit alms [wherever the image stops, with representatives of Catholic Action collecting the offerings]. Certainly it is very significant because the men always are with the image of Jesucristo, and the women always console the image of María.

When all of this is finished, some residents form groups to drink. But also some form groups who do not drink liquor. Instead they eat things like bread and white honey or preserves. But the majority drink their drinks because it is well noted that those who assist in these events do not arrive at church on Saturday.

But not one of us in the *cofradía* of María Concepción drank liquor. My companions and I agreed that not until Easter Sunday were we going to drink some *tragos*, when the whole fiesta is over. Thus was Easter Sunday, when they celebrated a mass. We went to the *cofradía* to eat lunch. It was not much. The *juez* and I bought a liter of *aguardiente* and gave some *tragos* to the *mayordomos*. And we drank also. We expressed our appreciation for all the service the *mayordomos* gave during Holy Week, and everyone went home.

Was Maximón celebrated?

A group of *alguaciles* had their celebration with Maximón on Wednesday and Thursday. They had their own procession, however, and they stopped at cantinas where they drank and also gave Maximón drinks and cigars. They made an image of Maximón for two days. The *cofradía* of Maximón had a private celebration of Maximón which was apart from from the one with the *alguaciles*.

José and I suffered a lot trying to bake bread. We have little money, but we were able to buy 50 pounds of flour to practice by ourselves. We were not able to hire a teacher, and it all turned out very expensive because we burned a lot of bread. We could not make up in sales the money we had spent on the ingredients. Still, we had to be persistent because we need to learn this business. To make up for the value of the flour, I had to sell some coffee that we had reserved for our own use.

With the money we lost made up for with the sale of coffee, we tried again to bake bread. We worked all night until Saturday, 24 April, dawned. But again we failed. Nevertheless, I told my son that we have to learn. We were very sad because we thought we could earn a few centavos, but it was not to be.

❧ I Am Elected President of the Cooperative
24 APRIL 1982

On this day we celebrated the third general assembly of the cooperative. The meeting began at 10:00 A.M. Most of the associates arrived to take part. All the expenses of the year were accounted for according to the statutes. Chickens, bread, and corn were bought, and then the female associates worked to cook lunch. Everything was very pleasant.

At 10:00 A.M. they gave us refreshments with bread. After refreshments there was a search to choose the new directors in accordance with the statutes. I was unaware who among the associates wrote my name as candidate for the president. When we were called to vote, I won the majority.

For everyone else it was a party. But for me to be thrown into the presidency was something else! I hardly need more work! At this moment I felt nervous, but at last I had to give in. There was much happiness on behalf of the associates and friends, but for me it meant a great responsibility.

We enjoyed lunch with the technicians of INACOP [who were there to check on the proceedings]. When lunch was over, we took possession of the offices that we won.

The technician of INACOP gave us the oath to complete faithfully the offices. And we said, "Yes, we swear." After all these events I spoke on the microphone to thank everyone who had voted for me, and at the same time I told them that to be able to accomplish the work I will need the help of all the associates and that I hope we will be able to work together to achieve something for our cooperative. Then those at the assembly said good-bye to one another.

These events took place in the assembly hall of the national school, Rodolfo Juan García. When they were over, we new directors went to the cooperative. Finally, I discovered that they had named me president of the board of directors because the previous board was never able to obtain the quota of coffee. For many months they were taking steps before the national association of coffee, but they were not able to get the quota. They lost more than $300 in expenses. Who knows whether I have their confidence or whether they want to see me fail the same as they.

❧Inquiring about a Coffee Quota in Guatemala City
27 APRIL 1982

On Monday I went to Guatemala [City] to inquire about the coffee business. I found the national association of coffee, located in Plazuela España, Zone 10. I chatted with the *jefe* of the department of marketing, telling him that we in the cooperative have taken 1,000 *quintales* of *café pergamino* [second-class coffee] to the *beneficio* of Homero Ordoñez in Santo Tomás la Unión. I told him that we have not sold it at a good price and that we want to see if it is possible to export it. The *jefe* told me to come back later to see about it.

It is true that the associates had sold the coffee but at a very unfair price. The associates negotiated the coffee for the whole town, but unfortunately they were not able to get the quota, and for that reason they sold it at a low price. Thus, we asked to export the coffee at a just price.

Can you explain the quotas a little more?

He gave me the *tarjeta de quota* [quota card], and I took it to the *beneficio* for a good price of 952 *quintales* for $10,000. The national association of coffee growers allocates quotas each year to the farms and cooperatives. Usually the cooperative gets only one a year, but a farm may get one each three months. The value of the quota varies, but our cooperative had sold the coffee at $45 per *quintal*, but with the quota we [henceforth] could sell it at $55 a *quintal*, and the *beneficio* could get $75. Thus, with the quota that one has to ask for at the national association one can get a better price. Each member of the cooperative, including my wife, got $100.

❧INTECAP Offers to Send a Baking Teacher
TUESDAY, 28 APRIL 1982

I chatted with Rolando Roldán, the representative of the Instituto Técnico de Capacitación (INTECAP). He offered to send a professional instructor of baking if I wished. I answered, "Don Rolando, many thanks for your good intentions. I am in much need because it is certain that I have an oven at home where I can work, but I do not completely know this occupation." Then we agreed that he would send me a teacher on Monday, 3 May. But I thought that these were lies because sometimes it happens this way.

❧ The Month of María
1 MAY 1982

This day, 1 May 1982, arrived. It is the custom to celebrate the month of María on 1 May. Thus on this day the Virgen María was taken out with much veneration and a procession through the main streets to the church. Before the procession, *atol* was given to all the *principales*. I did not know how many persons were accompanying the procession. After drinking the *atol*, they organized the women in files to accompany the Virgen María. Also, the men made two files, but the women went first, and the men went behind. The women are the ones who are in charge of carrying the Virgen to the church. They took up the whole road as they went, sprinkling flowers with much respect.

During the month of May the Virgen María is venerated by the women and by the boys and girls for being the mother of Señor Jesucristo. And for us, she is also our mother. During these 30 days, there are many groups of women praying daily before the Virgen María. When the month ends, those who are in charge of bringing it back from the church are the members of the *cofradía* of María. At this time there is no fiesta.

❧ The Teacher, Juan, Arrives
MONDAY, 3 MAY 1982

This was a day when I went to plant onions. I was nearly finished when Ramoncito arrived to tell me that some señores needed me. Then I ran to see who these persons were. When I arrived I saw my great friend Rolando Roldán, who said, "I would like to introduce Señor Juan Roberto Romero Morales."

"I am very pleased to meet you," I replied.

Don Rolando said, "Here you have at your service the instructor of baking."

"How many persons do I need?" I asked him.

"Just those in your family," he responded.

"May others participate also?"

"Yes."

Then I went to the municipality to make a public announcement advising all those who want to learn the occupation of baking to sign up. This is how 24 aspirants received the opportunity to learn the production of the sacred bread.

For eight days in my house we learned theory, and we calculated the money needed to buy the materials. We divided the expenses and organized into two groups, with each group having its committee. I was the coordinator of the two groups. But it was difficult to raise the money. By the grace of God and the good heart of the good maestro, Juan Roberto, we were able to buy the materials. He lent us the money and went himself to Guatemala [City] to buy them.

Juan Roberto returned from Guatemala [City] on 11 May. He brought flour, lard, sugar, and other ingredients for the production of bread. The participants went to San Martín to get the cargo. Since it was somewhat heavy, they had to pay [the owner of] a pickup to bring it to our town. Everyone was very happy when they arrived. At the same time we agreed that tomorrow Don Juan would begin the first practical classes.

Thus on 12 May, Don Juan met with the first group. We agreed that each group would meet every other day. The bread that we would make during the training would be divided among the participants' families. The practical classes of explanation ended on 19 June of the same year. [The actual practice of baking came after eight days of lecture.]

Making and Selling Bread During the Training
20–23 JUNE 1982

On 20 June we began to bake bread to sell. We did the same from 21–23 June. By the grace of God, we sold the bread well. A lot of people in my town bought the bread. Also, the boys made bread to use during the fiesta in their own families, not to sell.

Juan and I worked very hard until night, and by the grace of God, it turned out well. We lost nothing. It is true that we made only a little money, but we did sell more than $200 worth of bread in three days. More than anything else the bread served us for the *cofradía*. Moreover, I had to help some friends, giving them bread on credit, because we are living in difficult times due to the low price for onions [that we sell]. These friends told me that they needed bread for the fiesta. I gave it to them because I understand the need of their families. Thus was 23 June [the eve of the main day of the fiesta of San Juan Bautista]. Also, I was in the church for my office in the *cofradía*.

In the afternoon we took out the images in procession to the church. This was a very big day because beforehand three different Catholic groups arrived in my house. The first two are from the village of Pachichaj. One is called Sinai and the other is Spokesmen of Cristo. The third is of the church in San José and does not have a name. It made the *cofradía* more joyful because there is enough space [in the house of the *cofradía*] for all of them. However, when we left in procession for the other *cofradías*, it began to rain, which disrupted everything. It was still raining when the procession entered the church.

This day, 23 June, was very much celebrated in town. All of the sports teams filed through the principal streets of the town. Also, the Martial Band of the Brigada General Miguel Tánchez Ordoñez of Quezaltenango participated. It was the first time in the history of the town that the military commissioners arranged the event.

We of the *cofradía* agreed to go to bed early and not to drink liquor because we will participate tomorrow in the procession. All of the mayordomos obeyed and went home to retire.

Two in the morning is the hour that everyone gets up and gets ready for the mass at dawn. But it was all under rain, and it dawned raining. Nine A.M. arrived, and it was still raining. The priest began the patronal mass, and it was still raining. We waited until 11:00 A.M., when the rain let up a little, before beginning the procession through the main streets of the town.

On 23 June my wife and a helper named Juana Toc worked all night cooking meat and making tamalitos. Although it was a lot of work, it is the *costumbre*, and we had to do it. Everything was ready by 4:00 A.M.

❧Celebrating the Fiesta with Plenty of Bread
24 JUNE 1982

At 4:00 A.M. the *juez* arrived, accompanied by the *mayordomos*. As a signal that they had arrived, they lit *bombas*. This is a custom practiced in the three [main] *cofradías*. In each fiesta the one in charge of gathering the members is the last *mayordomo*. [He goes to the first house, then the two arrive at the next house, then the three arrive at the next house, and so on.] If the last *mayordomo* is clever, he begins to get them very early. Also, the *cofrade* who lights the first *bombas* is complying with good *costumbres*, and he merits the honor of the *alcalde* because he is setting a good example for his fellow *mayordomos*. The one who is in charge of buying the *bombas* is the *juez*. When the *bombas* have all exploded, the *alcalde* arrives to greet the *juez* and the *mayordomo*. The *juez* kisses the hand of the *alcalde*, the first *mayordomo*, the second *mayordomo*, and all the rest in order. Then they sit down, and the wife of the *alcalde* gives them chocolate and bread.

When we finished eating bread, I ordered the *juez* to order the *mayordomos* to the kitchen. Then my wife gave them baskets of tamalitos and pots of broth with meat. It is the custom to put two or three pounds of meat in each pot. Because we are short of money, my wife put only two pounds in each pot. But we did comply with the *costumbre*.

When they all had their baskets in hand, I told them to take their baskets and pots to each house [of the members], but always interchanged.

This was not finished until 7:00 A.M. Then we went to the church for mass. When the mass was over, we all went home.

About 1:00–2:00 P.M. we began the procession, taking the images from the *cofradía* to the church.

Now there are certain changes in the *costumbres*. In previous years they took out the image in procession again on 27 June and returned it on 30 June to be taken to the new *cofradía* on 1 July. This year only one trip was made on 23 June. I have said many times before that there is a group of catechists who do not want the townsfolk to continue the *costumbres*. This year they told the priest that these *costumbres* now serve no purpose and that they have needed changing for some years. The priest then allowed them to demand that the image be taken to the new *cofradía* on 24 June. And it was done as they had arranged it. This year they were able to get their way with the president of Catholic Action. To avoid problems, we arranged it with the other *cofrades*. Thus, this year the new *cofradía* received the image on 24 June. But who knows whether they will do the same thing in another year or whether with another president they will continue the *costumbres* of our ancestors.

❧ The Second Course in Baking Begins
7 JULY 1982

On this day the second course in the production of bread began. Until now the boys and the instructor needed a rest. When we began the work, it was difficult to collect the money. The first course cost $11 per student, and Don Juan said that the same amount would be needed for the second course. But not everyone was able to raise the needed $11. Then we asked the instructor the favor of lending us the money. It is certain that the boys are interested, but they do not have the money. The good man Juan lent us $155 to buy the ingredients. Only then was it possible for us to buy the needed materials.

In the first course we spent the sum of $264, and the same happened in the second course. In total it cost us $528. Also, each person brought wood for the afternoons when the practice began. I provided the oven and a little material that we have. Moreover, I provided the light [electricity] without collecting a single centavo [from the others]. My conscience would not permit it because I know that my people are not able to pay. Moreover, my thought was that we all would learn a job for the future and we all could do something for our town.

Because of my commitments in the cooperative, I did not participate in all the practices, but my son took advantage of the opportunity because when I was not participating, he was there in my place. I do not know, but I think the youngster has learned the most of all [the participants] in the course, because I already have proof of his ability and he works well without my having to be with him. Well, I always have thought that the occupation would be better for him because he is growing.

❦ Don Jaime Arrives in San José
27 JULY 1982

On this day I was ready to make a trip to Panajachel to settle some matters of the cooperative. When I went to the shore of the lake to catch the launch, I saw my good and unforgettable friend James D. Sexton disembarking. We greeted one another, and I thought it better not to go. Instead, I sent José Carlos to take care of the errand, and I gave him travel money. Then my friend and I went to my house.

When we arrived, my family was still sleeping, but when I told them our great friend James Sexton was here, they got up because the youngsters wanted to see him again, because when he came to Guatemala two years ago he did not come to San José. For that reason, my family was surprised when we arrived home, and they greeted him.

We chatted, and I showed him the house where I am producing bread. When I asked the señor if he would like to eat breakfast with us, he said yes and gave me $10 to buy things to eat. But I thought $10 is a lot of money, and I took only $5 to give to my wife to buy food.

Then the maestro of baking, Juan Roberto Romero Morales, arrived, and we three ate breakfast together. After breakfast Don Jaime
and I went walking through the town to take some photos of the
people [and places].

We went to see the new municipality and post office. Then we
went to the cooperative, and from there we went to the place called
Telnic, where the detachment of soldiers had been in San José [in
1980]. Then we walked some more, looking over the Hill of Chuitinamit. [After examining the agricultural nursery of the cooperative] we
returned through different streets until we arrived at the street where
they killed the woman on 19 August of last year (1981). I wanted to
show the house to Señor Sexton, but it was impossible because across
the way came a son of the deceased. I thought it better not to show it
because they could think badly of us. Then we entered the shop of
the cooperative to drink a soda because it [the temperature] was very
warm. Not until we left the tienda did I show him the house where
they killed the woman. Then we returned home for lunch.

On this day a *mozo* was making bread. Neither I nor my youngster was able to do it. But when we returned from our walk, I had to
go to see how the work was going. When lunch was ready, again the
three of us ate together. What grieved me was that my wife was not
able to cook better. She is able to cook only typical food.

After lunch we talked about a lot of things. And we did not go
anywhere else. My friend Sexton told me that when he returns to his
country he would leave me a typewriter and a dictionary (Larousse,
Diccionario Moderno). Another thing is that when he arrived at my
house he gave me a Timex watch and the case with instructions, for
which I thanked him and secretly thanked God. When we finished
lunch, my youngster [José] was ready to go to school. I gave him the
watch I was wearing and put on the watch that Jaime gave me.

In the afternoon when it was time for the launch, the whole family went to the wharf to send off our friend. Also, Jaime and I agreed
that I will go to Panajachel on Wednesday, 28 July, to work on the
pages in arrears.

On this day was the birthday of the baby, Anica Catana, who is
three years old. For us this day was very nice.

℘ A Trip to Panajachel
28 JULY 1982

On Wednesday I barely made the launch to Panajachel because
it arrived very early. When I arrived in Panajachel, I went to the

house of my friend Sexton. We drank some coffee and then went to
eat breakfast. Afterwards, we began to work very hard through part of
the night, resting only when we went to eat.

ᕫ Three Dreams While Working with Don Jaime
31 JULY 1982

*During this three-week session of work with Ignacio, he seemed
much more tense than usual because of the situation. He would
stop and listen when he heard strange noises. I too felt more
uneasy than on previous trips, but I tried not to let it show. Ignacio told me about his dreams in the morning when he woke
up. First I taped them, and then Ignacio wrote them out in a
briefer version. What follows is primarily the version that I
taped.*

When I was in Panajachel working with Dr. Sexton, I slept well
all night long. I woke up and thought that it had dawned, but I looked
at my watch and it was 2:20 A.M. I went to sleep again, and that is
when I dreamed I was in San Luis just to visit. In my dream I was
walking around when suddenly they told me that three more important persons had been killed who were either *principales* or directors
of the church. I did not give it much importance, and they immediately said, "Go see! The bodies are already at the cemetery!"

"All right, I'm going to see what's happening." I met them on the
road to the cemetery. The three bodies were in their respective coffins, but one of them was very long. "*Púchica!*" I said. "Who's there?"
It was a very long body that they could not bear to carry.

"Well, a dead person, but he can't be lifted because he weighs a
lot."

Then in my dream I saw Padre Pablo (who had earlier been
killed in San Luis) with some nuns, none of whom I knew. I just knew
Father Pablo because much earlier he had come to San José. For that
reason I knew him in my dream, and he was attending the dead persons. But he was not able to lift the bodies because they weighed a
lot. Then I told the nuns and the father, "If you like, I'll help you."

"We don't need you," they told me. "We don't need you. Go!
Move back!"

And I told them, "Very well." Then I withdrew from them, and
a lot of people arrived—a lot! There were so many that together they
hardly felt the weight of the three dead persons, and they carried the

coffins as if they were empty. They went to the cemetery, and I returned to the town center again. I do not know if it is the madness of my dream or if it means there will be a massacre in this town.

After this dream I did not get up. I continued sleeping. In the dream that followed, Señor Mario, my father-in-law, appeared. In this dream he told me that he wanted to give me a piece of land as an inheritance for my sons and me. I told him, "Look, I tell you, do not say such things because I know your attitude. Forgive me, you are a liar. Many times you say these things and afterwards you do nothing. We are not asking for your land."

"No," he told me, "this time it is not a lie."

"Who knows," I said, "who knows. Excuse me, but I know that it is a lie. You are the father of my wife, but I don't like your attitude."

"But you need some land!"

"Well yes, we need it, I tell you. But it is better for us to rent. I don't want you to offer us any. Many times you have offered things to us, and we become content, but later there is nothing. And we don't want problems with you. We are thankful that you know you are our father, that we are your children, but let's not discuss land. Of course, we need land, but we don't need your lies."

Then this developed into a problem. He became very angry with me, and I with him. Then he disappeared. For sure I do not know the meaning of this dream.

I continued sleeping and had yet a third dream. I was swimming in Lake Atitlán. I felt as if I were almost in the middle of the lake where it is very deep. I looked to one side and the shore was very distant. On both sides there was a lot of *paxte* [plants like seaweed], *paxte* to my left and *paxte* to my right. But in the place where I was swimming, it was purely crystal, crystal, crystal. Behind me was a lot of *paxte*. Then I said, "If I go to the right, *paxte* will grab me, and it can kill me. If I go to the left or behind, it is the same. There is no one who can help me; I'm just by myself. There is no launch or canoe, just me. But if I swim I can reach the other side." But I felt the area I was swimming in was crystal clear. Then while I was swimming a breach opened for me like a path—blue, blue, blue! But it was shining as if the sun was reflecting on it. Then I said, "There is where I am going. Now I have found a path. And as I swam I was where it was white and blue and clear. I began to feel the freshness of the lake. I swam and swam, and I felt I suffered a lot swimming and thus fleeing from the lake. And I reached the beach. When I awoke, it was 5:00 A.M.

I have faith in God that this last dream means something good.

There are some bad things because otherwise why was there *paxte* on the right and on the left and behind me. But where I was swimming, everything was all right. Then suddenly on the right the breach opened for me, and everything was shining blue. Thus, my thoughts are that without doubt some bad things will happen. But they will pass, and I will be able to choose a path that will help me.

These are my thoughts. I do not know for sure what in the dreams will happen or if it is just the madness of dreams or if they have some other significance. What is most interesting is the third dream because it was already about to dawn. When we dream at dawn, it is significant. At times it turns out to be true. These were my three dreams.

❧Returning to San José for a Baptism
1–4 AUGUST 1982

Don Jaime and I worked on the pages until Saturday. Then I told him I would have to go back to San José because I had committed myself to be the godfather of a baby for baptizing. Thus, I had to take the launch in the morning. When I told him I would have to leave, my friend gave me the sum of $40 for the value of my work.

When I arrived home, I told my wife about the money, and she was happy. When it was time for the mass, we went to the house of the parents of the baby. But the truth is that I did not know anything about baptism because, as I have said many times, I am not very religious since I go to church only once in a while. I have seen only that one has to respond to what the priest says in the ceremony. Thus, as we were going to church, I asked a religious person, and he told me the answers. This is what served me at the hour of baptism.

When we left the church, the parents of the baby invited us to breakfast. Before breakfast they gave us some shots of liquor that my wife and I had to drink to show respect for the baby. We also bought a beer to drink in their house. After breakfast we went home. During the night, I had to attend a meeting of the cooperative.

Don Jaime and I had agreed that I would return Monday, but I could not because I had to do other things in the cooperative. And before leaving, I had to arrange for some boys to work for me. For that reason, I did not return to Panajachel until Tuesday.

When I arrived, we went back to working very hard all day long.

We had to bear it because the stay of my friend was for only three weeks.

℘ A Dream of an Earthquake in San José
3–8 AUGUST 1982

About 3:00 A.M. I dreamed that we were having a big earthquake. In the dream I said that this is a big earthquake almost equal to the one of February 1976. In the dream many trees were breaking and falling. We nearly fell into the earth due to the big movement. In my dream I said my prayers to God.

I do not know whether this is going to happen or perhaps it was because of my weariness from working so much yesterday [when I was in San José]. During the day, I worked in the milpa until 3:00 P.M., and then I worked in the bakery until 1:00 A.M.—16 hours of work. Perhaps it was my weariness.

I was able to work through Friday, 6 August. On Saturday I had scheduled a meeting in the cooperative concerning the construction of a house for the said cooperative.

On Saturday, when I arrived, they told me that my companions had met the day before to decide not to complete the construction of the office because of lack of time and money. When I heard this news, I was very upset because two federations had already offered me help. But all of this [effort] is lost. Thus, the meeting scheduled for this day [Saturday] was not possible. More than anything else I felt angry because when a person wants to work, there are always lazy persons who do not wish to. They say they do not have time or money, but I know very well by experience that a man never works when he does not feel like doing it. They say that there is no money, but I know very well there is $2,000 in the treasury, although this is enough only to begin [the construction]. But for them it is better to save the money and not use it. On this day I thought a lot of things because I want a lot for the cooperative, but the others do not. Well, from now on I am not going to discuss the construction with them. I just want to see when they will have time and money and end their laziness.

On Sunday, 8 August, I was working in the house on some data for the cooperative. In the afternoon I was in a meeting but of a different nature, which did not end until 10:00 P.M. We had to draw up a memorandum of permission for me to be absent from the cooperative beginning on 15 August for 15 days to participate in a course at the

Rafael Landivar University. The course will be about the techniques and dynamics of group management as a *promotor social* [social promoter].

❧ Return to Panajachel
MONDAY, 9 AUGUST 1982

Again I returned to Panajachel to work with my same friend in the house he is renting in Panajachel. First we went to eat breakfast, and then we worked very hard all day, stopping only to eat lunch and dinner. After dinner we were too tired to continue [writing and translating new pages], but we were able to settle some questions or doubts.

> *On this day I recorded on tape more information concerning Rafael Bizarro, the student who is kin to Ignacio and who was kidnapped by the army.*

Imagine, Don Jaime, last night I went to look for a cousin of mine named Renaldo Bizarro Pérez, who was the owner of Foto Maya in San Luis when Rafael, who was staying with him, was kidnapped. Since he was living in the same house where Rafael had disappeared, he was afraid to remain in San Luis. He went to the capital to live and work taking pictures in the public park in the city center near the National Palace. I had sent $5 with my youngster for a large photograph, and it was ready, so early in the morning Renaldo wanted to talk to me. We chatted as we took the same launch to Panajachel together, and I asked him if he knew anything about Rafael.

He told me, "Yes, Rafael is alive. About 15 days ago I talked to him briefly. He was with an army captain, and I wanted to talk to him a little while. He told me no more than, 'Buenos días.' And I said, 'Buenos días, how are you?' Then the captain told him, 'Get in the car. Let's go!' I stayed there, but the captain did not allow us to talk. But I am his cousin. What I have doubts about now is whether he is imprisoned or detained or working. But I saw that he was assigned to someone in particular." These are the words he told me about the particular subject of Rafael. Indeed he lives, but no one knows whether he is working or whether he is a prisoner.

> *You also told me that men from 18 to 30 were doing military exercises yesterday. What was going on?*

This was an unsettling observation that I made yesterday, Sunday. Well, for me it is somewhat loco, true, because this does not have merit. But [it's a] pity that these boys are obliged to enroll for training as soldiers. They are treated hard, like soldiers. It took place where we were 15 days ago at Telnic. They were there yesterday training. Perhaps they are going to act like soldiers. If I am not mistaken there were about 150 boys, and they say that some were absent. I do not think it is part of the *autodefensa* [organized civil defense against guerrilla intrusion in the town] because I am part of that, and I am not in the 18-to-30 bracket. It is probably something that the military commissioners have organized. Maybe later I will be able to write about what is happening. I was too busy with the cooperative and lining up the vice-president to take my place to investigate.

A Radio Patrol Gives Me a Great Fright
TUESDAY, 10 AUGUST 1982

I was working peacefully with Jaime [in Panajachel]. About 5:00 P.M. I left in the afternoon to go on an errand to the office of INTECAP to see whether the representative already had left [for San José] to take the diplomas for the future bakers. But when I went out the iron gate, I saw two women from my town. These women were standing in front of the tienda Doña Rosa. When they recognized me, they spoke. I greeted them, and we began to chat.

I had talked to them only about two minutes when a private pickup with five soldiers and a radio patrol of the army stopped where we were standing. This frightened me very much. I thought something bad was going to happen. There we were, but the women were not able to speak and neither was I. It really scared me! But by the grace of God, nothing happened. We had not done anything wrong, but at times they get confused when they want to take someone else. We gave thanks to God when these men left.

We continued to chat very nervously. One of these women is called María, and the other Elena. María says that she had problems with her husband. Finally it ended up at the court of the first instance to get the man to pay for the upkeep of their baby. But the husband did not want to pay alimony. She says that the judge told her that [since she had been living in San Martín] she had to find a *Martinero* who could say in the courtroom that this man had property to apply to the law. Thus, she contracted Señor Ignacio Puzul to give testimony

to the court and help in the situation. She says that her husband went
to the headquarters of the military reserves before Ignacio could give
his declaration in court. Then Ignacio was captured by the military.
She says that her husband went to tell the military that Ignacio Puzul
is a subversive who has commitments with the guerrillas. They took
the poor fellow away for interrogation before he could make his declaration. But this was a *calumnia*, because this man is a collaborator
with the army. When there was a confrontation with the guerrillas and
the military, he came in his truck to carry the wounded soldiers.

The next morning on the launch to San José, they told me at
11:00 A.M. that the military had given Ignacio his liberty at 7:00 P.M.
[yesterday]. He came in a truck to Panajachel. Only then were the
women consoled.

But how are things [of this world]? Señor Ignacio always has
liked falsehoods, because I remember well in the month of February
1979 this man accused me falsely to the judicial police. The refrain is
true: *Con una mano lo haces y con la otra lo pagas* [One hand pays
for what the other hand does].

❧ Returning to San José to Participate in the Graduation
11 AUGUST 1982

The course in baking was concluded on Wednesday, 11 August.
It was true that I was working with my dear, unforgettable friend
James D. Sexton. I had to tell him that I was going to San José to
attend the closing. I felt a little sad at the thought of not participating.
When I arrived in the morning of Wednesday, the boys were waiting
for me to arrange things with them.

This course was very nice for us because we did not pay a thing.
True, we bought some materials, but the bread that we made we ate
ourselves. To be more frank, the bread we made for practice we sold.
I recouped part of what I had spent on the course. Moreover, my two
youngsters, Ramón and Erasmo Ignacio, observed. When we worked
they helped as if they were participating in the course. Also, we got
to know 24 persons who are not kin to us.

We prepared some tamales to eat after passing out the diplomas.
The fiesta, which was in my house, began at 8:00 P.M. First we all
sang the national anthem. Then we heard some words from the representative of INTECAP, Señor Rolando Roldán. Next we heard some

words from the maestro of baking, Juan Roberto Romero Morales. Then the secretary of the municipality spoke. Then these three persons brought the diplomas. Also, there was a group of musicians composed of just young *Joseños* [who played string music—first violin, violin, large guitars, double bass—and sang]. There were a lot of people. The street was almost full because there was not enough room for them in my house. When they finished passing out the diplomas, they asked me to say a few words of thanks [to the representative of INTECAP, the maestro, the secretary, and those who got their diplomas].

What did you say?

In my words of appreciation I said these things:

Señor Representative, Señor Municipal Secretary, representative of the municipal mayor; Señor Maestro of Baking, Juan Roberto Romero Morales; Public; Invited Persons; and Dear Companions who participated in the course, good evening to all of you. In name of God and the Instituto Capacitación y Productividad, through your means we have been able to finish a course that we never thought would come to a happy conclusion. But now we have completed it. At the same time I ask forgiveness of the maestro for all the mistakes we have made. It was not that we were disobedient. Mainly it was I who was at fault with a lot of other jobs. Dear companions, all things have their beginning and end. Here we have finished a course. Receiving a diploma means we have completed a course, but it does not mean that we must stop with that. Only if we go forward with our training will it be valuable. You may use the oven and the house for practice, although I do not have the materials [to provide] for the production. But we can work tomorrow as yesterday and today. I want us to be brothers. By the grace of God, I am neither envious nor selfish. You know well that during the last three months I have never charged a single centavo to pay for the electricity or the materials. For that reason, I am happy to be able to help serve you in something. Thanks to the señores for having participated with me. Many thanks.

These were my words.

It seems that it all went well. The municipal secretary then declared the event closed, and they sat down to eat tamales and bread. This party continued until 11:00 P.M.

Gradually it ended. The maestro, Don Juan Roberto, said good-
bye to my family. It was very sad for my children, my wife, and me
because he always arrived every day when we were working. On this
night I nearly cried, but my wife indeed was caught up in tears. She
cried a lot. She said that she was not going to do such things again,
but I told her to be more calm. She said she needed a beer, and I
agreed.

One of the bakers, named Haroldo Zacarías Ramos, was also
thirsty for a beer, and we went to a tienda. I bought ten beers, and
we went home to drink them. We talked a lot about what we had
learned in the course and about other kinds of occupations. We drank
very modestly and recalled all the suffering we had endured taking
this course because many times we were oppressed by the military
commissioners. We worked in the milpa during the day, and our practical training in baking did not begin until 4:00–5:00 P.M. We did not
finish until 11:00 P.M. because we had to wait for the dough to rise.
We were oppressed because to work in the production of bread we
always had to ask permission from the *jefe* of the military commissioners. At times he answered us with bad words, but we were not doing
anything bad—we were just learning a trade. Then they would come
and tell us that no one could leave the house where we were working
because there could be a *balacera* if someone was seen walking. But
my companions left for their houses after finishing the work anyway
because there was no place for them to sleep and because we are all
of the same town. When we finished talking, it was past 2:00 A.M.
Finally, we went to bed, but I was overcome by a deep sleep. When
I awoke, it was already 6:00 A.M. The launch had already left. For that
reason, I was not able to return to work with my friend Sexton, although I had told him I would arrive early Thursday. But always one
has faults, and I hoped he would forgive me.

Is a balacera *a discharge of arms? Was there a curfew, and if so,
what were the hours?*

Exactly, a *balacera* is a discharge of arms or when two forces fire
at each other. There was no curfew, only a threat from the commissioners. They said [for example] that on the Hill of San Jorge they met
a group of guerrillas. Then they sent for the army in San Luis. The
soldiers arrived at 11:00 P.M., but they only passed through on their
way to San Jorge. With the army there are no problems, just oppression of the commissioners, who want us to give them money for permission to work at night.

❧ Spending My Birthday Working with Jaime
13 AUGUST 1982

On Friday morning, my birthday, I left for Panajachel on the launch. The day was made more beautiful when I arrived at the house of my great friend, and he gave me two gifts—a manual for studying typewriting and a pocket calculator. I felt very happy when he told me, "Ignacio, happy birthday," and gave me the presents. Then we went to eat breakfast, and afterwards we continued working on the pages.

At 10:00 A.M. Señor Sexton went to conduct some interviews with some students, but I remained working on the pages. Within 5 to 10 minutes after my friend left, I heard a lot of gunshots very near the town. I was very scared that something might have happened to my friend. I gave thanks to God when he returned. Only then did I feel relieved, because the shots continued until 12:00 noon. I heard very well that some were shooting close to the town, and others were shooting farther away. Without doubt the two groups were firing at each other. But by the grace of God, there had been no deaths. When lunchtime arrived, I left with my friend with much fear. I did not tell this to him because I did not wish to frighten him. Here in Guatemala many misfortunes have happened.

> When I showed Ignacio the interviews I had conducted with the elementary students, he read a question dealing with the belief in naguales, or some persons having the ability to turn into other forms. He then told me the following story he had heard while riding in a canoe from San Luis to San José.

Many people say that the *nagual*, or *xibinel*, does not exist. But Don José Puzul told me that yes, indeed, it exists. I began to chat with Don José Puzul when the two of us were on the lake in a canoe one night. This señor of San Luis, a Tzutuhil with a lot of strength, was rowing us across the lake in his canoe. He is not afraid of crossing the lake at night.

Then he asked me, "Ignacio, are you afraid of going out at night?"

"At times," I answered, "because they say the *xibinel* or *nagual* goes out at night."

"Well, it is true," Don José told me. "In the time of General Ubico, when I was an *alguacil*, we were patrolling the town making sure no one would go out after 9:00 P.M. I had to guard the canton of

Pijuy with other companions. But one of them told me that a woman lived in this canton who was a *xibinel* and who went out [at night]."

Then Don José said that he told his companions, "Let's go verify whether there is a *xibinel*." But his companions did not want to go. However, he insisted that he and his companions go near the house of this woman.

"When we arrived," he said, "we smoked cigars to stimulate our bodies and overcome our fear. Little by little we got near the house."

Don José said that when they arrived across from the house they saw a woman and a man sleeping. José could see them very well because these people were living in a rustic, cane house. In about a half hour the woman got up and wiped her face with her hands. Then she crossed over her husband four times [with her whole body], but the man did not realize what she was doing. After doing this *secreto*, she covered the face of the man with a sheet. Then she took the arm [*mano*] of the milling stone and wrapped it in a sheet and left in the place where she slept with her husband. Softly she opened the door, and she left to who knows where.

But José and his companions passed the time and continued smoking cigars. None of them had a watch, but they thought it was about midnight when they saw her returning to her *sitio*. He said they grabbed her and hit her with leather whips. After whipping her hard, they let her go, but she left as if nothing had happened.

Then they went to watch her again, but when they arrived across from the house that she had entered, they saw her crying a lot. She told her husband to make a fire and to cook her some medicine. The man asked what was causing her to ache, and she replied that she had a high fever and stomachache. But it was certain that she had neither a fever nor a stomachache but aches from the lashes they, the *algua-ciles*, had given her in the road.

Don José said that in 20 days, this *xibinel* died. He told me that if I see a *nagual*, or *xibinel*, not to be afraid. Just strike it. He also said that the *nagual* can kill a weak person. But he said that I should not be afraid of the *nagual*.

☙ Reflections on the March Coup and the State of Siege
13 AUGUST 1982

For coherence, I decided to leave this episode as Ignacio typed it out rather than break it up and put it in strict chronological order.

On 23 March 1982 my companions of the three *cofradías*, San Juan Bautista, Santo Domingo Guzmán, and Virgen María, and I went to the edge of the lake to wash two goatskins for the *tun* [drum]. This hide cost us $30, which we had collected among the six *alcaldes* and *jueces* of the three *cofradías*. Holy Week was near, and the *tun* is the main signal of this event. The old skins were completely torn, and that was the reason we bought new ones.

We were going to the beach to wash the skins so that they would not be difficult to put on. We left at 8:00 A.M. and did not return until 12:00 noon. The *alcalde* of San Juan Bautista prepared a lunch for all of us, and we intended to buy a liter of liquor, so my *juez* and I went to get it.

Then, while we were eating, we heard the news on the radio that the military had ordered all employees of the National Palace to leave their offices with their hands up and not take even a pencil with them. First they took over the station TGW, Radio Nacional de Guatemala, and then they connected up with Nuevo Mundo. The radio was saying that a group of young military officers, who will be the next government, have arrived at the palace.

Then we continued eating and drinking, but in a few minutes we learned that the situation was more serious. We learned that already power was in in the hands of three generals—Efraín Ríos Montt, [Horacio] Maldonado Schaad, and one with the surname of Martínez [Colonel Luis Gordillo Martínez]. They confirmed that General Fernando Romeo Lucas García was overthrown.

It caused a great fear in the towns because the people were thinking grave things could happen. There was a lot of gossip. They said that all those on the side of Lucas will be imprisoned. They told me to burn all the books of the party because within three days they would shoot those who were with the overthrown government. But I thought, "Why burn the papers? I do not believe in fear because I have not been employed by or received money from the party. Thus, I will have no more problems." I was actually happy when the government of Lucas fell because it allowed me to get out of politics.

Many *Joseños* against the regime of Lucas began to murmur [about mistreating those in office]. I told them, "No, boys, have patience. The military is the same because one general goes and another comes." Then we talked much more sensibly. I told them, "These things are well arranged because General Lucas made a lot of propaganda about the works he had accomplished during his government such as, 'Lucas promised and Lucas delivered.' But General Lucas did not agree to say these things because he still had five months to complete his term of office." [Actually, at the time of the coup Lucas had

100 days remaining in office until he was to be replaced by General Angel Anibal Guevara Rodríguez, whom the junta accused of winning the 7 March 1982 elections fraudulently.]

On all the radios of the country they said that Lucas promised and Lucas delivered. But keeping a promise is when one finishes his work. Thus it was apparent that these things were clearly arranged because when these things happened, the minister of government, *licenciado* Donaldo Alvarez Ruiz, was in the United States [three days beforehand]. It was clearly apparent that what they have done is to make it such that the people will say that the president has changed and the government will be better. But without doubt what has happened is that the only things that have changed are the faces—nothing more. Three days after the overthrow of General Lucas, General Ríos Montt said that we would never see bodies again; never would one see massacres as in the time of the ex-president Lucas; all Guatemalans would have peace because they had a new military junta and dynamics to end the subversion and terrorism; all the products will be lowered in price; all exploitation of the *campesino* is over; there will be better treatment for the poor people; and it will all be a new Guatemala. It is true that for a few days the price of sugar and gasoline was lower. All the people were very happy because they saw that the orders of the president of the junta of the government were being carried out. But these things were a fantasy. Only some 20 days later the prices went up higher than when Lucas was in power. Then the people saw it was the same. They realized nothing had changed. The same continued, if not worse.

About 10 days after the ex-president was overthrown, the forces of the army and national police and others went to break into the house of the ex-minister, Donaldo Alvarez Ruiz. According to the news of the press [*Prensa Libre*] and on the radio and from a *Joseño* who is a policeman in the capital, they broke into the house of this man. Inside the garage were 22 armored cars, which the ranking individuals took. Many people seized a number of things inside the house such as communications radios, television sets, and wardrobes. Nothing was left inside the residence.

This is very reprehensible because they are the same as authorities who do not respect property [of someone else]. If this man committed a crime, there are laws to punish him. But I believe that when they act in this manner they are not acting as authorities—they are the ones who are teaching how to rob the people.

A little after that, the government said in a decree that on 15 June there will be changes of the *alcaldes* in all the towns in the entire country. In my town this created a big problem because there are a lot of of people who would like to be mayor. But the priest from San Martín arrived on the Sunday of the resurrection to celebrate mass. When he was finished, he called a meeting for the *cofrades, principales*, and catechists. He told us that we had to take note of the needs of the town. These were his words:

> I say to you, señores, the government has decreed the removal of all the mayors in the country. I want you to look for a man who is Catholic so that the church can depend on the mayor when it needs to. Also, it is necessary to ask the mayor for permission to have a meeting for the town to name the person who will be mayor.

Then the priest left and went to San Martín.

They named me to go to Sololá to draw up a memorandum with a lawyer. I told them I was not able to go on this assignment because I have a lot of work to do. But finally the *principales* convinced me. But I told them I agreed to do it only if they named one of the directors to accompany me, because I did not want the sole responsiblity. They named two catechists, Agustín Méndez Pantzey and Mario Ovalle Tuc. They gave us $5 each, but when we arrived in Sololá, they charged us $5 for each memorandum. [One document was for the mayor, and the other was to send to Ríos Montt when the town had chosen the new mayor.] It was good that I carried $5 of my own money because the $5 they gave us just covered our travel and food.

When we arrived home, I just left my bag and then took the memorandum to the president of Catholic Action. He told me that tomorrow he is going to deliver the memorandum into the hands of the mayor so that the town can select the new tribunal on 15 June in accordance with the decree of the new junta. But before delivering the memorandum, the mayor began to throw the president of Catholic Action, Agustín Méndez Pantzey, and Mateo Sicay Vásquez in jail because the mayor said they wanted to replace him, which is against the law. He completed the *indagatoria* to jail them. But before the law of the country and before the law of God, these persons had not done anything wrong because they had only asked that the townspeople participate in the naming of the person.

It was a big problem in the whole town. Included in this memorandum were signatures of 50 men and 150 women. The mayor said that these women were Communists who had united to turn the people against the mayor and the military commissioner to make bigger problems. But I know that this is not a crime because the people were only asking that he comply with the statutes of the military junta of the government. The citizens were very much afraid because they were thinking that they had committed a big crime. Then the mayor and the commissioners assembled the townspeople to declare that the members of the Catholic Church had committed a great crime. I was just waiting and had not said anything because I had a copy of the memorandum that honorably addressed the mayor.

The mayor succeeded in gathering all the townspeople in the assembly hall of the church. He said, "These persons who want to remove me from office have committed a great crime just because of my religion [which is Protestant]. I am taking steps to send them to prison because it is clear to me that these persons are enemies of the municipal corporation." Also, the *jefe* of the military commissioners said that, if he wanted to act bad, these persons would be sent to a military detachment. The señor *jefe* spoke badly of these persons who had signed the memorandum. All the townsfolk were humble. No one spoke. This was when I had to say something in front of everyone:

> Dear people of San José, today we are here in this assembly hall of the church for a meeting that the mayor has called. Dear residents, do not be afraid. I know very well how these things are because I have a copy of the memorandum that has not yet been presented to the mayor. It is a pity what he is doing to frighten the people who signed this memorandum. But this memorandum is in accordance with the order of the president of the military junta of the government. The memorandum is not offensive nor does it remove the mayor. It is just for the people to choose the person to take over the office on 15 June. Let's be clear and not hypocritical. You who signed the memorandum are supporting what the government has decreed. In this case, residents, the mayor and the *jefe* of the military commissioners do not want to support the government. Well, you, before the eyes of God and the law of the country, have not committed a crime. It is clear that the mayor and the military commissioner are oppressing the town. If these men send anyone to prison, well, with much pleasure, I offer my service as a witness to these things before whatever appropriate tribunal. And do not be afraid.

After I spoke, the mayor and the *jefe* of the military commissioners became very angry and said they were going to sentence me. I told them, "It is very well that you sentence me if I have committed some fault."

After I said these words the townspeople, especially those who had signed the memorandum, felt consoled. Then this meeting was not valid because those who were condemned before the people were the mayor and the head of the military commissioners. The meeting did not end until 11:00 P.M.

Did you sign the memorandum, too?

I did not sign it for their protection and so that the mayor could not find anything to sentence me for.

After I went home, many of those who signed the memorandum came to ask whether they had committed a crime, and I told them the same things that I had said at the meeting. On this night the people saw that I indeed have the courage to confront whatever circumstances when the truth is worth the bother.

The problems continued on 25 April with another group of residents who are about ten in number and headed by the ex-mayor, Juan Mendoza Ovalle. They asked for a meeting of the townspeople to elect a person for the office of mayor on 15 June. But the town realized that the leader of the group is interested in being mayor again. But he did a lot to the inhabitants when he was previously in office. This meeting was nothing more than a feud because everyone told him of the bad he had committed—a lot of people had given him money when he was offering lands and demarcating the landmarks. Nearly all the people shouted at this man. Thus the meeting went. Nothing more happened than the mistreating of Señor Juan Mendoza. Everything was in disorder, and no one appreciated this meeting.

There is another señor, named Sebastian López García, who also was mayor twice and wanted to be mayor again, but he did not make a fuss. He sent his name directly to the governor asking to be named mayor again. But his attempt was futile. Without doubt, this man was given bad recommendations to the governor by other residents.

When it was near 15 June, the commissioners gave the names of their companions, and later they said the governor chose them [the mayors]. But I know well that they were selected by the military commissioners. It is very apparent that the military commissioners chose them. We are not able to believe that the military commissioners just happen to have a lot of luck because in my town the mayor who was named is Andrés Bizarro Mendoza, who is the assistant of the military commissioners. Also it was the same in San Martín, San Jorge, and San Luis—just helpers of the military commissioners. Then the towns realized that all of it was arranged by the military commissioners. For us what happened has happened, but who knows who will lead the people to a better future.

How were the names selected?

One day the military commissioners called a meeting when most people, including me, were working. There were not more than 30 people who attended, and most of them were women. Those present provided three names, and the fourth name was chosen by the military commissioners. The names went to the palace and to the governor. According to the radio, the names were chosen in a lottery. The governors were not replaced until later.

When General Efraín Ríos Montt joined the coup [23 March 1982, but actually it could have been hatched in January 1982, according to the *Christian Science Monitor* (25 March 1982)], he was declared the president of the military junta. Later [9 June 1982] they declared him president [of the republic] without consulting the towns. Many say that General Ríos Montt usurped the rights of the citizenry, because the president of the republic should be elected by a popular vote and never by electing himself. But in the end the townspeople have to conform because we are not able to talk about these things because the military indeed has a lot of power. The civilian population is not able to do anything.

During [the 30 days of] the month of June, the government declared and decreed that all Guatemalans committed to the guerrillas could lay down their arms and return to work and the government would give them money. Also, they said that they would give them employment and peace in all Guatemala. The same government ordered all the institutions and organizations like the Red Cross, Catholic Church, Evangelist Church, tribunals, and the command of the military reserves to give refuge to the guerrillas during the next 30 days. All the radios in the country announced this every other moment, as did television. But the revolutionaries hardly want what the government offered. They say that some accepted, but without stating the number. After granting the 30 days of amnesty, the government declared 30 days of an *estado de sitio* [a state of siege, beginning 1 July 1982], or suspension of [constitutional] guarantees [already limited by the March coup], in an attempt to end the subversion. An *estado de sitio* is to say that one remains subject to the orders of the supreme government. There are no rights to organize meetings without prior permission of the military authority; there is no liberty to walk at night. Where there are more than five persons in a meeting, they will be investigated regarding the nature and motive of the meeting. There is an order to penetrate whatever *sitio* to see whether there are truly subversive persons. But by the grace of God, in the the towns of the lake there aren't any because all the men are dedicated to their work in the milpa. And the truth is that the military do not bother us. There are a lot of kidnappings, but one does not know which of the two groups—the right or the left—[is responsible]. Many say it is the army, and many say it is the guerrillas. What is most clear is that there are false accusations for very personal reasons—suits or arguments over land, arguments over women, envy that another person has money, or does not pay a debt. For these reasons, they are accused of being guerrillas. That is the origin of these things. Right now [August 1982] these things continue in San Luis—always people continue to disappear, every two days, or every week. Now there is imposed a state of siege, but the same things continue [as before]. But definitely it is not known which of the two groups is responsible. Or perhaps both are.[30]

You also told me that you dreamed about the government of Lucas.

Yes, this was 15 September 1981. I do not have it in my diary because they could discover my diary and think I was against the government. On a separate piece of paper I just wrote down the date and the title of the dream, "About Lucas." And who would know which Lucas. I remember the dream very, very well. It was a very, very, very strange thing. Lucas hardly knew he would be overthrown. I dreamed about 2:30 or 3:00 A.M. Suddenly in my house there were were a lot of photographs of Lucas, plenty of Lucas. And across the street there were photographs of Lucas, the president. Then I said, "There are a lot of photographs here. *Púchica*, who put these up! I did not see who did. I have a picture of the president that is large, but who put more photographs here and outside?"
Suddenly some men arrived dressed in military green who said, "Are these photos of the president?"
"Yes," I answered.
"Who put them up?"
"I don't know!"
"Look, it is your house," they told me.

"Well, I don't know. Someone came in and put them up. I have only one photo. It is this one."

"Ah, it is this one."

"Yes."

They took a marker of a prominent color of ink and wrote, "Lucas will be overthrown. Lucas is a pure shit president."

Púchica, I felt scared. "Señor," I said, "don't do this to me because the government may kill me. They may think I am mistreating the president," I told him.

"Ah, you are one with them."

"No, it is that I have the photo here for respect."

"This photo is worthless."

He began to tear up all the photos that were in my house, and they left through the door and began to tear up all the photos that were outside. "Lucas is worthless! Lucas is worthless! Lucas is worthless!" one was writing, and the other was tearing up the photos.

"But you are messing up my house," I told them.

"Yes," he told me, "why are you with the government also? Be thankful that we are not going to kill you."

"Señor," I told him, "but I'm not at all to blame. I have not done anything. I intended to renounce, and they told me the same thing, that they are going to kill me if I resign from the party. Then there is no solace for me. You are telling me that you are going to kill me for being with them, and the government tells me that they are going to kill me if I resign. To whom can I turn?"

"Don't worry," he said, "don't worry. In a little while Lucas will not be president." But the man was very angry, very angry! And his companions were there ready. "Positively, we are going to remove Lucas! Lucas we are going to get rid of!"

"That is all right. It is your thing of which I know nothing," I told them in my dream.

"Good, we need to go to the courthouse and do the same thing," they said.

"You," I said, "not me. I'm not going to tell you not to go. You have bothered me. You have dirtied my house, but I can clean it," I told them.

"Stay. We are carrying out an order." And they left.

Still, I went out the door to see which path they took, to see whether they went to the central part of town. Then I said, "I'm going to look for a paintbrush." Then I was painting over the bad things they had written on the wall. It was as if I had been given a job to do. "God knows when I will have the wall repaired again!" And this is when I woke up.

I told my family, "Look, I dreamed that Lucas is going to fall."

"Is that so?" said my señora. "But how?"

"The guerrillas," I told her. "I dreamed they were guerrillas. They were in the same dress as the army and they had good arms."

"Is that so?"

"Guaranteed!"

Later, in a meeting, the boys of the cooperative were assembled, and we were talking about the situation. I told the boys, since there is a military commissioner in the cooperative. I told them, "I dreamed a very important thing. Does anyone know that Lucas is going to end his time? It seems that they are going to remove him. I dreamed such a thing."

"You are loco, Ignacio. More than anything else you are loco," he [the commissioner] told me. "Why is Lucas going to leave if he has the whole army? Lucas is the strongest man in Guatemala. I do not much believe there will be an overthrow."

"It is not certain, but I recommend that you do not do undesirable things because it can provoke a problem. I had this dream, and I am not going to bother much more with the parties. I will fulfill a requirement so that I can say I'm not against them, but I'm not going to struggle a lot for them because it can cause a serious thing for me or the town. Better not," I said. "I'm advising you of this."

"Ah, how can this be, hombre? We know well about Lucas because we always have communication with the army," he told me. "There is nothing."

"Very well," I said.

Thus, this was my dream. And on 30 September I dreamed the same thing. But in my dream I was in Sololá on an errand. Suddenly some hombres came and assembled the whole town with a loudspeaker. "Today is going to be a new thing. There is going to be a new thing, good things."

I said to myself, "Good things, what good things?"

Well, all of us were assembled. I was there, the government was there, the governor, and the *jefes* of the military were there.

With the loudspeaker, they began to say, "Right now comes the real good. So we have invited the students, the children, the poor, and the rich to come hear these things—all that the government of Lucas has done."

Púchica, I was scared, because I had had something to do with the government. But I had not done anything. More than anything I had suffered because they had not given me a single centavo. I was like a horse with a load, and I received nothing for it.

Then the governor said that they had considered it and they were going to accept. Then he left, and another took his place.

"Thus, it is that the government of Lucas is worthless. Right now we are replacing the government." Then the man moved away and began to tell all the bad things Lucas had done and all the bad things that the members of the government had committed. Then I saw that all the people there in front were applauding, but they were not applauding the army. They were applauding, "Long live the guerrillas! Long live the Organización del Pueblo en Armas! Long live the trade unions!"

"*Púchica*, what is this?" I said, "Long live the trade unions. I hardly know what a trade union is!"

"Long live the people now that the hombres who esteem the people are in power."

"My goodness," I said. Then the students and children got up and began to sing the national anthem. And in my dream I was singing with them. And thus was my dream.

It seemed that I understood in my dream that the government of Lucas was worthless. When I woke up I told my family what I had dreamed and that without doubt Lucas was going to lose.

"Ah, will it be true?" they asked me, because at times they are afraid my dreams will come true. And in seven months the government of Lucas fell. I do not know why I dream these things. At times it is surprising to dream things that come true. Perhaps I need a person to tell me why this is.

℘ We Work Hard to Finish the Pages
SATURDAY, 14 AUGUST 1982

We continued working to finish the papers, but there were a lot of them and it was exhausting. We were pretty tired, but it was true we had worked a lot. At times I felt too tired to write anymore, but we were obliged to complete it. Although it was already Saturday, we still had pending the story of the founding of the cooperative.

In early afternoon the señor began to arrange his suitcase and all the pages in his briefcase. I was still typing more pages. When he was through arranging all his luggage, he packed the typewriter [in its original case]. He told me he was going to leave the typewriter with me, but I doubted him because I had no money to pay for it. But later he told me he was leaving it as a gift. I felt like a child who did not understand or could not control his happiness. Then my friend signed a document that said he gave the typewriter as gift to Ignacio Bizarro Ujpán.

When I retired to the room where I was sleeping, I thanked God and Jesucristo for the things he was giving me, which included a modern dictionary. These things are very expensive and valuable. Many thanks [go] to the good heart of this dear friend and his wife.

∿ Jaime Sexton Leaves
15 AUGUST 1982

When Sunday dawned, we got up at 5:00 A.M. We showered and drank coffee. Then I went to the beach to meet my wife and children because they had agreed to bring me my clothing to take to Guatemala [City]. Since the launch had arrived already, I found my family in the street. Then they entered the house to greet Señor Sexton. My wife said that she wanted to say good-bye to him when he returned to his country. I told her he was ready to go, so Anica, José, Susana Julia, and I all greeted him. Then we went to the restaurant to eat. [Ignacio and his family also said a prayer for my safe return, and his wife, Anica, gave me a small suit of typical clothing that she had woven and sewn for my five-year old son.]

My wife did not much want to enter the *comedor*. "Ignacio," she said, "let's not go into a *comedor* because we do not have money to pay for breakfast." But our friend paid for it.

In the restaurant we met a bilingual maestro of San Luis named Ricardo Pantzay Yoc. This boy was going to Guatemala [City] to take the same course that I was going to take. I told him that we should go together, but he told me that he would have to wait for his papers for admission to the university.

When we returned to the same *sitio* where Don Jaime and I had been working, my friend tried to finish the papers on the history of the cooperative, but it was not possible because it was too long. Still, we were able to go over part of it.

Since it was the fiesta of Sololá, we were told that there were no direct buses to Guatemala [City]. Then we boarded a bus of the Mendoza of Chichicastenango line, which eventually let us off at Los Encuentros. I was a little sad to leave my family in Panajachel, but I did not tell them to go to the fiesta in Sololá with me because I was accompanying the best friend of all my life.

When they collected our travel money, my friend paid. When we arrived in the capital, the bus let us off at the Trébol, and then a taxi took us to La Aurora Airport. He charged us $6, which to me was very expensive.

When we arrived at the airport, there was still some time before the departure of the airplane. We sat down in a restaurant in the airport, and my friend finished reading the history of the cooperative. We corrected some errors, but still some parts were not clear. [Ignacio later cleared them up by answering some questions I sent him in a letter.]

When we finished lunch, we left the restaurant. Because the hour of departure of the airplane had arrived, we said good-bye. My unforgettable friend left me so that he could enter the departure gate. I left with tears in my eyes and much sadness, because I do not know whether we will see one another again. But what can we do?

This friend paid me well during the days I worked with him in Panajachel. With this money I was able to cover the expenses for my family and for the course in the university that I was going to take.

In the afternoon of this Sunday, but not until 3:00 P.M., I was with other friends from San Miguel, Santa Apolonia, and my friend Yoc from San Luis. We went to the Federación Guatemalteca de Cooperativas de Consumo [Guatemalan Federation of Cooperatives of Consumption]. But since it was Sunday no one was there. Finally we asked permission of a señor to take us to the university. He charged us $2 just for the diesel. It seemed distant to go to Zone 16.

They admitted us at the university and told us that no one was able to leave because of the situation that the country was experiencing. Also, they said that if we did not obey their orders, the university would not be responsible for [what might happen] to any of the participants. They gave us a bed, bedclothes, and food. And they introduced us to friends from other countries who have a very distinct manner of speaking.

A Shaman Resists Abduction
16–23 AUGUST 1982

We ate breakfast quietly, and they gave us a chance to get to know one another by name. The professors were very good persons because they let everyone participate. But I delayed participating for three days. I mainly observed to learn better. At times I wanted to speak, but at the same time I thought I had better not because I was among highly educated persons and I am hardly educated. But later I participated a lot in a lot of things.

In the afternoon of this day I heard the news that there had been another misfortune in San Luis. My friend, Ricardo Pantzay Yoc, scarcely ate because the persons who were eliminated were his neighbors. Thus went the day.

On 17 August the boys gave us news that the department of Sololá was in a very delicate situation. No one was able to walk outside past 8:00 P.M. But this was a falsehood of the reporters, who said that the government had decreed a state of siege and curfew only in the department of Sololá. When we heard this news, it alarmed us very much because the radio repeatedly said that the department of Sololá was in a dangerous situation because bad persons had been found in San Luis.

Well, we continued to take our course, but we constantly worried about our families. Then my friend Ricardo asked permission to travel to San Luis on Sunday. The coordinator of the course, Señorita Angelina, gave Ricardo permission to go see about his family. Then, on 22 August, Ricardo left the university very sad to go to San Luis.

This Sunday, together with other friends, I asked permission to go to the stadium to watch a game of soccer between a team of Guatemala and a team from Washington, United States. It was the first time in my life that I had ever gone to the Mateo Flores National Stadium. Well, all went well. [But] Guatemala lost.

When we left the stadium, we went downtown to eat lunch. At 5:00 P.M. we returned to the university, where they confined us once again. We ate dinner, but I continued to worry about my friend Ricardo.

Monday dawned, and we ate breakfast. Then we continued with the course. Ricardo did not arrive until 10:00 A.M. I did not chat with him because we were busy. During lunch hour, however, we were together, and he told me that after lunch we could retire more inside the garden to talk a little about what had happened in San Luis. He told me this so that no one else would be aware of what we were talking about. I was attentive to what he was telling me.

After lunch we went back a little out of view where he told me, "Ignacio, I am going to tell you these things because you are an honorable person, but I do not want you to tell any of my companions in the course what happened in my town."

Ricardo said that in San Luis there is a shaman named Coyoy
Temaj, who is one of the best of the Tzutuhil shamans. But without
doubt some among them [the shamans] were not in accord with what
he was doing, and they denounced him to the military detachment
nearby (about two kilometers away), saying that he was a Communist
because he was doing *costumbres* for those who are of the left. This
took place at night. When Monday, 16 August, dawned, a man from
San Luis accompanied the military and in *lengua* woke up the shaman,
saying that he had a sick person in his family who needed a *costumbre*.
Coyoy did not want to get up because he knew the situation was delicate. But the man from San Luis was urging him do a *costumbre* before his sick person died.

Finally, the shaman got up, but when he stepped out of his house
he was captured by some men (soldiers). When they grabbed him, he
shouted, and his wife came to help. When she came out, they began
to hit her. The soldiers wanted to kill the woman, but it was incredible
that their arms did not discharge. That is to say, they were not able to
kill her. Then she got more courage and hit them, gravely wounding
the two of them. Possibly the *naguales* of the shaman and his wife
entered the third dimension, because they put up a tremendous fight.
The two evildoers remained in the *sitio* unable to walk. But then a
military commissioner, himself of San Luis, arrived and shot the shaman, but he was not able to kill him although he left him gravely
wounded. This same man carried the two wounded men toward the
encampment. The people say that they know well that they were
members of the military because it was almost dawn when they left
town. They were not able to walk because they were wounded in the
testicles.

What is the third dimension?

The word [third] dimension is when a person or *brujo* changes
into something mysterious or is when the *nagual* goes into action,
because they say that each *brujo* has his *nagual*. When the moment
comes for the *nagual* to work, the *brujos* turn into animals like jaguars, cats, or birds, but they say that they do this when they want to
hide from the enemy to conquer him. And they say that the *nagual*
disappears into the air. That is what they call the [third] dimension—
nagual, or power.

When it was completely daylight, the woman presented herself
before the court asking for a town meeting so that she could tell what
had happened. When the townsfolk were assembled, she began to

explain in Tzutuhil that she and her husband had been taken out of their house, and she presented her husband, who was wounded in the leg. Then she asked the help of the mayor for the protection of the people. But when she finished her declaration, the mayor did not speak a single word.

In San Luis a small group of *bomberos*, made up of local teachers, had just been organized. Their first service was to transfer the shaman to the hospital in Sololá. Unfortunately, when they were passing the bridge [over the Panajachel River] near Panajachel, they were fired at with an incendiary bomb. The car was totally consumed by the resulting fire, and the driver and the shaman were burned. The only one who escaped from the fire was a companion, who was hit by a splinter. It was he who provided the information that the bomb was fired by some men of particular dress. The people of San Luis say that the bomb was fired by soldiers so that no one would arrive to describe what had happened; that is, the shame that they had suffered in the *sitio*. They were not able to kill the shaman with arms; it took a bomb!

These things my friend, Ricardo Pantzay Yoc, confided in me. They are true, because he had to go to his town to find out about what he had heard on the radio.

In this course we made a lot of friends with people from other towns. This course was very strict; two Colombians were expelled for infractions. They asked permission to leave, but they stayed out past the hour. A person from Jutiapa had to leave for two days because his brother died. But he returned and received his diploma.

ꙮ The Closing of the Course in the University
26–29 AUGUST 1982

This day was very pleasant. They prepared a special lunch for the closing of the course at 5:00 P.M. All day I was dressed in the *traje* of San Luis because my friend Ricardo had managed to carry back some suits when he went home.

Also, in the afternoon we presented some folklore about the *costumbre* of Maximón and his miracles. Maximón in *lengua* is *Rij Laj Mach*. That is to say, a powerful man with a white beard.

The organization of the [cast] of the folklore was: Maximón, played by my friend Benito Sáenz Yojcon, of Santa Apolonia; the most powerful shaman, who was in charge of carrying Maximón on his shoulders, played by myself; a shaman making a *costumbre* before Maximón to consult a cure for a sick person, played by my friend

Ricardo Pantzay Yoc; the sick person, played by my friend Nataniel, of San Miguel; and the mother of the sick person, played by a companion from Chimaltenango. Accompanying the presentation was music of a pure marimba.

We came out of an office with Maximón on my shoulders. I entered and danced toward the audience, which was very amazed. I had to dance for about five minutes. Then we lowered Maximón and with much respect set him in a chair. Then the shaman began to make the *costumbre* for the health of the sick person, who was laid out moaning with much pain. The shaman presented a lot of offerings such as candles, *tragos*, and myrrh incense.

The day before, during the hour of rest after lunch, I looked for some animal to [pretend to] kill during the play for the act of witchcraft. I found a small lizard in the garden. I caught it and kept it inside a pail and fed it with some insects. Thus, when it was time for [the presentation] to begin, we put the lizard inside some plastic and placed it in the clothing of the sick person. When the shaman performed the witchcraft, the animal came out alive from inside the clothing of the sick person. It astonished the audience. They thought we really were *brujos*, because the animal came running out of the clothing of the sick person to the shoulder of the shaman, who did the *costumbre* with the animal on his shoulder. When it was finished, I grabbed the animal and returned it to the place where I had caught it.

The presentation gave us international fame. That is to say, there were persons from other countries who could not do the same things. When this was all over, the director and the professors of the course called us the teachers of the shamans of San Luis. We answered that the two of us were almost shamans, and they believed that it was true. But after the questions, Ricardo and I just laughed because neither of us is a shaman. It was just the force of the blood when we did this presentation, but it was nearly real. For that reason, the participants were very amazed at what they were seeing.

When this folklore was over, a lot of señoritas invited us to dance, but I am not accustomed to dancing. Still, I had to accept a dance with a señorita named Judit Francisca, who came to the course representing El Salvador.

After the dance they gave us the diplomas of Self-formation for Social Promoters in Techniques and Group Dynamics. I was very happy, because the diplomas are signed by the director of the university and the secretary-general and director of the course of CAPS of the Rafael Landivar University. I had some discussions in Spanish and others in *lengua*. After all of this we went to eat dinner.

At 8:00 P.M. the fiesta continued, and a lot were dancing. But I did not wish to dance anymore. I went to bed at 9:00 P.M., but not peacefully because there was a lot of racket, which did not end until 11:00 P.M. And when they came into the room, they continued chatting until midnight. I hardly slept.

We got up at 5:00 A.M. and handed in the bedding. Then they gave us breakfast. Afterwards, we said good-bye to our companions in the course, and each one took his own road. Well, we companions of San Miguel and Santa Apolonia did not say good-bye until Panajachel, where I caught the launch to San José.

When I arrived home, my family was surprised. They thought I would not be coming home until Saturday afternoon. But by the grace of God, they let us leave Friday. I have another obligation in the *cofradía* to celebrate the beheading of San Juan Bautista. This was all completed with my companions of the *cofradía* on 29 August.

❧Examples of Evil Spirits
30 OCTOBER–6 NOVEMBER 1982

Many people do not believe in spirits, but two things happened that are true. First, in the town there is an organization of *autodefensa civil* [civilian self-defense] that goes out each night to protect the people [from guerrillas]. It is very well organized. Some have turns from 9:00 P.M. and others from 1:00–4:00 A.M.

On this night, two days before the celebration of the Day of the Dead [30 October], my first cousin, Gilberto Bizarro Salazar, and some others took their turn. They were in front of the cooperative when suddenly they saw a woman leave a house, but they say she left about two feet above the ground. That is to say, she was almost in the air, and gradually she got closer. However, they could not see her face well—it was like a ghost. But it was clearly in the form of a woman. Gilberto and his companions say that, when the woman got close to them, they wanted to fire their weapons, but their arms would not discharge. In a blink of an eye it disappeared.

A possible solution [to this puzzle] is that Señora Luisa Sisay Bizarro died in this house in the month of February of this year. I know well that it was the month of February because we *cofrades* buried this señora. Without doubt it is the spirit of this woman who appeared in this place.

The same thing happened to my son José. Four days had passed since All Souls' Day. That is to say, it was 6 November. During the month of November, here in town they celebrate mass in honor of souls in purgatory. Thus, in this afternoon, they celebrated mass, and in the night I went to the cooperative for a meeting. After the meeting, I went with Abraham to the house of his father, who is gravely ill. We took care of him until 1:00 A.M. When I finally arrived home, my wife was very frightened, and she told me what had happened.

She had been sleeping from 9:00 P.M., since none of us had gotten much sleep because of our activities in the *cofradía*. But José had gone out for a walk through the street. He returned about 9:30 P.M. and went to his bed to go to sleep. However, he did not go to sleep. He was lying down in bed when suddenly a woman opened the door and entered the house calling the name of my wife. José said that he saw the woman well because the light was on, but suddenly she disappeared. It scared him very much, and he began to wake up his mother. But my wife says that while she was sleeping, she dreamed she was chatting with my Aunt María [Ignacio's foster mother], but this señora has been dead for 14 years. My señora says that she does not remember anything about the conversation because she had just begun to chat with her when José woke her up and interrupted her dream.

What we believe is that the spirit of the dead always exists. What happens at death is that the soul leaves. This is because the body is corrupt but not the spirit. José says that he saw the woman when she opened the door. But when he woke up his mother and together they went to close the door, it was already completely closed.

By 1:00 A.M., when I arrived home, my family was awake thinking that something bad had happened to me because the situation is very delicate. But the reason for my coming home late was that we had to care for the sick person. These things are true.

❧ A Dream Is a Foreboding of Danger
14 NOVEMBER 1982

This is a difficult story that happened to us on Sunday, 14 November. At 4:00 A.M. I had a dream, and when I later got up I told my wife. In the dream I saw that I was in a canoe, rowing with my friend Eduardo Flores Sicay. Then we saw a skeleton of a dead person, but it was distant. Then I told my companion that we should head back to the beach. When we arrived at the beach, we again saw the skeleton.

After I told my wife about the dream, she warned me not to go to Panajachel for a meeting because something bad might happen. But since I was committed to other members of the cooperative, I had to go.

We left San José at 6:00 A.M., but the wind was tremendously strong, and we were nearly killed. The motor was not moving the launch. This worried us because only by the grace of God were we gradually able to edge close to the shore until we succeeded in arriving in Panajachel.

The commissioners [who came with us] carried their arms because nearly everyone had come, and they were afraid if they left their arms [in San José] someone might steal them. But no one advised the police in Panajachel that we were coming. Very confidently we took the main street of the town without realizing what the inhabitants were thinking of us.

Well, in front of the Texaco gasoline station, we met an American, who took pictures of us. Then he asked us if we were guerrillas, and we answered no. Then he told us the pictures were worthless because he wanted pictures of rebels. Not until then did we feel foolish, because the people believed we were leftists. We were unaware that someone had gone to advise the police [that rebels were coming].

When we got near the headquarters of the police, the police had already taken positions to confront us with arms. Also, police in a jeep were ready to shoot grenades at us. We did not realize what they thought about us. Then they told us to halt and ordered that only one person advance to identify our group. The captain asked if we were ORPA [Organización de Pueblo en Armas] or EGP [Ejército Guerrillero de los Pobres] and said that we should not use our arms. Then a military commissioner said, "We are of the *fuerza permanente egresados* [active reserves] of the national army, and we came to participate in a meeting with the *comandante* of the military reserves of Sololá." Only then did we meet the police, but we continued advancing toward them because they did not ask us for some kind of identification.

This capture of the police was very interesting because, a little while after we met them there, a very drunk military man arrived who thought we were guerrillas and who thought he could kill us with his rifle. But as we were many, the rest of my companions intended to disarm him. But I told them it is not possible to argue with a drunk and to leave him be. The drunk military man heard and understood what I told my companions. He shot at the ground and left. It was very funny because in that town they took us for guerrillas, and luckily they did not kill us because the boys carried only four 12-gauge shotguns and five .22 rifles. These were very light arms compared to the arms of the elements of the government. They could have pulverized us.

The reason for the meeting was to let us know that there is the probability that the government is going to sign up those of us who have done military service (*egresados del ejército*), but for just six months. The reason is that the soldiers in due time are going to be very tired of fighting the guerrillas, and he [the *comandante* of the reserves] could not send persons who are not familiar with arms. Thus he needs persons who know how to handle automatic weapons. They will get a salary of only $75 [a month] plus $25 for [dependents such as] parents or wives.

For me the trip was all right because I was able to find out directly about the situation of the *Martineros* when they were talking to the *comandante* of the reserves. What I saw in Panajachel will be in the pages that follow.

I wrote to Ignacio asking whether the egresados, *including himself, would have to serve for six months in the army or as reservists. Also, I asked if this would be for all the* egresados *of Sololá and if the age of each was important. He responded in the following manner.*

This was my fault. I should have said the government is going to sign up those who have served in the army for six months or military service as active soldiers in the barracks in the state or in the detachments so that the old soldiers will be selected with the young ones for a good formation, not just in Sololá but in the whole country.

They said that the age of a person was not important, only that he be in good health if he was obliged to do the six months' service. Almost the majority of the departments, or, better said, the *egresados*, of the departments indeed served the six months of military service, but not just in the department of Sololá and not just in the towns on the shore of the lake. But this [program] now [10 March 1983] has been eliminated. Now there are only young soldiers in the barracks.[31]

❧ The Situation in San Martín with the Military Commissioners
SEPTEMBER–DECEMBER 1982

Now I am going to write an episode about the situation of my neighboring town of San Martín la Laguna, hoping that whoever reads these things will have pause for reflection. At times we talk about things without knowing what is really happening. All of the towns on the shore of the lake said that the army was the cause of many kidnappings of the humble campesinos. But the truth is that it is not the army. If the army executed a sentence, it was because someone had accused a person.

In San Martín la Laguna, the first kidnappings began on 20 September 1981. First the baker Bernabé Ajacac was kidnapped. Then on 13 November the same thing happened to the campesino Jacobo Salas. Their bodies never appeared. In March of 1982 the farmer Oscar Tzep, who is a tailor, was kidnapped. His religion was evangelist (Protestant), and he was a decent man. He was kidnapped when he returned from an evangelistic meeting in San Jorge la Laguna. His body appeared on the highway to Cocales. The negative version that his family gave was that the kidnappers spoke *lengua*. After he was kidnapped, they searched his house and carried away $300. There was no more investigation, but the *Martineros* said that those who carried out the kidnappings were Indians.

During this same month a humble peasant by the surname of Xico was kidnapped, and his body disappeared. In the same year two humble stonemasons were kidnapped. One was a native of San Martín, and the other was a native of San Luis who was living in San Martín. First they were threatened so that they would give a sum of money, but they were unable to pay. A little later they were abducted, and their bodies did not appear. These persons were poor, and their lives as stonemasons were very hard in construction work.

The townspeople were alarmed because they heard that there were more blacklists. But there were doubts [about who was responsible]. Some said members of the army while others said the guerrillas were doing the kidnapping.

But later a famous *Martinero* by the name of Ignacio Cojox was abducted. They kidnapped him only because he fought the military commissioners and gave them trouble. His body disappeared.

A little later the news emerged that many *Martineros* were threatened with anonymous letters accusing them of having contact with the guerrillas and saying that in a little while or so they also would be kidnapped. What these men did was ask the commissioners to prevent such kidnappings, and then the commissioners asked for large sums of money to have them erased from the blacklist. It was no more than that they [the commissioners] had fabricated anonymous letters to scare the people. When the people received the letters, they went to the commissioners to pay large sums of money.

Thus, the people little by little came to realize that the commissioners were the cause of many misfortunes. The person who could not pay the quantity of money they were demanding would disappear for sure within a few days. Many people sold their land simply out of fear that they were going to be killed. The townspeople wanted to investigate, but the person who was in charge of the investigation was kidnapped. This was when the people realized that they had no [local] support and that they had to go beyond the commissioners.

For the commissioners it was a business, because they did not work; they lived off what they extorted from the people, just drinking and womanizing. Two of the commissioners were now equipped with two women. They first threatened the husbands of these women, and the poor husbands did nothing as their women went to live with the two commissioners.

Thus, more *Martineros* were disappearing, but no one had the courage to denounce them because of fear of becoming victims of this cruel savagery. The commissioners were content because they were not without money. They continued with this machismo without realizing that some day they would be discovered by the national army.

It was after the fall of the government of General Lucas García that the illustrious *Martinero* named Bartolomé Yac, a man of much courage, went from house to house of the *Martineros* who had given money to the commissioners. This man wrote down the names and the amount of money they had given. Then, along with Santiago Yac, he went to the capital of Guatemala to denounce the commissioners before the supreme government so that they would investigate and clarify why so many kidnappings were taking place.

Thus it was for some months. The commissioners continued with the same business without realizing that later there would be a grave thing for them.

Also, they went to San Jorge to kidnap the merchant Ignacio Piloy Tobar. The commissioner of San Jorge made contact with the commissioners of San Martín. Then during a night the latter went to that town. The house of the señor was very simple, and it was very easy for them to break in and take out the said señor and then search his house. They took $250. These men operated in two groups—one group kidnapped the persons, and another group used masks to rob the house. Thus it was in the house of Señor Piloy.

However, the residents realized that they had kidnapped the owner of the house, and they set out to catch the kidnappers. But when they got near to where they were torturing the man, the commissioners fired their arms five times. The residents then did not have the courage to get close to them. They tied the man to an avocado pole and left him nearly dead. There was an ant nest there, and the ants began to bite Señor Piloy. But gradually he recovered, and he realized that the kidnappers were Indians, because they spoke in *lengua*. And he was aware when they divided his money. He said that he acted as if he were already dead because it was true that they had beaten him severely. But by the grace of God, they did not shoot their weapons. He said that he heard when one of them asked whether to finish killing him. One of them (a leader) said, "No, leave him thus," [because] they had already obtained a little money.

This was when the *Jorgeños* realized it was *Martineros* who were doing these misdeeds. But, as I said earlier, no one had the courage to denounce them because he who denounced the commissioners, they say, would have his whole family killed. Thus, all the people were afraid.

When the commissioners did not have money, they just sent a letter to ask for money of another person, and if this person denied them, they accused him of being a guerrilla fighter. It was certain that they would take this person out to kidnap him. These evil commissioners committed many disgraces in this neighboring town, including threatening the poor women at the point of a pistol. The women had to allow them to have sexual intercourse even though they were married. Their husbands did not have the means to bring action against these men because presenting their demands meant their death was certain.

This is what happened to Señor Guido Vallejo. This man had a little money because he is the owner of a small inn. One night they came inside his house and tied him up and began to search his house. But they say that this man had his money in another house. When they saw that they would find nothing, all of them raped the wife of Guido Vallejo. When they finished raping her, they untied her husband and told him not to say anything because he would suffer the consequences. This poor husband thus did not do anything. What was even more lamentable was that Guido Vallejo was the mayor of the town, a person respected by the *principales*. Moreover, he is the father of one of the teachers of the primary school. But the commissioners, like animals, respected no one.

Later they kidnapped another person whose crime was that he had married a student, but this boy whom they kidnapped was also a student. The boy's surname was Cumatz Cojbx, and the girl's name was Tobías Flores. This happened recently because for about two months the body of the boy has not appeared. The *Martineros* say that without doubt one of the commissioners wanted to be with the girl.

In the middle of the month of October of this year [1982], they carried out their last kidnapping [when they abducted] the municipal

commissary, Santiago García Ajacac. They say that, days before, he
had had a discussion with the commissioners, and in the same week
the commissary was kidnapped. The *Martineros* say that when night
fell, the commissioners arrived to arrange the shifts guarding the
town. They say that they took all the *alguaciles* to the landmark of San
José to prevent enemies from entering. They left only three *alguaciles*
with the commissary waiting for litigants or petitions [of whatever residents who came to the municipality with a grievance]. But according
to the *Martineros*, the commissioners already knew what was going to
happen because another group of their companions were in charge of
kidnapping the commissary. The landmark of San José and San Martín
is at a summit, or peak, that towers so that one can see both towns.
They were there when suddenly a great uproar began in the town.
They told an assistant commissioner to go see what was happening.
When the assistant commissioner arrived, he saw the *alguaciles* and
two of their companions tied up by their hands and feet in front of the
municipality. Then the assistant ran to tell the rest of his companions
what had happened. They did this to confuse the *alguaciles* who were
walking with them so that the people would say that they did not know
the kidnappers. However, they say one of the *alguaciles* saw that the
companions of the commissioners were those who kidnapped the commissary. Then the townsfolk became alarmed and began to look for the
other commissioners, who then could not be found in the town. This
confirmed that they were divided into two groups when they orches-
trated the kidnapping. The kin of the kidnapped García Ajacac and
the townspeople tried to find his body, but it was futile.

The commissioners of San Martín tried to make contact with the
commissioners of this town, but it was fortunate for the *Joseños* that
the *jefe* of the commissioners is a member of the cooperative who is
secretary of the board of control. Well, in the cooperative we have
discussed only good things, or, better said, we have made good recommendations for not staining the town. Each time the commissioners [of San Martín] were looking for a contact, one of our commissioners advised me of what they [the *Martineros*] tried to do.

By the grace of God, among the commissioners of San José, I
have two first cousins. I always recommend their not doing anything
with the *Martineros* because I know very well the bad attitude of the
Martineros, a lesson I learned when they accused me falsely. From
that time on, I quit being their friend. And I always tell the commissioners of the town to take more care so that no one will accuse them
of misdeeds before the guerrillas. It seems that they paid attention to
me because without my recommendations, who knows how the commissioners of this town [of San José] would be.

The people of San Martín had already forgotten the petition that Bartolomé Yac had presented. For his protection, Bartolomé very confidentially made the list of names and money given to the commissioners because if the commissioners had realized that Bartolomé was their enemy, without doubt they would have killed him earlier. But Bartolomé acted very serenely with them and as if he were their great friend.

My wife and I knew very well that the petition was presented because one day Santiago Yac chatted with my wife telling her these things:

> We *Martineros* are suffering a lot in our town because of the commissioners. First they killed my son-in-law, Oscar Tzep, and immediately they took money from my son Diego. We had to do what was possible to pay the quantity of money they asked for, and they wanted more. But we do not have any. Then with my cousin Bartolomé I went to Guatemala [City] to present a petition to the Señor President of the Republic. When we arrived, the president received us well and told us the investigation would be later. But when we went to Guatemala [City], we did not tell anyone so that no one would know what we were doing. These things I tell you, but please do not tell anyone but your husband, Ignacio, because I know that this person deserves to know these things.

My wife said, "Thanks, Don Santiago, for the information. We will keep it to ourselves."

Then in the afternoon my wife told me these things, but I did not pay much attention to them. I said more than anything else they were lies because Don Santiago Yac is an ignorant man and moreover he is about 80 years old. Also, Bartolomé was very active in politics, and those of his town say that he was a fool there. Thus, I had doubts, but later it all turned out to be true.

It happened that at the end of October of this year the news spread that the soldiers had come to capture the commissioners to take them to an encampment for interrogation. It is true that they had committed too many evil deeds in the town. The commissioners were ignorant of their own whereabouts for 10 days [during the interrogation]. On this same day Bartolomé Yac was taken prisoner for the investigations because it is certain that he had presented the petition. But Bartolomé was taken to the jail in Sololá, not with the others.

It is not known where the seven military commissioners were for a period of 10 days until Sunday, 7 November, when a military commission brought them before the people of San Martín. The military commission confirmed that the commissioners had been interrogated in the encampment and that indeed they had committed certain crimes. Then a high military *comandante* asked the people of San Martín what they wanted to do with these wicked men. The whole town asked that they be given equal sentence to the sentence they had given many innocent townspeople. Moreover, the town said that they had swindled many people in the town. Then they made a list of all that had been cheated from the people, and they realized that the commissioners had robbed more than $3,000—and what is more, had taken 17 lives! The townspeople said that the commissioners should not be supported anymore because, if one thought about it, the commissioners could finish off the whole town. The people declared their serious repudiation and asked for the death of the seven men. They were once *desconocidos*, but not now!

When the high military leader saw that nothing could be done to free the commissioners, he left them locked in jail awaiting further orders. They were in jail for four days. But according to the information of several townsmen, no one was permitted to visit them other than to give them food. But they say none of them wanted to eat. They say they were aching because of the grave interrogations (torture). One of them had his ribs broken but was not permitted to receive treatment.

During the four days that they were in jail, they did not have formal communication with their families. One version says that they were drugged. Another says that perhaps they were suffering much regret. [In any case,] the people say that these men [now] seem crazy.

In the morning they were taken to the jail in Sololá. They took them in a launch. On this day, Thursday, 11 November, they set free the accuser, Bartolomé Yac. When he arrived in his town, the people jumped with joy, lighting firecrackers and exploding *bombas* and putting up a marimba.

It was made known that Bartolomé had seen that there were savages in his native land and that he had made the decision to denounce them. Then the people said that the national army is not to blame for what is happening in the towns. More than anything else, they said those responsible are the military commissioners. Now in these last days we are seeing that there are fair investigations, because the military commission took a boy with the commissioners for complicity but he proved that he had nothing to do with the commissioners, and later he was set free. Right now this boy is physically well.

The bad that these commissioners did was that they asked for money in the name of the national army, but it was not the army [who wanted it]. It was they who conceived the evil idea of robbing their own people.

There are two versions [as to what will be their fate]—one says they will go before a firing squad, and the other says that they will go to prison for 20 years, but on this date [12 December 1982] it is still not known what sentence awaits these men. Many are asking capital punishment; others a jail sentence [for these men]. But the truth is that no one knows [what will happen], because these things take a few days.

This Saturday the *comandante* of the naval detachment [*naval de la marina de guerra*] requested names of 15 persons to replace the military commissioners. Some of the former commissioners wanted to remain and continue the same disgraces, but the townsfolk did not support them. They saw the need to organize new commissioners. Nevertheless, Santos Alvarado, a companion of those who are imprisoned, and two others insisted that they remain commissioners. He carried a list of potential commissioners to the *comandante* of military reserves in Panajachel to try to annul what the townspeople had done the previous day. I am witness to these things because [I observed them] when we members of the *fuerza permanente (egresados del ejército)* [standing forces, or standby reserves] were called to Panajachel for a meeting, which was held on the beach.

All the towns on the shore of Lake Atitlán participated, but San Martín arrived very late, at 11:00 A.M., when the meeting had already ended. But when we arrived at the beach, Santos Alvarado was already there telling the colonel that the entire town was in favor of his remaining as commissioner. And the colonel accepted him because Santos said the people supported him. Then I stayed to find out what was happening among them.

When the *egresados* of the national army and the *comandante* of the naval forces in San Luis arrived, they presented themselves before the colonel. But they learned that the *Martineros* had been undermined by the lying Alvarado. [They were furious. But] gradually the colonel was able to calm their fury. Then the other *Martineros* explained what had happened. They also told the colonel that the commissioners chosen by the people were waiting to be sworn into office. Then the colonel realized that Alvarado was a liar. The colonel promised to go to San Martín and find out which of the two groups [of proposed commissioners] has the majority [of the townspeople behind them].

I heard all that the *Martineros* told the imprudent Santos Alvarado who wanted to remain commissioner. I very well realize that they told him that he was one of those who participated in the kidnappings and that his car was used to toss out the poor bodies. But he claimed he was just an observer. [Nevertheless,] when the meeting ended, Santos had a distorted face, very sad and nearly crying. He was unable to speak.

Then a *Martinero* told me how they [the commissioners] had been living a dissolute life. He said that the ex-commissioners who are imprisoned confessed before the military tribunal and the local tribunal that they had committed certain kidnappings and that after the painful tortures the bodies did not appear because they put stones around their necks and threw them into the lake. He also said that this is why the *Martineros* are very grieved. I did not much want to talk anymore with this man because I know that they are very barbaric persons.

On Monday, 15 November, I did not go to San Martín, but I sent my cousin, José Manuel Bizarro, to observe what was happening in this town. He went on my behalf because I was very much interested in writing something about this day. At 5:00 P.M. my cousin arrived to give me all the information.

He says that not a single person stayed home. There was not enough room for all the men, women, and children in the municipal atrium, so many were in the principal streets of the town. The reception of the *comandante* of the military reserves of the departmental capital of Sololá was immense. He says that the colonel asked the people whether they were in accordance with Santos Alvarado, but the town told him to kill this disgraceful man because he was an accomplice of those imprisoned. Then the colonel asked whom the people wanted to be the military commissioners, and they responded that they wanted for sure those men they had listed. They insisted that the colonel comply with what they had done on Saturday when they elected these men for this office [of military commissioner].

Not until then did the colonel realize the unity of the townspeople, and he did nothing for Santos Alvarado. Instead, he swore in the new commissioners of the town. At the same time they began to light very expensive *bombas*, and they joyously set up a marimba. Also the people said that they support the national army because it was not the army that had caused the bad things to happen. Those guilty were the ex-commissioners.

José Manuel says that then the townspeople declared that from this date on the *Martineros* are going to sleep tranquilly in their homes because the commissioners are different men. The people said that before now their grief came when night fell. No one had slept peacefully until the hour when the bus left for Guatemala [City], [which was early morning]. Thus, they were able to sleep only one or two hours a night. And it had been so for two years.

José Manuel says that in the afternoon hundreds of men drank their drinks peacefully—some from happiness, because there is a new military authority, and others for the sadness of the sons or kin who were victims of the violence. On this day, Monday, it was more than anything else a day of celebration for all the men and women [of San Martín].

The new *jefe* of the military commissioners is named Gaspar Yotz Ajacac. In total there are 15 [commissioners].

Since the new commissioners took possession of their offices, there have been a lot of changes in San Martín. All the townsfolk and the religious organizations are very coordinated. Many evangelists are now enjoying the preaching of the evangelism. Also, the members of the Catholic Church want to do their fiestas. And for us *Joseños* there is not much grief. Now we are able to leave at 1:00–2:00 A.M. to catch the bus to make trips.[32]

❧ Bartolomé Yac Is Threatened with Death
12 DECEMBER 1982

At noon my friend Abundio Yax of San Jorge la Laguna arrived to visit while passing through the town. He says that he went to visit Señor Bartolomé Yac, who denounced the commissioners of his town, San Martín. He says that Bartolomé is very sick and does not have money to pay for a doctor. All of his money went to the *fianza* [bail, or deposit]. But Bartolomé says that he is very content because he freed his town from the hands of these evil men.

But who knows why his townspeople do not want to help him buy medicine? It is certain that the town is free because of him. Since they imprisoned the commissioners, there have been no more disgraces. Many say that Bartolomé is a prophet because he liberated his people. But if his people consider him a prophet, why don't they have the conscience to help him?

Also, Abundio says that the kin of those imprisoned are threatening to kill him. But Bartolomé is saying these words:

> My body is lost. The enemies of my town can do what they wish. They can kill this corrupt body and feed it to the animals, but never [can they kill] my spirit, which will appear before the

tribunal of God to confess any real harm I have done. I know very well that my God loves me because I have defended all those who have already died because of these evil men. It is more important that I die so that my people be free of violence.

Thanks to God, the situation in Guatemala has changed. The guerrillas have been losing before the national army because these months there are not as many as before. Moreover, many have surrendered to the army. The majority of them are of the Quiché and Cakchiquel race. They say that they felt it necessary to commit crimes. They were living poorly, and the only way they could achieve the good [life] was to become guerrillas and kill off the persons who have large farms. Only in this manner could they become property owners themselves. That is why they became guerrillas. But they say they were weakened [encouraged] by foreigners. Now [the army] is looking for a Jesuit priest and a medical doctor and two Ladino women who took advantage of their knowledge to induce the indigenous people, although some of them [the guerrillas] are Ladinos.

❧ Reflections on Protestant Pastors and Catholic Priests
29 SEPTEMBER–31 DECEMBER 1982

Those who say they are perfect are the ones who are the most exploitative. Señor Alejandro Ramos Cholotio of San Diego worked ten years in San José for El Comité Pro Ciego y Sordomudos [The Committee for the Blind and Deaf-and-Dumb], which is based in Quezaltenango. His salary was $80 a month, but that was not enough because he and his wife went on big drinking sprees. People suffering with their eyes gave them money for treatment, but Señor Cholotio had more children than he could support on his low income. Thus, this man had to ask the people of San José for loans. However, when they asked to be repaid, he could not do so because he had wasted his money on alcohol. Thus, he began to lose the confidence of the Joseños. Also, he stole many chickens for his family to eat. Whenever a resident had a missing chicken, he went to ask Cholotio whether the latter had seen it, but Cholotio would threaten to kill him because he had a little sway with the authority [the mayor], and moreover he was the *comisionado militar*, so he had his own authority.

For that reason, the people to whom he owed money could do nothing about it. And Señor Cholotio had a revolver. But thanks to

God, his ten-year contract with the eye clinic ended, and he returned to San Diego, his hometown. But the people realized that he had left with many debts in the tiendas and cantinas.

In San Diego, Alejandro got a job collecting garbage in the homes of the people of San Diego with a pickup owned by one of his sisters. Seeing that this occupation did not pay much, he got the idea of converting to Protestantism, but deceitfully since he never admitted what he had done in San José. Nowadays, they say that he is internationally famous as an evangelist. If his Protestant brothers had known his earlier lies, however, they might not have accepted him. Also, they say that he has a power to cure illness. But this is a lie.

In the month of August 1982 Cholotio came to San José and belittled the other religions, especially the Catholic religion. He did not come to preach what is in the Bible. Instead, more than anything else, he acted like a savage.

Members of the Assembly of God Church presented a woman to him who is about 45 years old and who is named Isabel Ujpán, a relation of my father. This woman has never been able to have a baby. The congregation told her that with the miracles of Cholotio she would bear a child for sure. Cholotio asked her whether she wanted a boy or girl. This woman was thrilled at what she was hearing, and she answered that she wanted a little boy. The poor woman declared that when she gave birth to her baby, she would name him after the evangelist, Alejandro Ramos. However, it is a pity that to this day [3 May 1983], she has had no signs of being pregnant. When this unfortunate woman realized that the lying Cholotio cannot perform miracles, she rejoined the Catholic Church.

On Cholotio's evangelistic tour of our town in August, which lasted five days, they paid him $400 to criticize the other religions. What was most lamentable was that he never went to visit the inhabitants of San José in their homes because he knew that he owed them big debts and that he had stolen from them when he was working in the town. The people waited for him in the streets to ask for their money back, but he did not show up. Also, most unfortunately, the $400 was collected from the small congregation, which is very poor. They had to sell their axes, machetes, and masonry tools to raise such a large quantity of money.

Before leaving, Cholotio told the congregation that he would have to return in December. On 5 December he did. He came back with his family, and he acted like a god. But the truth is that he came only to mistreat the people. This time most of the people who had heard him earlier were on the coast trying to earn a little money.

Realizing that Cholotio was abusive with his words, the civil and military authorities disconnected his megaphone. Since only a few had come to hear him speak, it was difficult to raise the hundreds of dollars for which he was asking. One of the leaders of the congregation had to sell some land to pay Cholotio for his service.

During the rest of the month of December, the Assembly of God Church was very low on morale because it had given all of its money to Cholotio. Pastors usually do not work, and they are supported with collections of corn, beans, and meat (money, in effect) for their services. After Cholotio left, the brothers had nothing more to give. The poor pastor, who did no other work, said that since the brothers had no more to give, he and his family would have to endure hunger. But this pastor was a liar. [Instead of staying and enduring hunger,] he told everyone good-bye and left one night for Ixtahuacán, another town. Since that date, the Assembly of God Church has been broke.

On 29 September, a Wednesday, Señora Lilian Chávez was critically ill. Her children and the directors of the Catholic Church went to San Martín to fetch the priest for the last sacraments. He came to San José, but not before going to San Jorge to celebrate a mass. When he arrived in our town, it was very late. Not until then did he give the sick person extreme unction.

When the priest was returning to San Martín, someone threw stones at his car when he was at the halfway mark between San José and San Martín. The priest did not see anyone, but the people suspected the culprits were insolent youngsters. The car was not damaged because the stones were small and probably the boys who threw them were very little. However, when the priest met two young students who were returning from San Martín, he spoke foul words to them. But truly these boys were just returning from school, and they responded in like manner. [Nevertheless,] all of this seemed trivial.

On Sunday, 3 October, the father was supposed to celebrate mass since it was the first Sunday of the month. The people waited for him from 8:00 to 11:00 A.M., but he did not show up. When they grew tired of waiting, the poor people sent a delegation of Catholic Actionists to ask why the priest was not going to celebrate the mass. When they arrived, the father wanted to fight with them, so they immediately left.

The priest was like a furious animal. He sent for everything that was inside the church, and he said that he was going to close it because there were malicious people in the town. Thus, they took everything used in the mass to San Martín.

In the afternoon, all the *principales*, catechists, and *cofradías* met to try to find out who had caused the damage. But no one knew. The people nearly cried because of the absence of the priest. They said that God was abandoning the town because the priest said that stoning a priest is like stoning Jesucristo. And for that reason this town is condemned.

I was a *cofrade* of the Virgen María, and I told them not to be afraid. If the priest did not wish to come, we could still worship our God in our own way. Furthermore, I told them it is not the priest who will lead us to God if our consciences are dirty. With or without the priest, God will hear us if we are his true children. We should not worry about this matter.

Still, the catechists went to San Martín for mass, and hundreds of baptized members of the church went daily to ask the priest to forgive the townspeople. This went on for two months.

Finally, it surfaced that those who had thrown the stones at the priest were two boys named Diego Bizarro Pichijay and Rojando Pichijay Pur. Both are members of the Central American Church, and the former is an assistant military commissioner. These two boys went to San Martín to tell the priest that they were the evildoers. Only then did the priest learn who had thrown the stones. There had been rumors that the culprits were members of the Catholic church, but they turned out to be lies.

The character of the priest is such that he offended all the Catholics in the town because two [Protestant] boys threw two stones at him. Thus, I am realizing that those who say they represent Jesucristo are the most delicate. If we note what the Bible says, Jesús was a real man who loved his enemies and bore the insults they leveled at him. What is most surprising is that these boys just threw some stones, and already the priest did not want to celebrate mass. And he says that he represents Jesús! I believe that in the various religions it is just a technique to earn money. And in spirit they are far from the truth.

❧ A *Comisionado Militar* Shoots Off His Own Toe
FRIDAY, 7 JANUARY 1983

On Friday, 7 January, the army brought provisions of corn, flour, beans, oil, and other things for the members of the *patrulla de autodefensa civil* of the town of San José and its three villages of Patzilín, Tzarayá, and Pachichaj. On Saturday they made a public announcement in the town that they were going to distribute the provisions on Sunday. They also went to tell the three villages.

On Sunday many people came from the villages. In total the members of the *autodefensa* comprise 700 people, but the army gave only enough for 300. From 9:00 A.M. to 2:00 P.M. the *comisionados* divided the provisions among the people of the villages. Then they gave the food to the people of the town, and they did not finish until late afternoon. The *comisionados* took advantage of their power because they gave very little of each item to those of the villages. They also pretended to give a little to the poorest of the town. But they saved plenty for themselves. After passing out the provisions, they began to drink in their headquarters.

On this day I had a meeting in the cooperative, and we did not finish until 10:00 P.M. Although I am on the list of the *egresados* of the army, I did not go to get any of the things they were giving out because I do not want to receive something now that is hardly worth it and be bothered later by the *autodefensa*, with which I do not agree. I decided it was better not to go, even though my wife told me to go and get some of the food.

During the night, when the *comisionados* were drunk, they gave their weapons to some assistants who do not know how to handle them. These individuals then split up and went to guard the town. When one of them, Julián Cholotio Tambritz, heard shots, he ran to tell his companions that shots had been fired near him. They all became frightened and in turn ran to tell the *comisionados*, who were drinking at their headquarters, to come and investigate whether leftists had fired the shots.

Then the *comisionados* ran to search for the enemy. However, one of them, Gustavo Angel Campos Ramos, was so scared and nervous he accidentally discharged his weapon and shot off his big toe. In vain the *comisionados* tried to find it. The same night they sent Gustavo to the hospital in Sololá.

Later, when the *comisionados* were investigating, they discovered that the same person who heard the shots had fired them. And they beat him brutally.

There was a lot of activity in the town, but I did not go out. I just heard the shots. I stayed home, but I was somewhat grieved because I thought that the guerrillas might have entered the town. I did not find out what had happened until Tuesday, when I talked to the mayor on the launch to Panajachel. When we arrived there, we met the assistants of the commissioners, and I asked them if what I had been told was true. They answered yes. They also said that the wounded man is in very serious condition and that he may be transferred to the military hospital in Guatemala [City].

[I also found out] that during the night when the *comisionados* were drunk, Señor Emilio Dardón and merchants from the southern coast were passing through the area in Emilio's truck with a load of nets and vegetables. After the assistant commissioner fired his weapon, the commissioners captured the owner of the truck, claiming that he and his fellow travelers were the ones who shot their weapons. But it was all a lie. The *comisionados* did this just so they could tell their *jefes* that their companion was shot in a confrontation. But the whole town knows the truth, because the mayor told me that a lot of people went to see what was happening. He also told me that the drunk commissioners nearly killed Emilio. But the government has ordered [the people] not to abuse, lie, or steal. Then why are such things happening?

❧ A Malicious Slander Against Me and the Cooperative
25 JANUARY–7 FEBRUARY 1983

Because I have had serious problems in the cooperative, I have not been able to continue working on my diary until now. We Indians suffer the illness of envy.

In November of last year, I was struggling to get our cooperative a coffee quota in the national coffee association. I agreed to go to the capital of Guatemala to solicit a coffee quota so that we would be able to sell our product at a better price. True, we do not have a lot of coffee, but nevertheless each member of the cooperative has some cultivation. Each of us produces about 20 to 40 *quintales* of *café pergamino* [pulped but unshelled coffee].

The national coffee association granted us a quota of 990 *quintales* for 44 associates—both men and women. Thus, on 27 November I went to Guatemala [City] to get the card.

As I have said earlier, at one of the meetings of our cooperative we decided to sell the coffee on the coast to Señor Homero Ordoñez of Santo Tomás la Unión, who agreed to pay us a good price, at least it seemed so to us. But the *Martineros* wanted us to sell our coffee to them at a very low price. When the powerful *Martineros* realized we were negotiating the price of the coffee on the coast, they sent an anonymous memorandum to the director of the national coffee association. The *Martineros* accused me of selling the quota card to an intermediary and using the money to buy a mill for the *nixtamal* and a well-stocked tienda. Furthermore, they claimed that San José does not have the capability of producing 50 *quintales* of coffee because the coffee groves in San José belong to the *Martineros*. Without doubt, when the director, Leonel Orellana, received the memorandum, he thought the accusations were true.

At 10:00 A.M. on 26 January, I was called to the courthouse. The *alguacil* told me to present myself immediately because some inspectors of the national coffee association needed me for an investigation ordered by the director. At that very moment, my wife and I were cleaning coffee in our homesite. I had to abandon my work and go to the courthouse.

When I arrived, six inspectors were waiting for me. They told me that they needed to talk to me about an investigation. They also said that they would need a typewriter to fill out their forms. I told them that with much pleasure I could supply a typewriter and that they could work in the cooperative if they wished. They accepted.

When we arrived at the cooperative, I sent my cousin Abraham for my typewriter. When he returned with it, the inspectors took out their papers and began to type, but they still had not told me the reason for the investigation.

First they asked me how the cooperative was doing, and I answered it was doing fine. Then they asked me how many members there were when I became president. I told them that since its founding until 24 April 1982 we had 44 members. From 24 April until January of this year we gained 50 new associates. In total the cooperative has 94 active members.

Then they asked me how many members had their own mills for grinding *nixtamal* and how many of the board of directors have their own tiendas, and, if they do, what do they sell in them. I responded that none of the associates has a mill or a tienda.

Next they asked me when I had sold the coffee quota card and why and to whom I had sold it. I answered that the card had not been sold and that it was deposited, because we are cleaning our coffee and we [soon] intend to do business in accordance with the stipulations on the quota card.

Next they asked me who had sold the coffee to the cooperative. I replied that we in the cooperative do not buy coffee because we have no money with which to buy it. Furthermore, we are cleaning only our own harvest. The inspectors were doubtful that I was telling the truth, but I did not know that there had been an accusation against me and my fellow officers of the cooperative.

When I offered the inspectors lunch, they accepted. The committee of control then became preoccupied with preparing it.

When lunch was over, the inspectors gave me the schedule of investigation. Then they told me I needed to call all the associates who have land nearby because they wanted to inspect it. I called them and organized five groups. Each group went with an inspector to demonstrate that indeed they had land. The auditor told me to go with him to inspect where the associates were cleaning coffee. Thus, we went to Panasajar.

Thanks to God, when we arrived, many members of the cooperative were sunning their coffee. Then the *jefe* of the inspectors told me to call my two companions on the board of directors—the vice-president and the treasurer. The rest of the associates stayed where they were, drying coffee.

Señor David Rodríguez told us that we must want to know what was happening. Then he took out a folder containing a photocopy of the memorandum, and only then did I learn of the malicious slander of the *Martineros*. Also, I learned that the papers said that the coffee quota of the cooperative had been canceled because the cooperative was engaged in illicit business. This demoralized my companions.

Señor David told me, "Ignacio, I am reading this copy to you, but I do not want you to take revenge against these persons who have made this malicious accusation."

I replied, "I never like to accuse persons or take measures of vengeance. God forgive them for their lies."

When we returned from the beach, the same señor told me to hand over all the legal papers of the cooperative. With much pleasure I gave him the title of the cooperative that was authorized by the national institute of cooperatives (INACOP), and the *personería jurídica* [paper of legal capacity] authorized by the local civil registry and by the *administración de rentas internas* [administration of internal revenue]. Later he asked me for the memorandum that states the associates have a coffee quota, and I gave him the *libro de actas* [minutes book]. Then he asked me for the list of associates and how many *quintales* of coffee each one had contributed. I gave him two books that list the name of the members and number of *quintales* for each. By the grace of God, everything was in good order.

This man also told me to take special care because my enemies want the quota to be canceled. At 6:00 P.M. the inspectors returned from their inspections. Then they ordered me to be ready to continue tomorrow so that they could be sure that the members actually have coffee groves, and they left for San Martín for lodging.

This afternoon was very depressing for us *Joseños* because we have just begun to learn the coffee business and already the *Martineros* are persecuting us. On this day I ate neither lunch nor dinner because the inspectors told me that I should be careful since the matter is very serious. All night I did not sleep at all. I stayed up putting in order all the papers of the cooperative for reassurance.

We do not all have the same capacity [to withstand stress]. My companions were demoralized and weak because they have never had such serious problems. But I had to work hard all during the night.

On Thursday, when the sun came up, I felt exhausted when the inspectors arrived. [Nevertheless,] I organized six groups to go to different places to point out *Joseño* coffee groves. Before leaving with the *jefe*, David Rodríguez, I instructed the women to prepare lunch at Paché. I told the other inspectors and guides that we would meet at this place when the smoke indicated they were cooking lunch. We carried chickens, meat, and drinks. Pack animals carried water. Everything that was bought was bought by the cooperative.

Thus, each group went to their coffee groves accompanied by an inspector and officer of the cooperative. Finally, I left with the *jefe* of the inspectors. We inspected Xechumil, Chixicay, Chixot, and Popabaj. Then we climbed up to Poptún and Tojchoc, and we descended through Pachay and Chimucuní until we reached Paché. Each time we inspected these places, the *Joseño* owner of the coffee groves was there to meet us. But the *Martineros* were also there guarding their own coffee groves. By the grace of God, there were no problems, because it is certain that the *Joseños* pointed out their own coffee groves. When the *jefe* and I returned to Paché, three of the other inspectors were waiting for us. The other two had gone very far away, and we had to wait until 1:00 P.M. for them to get back.

By the time all the inspectors had returned, several *Martineros* had joined us to find out what was happening. But they were mainly there to make sure that *Joseños* did not claim *Martinero* coffee groves as their own. For that reason, before eating, the *jefe*, David Rodríguez, made the following speech:

> Residents of the two towns—San José and San Martín—we are here to find out whether it is true that the cooperative has enemies. We want to make it clear that we have brought a photocopy of a memorandum that was sent to the director of the [national coffee] association accusing the president of the cooperative of conducting illicit business with the coffee quota card. Also, it says that the people of San José do not have the capability of producing 50 *quintales* of coffee. Señores, this is a lie, because

yesterday and today we have traveled a lot inspecting the coffee groves of the *Joseños*, and indeed they have coffee groves. Señores, I am not able to say whether the accuser is from San José or from San Martín because the memorandum does not have a signature. I declare, señores, that the tongue God gave you is for saying good things and not for slandering others. And if your tongue does not serve you well, cut it out and throw it in the trash can so that you will not condemn your fellow man. We inspectors of the national coffee association are investigating this matter. For the second time I say to you, members of the cooperative, please say so if the president or some other member has engaged in illegal business as this paper claims. Say whether it is true that the president bought his own mill with money from your coffee quota! Say whether he has his own well-stocked tienda!

The associates selected an active member, Roberto Mendoza Pérez, to respond. On behalf of all the associates, this is what he said:

> All the accusations in the memorandum that you are carrying are lies, because the president actually has demonstrated his [good] work and education. Moreover, the claim that he has a mill and a tienda is false. We are witnesses that he has nothing. It is true that there is a mill, but it is the property of the cooperative, as is the tienda. Moreover, the cooperative is more than four years old, and the mill is only three. But it is [the result of] the effort of all of us, not the money of just one member. We are witnesses that he never did business without our knowledge. Thanks, señores, for having made these things clear to us. Never have we thought badly about the president because we have never seen him work badly. We have given him our confidence, and we have drawn up a memorandum of agreement that he is the one who should work as head of the cooperative.

After all of these things, lunch was served to the inspectors and to all the associates of the cooperative. I told the cooks to serve a little to the *Martineros* if there was enough. However, one of my companions said that the cook should not give anything to the *Martineros*. But I told him that he should remember that we have said that we should never judge or be vindictive, and that we should put the matter in the hands of God. I told him the proverb that says, "*Dios tarda pero no olvida* [God may take a long time, but he never forgets]." Only then did I convince this companion who nearly wanted to fight with some *Martineros*. But when I told him these things, he thought them over. And we ate lunch peacefully, at least some did. I, however, stayed upset because I wanted to know who had written the statement against me. But I was unable to find out.

When lunch was over, we were able to rest a little in the shade. At 3:30 P.M. we arrived back in our town. Then the inspectors began to record what they had seen.

Well, it was a general inspection because they also investigated those who do not belong to the cooperative. They inspected about 200 pieces of property that do not belong to the members of the cooperative. On this day the inspectors calculated the formulas for how many *cuerdas* of coffee each person has and how many *quintales* of coffee each *cuerda* produces. They also included how many *mozos* are employed to pick the product and other requirements. They were able to work until 6:30 P.M.

When the inspectors went to San Martín, my companions on the board remained very depressed because there are even some *Joseños* who also would like to see us bankrupt—people of the same town as us! They feel we are enemies because the cooperative has backing. We were told that one or two *Joseños* helped the *Martineros* write the memorandum. But I did not pay any attention because sometimes such things are lies. To forget these things a little, we went to a cantina to drink some *tragos*, but not a lot because the following day our obligations would continue. We went to bed at midnight.

When Friday, 28 January, came, I went to the cooperative to buy some things for lunch. At 8:00 A.M. the inspectors arrived. Then they began to fill out some papers on persons who are not in the cooperative. Well, I did not have to be there because the inspectors were talking to nonmembers of the cooperative, but they wanted me to help direct the people and translate for those who do not speak Spanish. Thus, I worked hard until noon, when they left [San José] for their homes. As they were leaving, they said they would come back on Monday to continue their work.

Almost no one in the cooperative had [yet] satisfied their formula because, as I told the inspectors, we in the cooperative do not have titles to the communal land and when we finish the work with the private property, we need to average the data for the communal land already inspected. The inspectors honored my suggestion because they saw that I was helping a lot with the data for the people who are not in the cooperative. I was not able to rest a little and recuperate until the inspectors left.

Saturday and Sunday I did not work at all because I had to prepare more data that they were going to ask for on Monday. During these days, I did not think about my work in the milpa, nor did I pay any attention to my children. I was just concentrating on how to come out ahead with the problems, because many people say that it is probable that the registration of the quota will be canceled. They say this because they know that we in the cooperative do not have titles to the land where we have planted coffee. And because of the memorandum, the inspectors demanded titles from those who are not in the cooperative, and the people think the worst is going to happen to us. This was their criticism.

When Monday, 31 January, came, the inspectors came again. And they called me again. They collected data regarding the number of *cuerdas* used and amount of coffee produced last year, how it was sold, and who sold it. And again each one provided his data. Then they asked for the titles to the land and whether each person was a member of the cooperative. Thus it went. At this time I did not much get involved because already I had instructed the people many times not to fail to answer the questions. This did not end until 7:00 P.M. Then the señores went to San Martín to sleep.

Also, on this day a lot of work was done. I ate only one time because I had no appetite due to so many problems. I felt like resigning as president of the cooperative because my patience was exhausted. For whatever little thing or problem, no one could help me. Well, it is certain that the boys of the cooperative worked, but they provided few ideas. I was nearly sick from concentrating so hard.

Tuesday dawned, and the inspectors told me to go with them to the three *aldeas* of Tzarayá, Patzilín, and Pachichaj. I had to obey them.

From San José we left at 7:00 A.M. in a car. When we arrived in Tzarayá, the inspectors told the people they would come back to inspect their property. When we reached Patzilín, there were a lot of people, but they told them the same thing. Then we got out of the car and took horses to Pachichaj. At 9:30 A.M. we arrived in this village.

The inspectors told me to organize three groups to inspect the coffee groves. And I did what they told me. While I remained chatting with some friends, they went to inspect the coffee groves. When they returned, they filled out their data. I had to translate for a lot of people who were unable to understand Spanish. We did not finish until 1:00 P.M.

After eating the lunch that they gave us, we returned to Patzilín, where the inspectors went to the coffee groves. They did not finish until 5:30 P.M. I worked hard translating.

At 6:00 in the afternoon, we arrived in Tzarayá. It was almost night, but the people were still waiting for the inspectors. When these men got out of their car, they did not inspect the coffee groves. They only wrote down the important data. While the señores worked, I rested, because the men of Tzarayá understand Spanish well. When the inspectors were finished, we returned to San José and arrived at 8:00 P.M. They let me off at my house.

Well, the inspectors asked me many questions on the road regarding why the *Martineros* acted poorly toward us *Joseños* and why they accused us falsely. I told them the following:

> The *Martineros* behaved badly toward us because they always have managed to take possession of all our products, including coffee, chick-peas, and onions. None of us knew anything about the business [of marketing our products]. The *Martineros* in the past have been clever. They have offered the price they wished, and the *Joseños* have had to sell to them. The merchants of San Martín realized big profits, and the *Joseños* just served as an escalator [without enjoying the earnings from the higher prices]. But nowadays we feel a little freer [from their control] because we are selling our own products at better prices. Taking the case of coffee as an example, earlier the *Martineros* paid us $3 to $4 a *quintal*. But when we organized in the cooperative, we discovered that coffee was worth much more. It was then that we registered in the national association of coffee to gain a better price. Last year we succeeded in selling our coffee at $78 a *quintal*. The *Martineros* lost their big profits. With the money that we earned we bought the *sitio* in the town center at the price of $2,200. Now they are upset because they have not been able to trick us into selling our products at lower prices. It is for that reason they misinformed you. The truth is that these days we are buying back some of our land [that we had earlier sold to the *Martineros*]. And the truth is that it is now harvest time, and the *Martineros* realize they have lost our business. That is why they would like the association to cancel our quota. They would like us to have to continue doing business with them. But I believe that it will be impossible for them to continue business with us because we are gaining more experience. As a proverb states, *Hombre sin problemas jamás llega hacer hombre* [A man without problems never becomes a man].
>
> I believe that these enemies will never be able to do something bad to me because I actually have not been bad. On the contrary, I have borne many injuries, but I have said that I never will take revenge. Only the power of God resides in me. In these times we are suffering, but it is so that our children will be better off in the future.

On Wednesday the inspectors were working with two other co-operatives in San Martín. These cooperatives are soliciting their own registration in the national coffee association, but they have not succeeded yet.

On this day, when our associates of the cooperative told me that we had overlooked five members of the cooperative and six who are not members, I sent a note to the inspectors in San Martín to see whether they wanted to return to talk to them. They answered that they would be happy to do so.

Thus on Thursday only three inspectors worked in San Martín. The other three returned to San José. By the grace of God, the inspectors included them in their report even though they had already finished in San José on Tuesday. We ate lunch together, and they told me that, if some problem emerges in San Martín, they will suspend their work there.

On Friday two inspectors visited me and said they have a lot to do in San Martín. But because the *Martineros* are very contrary, the inspectors were unable to complete their work. They had to tell the *Martineros* they would suspend their investigation until next week. But the inspectors told me that the *Martineros* have lost their confidence and that they do not intend to return to San Martín. Indeed the inspectors told me that they have detected the bad attitude of the *Martineros*.

On Monday the *Martineros* were waiting again for the inspectors because the latter told them they were coming back on this day. But I knew that they were not going to return. In the afternoon I went to San Martín to see what was happening, and many people were still waiting.

❧ The Case of the Elderly and of an Incredible Pastor
JANUARY–MARCH 1983

Don Mauricio Quit was born in Santa Ana la Laguna of Quiché origins. He is a wealthy man who owns a lot of land. His wife was from Totonicapán, and she and Mauricio had many sons and daughters. Mauricio's wife died of old age, and this man converted to an evangelist preacher. Every Tuesday and Saturday, Don Mauricio preached in the market of Santa Ana. For about 15 years he preached the message of Jesucristo.

Don Mauricio, who is definitely 102 years old and has long hair and a beard, began to mistreat people who did not take his advice.

But nothing happened to him until recently. Because of his preaching, he offended people of the other religions. Without doubt, they accused him, but it is not known whether his accusers were leftists or rightists.

They say that a group of men arrived at his house and punished him by cutting off his hair and beard and warning him not to preach anymore if he did not wish to suffer serious consequences. Therefore, Mauricio quit preaching in the market, and he became afraid to live in his own house. For that reason, he went to live in Patzilín in the house of a son-in-law.

He lived happily there for some months, but later he began to tell his son-in-law that he needed a woman to marry. But the son-in-law thought it was a joke because he was very old. But Don Mauricio insisted on having a woman so that he could live happily.

Thus, the son-in-law and the daughter of this señor discussed the matter with his other children in Santa Ana. They decided to look for a woman for their father.

It was difficult for them to find Magdelena Xico—an 85-year-old woman of the village of Tzarayá. They persuaded her to go to live in Patzilín as the woman of the elderly Mauricio Quit. But since Mauricio was an evangelist, he wanted to be married in the civil court of San José la Laguna. But the municipality said that they could not marry these persons because they were too old and the law did not authorize them to do so. They told them to go to the appropriate courthouse in Sololá. But Don Mauricio did not wish to go to Sololá, and he ordered his children to bring Magdelena to him anyway. They began living together without marriage.

Mauricio forgot that he was an evangelist preacher. The evangelist religion prohibits uniting in fornication. Thus it was with them. Since they were both old, the son-in-law provided their food. Their work was to eat and sleep.

They say that Mauricio became very happy when he had his own woman. But it was amusing in the town and the villages because Magdelena could not tolerate Mauricio. He did not let her sleep. Mauricio was sexually energetic, but the poor woman was very weak. Thus, she had to abandon her mate. They began to live together in January 1983, and they parted in March of the same year. So this case just happened.

A lot of very old people criticized Mauricio and Magdelena. The old women claimed that the end of the world was coming because nothing like this had happened before in these parts.

Also, I am going to write about the case of Pedro Miguel Rocché of the village of Patzilín, who is pastor of the Prince of Peace Church. For many years, Pedro Miguel was a big director in the Catholic Church. Then he quit his directorship and went to take part in the charismatic movement. Because he was too demanding, he did not put up with the charismatic congregation. He joined the Prince of Peace Church, and a little later they ordained him pastor. Thus he was for some years.

Later his woman became sick, but they did not give the poor lady medicine nor did they take her to the hospital. They said that she could be cured only with prayer. They prayed hard, but it was useless. The poor woman died. But they said that it was good that she died because her soul went directly to God since she had not taken any medicine. Pedro Miguel was left with just his children, but it was difficult for him to fix their meals.

In a few months one of Pedro Miguel's sons, Santiago Rocché, courted a girl named Juana Vides in the village of Pachichaj. For a time, she had lived as the woman of Carlos Rocché, Pedro Miguel's nephew. She was working for Señor Manuel Temó when Santiago convinced her to become his wife.

A little later Pedro Miguel fell in love with his daughter-in-law, Juana. He took her away from his son. Thus, Santiago had to give up his woman to his father. It is incredible but true that this evangelist pastor has his daughter-in-law for his own woman and his poor son until this date [10 May 1983] has not found himself another woman.

❧ Factionalism in the Catholic Church
3–7 APRIL 1983

The Catholic Church continues to have problems because of its directors. As I have said earlier, there are two groups in the Catholic Church—a small group of 5 to 10 persons and a big group composed of a lot of persons. A new thing is that the priest has meddled in these problems.

This Holy Week, which comes at the beginning of the month of April, there were serious problems for the whole Catholic population. The problem originated some years ago, but it really did not surface until this year.

The first group is made up of the director, Abraham Bizarro, and about 5 to 6 catechists. They are always exempt from other offices of the church. They just come to do the ordering; that is, they always give orders, but they do not work. The larger group belongs to the same church. This larger group indeed works because there are plenty of them, and they always celebrate the fiestas. When this group organizes some religious activities, the smaller group impedes their activities. Then they go to the priest to tell him that they are actually doing something against the church and they are violating ordinances. But this is not true. It is just an obstacle to block or break up the activities of the larger group.

Before Holy Week, the big group organized the processions for Holy Thursday and Holy Friday. Thus, this group bought a large portable platform for $400 [for carrying the image of Jesucristo]. They bought it eight years ago with money from 45 contributors. A *principal* named Alejandro Morales contributed $50, and the rest contributed smaller amounts. The leaders of the promotion were two men who had worked with the priests in Guatemala [City] and who realized that the procession was more solemn when the image was carried on a platform that required many bearers. When these men came back to San José, they gradually organized their companions to buy the platform. They bought it from the Santa Terecita Church because this church said they did not use it anymore. The platform was merely used, not old.

Since there was displeasure among the smaller group of Catholics, they bought a new glass platform for $200. This was overdoing it, because they were just few in number, and still they bought a glass platform. Thus, for three years they have used the new platform, which requires six bearers. They did so with the permission of the priest. And the larger group had to stop using their larger platform. They could not do anything about it.

In 1982, when I was head of the *cofradía* of María, three weeks before Holy Week the *principales*, *cofradías*, catechists, and board of directors of Catholic Action met to decide which platform to use in the procession. We decided to use the larger one. Thus, when Holy Thursday came, there was no problem because it had been decided in advance. All of the service of the passion and death of Jesucristo took place without any problems.

But this year there was a misfortune because on Holy Thursday they began to have big problems. The larger group said they wanted to use the larger platform, and the smaller group said they wanted to use the smaller one. The latter group claimed that it was more appropriate to put the image of Jesucristo inside glass. Both groups threatened to hit the directors if they did not comply with their wishes.

On Holy Thursday they took out the image of Jesús of Nazareth in procession with the platform that requires 18 bearers. That is, the larger group won. But the smaller group wallowed in envy.

On Holy Friday, as is the custom, they took out the image of Jesús in procession in front of the church for the crucifixion. But in this procession there was a debauchery. Customarily, after the procession, they crucify the image of Jesucristo in the middle of the church and say prayers at the foot of the cross. However, this Holy Friday, after crucifying the image of Jesucristo, a great uproar broke out over the platform when they were all inside the church. Certainly, on this Holy Friday the Catholic church was not in accord with the passion and death of Jesús. They gave more attention to fighting over the two platforms. When they took down the image of Jesús from the cross, as is the custom, they wanted to take out the image in procession as if they were crying at the burial of Jesús. But both groups insulted each other inside the church. Each wanted to use its own platform. Finally, the larger group won. But the smaller group then did not want to take the image out at all, so that neither of the two groups would have the satisfaction of using its own platform. Finally, the procession took place at 8:30 P.M.

The smaller group, which lost, was not able to use the glass platform on Easter Saturday. Then they went to accuse the bigger group before the priest of San Martín la Laguna. He had scheduled a divine mass at 5:00 P.M. The church was full of people, since about 95 percent of the Catholics attend the masses. But the priest got mixed up in the fight over the two platforms, and he did not want to celebrate the divine mass. When the people saw that the priest was not coming, at 6:00 P.M. they left, criticizing him.

Also there was an Easter Sunday mass scheduled, as well as a marriage and a baptism. But on Sunday the priest did not perform any of them.

I do not know why the priest meddled in the problems of the people when he says that he represents Jesucristo on earth. But these days one can see that the priest is a liar. As minister, he has no business getting mixed up in such problems. He should have fulfilled his mission of celebrating the two masses that were already on the program. I was just an observer of these things. True, they asked me to participate in all these services of the church, but I told them no, because they only cause problems. Many years of such experience have taught me not to participate with either group. I do not know why the people do not understand such things better. They say that they are children of God because they attend church, and attending church is enough for salvation. But what kind of salvation can they achieve when all they do is fight one another in church?

Many things are going on here. They say the priest is the representative of Jesucristo. But the townsfolk are just respecting their traditions. Still, they have to ask permission to do something. The priest says that without his permission, whatever service they celebrate will not be received by God because it is not authorized by the priest. Even just to play basketball in front of the church, the priest has to be asked 5 to 6 days in advance. Without his permission, he does not allow this sport. Everyone has to get permission from the priest. The town itself has no say. San José is losing completely because of the religion—or, that is to say, because of this priest.

The priest is the biggest liar and exploiter because they give him their earnings. There are afternoons when in one hour he celebrates a mass that costs $12. And if it is a mass for the deceased, it costs $15. The priest says that it costs more because it is to free the soul of the dead from purgatory. But I have observed that whether it is a sacred mass or a death mass he takes the same amount of time and he says the same words. The priest does this because he firmly dominates the indigenous people. Positively, the priest does not do anything to free the soul of the dead. It is a lie.

Also, they say that when a person commits a serious sin, it is forgivable by God but only if the person confesses before the priest. Also, they say that a person is able to commit a number of sins and confess them a number of times and to be forgiven a number of times. My thought is that a person could confess indefinitely, but if his conscience is dirty, it will never be cleaned, because God is not a plaything. If we say to God, "Forgive me today because I am going to commit a serious sin," and then God forgives me, tomorrow I will ask God to forgive me again and commit again the same sin for which I was forgiven yesterday. But God is not a toy! Let us suppose I say, "My Father, forgive me. I have stolen $200 because I needed it." I am sure that my Father is going to forgive me, but tomorrow I just say the same thing. And if the day after tomorrow I say the same thing, I am sure that my Father is going to disown me and treat me like a thief and not forgive me anymore. Well, what I am saying is that one being able to commit numerous sins and have them forgiven with just a confession is a lie.

They say that if a person mistreats another and confesses it, it is pardonable. But in the fifth commandment that God gave Moisés, he says, "Do not kill." And if we kill and if we confess to Him, can it be that He will forgive us? He is not going to pardon us, because the same God commanded us not to kill. God cannot be a mocker. Well, the señor priest says that they absolve their sins. But who knows if God is going to forgive them? They may be the most condemned! The same Bible says damned is the man who knows good and does evil.

A case in point is that of Señor Jesús Fernández. He is the richest man in town with lots of land and money. He has been married 35 years to Laura Menéndez. Both are of my Indian race. He is very Catholic but also very given to adultery. He has destroyed many marriages. Every time he is discovered, he confesses to the priest and asks forgiveness, but then he goes back to doing it again.

This Holy Tuesday, 29 March, he committed adultery with Engracia Meza. The husband of the woman complained to the directors of the Catholic Church. Then Señor Jesús Fernández declared that he for sure was going to confess and never commit adultery again in his life. But during his life he has committed 35 adulteries with 35 women. Nevertheless, his poor wife was convinced that he was going to confess to the priest and never commit adultery again.

But it happened that this Easter Sunday, 3 April, Jesús started sipping liquor with his friends, including the husband of Engracia Meza. When Jesús saw that the husband of Engracia was good and drunk, he left with this woman. Later Engracia's husband realized what they were doing, and he went to complain in the municipality. Jesús was taken out of the house of the woman at 10:00 P.M., and he was fined $60 the following day.

❧ More Information on the Ex-Commissioners
6–25 APRIL 1983

After the municipal elections in 1980, the ex-mayor, Juan Mendoza rejoined the national police, but he went to work on the frontier of Mexico. When the Lucas government fell after the coup, there was a change of *jefes* in the police corps in different parts of the country. In this manner, Señor Mendoza was discovered to be dealing in the black market running products of Mexico to the frontier of Guatemala. Since the smugglers were paying sums of money to the police, they had no problems. However, when the new *jefes* discovered what was happening, Mendoza was fired. He tried to get reinstated as a policeman, but they say he is on a blacklist.

He came back to San José, but he is unemployed. What he does for a living is to stir up litigation and then act as a legal counselor. When married couples are having problems, he tells them to take action before the appropriate tribunals instead of helping them settle their marital disputes amicably. He takes them to Sololá, which costs them more. However, several times he has lost his cases before the tribunals. Thus, many people do not respect him.

Such was the predictable outcome of the case of Señora Consuelo Temó. With the help of Mendoza, she was suing her husband, Edgar Cojbx Cotúc. Although Mendoza acted as counselor to Señora Consuelo Temó, his efforts were futile. Señor Edgar Cojbx won. Also, Mendoza has done the same thing with the people in the villages of the municipal district of San José.

In San Martín la Laguna there are many clever persons who could do something to save the imprisoned *ex-comisionados*. But the people witnessed the wicked deeds of these men, and no one tried to defend them before the tribunals. The one who decided to try to do something was Juan Mendoza, who acted like an attorney for the imprisoned. The poor women of those imprisoned brought Juan things like choice cuts of meat, chickens, liquor, and money so that he would do something. He went many times to Guatemala [City] to present briefs in the defense of the guilty. Each time he returned, he said that they would spend only a short time in jail. He assured their wives that he would be able to get these men out of jail.

However, all of his efforts were futile because there are 55 formal accusers against the ex-commissioners. Moreover, when the court asked the town for 500 signatures in favor of their death, the accusers collected 800 from honorable persons. This is when the *tribunales de fuero especial* [tribunals of special law] proved that the *ex-comisionados* are guilty of these crimes.

Yesterday, which was Tuesday, 6 April, on the first radio broadcast of Nuevo Mundo at 6:05 A.M., it said that the prisoners of San Martín la Laguna of the department of Sololá are going to be convicted and sentenced to death. At the same time a copy of the petition presented by the people of San Martín was read which asked for the penalty of death for the eight prisoners. But the news did not say when the execution will take place or whether some of them will be set free or all of them executed.

Earlier I said there were seven imprisoned ex-commissioners. But in the month of January of this year, another was jailed. As is the custom in this town, the fiesta of Esquipulas is celebrated by almost everyone in the month of January. Thus, Federico Yojcom, who was a friend of the prisoners but who was not known to have actually taken part in the swindles and kidnappings, celebrated the fiesta of Esquipulas.

Federico was happy, and he invited many persons. Then he began to drink excessively. No doubt because of his drunkenness, he began to say that he was one of those who participated in the robberies and kidnappings. Also, he said that he had committed assassinations along with those already imprisoned. And he said that if he wanted to kill someone it would not be difficult because he certainly had practice.

This was how the people discovered what he had done, and they denounced him to the authorities. The following day they took him to an unknown place. Later, it was discovered that he had joined his companions in jail. According to the *Martineros*, Federico was the one who confirmed that the eight prisoners had killed a lot of people and extorted a lot of money.

The most tragic thing is that some of those whom the ex-commissioners massacred in this town were their own kin. Now the kin of the murdered are pursuing the accusations against the ex-commissioners, who are also their own kin. First the nephews killed the sons of their uncles. Now the uncles are asking that their nephews to be sentenced to death. It is all very crazy!

A small group of people support the prisoners, and these people want them to be punished with only 15 to 20 years in prison. But the majority are asking that they be shot by firing squad. Also, the president of the republic has received an appeal to initiate new proceedings. However, it is certain that the *tribunal de fuero especial* will conduct the trial well.

Since the ex-commissioners have been locked up, there have been no more misfortunes in this town, which [seems] to verify that those arrested [indeed] committed the violence and terror. One version says that they fabricated clandestine leaflets with subversive words and then accused their own neighbors of being guerrillas. They did this so that they could extort money from them. When the falsely accused refused, the ex-commissioners assassinated a lot of them, including students, teachers, and finally a *universitario* [university student] of the surname Cumatz Cojbx.

I am awaiting information as to whether there will be a firing squad. It seems to me that the sentence will be announced this month because there is a lot of activity in the town of San Martín.

❧ Guerrillas Crucify a *Comisionado* of Santa Bárbara
16–19 APRIL 1983

They say that when a *comisionado militar* was working in his milpa with two of his children, some men dressed in military uniforms arrived and asked him for his identification papers. But this man was not carrying his papers. He said that he did not need to carry any papers because he was a military commissioner. Without doubt this man thought those who had arrived to talk to him were the military.

He began to tell them that he had collaborated a lot with the army and had eliminated persons who were on the left. The men in uniform asked him for a lot of information, and they told him that they were members of the national army. This man told them everything he had done. After hearing all of this information, they took him and his two children toward the Hill of Xecam. When they arrived at this place, they told the two youngsters to go home and tell the rest of the family that their father would not return—his life was over.

Then those in military uniforms told them they were not soldiers of the army—they were members of the guerrillas (ORPA). When the two youngsters arrived home, they told what had happened. The people of the town wanted to find this man, but in the end they did not have the courage. They were too scared because they say that there were 300 guerrillas.

The townspeople did not go to look for him until Sunday. When they found his body, they discovered that the guerrillas had given this poor *comisionado militar* a horrible death. They had cut off his fingers, cut out his tongue, cut off his testicles and hung them around his neck, and crucified him to a tree. The people had to take the body to Sololá, and they did not bury him until Tuesday. This event happened in Santa Bárbara, which is six kilometers from San José.

❧ More Information on the Jailed *Comisionados*
25 APRIL 1983

On 25 April I received new information about the prisoners from San Martín. The *Martineros* submitted a petition to the special tribunal, or, better said, to the administrator. The petition contains the signatures of 800 *Martineros* who asked the president of the republic to give the penalty of death to the eight prisoners. The verdict still is not known. The newspaper said that 800 *Martineros* had signed the petition, but yesterday I went to San Martín and chatted with the civil registrar. He told me that there are only 600 signatures, including women and children.

Another version says that the families of the imprisoned are trying to raise money to give to the officials to obtain a favorable verdict. They say that they need $500 per prisoner. It is certain that they are looking for money [because I know someone whom they asked].

❧ We Are Required to Have Passes to Leave the Town
10 MAY 1983

On 10 May they gathered all of us in town who are from 18 to 60 years of age. They told us we will have to be inspected when we leave the town. We will have to have a pass to leave.

In this month they inaugurated a new barracks in the town of Sololá, the seat of the department of Sololá. They are going to call it Military Zone Number 14. It is not known if they will later rename it.

Epilogue

❧Epilogue: The Crisis Continues, 1983-84

One of the programs to which the Guatemalan government wanted to attract returning refugees to build a new country was a scheme that would transform the Indian highlands under Colonel Wohlers, who headed PAAC, the social side of Ríos's "guns and beans" program. In the summer of 1982 the army placed several highland villages thought to be guerrilla strongholds under permanent military control. Under previous governments, the army would leave a village only to have the subversives return. With the help of the defensa civil, *which is mandatory for all males between 18 to 50, the villages would remain occupied. The first stage of the PAAC was to give small farmers credit to boost food production to meet local demand and to employ the displaced and jobless in food-for-work units that built roads and irrigational facilities in exchange for daily subsistence and food rations.*

The second stage of development was to step up colonization and the use of existing cooperatives to boost new forms of agricultural exports of crops such as frozen broccoli, Chinese cabbage, watermelons, and 15 new crops. Also planned were huge plantations of fruit and vegetables with storage and processing facilities and refrigeration plants. The Guatemalan government had provided $12 million in new financing, but much more was needed, and USAID approval was pending as of 6 May 1983. The model is that of the Taiwanese cooperative and Israeli kibbutz, which were seen as examples of efficient land use. However, Moore Lappé and Allen (1983) point out the *pitfalls of overspecialization and the dependence of campesinos on outside buyers such as Alcosa, a Guatemalan subsidiary of Hanover Brands, a corporation based in the United States.*

Concerns over whether peasants persuaded to cooperate in new schemes of agricultural development will be adequately protected with regard to overspecialization and the vagaries of international markets for export crops are likely to be overshadowed by the lack of funds available for such grandiose plans. By mid-May 1983, Guatemala had slipped from a healthy growth rate to bankruptcy, for all practical purposes. When a delegation from Guatemala went to Washington to try to secure a $125 million loan from the International Monetary Fund (IMF), the officers of IMF pointed out in clear terms that extra sources of revenue had to be secured before they would consider the loan in August of 1983. To raise revenue, Ríos Montt introduced a value-added tax (IVA), which was a 10 percent sales tax that took effect on 1 August 1983. This tax angered both the country's businessmen and poorest sectors of the population.

By 6 May 1983 a political initiative had divided right-wing opposition but also encouraged the reactivation of old parties and proliferation of new ones. New ground rules prior to election plans included disbanding all existing parties and requiring them to register again by collecting 4,000 signatures from literate citizens among 50 towns in at least 12 of Guatemala's 22 departments. Also, 50 literate citizens could form an organizational committee leading to the eventual formation of a new party.

The new parties included the Partido Petenero and a new party of the Partido Social Democrático (PSD), in addition to the authentic PSD led by Mario Solórzano and linked to the URNG guerrilla alliance. The older parties that became active again included the PR, PID, and the FUN. The MLN called the plan a farce and threatened holy war against Ríos Montt. When the MLN reneged on its position, Leonel Sisniega Otero, who had helped to engineer the Lucas coup but who was kept from power and subsequently was involved in a number of coup attempts against Ríos, is reported to have pulled his faction out of the party. The Christian Democrats accepted the legislation even though the government refused to meet its demand of ending the special courts. Right-wing dissidents of the DC were attempting to pull out and join a new pro-government Partido Social Cristiano.

The private sector was showing disillusion with all the political parties and was beginning to solve its problems directly with the government or the army. According to some observers, all of these devel-

opments favored Ríos Montt (Latin America Regional Reports Mexico & Central America *1983d, f, h*).

By the end of his first year of office, Ríos Montt had survived a number of attempted coups by officers sympathetic to the far-right MLN, which was more aligned with ex-President Lucas García and sectors of the business community. All of the political parties demanded elections. Mario Sandoval, an angry presidential hopeful of the MLN, warned, "He who rises by coup can fall by coup" (Nelson 1983). In an abortive coup in October 1982, Colonel Francisco Gordillo, an original member of the junta which had ousted Lucas, and a key army contact for the MLN, was arrested.

Under Ríos, the army had strengthened its role in administration. It had taken over a number of state dependencies, including the Instituto Guatemalteco de Seguridad Social (IGSS), and the ministry of defense had become a private army at the service of the corrupt interior minister, Donaldo Alvarez Ruiz. The G-2, army intelligence, was doing much of the dirty work that formerly had been carried out by the hated policía judicial and detective corps (Latin America Regional Reports Mexico & Central America *1983b:7*).

The army had hardly been touched by the anti-corruption campaign. Most officers sympathetic to ex-President Lucas were still on active duty. Also, the officer corps, which for the most part is fiercely nationalistic and anti-communistic, was less enthusiastic about Ríos's efforts to restore law and order and improve Guatemala's human rights image. They wanted a free hand to fight the guerrillas. This situation made the president most vulnerable because the army did not trust two of his close advisory groups—centrist technocrats such as Jorge Serrano, president of the council of state, and pastors of El Verbo, the president's Protestant Church (Latin America Regional Reports Mexico & Central America *1983b*).

By July of 1983, Ríos Montt was struggling against some of the most powerful and diverse groups in Guatemala to hang on to his presidency. Senior officers in the army were becoming increasingly dissatisfied with the influence of the six junior officers acting as an advisory staff to the president. The Catholic Church was against the aggressive influence of advisers from the El Verbo Church, based in California. These ill feelings only increased when President Ríos executed six suspected terrorists despite the pope's visit to Central America to promote respect for human rights. Ríos seemed to be rubbing in his ill feelings toward Catholicism when he refused to provide funds for a specially built car for the pontiff. Finally, Ríos had to contend with rightists who thought he was too moderate and leftists who *thought he was too conservative. Both leftists and rightists thought Ríos was not sharing power (Kohan 1983; Latin America Regional Reports Mexico & Central America 1983e; Kelly 1983).*

On 29 June 1983 a significant abortive coup took place when the commander of the Quezaltenango garrison refused to carry out a presidential order to bombard a village that had fallen under guerrilla control. Commanders in three other zones of conflict, Huehuetenango, San Marcos, and Santa Cruz del Quiché, joined the rebellion, as did the Guatemalan air force. When General Oscar Mejía Víctores, who had been promoted from vice-minister to minister of defense in September, toured the area, he learned that not only were the officers against the indiscriminate killing of peasants, which had drawn worldwide protests, but also that the commanders wanted the removal of the six military advisers making up the young officers' council as well as an early date for elections and a return to constitutional rule. On the same night Colonel Francisco Gordillo stated on national television that Ríos Montt thought it was God who made him president, but in reality it was "we who appointed him." Gordillo announced that he was going underground to bring down the government. On the same television program, Leonel Sisniega Otero criticized the president. Ríos Montt responded by dissolving the body of junior officers and dismissing the evangelists who were advising him. He also dismissed about 50 army officers from government jobs, and he set 1 July 1984 as the date for an election of a constituent assembly. However, he also reimposed a state of alarm that suspended many civil liberties (The New York Times 1983b; Latin America Regional Reports Mexico & Central America 1983e; Chavez 1983).

On 8 August 1983 a successful coup finally ended Ríos Montt's 17-month rule. The same force that put him into power took him out — the military. General Oscar Humberto Mejía, President Ríos's defense minister, replaced him. On assuming power, Mejía stated that he would remain minister of defense as well as chief of state but that he rejected the title of president. Mejía insisted that the change was not a coup, just a change in government, suggesting that the new government would differ mainly in style rather than substance.

It was possible that Mejía did not have the total backing of the military that he implied at his swearing-in ceremony. Mejía and the army chief of staff, Colonel López Fuentes, were the leading figures of the core of the higher echelon of survivors from the Lucas García administration. The young officers who supported Ríos Montt were still against the burnt-land strategy and military doctrine of occupational force. Guatemalan military sources said that armed resistance to the coup might have been fiercer if the U.S. ambassador had not intervened. (A day before the coup General Mejía met with the second-ranking officer in the U.S. Southern Command and his peers from Honduras and El Salvador. Also, Major William Ricardo, assistant U.S. military attaché at the U.S. embassy, appeared on Guatemalan television talking on a walkie-talkie while Guatemalan troops surrounded the palace.) Nicaragua's Sandinista government accused the Reagan administration of plotting the coup in order to have someone in power in Guatemala who would be more aggressive toward leftists in the region. Vinicio Cerezo, leader of the DC, accused the U.S. of meddling, at least by default, because the coup took place after the U.S. said it would not disapprove of the plans (Associated Press 1983b; Nelson 1983; Latin America Regional Reports Mexico & Central America *1983g).*

*The attempted coup in June seems to have been the product of two coordinated attempts of the right headed by General Echeverría, Colonel Gordillo, and Sisniega Otero. It apparently was supported by Mejía and Fuentes López because of resentment against the president and his clique of junior officers. The other base of support was that of the large-unit commanders, mainly in the zones of conflict in the west, who rose more against Defense Minister Mejía and Fuentes López than against Ríos Montt. They were unhappy with the emphasis on a military solution to the guerrilla problem. Still other officers supported the June attempted coup because they wanted experienced officers to return from administration to their field posts at a time when it seemed that the guerrillas were gearing up for a new offensive (*Latin America Regional Reports Mexico & Central America *1983f).*

In addition to having internal problems with the military, Ríos Montt, a one-time Roman Catholic who converted to the Christian Church of the Word a few years ago, alienated both progressive and conservative elements of the Catholic Church with his unabashed preference for his Protestant Church in a land that is predominantly Catholic. The progressive Catholic sector was further agitated by Ríos's not staying the execution of the six condemned men on the eve of the pope's visit and the conservative element of the Catholic Church was offended by Ríos's overt proselytizing. Critics dubbed him the Ayatollah of Guatemala. Even his own elder brother, Roman Catholic Bishop Mario Enrique Ríos Montt of Escuintla, worried that a religious war more serious than the current political war could erupt if the people's religious sentiments were manipulated (Simons 1982b). Finally, President Ríos did not placate the U.S. He was reluctant to get full U.S. military and economic aid restored, his stance toward

Nicaragua was neutral, and his policy toward El Salvador was non-involvement with the Salvadoran army. He assumed this position just when Guatemala most needed economic and military support from the U.S. (Nelson 1983; Latin America Regional Reports Mexico & Central America *1983f*).

In Mejía's brief acceptance speech, he referred to Ríos Montt's errors of promoting a fanatical and aggressive fundamentalist group of Protestants and relying on his junior officers. He also announced that there would be a quick return to social, economic, and political democracy. Specifically he declared: (1) the state of alarm imposed by Ríos Montt in June was lifted; (2) Ríos Montt's controversial secret military tribunals were abolished; (3) there would be new freedom for political parties; (4) the electoral schedule set by Ríos for elections of the constituent assembly on 1 July 1984 would be followed, although there were hints that the date might be moved up; (5) Mejía would try to improve relations with the United States, which had been reluctant to supply more military aid because of human rights violations; (6) he would preserve the unity of the army with the traditional principles of military hierarchy and subordination of junior officers; (7) he would use all means at his disposal to eradicate the Marxist-Leninist subversion that was threatening Guatemala's liberty and sovereignty; and (8) he implied that he would not mix politics with evangelism (Vasquez 1983; Kelly 1983).

General Mejía's rise to power was not as enthusiastically greeted as that of General Ríos Montt either in Guatemala City or in Washington. In Guatemala a centrist politician, Leopoldo Urrutia, leader of the party Alianz Democrática, called for the formation of a civic-military junta, which led some analysts to believe that there might have been powerful military support behind Urrutia's statement. And if Mejía cannot overcome divisions within the military, he could be toppled, too (Latin America Regional Reports Mexico & Central America *1983f*).

In Washington, observers noted that Mejía might be a setback to bolstering an anti-Communist regime because he represents a military government with close ties to the far right, including the MLN. For example, the MLN's leader, Mario Sandoval, has stated that it may be necessary to kill a half-million Guatemalans in order to pacify the country (Nelson 1983). And the still unresolved kidnapping of Ríos Montt's sister, Marta Elena Carlota, is widely suspected to be the work of the MLN. Representative Clarence Long, chairman of the appropriations subcommittee on foreign operations, described Mejía as arrogant and mean and stated that his committee could see to it that no military or economic aid goes to his crowd. Mejía retorted that Long sounded like a member of the EGP (Latin America Regional Reports Mexico & Central America 1983e, 1983f, 1983g).

Nevertheless, Reagan supported Mejía, and the first thing Mejía did was to dismiss Foreign Affairs Minister Eduardo Castillo Arriola, executor of Ríos Montt's policy of neutrality toward Nicaragua and non-involvement in the Salvadoran army's war against the guerrillas. Mejía also stated publicly that the Contadora group had nothing to do in Central America and insisted that what was needed was support for the struggle against the Sandinistas in Nicaragua (Latin America Regional Reports Mexico & Central America 1983f).

In November, Chavez (1983a) filed a report noting that violence under the Mejía's three-month-old regime was weakening his government. A sharp rise in political violence against the Roman Catholic Church had begun to undermine the government at the same time that the Reagan administration was trying to resume military aid and economic assistance. On the first of November, the body of Rev. Augusto Ramírez Monasterio, a Franciscan church leader in Antigua, was found in the capital just a day after Mejía had publicly accused some members of the Catholic Church of cooperating with the guerrillas. Mejía denied that the army was involved and promised a full investigation. On 26 November, however, Prensa Libre (1983) reported that Monseñor José Girón Perrone, vicar-general of the archdiocese appointed by the government in the absence of the vicar-capitular, stated that no news had been given with regard to the investigation of the murder or of the murders of 12 other priests since 1978, when Lucas was in office. None was killed under Ríos Montt, and this was the first priest killed under Mejía. One diplomat stated that it did not matter whether the military was involved and that Mejía's statement could have been taken as a signal by a paramilitary group to go ahead with the killing.

Under Mejía, the press has been freer with the state of alarm lifted. Also, Mejía transferred two regional commanders for violations of human rights. However, the new chief of state did not seem to be in full control of the country, and there was talk that he too could be ousted soon. According to Vinicio Cerezo Arévalo, most of Mejía's problems were due to his lack of control of the military. After two coups in less than two years, the divisions in the military are deeper. Since the latest coup, three Christian Democrats have been murdered, but Cerezo said it was not yet as bad as it had been under Ríos Montt, when 30 local party officials were killed. Cerezo said, however, that he had been warned by the military that he and other moderate

*politicians could be targets of right-wing officers trying to destabilize
the government and gain a pretext for yet another coup that would
delay the electoral process. Violence was increasing not only in the
urban areas but also in the country (Chavez 1983a).*

*Chavez (1983b) also reported the existence of reorientation
camps in some areas, such as Cobán, Alta Verapaz. They are filled
with Indians who supposedly have been close to guerrillas. After a
seven-month indoctrination against subversion and attending classes
in Spanish, woodworking, and agriculture, they are to be resettled on
large farms. As long as the Indians are under the army's supervision
in large camps, the guerrillas do not have access to them. The camp is
described as a model farm with electricity, running water, and available land. As Chavez concludes, for the moment the camps may be
the better alternative. If the villagers go home they risk being ha-
rassed by the army or by the guerrillas. The army diminished guerrilla support in Alta Verapaz with an offensive in 1982 that left many
of the Indians dead and chased thousands of others higher into the
mountains or over the border into Mexico. Those who remained were
enlisted in the civil defense patrols, and others were either captured
and brought into camps or willingly asked for amnesty. The army
strategy is to starve the guerrillas and deny them support of the population (Chavez 1983b).*

*Krueger and Smith (1983) describe the highlands as militarized,
with civil patrols, army penetration, and camps controlled by the
army. Army personnel are concentrated mainly in municipal capitals
and camps established as holding areas or in regions of permanent
resettlement where conflict has been most intense. Camps exist in the
Ixil area of El Quiché near Nebaj and Chajul; in Xemetebaj, Chimaltenango; and in Godínez, Sololá. Large numbers of the inhabitants of
these camps are widows and their children. Often they receive aid
through Protestant and Catholic church resources.*

*In the department of Sololá many people who had left their vil-
lages returned. Civil patrols have been organized. There have been
recent reports of kidnappings but no reports of sweeps by the army in
search of guerrillas. But some areas, such as Alta and Baja Verapaz,
still had intense army activity.*

*By November of 1983, the Guatemalan economy was in
shambles, especially in the western highlands. Even areas less affected
by the violence are facing severe handicaps. Due to the violence and
lack of workers, crops have either been destroyed or not planted.
Grains are thus scarce and expensive, selling for $18 to $20 per 100
pounds, about twice the price in 1980. Campesinos who once de-*

*pended on seasonal work on the coastal plantations are having diffi-
culty finding work because displaced persons permanently reside on
the southern coast and because violence and depressed world prices
have lowered productivity. Wages are down to $1 a day from the 1980s
average of $2 (despite the legal minimum of $3.20 per day). Artisans
are unable to sell their work to either local farmers or tourists. Participation in the civil patrols takes valuable time away from other economic activities, and it is served without pay. The depressed economy
has resulted in higher levels of malnutrition, illness, hunger, and even
starvation (Krueger and Smith 1983).*

*On 20 November 1983 another USAID linguist was reported
seized. Two had already been found dead. An official of the ministry
of education said there were powerful groups in the country who
think that anyone trying to improve the lives of the Indians is a Communist. Some officials of the Guatemalan government think that the
deaths of the USAID workers were the prime reason that the U.S.
Congress cut off $53.5 million of economic aid. The $3 million bilingual project was to have been expanded in 1984, but the request was
part of the package that Congress excluded* (The New York Times
1983c).

*On Sunday, 1 July 1984, Mejía carried out his promise to hold
national elections for a new 88-seat constituent assembly, the fourth
in 30 years* (Latin America Regional Reports Mexico & Central America 1984c). Time *(16 July 1984:40) described it as the country's most
open and fraud-free elections in more than a decade. Voters strongly
supported moderate civilian political parties and sharply rebuffed the
military and landowning oligarchy that has ruled the country since
the CIA-backed coup in 1954. A big winner was Vinicio Cerezo Arévalo's Partido Democracia Cristiana Guatemalteca, which won 22
seats in the assembly. However, Mejía warned the assemblymen that
their mandate was limited to writing a new constitution and preparing
for presidential elections in July 1985. Ten days before the election,
Mejía had appeared on television, flanked by 27 armed forces commanders, to declare that he would not allow the new constituent assembly to replace him with a provisional president.*

*Although 1.8 million voters turned out for the election, Long
(1984:10) cautioned that voting is mandatory for literate Guatemalans. Those who do not vote and receive stamps on their military cards
are subject to $5 fines, which the people fear. Raúl Molina Mejía,
leader of the Representación Unitaria de la Oposición Guatemalteca
(RUOG, the political and diplomatic wing of the four guerrilla forces
operating under the banner of the Unidad Revolucionaria Nacional*

Guatemalteca, URNG) told Latin America Regional Reports Mexico & Central America *(1984d) that individuals voted because they feared that if they did not they would be taken as subversives and condemned to death.*

After the election on 1 July 1984, Mario Sandoval Alarcón, a leader of the MLN, was disputing unofficial figures that gave his party fewer seats than the moderates. But a spokesman for the tribunal said that the official results would not likely change significantly. Sandoval rejected allegations that the MLN, supported by the country's most conservative landowners and industrialists, is linked to death squads. He said, "That is not true. I have ten men looking after me. That is not a secret army. The arms that we have are for personal use. Few of us have machine guns" (United Press International 1984:10).

As of August 1984, Guatemala continued to have one of the worst human rights records in the hemisphere with 100–116 political killings a month. The election of 1 July 1984 was likely to be considered progressive by some members of the U.S. Congress. And Congress was studying a request by the Reagan administration to give $10 million in military aid, which it considered nonlethal, to Guatemala after a seven-year embargo on such assistance (Time 1984:40; Latin America Regional Reports Mexico & Central America 1984b). Finally, the events unfolding in San José, Sololá, continued to be recorded by Ignacio Bizarro Ujpán.

～Notes

1. As Gwertzman (1983) reports, the opposing testimony of senators Daniel Inouye and John Stennis illustrate this point. Senator Inouye announced that he would no longer support open-ended funding for El Salvador just because it claimed to be anti-communistic. He warned that the U.S. was repeating the mistakes of the 1950s, when it supported Fulgencio Batista, the Cuban dictator whom Castro ousted. Inouye stated that by supporting Batista, whose utter corruption we were aware of, we played a part in the creation of Fidel Castro. Inouye warned that we may be creating another Castro in El Salvador. He added that we are inviting revolution there and that it is time for us to support those who are being slaughtered.

Stennis said that the lessons of the Vietnam war led him to believe that more force should be applied in El Salvador, even considering a blockade to stop the flow of arms to insurgents of that country. Senator Dennis DeConcini supported Stennis by urging an all-out American military involvement in the region, warning that piecemeal aid to El Salvador would only be wasted. Senator Barry Goldwater holds similar views. On CBS television he stated, "If I were the president . . . I would say, if it becomes necessary to save Central America, we will use our troops, our aircraft, our forces. It's that important" (Associated Press 1983a). However, some sectors in the Pentagon are reluctant to get involved again with combat troops where there is no broad national support for the government in power (Pastor 1982).

2. One analyst, William M. LeoGrande (1983:99) adds that, because the war in El Salvador looked like an easy victory, it was a splendid little war for an administration who wanted to demonstrate a willingness to use force in foreign affairs, de-emphasize human rights, and show its resolve to contain the Soviet Union. It was a perfect way to repudiate key elements of Carter's foreign policy.

In a reassessment of Vietnam and its lessons, Summers (in Butterfield 1983:54) quotes Weygand: " . . . there is no such thing as a 'splendid little war.' War is death and destruction. The American way of war is particularly violent, deadly and dreadful." For that reason, the American people should weigh carefully whether it wishes to send combat troops to any small country.

3. Although some companies, such as the Michelin rubber corporation, made millions of francs in profits, the French government spent millions of francs to conquer, pacify, and later defend Indochina. Even though it was a source of enormous profits for a small group of financially powerful Frenchmen, for France as a whole it was an everlasting drain on its resources (Buttinger 1968:166, 170–171; *Vietnam: A Television History* 1983).

According to Hanley (1983), business executives with an interest in Central America would be perfectly happy if the Nicaraguan government were overthrown, and those involved in Latin America seem to back Reagan's policy of military support for the governments in power in El Salvador and Honduras. The influence of big business in Central America is demonstrated in part by Senator Jesse Helms's reading into the *Congressional Record* in October of 1981 a piece by Edward Walsh (1983) that argues that U.S. companies have provided investments that have built factories, roads, hospitals, and schools and have provided jobs for thousands of Central Americans.

4. Both Reagan and Dodd were criticized as being demagogic. Anthony Lewis (1983) wrote that President Reagan gave no indication that he had a clue to the reality in El Salvador. "Instead he offered demagogy: a mixture of half-truths, Red-baiting and jingoism."

Jeane L. Kirkpatrick (in Weinraub 1983b) declared that Dodd's comments were both demagogic and irresponsible, claiming that Dodd's figure of $1 billion was off by 40 percent and that most of our aid—in a ratio of 3 to 1—goes for economic assistance to help the poor people that Senator Dodd says he wants to help. However, Luis Maira (1983:81) has pointed out that Kirkpatrick sees maintaining order as a crucial variable for a government to maintain its status. For example, Maira points out that Kirkpatrick has written that to many Salvadorans the violence of the repression under General Hernández, which cost 30,000 lives in El Salvador, was less important than the fact that order was restored and that 13 years of peace followed.

Still, Kirkpatrick agrees that the trouble in Central America is primarily economic and social: poverty, hunger, illiteracy, and disease win masses of recruits for Marxist revolutionaries. She has long advocated a Marshall Plan for Central America. Her opponents in the state department have mainly argued that, unlike Western Europe after World War II, Central America does not have the skilled workers and political institutions to make good use of a sudden influx of financial aid (Weinraub 1983a; Church 1983:24) and that there are no assurances that leaders in the area will use the funds equitably and justly (Kaiser 1983). For example, a Salvadoran governmental audit of the Institute for Agrarian Transformation, an agency overseeing the land redistribution program, grossly mismanaged its $6 million in funds from Washington. The audit found "doubtful investments, exaggerated expenses, others improper, some laughable, and others not legally admissible from an accounting point of view." There were accusations that some of the money went to private farms and military commanders. In 1981 the institute's president, who, according to aides, was planning to expose corruption in the agency, was assassinated along with two American advisers (*The New York Times* 1982a).

5. In essence this had been U.S. law until Reagan vetoed on 30 November 1983 legislation that would have extended the link between military aid and human rights. Reagan rationalized his veto by stating that such a requirement infringes on a president's ability to conduct foreign policy and that the certification process was generally a farce (Skelton 1984).

6. In an eloquently reasoned article, Robert Pastor (1982) argues that the basic cause of the Central American crisis is not just poverty and injustice nor is it primarily Soviet-backed Cuban terrorists taking advantage of worsening economic conditions (the surge in oil prices after 1973 flamed severe inflation, and a concomitant world depression lowered the price of major exports of the region such as coffee, bananas, sugar, and cotton). Rather, Pastor argues that the instability in the region stems from the incongruence of remarkable economic progress and political stagnation. Between 1950 and 1978, the six nations (excluding Belize) averaged an annual growth rate of 5.3 percent. But when groups with new wealth sought political power commensurate with their new economic power, they found their path blocked by the old wealthy, ruling elite. When the people with new wealth failed to achieve political power through legitimate channels of political parties and elections, they turned to subversion as the only opposition available and attempted to enlist the support of the disaffected masses of peasants.

Pastor believes, along with several other analysts, that resorting to unilateral troop involvement (as the U.S. did in Southeast Asia when massive military assistance failed to stabilize the area) will be so internally divisive in the U.S. that the Vietnam demonstrations of the 1960s will seem only a minor historical prelude to the anti-war riots of the 1980s. And Pastor believes that U.S. combat troops in Central America would provoke such a hostile national reaction that it would be the best gift the U.S. could give the left. Again, the U.S. would lose both at home and abroad. According to Pastor, the best way to defeat the Marxist-Leninist left in Central America is to break the hammerlock of the traditional power centers of the right. Furthermore, the way for the United States to have more influence in the struggle for Central America is not to join the fight but to put more distance between itself and the region, using Panama as an example of how democracy can be promoted— for such was the effect of of turning the Panama Canal over to Panamanians, even though there were cries from conservatives that such action would assure that the vital canal would fall into the hands of unfriendly forces.

7. As in El Salvador, by 1984 insurgency and counterinsurgency had devastated the economy in Guatemala. Therefore, the people urgently need the economic aid proposed in the Jackson Plan.

8. Farnsworth (1983) reported that exports to Latin America as a whole dropped by nearly one-fourth in 1982. He cites Sanjay Dhar, an economist with the Federal Reserve Bank of New York, who stated that declining exports to Latin America accounted for the loss of nearly 250,000 jobs in the U.S., and he estimated that 150,000 more jobs would be lost in 1983. De-

clining exports are accounted for mainly by the restrictions placed on Latin American countries with heavy foreign debts. The commerce department estimates that 25,200 jobs are generated by each $1 billion of American exports.

9. John Early (1982:66) notes that the Maya in the western highlands have lost land by being taken advantage of by Ladinos with superior understanding of complex legalities, and by selling it to finance drinking habits, pay for expensive curing rituals of shamans, pay for burial expenses, or pay off debts incurred while holding civil and religious offices of towns and villages.

10. The Partido Guatemalteco del Trabajo (1983) published a manifesto in *Prensa Libre* citing a UNESCO figure for infant mortality of 81.1 per 1,000 and stating that even in the urban areas 26 percent of the deaths occur because of lack of potable water and minimum sanitary conditions.

11. As in *Son of Tecún Umán*, I have tried to stay as close as possible to Ignacio's own words, but again I have employed a free translation where needed for stylistic and grammatical reasons. In translating, I have relied mainly on Ramón García-Pelayo Y Gross and Micheline Durand (1976), Daniel Armas (1971), Louis A. Robb (1980), and Jorge Luis Arriola (1973) as standard references. Spanish and Indian words and local expressions are italicized. For the reader's convenience, they are also indexed, so that definitions may be easily looked up if they are forgotten.
Since the entire document of Ignacio's life in *Campesino* is taken from a diary he kept, there was little need to rearrange events in chronological order. However, for ease in reading, some of the information within an episode was sometimes rearranged. For example, if Ignacio listed all of the characters at the end of an event, I would move their names to the beginning. Also, as in the first book, I deleted some repetitious descriptions of routine events of holidays such as Christmas and All Saints' Day, the kinds of meals he ate each day, saying his nightly prayers, his daily work routine, how well he slept, and common illnesses such as colds and headaches. However, I left enough of this information in the text to give the reader an authentic picture of daily life. The story itself provides additional information on the manner in which Ignacio recorded his story in Spanish and in which I translated and edited it into English from handwritten, typed, and taped accounts. As in the first book, I have indicated when my questions elicited more detail and when I constructed an episode from both a written and a taped version. Most of the subtitles in the text of the diary were added by me. Throughout the text, I have included notes that provide information that makes it clear to the reader what is going on in Guatemala at the national and international level at the time the reader is seeing events from a local Indian perspective.

12. A detailed, thematic analysis of *Son of Tecún Umán* and *Campesino* combined appears in Sexton (1982). A holistic ethnographic summary of the general setting appears in the introduction to *Son of Tecún Umán* (Sexton 1981), and discussions of the research on modernization and development (from which Ignacio's life history documents are an outgrowth) appear in Sex-

ton (1972, 1978, 1979a, 1979b), Sexton and Woods (1977, 1982), Woods and Graves (1973), and Woods (1975).

13. When I sent Ignacio a letter on 30 August 1978 informing him that I had received an encouraging letter from the University of Arizona Press to revise a draft of *Son of Tecún Umán* and resubmit, he wrote a short section on 26 September 1978 reflecting about his early childhood in the 1950s. Although he told essentially the same story in the introduction to his autobiography in *Son of Tecún Umán*, the second version has new information that Ignacio recalled the second time he told the episode. He said he forgot to include the new details in the first book, but nevertheless thought they were important to include in his life story in *Campesino*, the sequel. Since Ignacio and I both see parallels in what happened politically in Guatemala in the 1950s and in the 1980s, I am including these viewpoints. Also, this information is not appearing in the chronological sequence in which Ignacio told it. I am placing it at the beginning of his story because it makes an appropriate introduction to the present continuation of the diary, which covers the period from 7 February 1977 to 10 May 1983.

14. See appendix, under "Before Castillo Armas," for a discussion of the events leading up to Castillo Armas's succession to the presidency.

15. At this time Ignacio was 36 years of age; his wife, Anica, was 30; his eldest son, José Juan, would be 10 in October; his eldest daughter, María, was 9; his next son, Ramón Antonio, was 5; his youngest son, Erasmo Ignacio, was 3; and his youngest daughter, Susana Julia, would be 1 in October.

16. The persecution that Ignacio experienced over his role in developing a cooperative in San José seems to have been instigated by an envious businessman in San Martín. During the 1970s and 1980s there was selective persecution of cooperatives by large landowners and government officials to suppress modest economic and political gains. For the historical background of the situation, see the appendix, under "From Castillo Armas to Lucas García."

17. The judicial police, who are distinct from the investigative force of the judiciary, are a separate entity from the national police force, but they function under the Ministry of Government, part of the executive branch of government. They perform the role of police intelligence and investigation. All of them are stationed in Guatemala City, and they only occasionally are assigned to provincial areas (Dombrowski et al. 1970).

18. When Lucas took over the government in July of 1978, there were only four legally recognized parties: the Partido Revolucionario (PR), Movimiento de Liberación (MLN), Partido Institucional Democrático (PID), and Democracia Cristiana (DC). After a ten-year freeze, his government decided to allow the registration of new parties in a cosmetic gesture to democratize the political system since more restrictions than ever were placed on the parties. The new parties petitioning included the Central Auténtica Nacionalista (CAN), the Partido Nacional Renovador (PNR), the Frente de Unidad

Nacional (FUN), the Frente Unido Revolucionario (FUR), and the Partido Social Democrático (PSD). Of these nine parties, only the FUR, PSD, and DC had a broad political center of moderate leftists and moderate rightists. The FUR, which was being organized by Manuel Colom Argueta, an old colleague of Vice-President Villagrán Kramer, seemed the most promising for a progressive attitude in the 1982 election. But most thought the MLN would embody the old trend. The other new party, the PSD, was more toward the left, like the DC. It was organized by Dr. Alberto Fuentes Mohr, a distinguished foreign minister who had been an outspoken critic of right-wing terrorists organizations that had flourished in the days of General Arana. It was widely believed that Fuentes and Colom would form a joint ticket for the presidential elections in 1982 (Montealegre and Arnson 1983:297). The Communist party, the Partido Guatemalteco de los Trabajadores (PGT), and the terrorists of the EGP were outside the system. Both the PGT and EGP were committed to violent revolution, but they were operating at a much lower level than in the early 1970s (Crawley 1980:163; Gleijeses 1983:189).

According to Crawley (1980:163), it was not the open struggle among these political parties that led the country back into political violence, but the overreaction of the right wing to the emergence of a new force—the unions. Most of the unions of the country had come together recently under the umbrella of the Consejo Nacional de Unidad Sindical (CNUS). In October of 1978 the authorities yielded to pressure from privately owned bus companies and authorized a 100 percent increase in bus fares. CNUS called for a strike and demonstration, but the Lucas government unexpectedly took a tough line and ordered the police to disperse the crowds. As Crawley points out, a mass demonstration in support of left-wing rebels in neighboring Nicaragua had gone unopposed. In the resulting clashes, 31 were killed, hundreds injured, and at least 800 arrested. Then six days later the government revoked the increase in bus fares. The reversal was explained by the influence of the moderates in the government, including Kramer. Some even claimed Lucas himself opposed the hard-liners, who were identified as Donaldo Alvarez Ruiz, the interior minister; General Otto Spiegeler Noriega, the defense minister; General David Cancinos Barrios, the army chief of staff; and Colonel Germán Chupina Barahona, the police chief.

Following the October 1978 bus-fare demonstration, a systematic program of terror and suppression began in earnest. The Ejército Secreto Anticomunista (ESA, Secret Anti-Communist Army), an extremely right-wing organization similar to La Mano Blanca and Ojo por Ojo (Eye for Eye) organizations of the Arana period, announced its appearance with the publication of a death list of 36 people, including opposition figures, trade union and student leaders, and, curiously enough, even the four most prominent hard-liners in the government (Crawley 1980:163).

The killings began almost immediately. In January of 1979, a few days before his PSD was legalized, Alberto Fuentes Mohr was assassinated in Guatemala City.

In March of 1979 Manuel Colom Argueta, the former mayor of Guatemala City and organizer of FUR, made an outspoken statement against the importing trade sector of the economy, which he claimed had strong links to General Ricardo Peralta Méndez and was behind the assassination of Fuentes Mohr. Furthermore, Colom Argueta stated that the agro-exporting sector was equally influential and that it included both the new rich from the cotton industry and the old rich from among the coffee growers, such as Raúl García Granados, who had organized La Mano Blanca in 1966, and Jorge García Granados, who was the leader of the PR and the real power behind the throne of President Lucas García. Colom Argueta also identified Colonel Enrique Peralta Azurdia as the visible head of the traditional monopoly of the industrial sector. Colom Argueta characterized the action of the members of these economic sectors not as rivalries between businessmen but as shoot-outs between rival mafias. Colom Argueta also stated that the military hierarchy and the oligarchy negotiate the presidential candidates and that the Lucas government no longer had the power to arbitrate inter-oligarchic conflicts; that corruption is the rule, and the army participates in major business deals; that the current strategy of those in power was to destroy organized popular resistance, especially by killing key persons; that more people were dying in Guatemala than in Nicaragua, but no one knew there was a war going on against the people; that in the last three months the 2,000 murder victims included persons killed on contract because of the inter-oligarchic disputes and selective repression of the government; that while the ruling class fought it out, the army did not murder within its own ranks; and that the army was the main political party in his country. Colom Argueta also stated that Mario Sandoval Alarcón, leader of the MLN, was a buffoon straight out of the middle ages. The army uses him and he uses the army and his dispute with the PID, the ruling party, is not over ideological issues but over how power should be shared. Colom Argueta closed his statement by declaring, "The government is attempting to give itself a democratic veneer, which is why they are recognizing my party (the FUR). But in exchange, they may want my head" (Colom Argueta 1983:122–124).

Perhaps Colom Argueta had had a premonition, because a few days later he was machine-gunned in Guatemala City on 23 March 1979, six days after his left-of-center party had been granted registration with the government (Simons 1983a:132).

19. This strike was called by the Comité de Unidad Campesina (CUC). It is interesting that Ignacio perceived the militant leaders of the CUC as guerrillas. After an estimated 40,000 cotton pickers and 70,000 cane cutters went on strike, the government raised the legal minimum wage of farm laborers from $1.12 to $3.20 a day (Davis 1983a). However, even with the new law, not all farm employers paid their workers the legal minimum wage.

20. As noted earlier, the FUR had actually been legalized at this time, but after the assassinations of Fuentes Mohr and Colom Argueta, their parties, the PSD and the FUR, respectively, began to feel the wrath of the Lucas regime. Both of these parties refused to participate in the municipal elections of 1980. Except for the rightist parties, the Democracia Cristiana (DC), which was the most moderate of the center-left parties, was the only party to participate in an election in which only 12.5 percent of the electorate even bothered to vote. Six leaders of the DC were assassinated during the campaign for the 1980 municipal elections. After the elections, dozens of DC mayors were murdered, and death squads killed members of the rank and file of the party (Bonner 1981; Gleijeses 1983:193). The popular secretary-general of the

DC, Vinicio Cerezo Arévalo, warned that the party would refuse to participate in the coming 1982 presidential elections unless the government
stopped the repression against it and guaranteed conditions for a free and fair
election (*Latin America Regional Reports Mexico & Central America* 1981c).

21. In addition to the successful example of the Nicaraguan revolution
in May of 1979, the public announcement of the Organización del Pueblo en
Armas (ORPA) in September of the same year fanned the flames of insurgency
and counterinsurgency. ORPA is another splinter of the FAR which had been
quietly organizing in the western mountains. Reported to have a significant
Indian following (Davis 1983a), ORPA announced itself publicly by occupying
the Mujulía Farm in the coffee-growing region of the Quezaltenango province. In addition to organizing a political base among mostly Indian campesinos, ORPA worked to build an urban infrastructure.

The founders of ORPA broke away from the FAR because they thought
the latter's position on the Indians was racist. Unlike the EGP, which is the
largest of the guerrilla organizations, ORPA has no mass organizations and
works purely as a military entity. Its military operations have been described
as brilliant, but critics claim that the lack of political organization reduces
their effectiveness (*Latin America Regional Reports Mexico & Central America* 1982d).

About the time that ORPA publicly announced itself, the FAR came
back to life as did the Partido Guatemalteco de Trabajo (PGT). The FAR,
which spawned both the EGP and ORPA, is one of Guatemala's oldest guerrilla organizations. After its *foco* strategy failed in the 1960s, it concentrated
on influencing the trade union movement. Its activists played a key role in
the formation of the Central Nacional de Trabajadores (CNT) and the broad-
based CNUS trade union alliance, which was effective in the bus-fare demonstrations. The FAR's influence was damaged when severe repression destroyed the CNT and CNUS between 1979 and 1980. Nevertheless, the FAR
maintains a structure in Guatemala City and Chimaltenango. The FAR's
fighters are also active in the Petén region (*Latin America Regional Reports
Mexico & Central America* 1982d).

The PGT is divided into three factions that by 1982 were all active in
the armed conflict. The main body, the PGT-Camarilla, began active participation in the war only in 1981, although it agreed to join the armed struggle
at its fifth party conference in 1969. Its failure to implement this line of action
and its tensions between the military and political elements of the party resulted in the splits, the most recent being the PGT-Nucleo de Conducción y
Dirección (PGT-Nucleo) and the PGT-Comisión Militar. Although active in
the armed struggle, none of these is strong militarily. The PGT has, however,
executed a number of impressive kidnappings, and it has strong international
links and residual influence in the trade union movement (*Latin America
Regional Reports Mexico & Central America* 1982d).

Unlike the first guerrillas of 13 of November Movement led by Yon Sosa
and Turcios, little is known about the leaders of the four guerrilla groups
operating today. Perhaps they learned an important lesson about revealing
their identities after the EGP suffered from La Mano Blanca during the Méndez regime. In any case, one diplomat is quoted as saying the Marxist-Len-

inist groups are "a pretty faceless bunch of people" (Rohter 1982:24). In a similar vein a chocolate vendor was quoted by Goodsell (1982a:10) as saying, "We may not always like the way the police and soldiers act, but we like the guerrillas even less, and part of the problem for the government is that it is striking out at a faceless organization. Who are these kids who bomb buildings?"

Some of their Salvadoran counterparts have also been careful with their identity. For example, Cayetano Carpio and other leaders of the largest guerrilla group wore hoods until recently to hide their identity even from one another (Sancton 1982:30). However, unlike their Guatemalan counterparts, some Salvadoran guerrillas have invited foreign correspondents to travel with them in the mountains where many of them have been fighting for ten years or longer. But it is widely assumed that the Guatemalan guerrillas wish to implant a socialist and possibly a Marxist-Leninist government (Bonner 1982b, 1982c).

22. Sancton (1980:38), Crawley (1980:163), and Gleijeses (1983:194) sum up what was happening in Guatemala at this time. In the later part of 1979, violence continued to escalate. Responding to the upheavals in Nicaragua and El Salvador and to news that the guerrilla groups had reached an agreement on joint action, the government stepped up its counterinsurgency operations throughout the country. The Ejército Secreto Anticomunista led the rightist backlash as the main source of violence, and it seems to have had the cooperation of the country's repressive military leaders. The goal of the ESA was to annihilate the left, which they defined as anyone from Marxist guerrillas to moderate reformers, including students, professors, union leaders, journalists, priests, and politicians in opposition. Many of them were tortured and mutilated. Vice-President Villagrán, at odds with President Lucas over Belize and the repression, announced in November of 1979 that he was resigning effective in January of 1980. (He later fled to Miami, where he was a key source in Amnesty International's 1981 report that linked repression directly to an annex of the National Palace.)

Meanwhile the armed leftists continued to make sporadic attacks, including the bombing in July 1980 of a military convoy truck in Guatemala City. Also, the leftists seemed to be winning some support among the impoverished Indians who make up over half the population.

As the violence escalated, Guatemala's relations with the Carter administration in Washington were sinking to an all-time low. However, like rightists throughout Central America, Guatemala's military rulers apparently dismissed the Carter administration in hopes that a Reagan victory in November of 1980 would reverse U.S. policy.

Largely because of increased nickel production and new oil exports, Guatemala's economy continued to grow by 5 percent a year. However, despite a growing middle class, most of the country's wealth remained in the hands of a small minority. Officials in in the U.S. state department believed the country's potential prosperity could prevent total revolution only if political and social reforms were adopted. Sancton (1980:38) quoted one frustrated U.S. official as saying, "What they don't understand is that simply killing Communists doesn't solve the problem."

23. Bonner (1982b) reports that in October, guerrilla forces overran Sololá and executed the army colonel who was the governor of the province. Afterwards, well-disciplined soldiers wearing Korean-made camouflage uniforms and carrying Israeli-made automatic rifles reportedly engaged in combat almost nightly with tough, predominantly Indian guerrilla forces. Bonner also notes that the leftist revolution predates Fidel Castro's assumption of power in Cuba and that the civil war has been spawned by years of repression, military governments, and economic inequality.

24. Guatemala's ruling elite hated Jimmy Carter for cutting off military aid in 1977 to protest human rights abuses. When Ronald Reagan was elected president in November of 1980, the oligarchy celebrated by lighting fireworks and hiring marimbas (Rohter 1982). Soon after Reagan assumed office, his new secretary of state, General Alexander Haig, announced on January 28, 1981, that U.S. foreign policy would shift the focus away from human rights toward the battle against international terrorism (*The New York Times* 1981).

25. Obviously, the tactic of taking the payroll intended for the workers was different from the strategy used by the FAR in its attack on the Jaguar of Ixcán, in which the guerrillas wanted to make a good impression on the peasants by not taking the payroll.

26. In June of 1981, a month before this meeting in San José, the Reagan administration sold the army 50 trucks and 100 jeeps for $3.2 million through the commerce department by removing them from a list that banned them from countries with human rights violations and putting them in a category for control of regional stability. Also during 1980 and 1981 the Guatemalan government spent $10.5 million for three Bell 212 and six Bell 412 helicopters purchased through the commerce department. At least two of them had been mounted with 30-caliber machine guns (The Institute for Policy Studies 1983:132). These sales were procured despite Amnesty International's incrimination of the Lucas Administration in February of 1981.

The morale of the military high command seems also to have been given a boost when security forces discovered a number of guerrilla bases of ORPA in Guatemala City, apparently after capturing key members of the guerrilla group. Also, two bases of the FAR were discovered in Escuintla. In the last three weeks of July, security forces destroyed 11 "safe houses" of ORPA, at least three of them in exclusive residential areas. The army claimed to have killed 32 guerrillas defending the houses, which served as central headquarters from which country-wide actions were coordinated. The government gave the affair wide media coverage, and an hour-long battle and bombardment in Guatemala City was even televised. The army claimed to have captured a huge quantity of arms from Chinese and Soviet-bloc countries and M-16s with serial numbers that matched those left behind by the U.S. in Vietnam (Rohter 1982). It also claimed to have captured medical supplies, details of army supply routes, lists of guerrilla sympathizers, and maps indicating guerrilla movements, especially in western Guatemala. Nevertheless, on 19 July 1981 ORPA and EGP seemed to be making rapid success in coordinated attacks on police posts and army convoys in Escuintla, Suchitepéquez, El Quiché, Huehuetenango, and Sacatepéquez. Also, an estimated

500 guerrillas occupied Chichicastenango in an action to celebrate the anniversary of the Nicaraguan revolution. Guerrillas claimed to have killed 40 soldiers three days earlier in an ambush on a military convoy in the Petén (*Latin America Regional Reports Mexico & Central America* 1981b).

Thus, despite recent success against the guerrillas in Guatemala City, the Lucas government was becoming increasingly alarmed at the guerrilla threat. And even President Lucas admitted that his regime was facing a well-organized rebel army. But many middle-ranking officers were beginning to question the effectiveness of the government's entire counterinsurgency strategy and militaristic approach. They argued that more use should be made of social benefits as a way of tempting peasant support away from the guerrillas (*Latin America and Regional Reports Mexico & Central America* 1981b).

27. Seven days later three Indians from the area were arrested and charged with the killing, which authorities said was committed during a burglary. The murder was widely believed, however, to be the work of a pro-government hit squad.

Father Pablo (a pseudonym) became the tenth priest to die in Guatemala in 18 months. During the same period 91 priests and clerics fled Guatemala after receiving death threats. One nun was kidnapped and murdered as a subversive, and 64 others left the country after receiving death threats. Six parish radio stations were destroyed or closed, 3 rectories were bombed, 4 parochial schools were closed, and 12 religious training centers were closed, along with 30 centers of Christian leadership (Melville 1983:26).

The earlier sale of jeeps and trucks in June 1981 along with funds to train air force pilots seem to have been designed to clear the way for larger military sales to Guatemala. However, the murder of Father Pablo, the first U.S. priest to die in Guatemala, upset the plans (*Latin America Regional Reports Mexico & Central America* 1981b).

Since Father Pablo's death, three more priests have been killed, including another from the U.S. named James Alfred Miller. Hooded men gunned him down on 13 February 1982. Ironically, Miller had asked for a transfer from Nicaragua because he opposed the leftist government. But apparently a Brother made the mistake of trying to save a Catholic youth from induction by the army [Associated Press 1982a; *Stevens Point (Wis.) Journal* 1982]. Davis (1983a) reports that, since 1978, six Protestant ministers also have been killed.

28. By the latter part of 1981, the guerrillas had stepped up their activities and so had the army in its countermeasures. A spate of bomb attacks received most of the publicity, but one of the most dramatic activities in November was the felling of hundreds of pine trees along the length of the Pan-American Highway between the capital and Sololá in an attempt to block the country's main artery. One diplomat estimated that it must have taken 500 people working all night to cut them down. Such actions helped the guerrillas to publicize nationally and internationally that a civil war was being fought in Guatemala that was similar to the one being fought in El Salvador (*Latin America Regional Reports Mexico & Central America* 1982a).

The counterinsurgency was led by Brig. General Benedicto Lucas García, President Lucas's brother, who recently had been appointed commander of the army. The forty-nine-year-old general had been trained by the French in Algiers. He was a strict disciplinarian who was said to be opposed to the unprofessionalism of the death squads, which act on behalf of the government but outside the army's direct control. Benedicto Lucas, a graduate of the St. Cyr Academy, the French equivalent to West Point, revitalized the Guatemalan Army. He sent the elite Kaibiles (named after the Mayan god of war) on mountain patrols of up to two weeks in duration, including frequent and effective night patrols. Benedicto Lucas planned to pacify the country with the same strategy the French used in Algiers and the North Americans employed in Vietnam. Under civic action programs, he concentrated on building schools and health clinics. However, large numbers of peasants were often killed to deny the guerrillas their support. For example, the Guatemalan press reported the massacre of an estimated 200 individuals, including women, children, and the elderly, in Zacualpa, just east of Santa Cruz del Quiché. The victims' throats had been cut by armed men in civilian clothes. The government denied that the massacre had taken place. Many killings were reported in the Guatemalan press as having been carried out by *desconocidos*, or unknowns, and the government routinely blamed the guerrillas. The U.S. state department's 1981 human rights report lists several Guatemalan villages in which circumstantial evidence links the military with the deaths of many peasants. At that time, apparently few Guatemalans believed that guerrillas were responsible for the killings (Bonner 1982b).

Also, in late 1981 there were constant troop movements along the Pan-American Highway. All vehicles and their occupants were subject to strict roadblocks and checks by heavily armed soldiers. All the buildings along side the road had been abandoned, including schools and hotels. Most of the small villages visible from the road had been razed, and the road itself was littered with burnt-out vehicles. At least one journalist who accompanied a search-and-destroy mission in December of 1981 claimed that the operation was far bigger than in El Salvador. The same journalist stated that some guerrillas were using captured antiaircraft guns and that the army was using napalm against the rebels. Also, refugees fleeing to Mexico reported army raids on villages in which the inhabitants were either killed or chased out. Then their homes were burnt and their villages sealed off (*Latin America Regional Reports Mexico & Central America* 1982a).

29. On 7 February 1982 the guerrillas stated that their four separate organizations—the EGP, ORPA, FAR, and PGT—were fighting under a united command called the Unidad Revolucionaria Nacional Guatemalteca (URNG). Within hours after the declaration, a series of bomb blasts almost blacked out Guatemala City. This action suggested that unification might have strengthened the estimated 3,000 to 5,000 armed guerrillas (Rohter 1982). The main objective of the unified command was to improve and consolidate its presence among the Indians in the western highlands, which it has code-named Vietnam and where it has set up liberated zones (*Latin America Regional Reports Mexico & Central America* 1982a).

As the guerrillas seemed to be growing in military strength and popular support, the Reagan administration grew alarmed that Guatemala rather than El Salvador might be the next domino to fall in Central America. In early

February the Reagan administration decided to test Congress by requesting $250,000 in military assistance for training in Guatemala (Gleijeses 1983:202). The request noted that Guatemala was facing a Cuban-supported Marxist insurgency whose goal was to overthrow the government and that Guatemala's challenge was to respond effectively to the guerrilla threat without the indiscriminate violence to which some segments of the security forces had resorted (The Institute for Policy Studies 1983:131).

30. For background on Ríos Montt's assumption of power and more details on his regime, see the appendix, under "Ríos Montt Takes Control."

31. For a discussion of military tactics and civil defense patrols in 1981 and 1982, see appendix, under "Military Tactics and Civilian Patrols."

32. A new uproar over the Partullas de Autodefensa Civil (PAC), a basic component of the counterinsurgency campaign, also emerged elsewhere in Guatemala. The problem is similar to the one that surfaced in the counterinsurgency programs in Vietnam (MacLear 1982). At the end of January of 1983 a delegation of campesinos from Quiché in El Quiché made a trip to the defense minister, General Oscar Mejía Víctores, to protest threats made by local militiamen against 150 peasants in the area. The delegation complained that the local PAC was operating an extortion racket for a local businessman, Tomás Calel Mejía. Also, Indian representatives on the council of state have protested the persecution of a number of their members (*Latin America Regional Reports Mexico & Central America* 1983a).

❧Appendix: The Struggle for Power, 1944-82

Before Castillo Armas

As Simons (1983a) points out, most contemporary accounts dealing with the present violence in Guatemala begin in 1954, when the CIA engineered a coup that ousted the liberal, reform-minded government of Jacobo Arbenz. Defenders of the role of the U.S. in this controversy point out that the U.S. was in the midst of a cold war with the Soviet Union in which there was a genuine fear of the spread of communism in the Free World. Furthermore, they argue that the openly socialistic government had well-known Communists in its organization and that it was stockpiling military arms from the Soviet Union and was responsible for countless mutilations, tortures, and murders. Opposers argue that Guatemala bought a shipment of arms from Czechoslovakia only after the U.S. cut off its supply. And they argue that there were not many Communist Party members in Guatemala, even though Arbenz included some in his government. Moreover, they add that the U.S. intervened in the internal affairs of an elected, sovereign republic for selfish economic interests (Sexton 1981). Thus, the U.S. shares the blame (Cockburn 1983) if not major responsibility as part of the problem (Fagen and Pellicer 1983) because of a long history of supporting authoritarian regimes that align themselves with the rich and block meaningful, peaceful social and economic reforms.

While there is some truth to the position of both sides, most recently published materials highly question past U.S. policy and emphasize the murky role of powerful U.S. business interests (Gordon 1983; Torres-Rivas 1983; Schlesinger and Kinzer 1983). To fully appreciate the relevance of the 1954 coup, one has to go back to the 1944 Revolution in Guatemala that led to Arbenz's gaining power.

While the U.S. and its allies were preoccupied with liberating Europe and Asia from Italian, German, and Japanese dictatorships, Guatemala liberated itself from the oppressive thirteen-year dictatorship of General Jorge Ubico. As Gordon (1983) notes, Guatemalans of many different walks of life—sections of the Ladino military leadership, members of the lower middle classes, students, intellectuals, urban workers, and peasants—joined to overthrow the Ubico dictatorship. They were encouraged by World War II rhetoric about freedom, the example of the social achievements of Mexico's Cárdenas regime, and an evolving nationalism that wished progress for Guatemala. Major Francisco Arana and Captain Jacobo Arbenz Guzmán played key roles and became the two military members of the interim junta.

Before the revolution, backwardness was most acute in the countryside among the Indians, who comprised well over a majority of the total population of the country. Eighty percent of the best land that surrounded the overpopulated villages was lying fallow because owners of the large plantations did not wish to use it. About three-fourths of the farmers had access to only small plots of land or none at all. Malnutrition was endemic, and Indian life expectancy was less than 40 years (compared to Ladino life expectancy of about 50 years). About 70 percent of the total population was illiterate, but among the Indians about 90 to 99 percent were unable to read and write (Gordon 1983:48).

The government believed that one path toward modernization was to insure labor for the expansion of agricultural development, especially on coastal *fincas*, or farms. Thus, vagrancy laws were passed that forced Indians to work up to 150 days a year on coffee plantations for five cents a day as well as three weeks on public roads without pay. Thus, the Indians were being treated little differently than they had been in colonial times under the *encomienda* and *mandamiento* systems that insured their cheap labor for various enterprises. In short, as Gordon (1983) points out, there was extreme peasant poverty, underutilization of labor and resources, and an economy that was almost wholly dependent on the U.S. coffee and banana markets. Also, there was the need to import foodstuffs that could be produced locally.

In December of 1944 Dr. Juan José Arévalo, a teacher living in exile, was overwhelmingly elected president—the first candidate to be elected under a democratic constitution in more than a century. Early the next year, just before the inauguration, the new constitution, based mainly on the revolutionary constitutions of Mexico and republican Spain, was approved. It divided power among the executive, legislative, and judicial branches; forbade military men from running for office; declared large plantations to be illegal; guaranteed individual liberties; and declared the first meaningful political and social reforms in decades (Rosénthal 1962:216; Gordon 1983; Schlesinger and Kinzer 1983:257).

Arévalo's government promptly developed programs of health and sanitation, a labor code that guaranteed the right to organize and strike, and improvements in education. His government made an effort to protect peasant rights to land by officially registering plots according to ownership and use to force both the government and the wealthy landowners to recognize them. He established the Instituto de Fomento de la Producción (Institute for Development of Production) to make credit, instruction, and supplies available to small farmers and to integrate the Indian into the national society while preserving his culture (Jonas 1974a; Gordon 1983; Schlesinger and Kinzer 1983).

The *Ley de Arrendamiento Forzoso* (Law of Forced Rental) was passed by Congress in December of 1949. This law, which was the most important agrarian measure enacted under Arévalo, was intended to force fallow land into productive use by allowing any farmer who owned one hectare (2.47 acres) to petition the right to rent unused acreage from nearby owners of plantations. The owner of the land could not charge more than five percent of the annual crop produced on the otherwise idle lands, and thus the renter would be protected from excessive exploitation (Whetten 1961:153).

Although Arévalo was supported by the Communists, he did not allow the Communist Party to acquire legal status. He ordered the United Fruit Company to negotiate at Bananera with the labor unions which had Communist members, but he did not attempt to break up the large estates and redistribute parcels to needy Indians.

Arévalo increasingly was the subject of criticism from the left, which thought he was moving too slowly, and the right, which resented his reforms. He began to rely more on the military junta which controlled the army and the country's finances. The leader was Francisco Javier Arana, Chief of the Armed Forces, who also became a presidential candidate supported by the Partido Unificación Anticomunista. Arana's assassination, which left Arbenz the strongest contender for the presidency, with the support of the unions and Communists, left allegations that Arbenz was involved. However, Arévalo refused to investigate the murder.

Not until Colonel Jacobo Arbenz Guzmán was elected in December of 1950 were any serious attempts made toward land reform. Arbenz introduced an agrarian reform measure (Decree 900) that permitted expropriation of unused lands of farms of more than 223 acres. The owners of the land were to be paid the same value that they had declared for their May 1952 taxes, and the compensation was to be in bonds at 3 percent interest, a standard rate for the 1950s. Even President Arbenz and his foreign minister, Guillermo Toriello, had land expropriated—the former 1700 acres, and the latter 1200 acres (Gordon 1983:52).

One of Arbenz's goals was to break the grip that foreign corporations such as the United Fruit Company, International Railways, and Electric Bond and State had on the Guatemalan economy. Since the constitution insured the right to organize, and the government encouraged such activity, by 1954 half the 600,000 workers were organized, including 100,000 in trade unions and 200,000 in peasant unions (Gordon 1983:53). Thus, there was a series of bitter strikes directed at the U.S. corporations, which were the largest and most resented employers. Important strikes took place against the United Fruit Company and the International Railways of Central America from 1946 to 1952.

However, United Fruit had powerful friends in the U.S. The company's offices were in Boston, and the company was closely linked with Boston's First National Bank, the Boston Registrar Bank for United Fruit, and the Old Colony Trust, its transfer agent. In 1949 Republican Senator Henry Cabot Lodge, whose family owned stock in the United Fruit Company, declared that the Communist-inspired reforms were causing a serious breakdown of the company (Gordon 1983:54).

Under the guidance of Edward Bernays, a master of public relations, the United Fruit Company launched a campaign to view their business problems in Guatemala more as a Red menace than as nationalists trying to regulate laissez-faire capitalism. Anti-U.S. sentiment in Arbenz's government grew along with Communist influence. This sentiment was reflected in the North American press (Jonas 1974b:59–61).

The fears of the U.S. government were compounded when the Guatemalan Congress sent letters of solidarity to the North Korean government during the Korean conflict. Guatemalan delegates to the Tenth Inter-American Conference in Caracas attacked U.S. foreign policy. At this conference Guatemala was the only nation to vote against condemning the spread of international communism into the Western Hemisphere (Adams 1970; Dombrowski et al. 1970).

In 1952 the Arbenz government legally recognized the Communist Party, known in Guatemala as the Partido Guatemalteco de Trabajo (PGT). The PGT entered the congressional elections and won four seats in Congress, but its influence seemed greater than its electoral support (Dombrowski et al. 1970). The Arbenz regime and the Communist Party planned to create a peasant militia and disband the army. Since their generals had already been purged, some members of the military were becoming alarmed at such plans. When the U.S. refused to sell weapons to the Guatemalan government, it purchased 4 million pounds of arms from Czechoslovakia in 1954. The army then demanded that Arbenz disassociate his government from the PGT, but he refused (Dombrowski et al. 1970).

Not only were elements in the army becoming disillusioned and alarmed at Arbenz's dependence on Communist sectors, the landowners resented the socioeconomic reforms. Their fears were reinforced when members of the PGT took active roles in the affairs of organized agrarian committees in the countryside and acted as field agitators. Also, some workers were abusing the labor laws intended to protect them. Employers who fired laborers had to pay indemnification. Since labor courts favored labor, workers could bait employers into firing them for indemnification. Because most rural employers worked with little capital and depended on loans to carry them through until crops were harvested, a rash of compensatory payments could bankrupt all but the most wealthy (Adams 1970:188).

During the Arbenz regime 340 of the 500 existing labor unions were on farms. The strongest were on the United Fruit Company plantations, but there were active ones on the smaller coffee farms. Union organization was often unsuccessful unless immediate results could be shown. This situation sometimes led to the filing of false charges against some farms and the pressing of questionable issues (Adams 1970).

Agitation in the south in 1954 led to the burning of sugarcane fields and the shooting of administrators and *finqueros*, or farm owners (Adams 1970). Firebrand Communist agitators such as Carlos Manuel Pellecer (Schlesinger and Kinzer 1983) urged peasants to seize land illegally. Between 1953 and April of 1954, more than 30 plantations were taken over by armed laborers (Dombrowski et al. 1970:35).

As the government increasingly favored the lower sector of society, the upper sector became more alienated. Businessmen, professionals, and clergy joined landowners and elements of the military in their antagonism toward unions, land reforms, and Communists operating in the government (Adams 1970:191). As criticism mounted, Arbenz was forced to rely more and more on the support of Communists, who found it mutually expedient (Adams 1970).

The death knell, however, was not sounded for the reform government of Arbenz until it began the expropriation of 240,000 acres of the United Fruit Company's holdings on the Pacific Coast and 173,000 acres on the Atlantic Coast. At that time the company had only 50,000 acres of its 565,000 acres in production. The Guatemalan government offered $600,000 as compensation based on the declared value for taxes, but the company had been undervaluing its assets to avoid taxes. It insisted that the Pacific Coast land alone was worth over $15,000,000, and it got the U.S. State Department to intervene on its behalf. But Guatemalan officials insisted on equal application of the law to foreign and native landowners and pointed out that the company's Pacific Coast land at Tiquisate had been given to it for a port that it never built and that the land on the Atlantic coast had been acquired by various manipulative techniques despite the protests of the municipalities (Gordon 1983:55–56).

The foreign policy staff of President Eisenhower had several key members who were or had been personally in the legal, financial, or political orbit of the United Fruit Company (Jonas 1974b:62–63). As Gordon (1983:55) writes:

> Secretary of State Dulles' law firm had represented the company in negotiations with the pre-1944 dictatorial Guatemalan regimes and had served as legal counsel for IRCA [International Railways of Central America]. John M. Cabot, Assistant Secretary of State for Latin American Affairs, was the brother of Thomas D. Cabot, a director of the First National Bank of Boston. Robert Cutler, presidential assistant for national security affairs and Eisenhower's liaison with the National Security Council, was president of Old Colony Trust prior to his Washington appointment. The board chairman of Old Colony Trust was also the board chairman of United Fruit.

Secretary of State John Dulles, who had a cozy relationship with the CIA because his brother Allan directed it, persuaded Eisenhower to overthrow the Guatemalan government. [He also convinced Eisenhower that he should support Diem's reneging on holding in 1956 a national election in Vietnam according to the Geneva conference (Karnow 1983; *Vietnam: A Television History* 1983)]. Thus, ultimately the United Fruit Company was able to convert what essentially was a business dispute with Guatemalan officials into an into an ideological East-West conflict (Simons 1983a).

With the backing of CIA, Colonel Carlos Castillo Armas directed a force of 300 rebels from Tegucigalpa, Honduras, to overthrow Arbenz. The plot that the CIA hatched included parachuting dummies into the countryside to try to convince peasants that Castillo Armas had a larger band of insurgents than he did; bombing of Guatemala City by CIA-hired pilots; broadcasting battle sounds from the U.S. embassy to simulate an attack on the capital; and payment of up to $60,000 in bribes to key military officers to turn on their commander. When Arbenz realized he lacked key military backing, he tried in vain to get Colonel Enrique Díaz to arm the people's organizations and political parties (Dombrowski et al. 1970; Schlesinger and Kinzer 1983).

U.S. Ambassador Peurifoy arranged to have Díaz replace Arbenz, but when Díaz vowed to continue to struggle against Castillo, Peurifoy forced him to resign at gunpoint. Then Castillo Armas entered Guatemala City aboard Peurifoy's U.S. embassy plane and later emerged as president (Jonas 1974a; Schlesinger and Kinzer 1983).

Castillo suspended the 1945 Constitution and began to rule by decree. Ubico's secret police chief was restored to his former post along with several other officials who had served in the Ubico regime. El Comité de Defensa Nacional Contra el Comunismo (The Committee of National Defense Against Communism) was established to urge citizens to turn in subversive neighbors, and it had unlimited powers of arrest. Warrants were not used, and the people lost rights of habeas corpus. Susanne Jonas (1974c:75) wrote that a conservative estimate of 9,000 were imprisoned, many of them tortured, and Edelberto Torres-Rivas (1983:43) stated that an estimated 8,000 peasants were killed in the first two months of the Castillo Armas regime. Large landowners took revenge and expelled legal and illegal settlers alike from the land. While there were some urban victims as well, the repression of 1954–1957 was primarily a vendetta of frightened and embittered bourgeoisie punishing the rebellion of their peons in the countryside. Most observers note that this was the first stage of violence leading to the present period of unrest (Gordon 1983; Schlesinger and Kinzer 1983; Torres-Rivas 1983).

The Agrarian Reform Law of 1952 was repealed, and landowners won back their land. The trade unions and peasant movements were destroyed. Branded as tools of Communist indoctrination, literacy programs were suspended, and hundreds of rural teachers were fired. The government ordered the burning and proscription of "subversive" books such as those of Miguel Angel Asturias, a Guatemalan novelist who later won the Nobel prize for literature in 1968, Fyodor Dostoyevsky's novels, and Victor Hugo's Les Miserables (Jonas 1974c:75). Arbenz was forced into exile, and right-wing military officers controlled Guatemala through most of the next quarter-century. Their policies of social and economic repression produced a revolutionary movement far more threatening to Guatemalan stability than the 1945–1954 governments. As LaFeber (1983:82) and Simons (1983a:134) have pointed out, a U.S. official was quoted in 1980 as saying, "What we'd give to have an Arbenz now."

Gordon (1983) adds an interesting footnote to the aftermath for U.S. business interests in Guatemala. Robert Cutler returned to Old Colony Trust as chairman of the board. Secretary of Commerce Sinclair Weeks went back to being a director of the First National Bank of Boston. Robert D. Hill, who as Ambassador to Costa Rica participated in the plan to subvert the Arbenz government and who earlier was assistant vice-president of W.R. Grace and Company (which had been active in Guatemalan commerce and had been having difficulties with the revolutionary regimes), became a director of the United Fruit Company. And as Schlesinger and Kinzer (1983) point out, Walter Bedell Smith, John Foster Dulles's undersecretary of state, was trying to land the presidency of the United Fruit Company even as he was urging the overthrow of Arbenz. The company later rewarded him with a seat on its board of directors.

Given the murky influence of U.S. business in the 1950s, it is not surprising that the roles of some officials in the Reagan administration have been questioned in the 1980s. Richard Stone, Reagan's envoy to Central America (who resigned after eight months on the job and was replaced by veteran diplomat Harry Shlaudeman) is a millionaire lawyer who is known for his hard-line views (Isaacson 1983:28; Whitaker et al. 1983) and whose experience in Central America includes working as a paid lobbyist for the right-wing government of General Fernando Romeo Lucas García (Abramson and Houston 1983), whose regime had an abominable human rights record (Amnesty International 1981). The public relations firm of White House aide Michael Deaver represented a Guatemalan group of businessmen and landowners named Los Amigos del Pais (Friends of the Country). *Latin America Regional Reports Mexico & Central America* (1980b) reported that the Guatemalan group paid the Washington public relations firm of Deaver and Hannaford $11,000 a month to spruce up Guatemala's national image and divert attention away from its grim human rights record. At that time General Lucas's leading adviser, Jorge García Granados, expressed hope that President Reagan might even make direct military intervention if the war showed signs of a popular uprising. However, according to Rohter (1982), despite the fact that Mario Sandoval Alarcón and Carlos Arana Osorio, both prominent right-wingers in Guatemala, mixed with Reagan's inner circle during his inauguration (Simons 1983a:133), Los Amigos del Pais seems to have been disappointed after the Reagan administration's first year in office because the American president had been persistent in demanding political moderation.

From Castillo Armas to Lucas García

A number of important officials considered Castillo Armas's victory a license to steal. They were eager to enjoy the spoils of victory, and such greed led to corruption and alleged collaboration with American gangsters in opening casinos. Even Castillo was accused of accepting a bribe that allowed officials to import unfit corn. In response, Castillo ordered a crackdown on critics of the deal. After workers booed government speakers at the annual Workers' Day rally on 1 May 1956 Castillo called a state of siege, similar to martial law, and authorized troops to break up potential strikes. Nevertheless, university students, already upset over the repeal of progressive social legislation, went on strike in various cities (Schlesinger and Kinzer 1983).

Although the change in government from leftist back to rightist put the brakes on revolutionary change, the direction of the change was not completely stopped. As Adams (1970:187) points out, important progressive elements survived. Perhaps the most important change initiated by the Arbenz government was the institution of electoral procedures that encouraged parties of opposition. In the Indian communities this reform had the special effect of undermining the traditional authority of the elders because younger, literate men were encouraged to run for local public offices. In Ladino communities parties chose their candidates without consideration to loyalty of the local upper class, and thus undermined the local power of that group (Adams

1970:187). Communist leaders failed to indoctrinate their peasant followers with Marxist-Leninist propaganda, but they did awaken the peasants and up-per-level sectors of the society to social realities, including the meddling of the U.S. in Guatemalan affairs. Even nationalists opposed to Arbenz had be-come uneasy about the role of the U.S. in toppling his government. Also, the Banco de Guatemala, the labor codes, and the labor courts continued. In-demnification for labor survived, although Melville and Melville (1971:139) point out that in some instances it was used as a vehicle to force peasants off their land. The Institute for Social Security survived, although the services were not comparable to those found in the U.S. A colonization program was started to replace the agrarian reform. Although it was more responsible in giving landed families more say, in training experts to run it, and in the se-lection of colonists (Rodríguez 1966), it was much slower in distributing land. And it did not keep pace with population pressures for land (Melville and Melville 1971:118).

For many peasants, the retribution for participating in the revolution-ary period was worse than the temporary benefits (Newbold 1956; Adams 1970). All the land that had been parceled out in the Arbenz agrarian reform was restored to the original owners, and many peasants were jailed or killed even though they knew little or nothing about Marxist-Leninist rhetoric.

Despite growing disarray and almost weekly plots against him, Castillo managed to hang on until July 1957, when he was assassinated at close range. The circumstances of his murder were suspicious, but most accounts say that he died at the hand of a disgruntled palace guard named Romeo Vásquez Sánchez, who shot him in the back and then committed suicide. According to Torres-Rivas (1983:38), the assassin was a member of Castillo's own party, and the killing was over a petty conflict of interest.

General Miguel Ydígoras Fuentes, who had been an ally of Ubico and who had run against Arbenz in 1950 for the presidency, was then ambassador to Colombia. Ydígoras believed that Arbenz had rigged the election in 1950 and that Castillo had failed to hold an election in 1956. Ydígoras felt cheated for a third time when Miguel Ortiz Passarelli was declared winner of the October 1957 election. Although Ydígoras had won the most votes, the ruling party, the Movimiento de Liberación Nacional (MLN), wished to retain power and claimed Passarelli the victor. Ydígoras rallied his supporters and in mass demonstrations intimidated the interim junta, which, in the presence of two U.S. military attachés, agreed to hold new elections on 19 January 1958. The MLN backed Colonel José Luis Cruz Salazar, who also received a $97,000 contribution from the CIA, but Ydígoras won a weak plurality and a confirmation by Congress (Schlesinger and Kinzer 1983:237).

With the successful 1954 coup, the CIA was given a new lease on life. Perhaps feeling overconfident, it decided, with the approval of the Eisen-hower administration, to engineer the overthrow of Cuba's Fidel Castro, who had ousted the corrupt government of Fulgencio Batista on 1 January 1959. However, the CIA needed a foreign base where it could train Cuban expa-triates for an invasion. In return for Ydígoras's having received U.S. support for his candidacy for president, the CIA asked to be allowed to train an invad-ing force at the plantation of Roberto Alejos, an old friend of Ydígoras who had been a former employee of both the United Fruit Company and the CIA and who was Ydígoras's representative for foreign aid programs, a potentially lucrative office. Also, Roberto's brother Carlos was ambassador to Washington, and he collaborated with the CIA in hatching the plot (Schlesinger and Kinzer 1983:238).

However, Ydígoras made the mistake of not getting the permission of the army. Several nationalistic officers opposed the plan to use Guatemala as a training ground for foreign invaders. Some even admired Castro for having the courage to stand up to the United States. On 13 November 1960 a group of officers who were under arrest at Fort Matamoros killed a colonel and a captain and escaped, taking with them about 100 troops and some weapons. The leaders of the plot in the fort were said to have been Captain Arturo Chuc del Cid and Captain Rafael Sessan Pereira. A government communique also implicated Mario Méndez Montenegro, a leader of the left-wing Partido Revolucionario (PR) who had been an unsuccessful presidential candidate in 1958 (*The New York Times* 1960). The rebels fled the fort and joined dissident forces in the northeast. Initially, as many as 120 officers and 3,000 soldiers were involved, but most of the conspirators failed to follow through (Frank 1974:179).

Fearing a Guatemalan coup would spoil the Bay of Pigs invasion (which on 17 April 1961 ironically turned out to be an embarrassing fiasco anyway), the CIA provided Ydígoras with B-26 bombers flown by Cuban exiles (Schlesinger and Kinzer 1983:239), but U.S. Ambassador John Muccio blocked Ydígoras's attempt to use Cuban troops to put down the rebellion (LaFeber 1982:82). President Eisenhower showed his support by ordering the U.S. carrier Shangri-la to patrol the eastern coast (*U.S. News and World Report* 1960). With such a show of force, the poorly planned revolt was quickly crushed. Not all of the rebels, however, submitted to the punishment of demotion and a reprimand from the president of Guatemala. Two leading insurgents fled to the mountains and eventually organized a guerrilla group. One was Marco Antonio Yon Sosa, a twenty-two-year-old lieutenant who had been trained by the U.S. in the Panama Canal Zone. The other was Luis Turcios Lima, a nineteen-year-old lieutenant who had been trained as a ranger at Fort Benning, Georgia.

According to Adolfo Gilly (in Melville and Melville 1971:141), an Argentine writer who spent some months with the rebels in the northeastern mountains, Yon Sosa claimed that the aim of the coup was to clean up the government, not to destroy capitalism. He also held that the Ydígoras's government had gained power through electoral fraud and was devoting itself to defending imperialism and the *latifundistas*, or large landowners, and to lining its pockets with national treasury funds. In a joint statement in 1962, Turcios and Yon Sosa declared that the Ydígoras government should be overthrown and replaced with one that represents human rights, saves their country from hardships, and pursues a self-respecting foreign policy (Gott et al. in Schlesinger and Kinzer 1983:240).

Also, according to Gilly (in Melville and Melville 1971:142), 800 peasants had requested arms when the rebel officers captured the military base in Zacapa. But such action had not been anticipated, and the officers could not decide whether to arm them.

On 6 February 1962 Turcios and Yon Sosa led their band, now called the Alejandro de León 13 of November Guerrilla Movement after a fallen comrade, on the first offensive in the history of this long, largely indigenously inspired guerrilla movement that continues in the 1980s. An intelligence report estimated that the size of the band was 100, which suggested that some civilians supported the guerrillas (*The New York Times* 1962).

The small guerrilla band raided an installation of the United Fruit Company in Bananera, taking an $18,000 payroll and food. Then the rebels attacked a nearby army garrison, killing the commanding officer and taking all the arms and munitions. Afterwards, the rebels raided small villages at night and clashed with national army units. Although leaders of both sides had been trained in guerrilla warfare by the U.S., which gave the regular army units some difficulty, Ydígoras was able to announce that the revolutionary movement had been smashed by 15 February. He felt confident enough to ease the curfew hours, which had been a part of the state of siege he had declared. However, not all the rebels had been completely silenced.

In the following month a second guerrilla group surfaced, led by a former Arbenz minister of defense, Carlos Paz Tejada. This group called itself the 20 October Front in honor of the 1944 Revolution. Its manifesto, according to Gott (in Schlesinger and Kinzer 1983:241), included condemnation of foreign military bases in Guatemala and the despotic rule of Ydígoras, which through its actions showed that it was unworthy of the people's trust.

As the movement grew in favor of overthrowing Ydígoras, President John Kennedy approved a pacification program for the most rebellious provinces of Zacapa and Izabal. Civic action programs included digging wells, building clinics, and providing school lunches. The U.S. also provided the Guatemalan Air Force with T-33 jets and C-47 transport planes. In May 1962 a team of Green Berets, all trained in Laos and of Mexican or Puerto Rican descent, established a counterinsurgency base at Mariscos, Izabal. Fifteen Guatemalan soldiers trained in guerrilla warfare accompanied them as part of the teaching staff (Melville and Melville 1971:143; Schlesinger and Kinzer 1983:241).

With U.S. assistance, Ydígoras's forces decimated the rebel bands of Turcios and Yon Sosa and of Paz Tejada. In the process, Ydígoras's forces killed and jailed hundreds of students, labor leaders, peasants, professionals, and ex-soldiers. In January 1963 two U.S. generals toured the area and declared the counterinsurgency program a success (Melville and Melville 1971:143; Schlesinger and Kinzer 1983:242).

Nevertheless, Ydígoras's domestic problems grew as different groups joined in criticism of his policies. Paul Kennedy (1971) felt that Ydígoras's frequent accusations that Cuba was the source of his problems and his declarations of states of siege to control unrest were attempts to mask deeper, socioeconomic problems. Ydígoras also apparently tried to divert attention away from his domestic problems by creating international incidents with Mexico and England. Mexico severed diplomatic relations with Guatemala after Ydígoras's planes strafed Mexican fishing boats. Ydígoras also threatened to go to war with England over Belize, claiming the territory belonged to Guatemala (Melville and Melville 1971).

Although President Kennedy had approved the counterinsurgency program to help Ydígoras, the American leader was unhappy with the rampant corruption in the general's regime. According to Schlesinger and Kinzer (1983:243), Kennedy did not think Ydígoras was cooperating with the social and economic goals of the Alliance for Progress. However, according to Mario

Rodríguez (1966:339), the Guatemalan right feared that Ydígoras was determined to implement the Alliance for Progress reforms. Like U.S. conservatives, Guatemalan conservatives feared the spread of communism, but they did not support a program of gradual social revolution that would eventually undermine the position of leadership in politics and society that they had enjoyed for centuries.

An attempt to introduce an income tax in late 1962 led to a rightist revolt in the air force on 26 November 1962. It was quickly crushed, but on the same day Arévalo, whom the conservatives hated, announced that he would return to Guatemala and run for president in December 1963. Arévalo publicly denounced Castroism and made clear his approval of the Alliance for Progress. But the right did not want such a moderate to return to power. They were backed by U.S. Ambassador John O. Bell, who remarked indiscreetly that Arévalo was a Communist and unsuited for the presidency. Bell's opinion apparently was influenced by Arévalo's book, *The Shark and the Sardines*, which depicted the U.S. as a shark gobbling up Latin American countries as if they were sardines. Arévalo wrote the book in frustration over the role of the CIA in ousting the Arbenz regime, but it was read by millions of Latin Americans, and Castro exploited this negative image (Rodríguez 1966; Melville and Melville 1971).

When Arévalo declared from his exile in Mexico that he was ready to take over the leadership of all the revolutionary forces in Guatemala, Ydígoras demanded his extradition and had his minister of the interior announce that Arévalo would be prosecuted for the murder of Colonel Francisco J. Arana. Later, Ydígoras apparently tried to outflank his political opponents by letting it be known that he would allow Arévalo to participate in the elections (Melville and Melville 1971:148–149). However, according to Rodríguez (1966:340), Ydígoras reneged on this position and announced on 21 March 1963 that Arévalo, a Communist whose party number was known by the government, would not be allowed to return. The supreme court ruled in favor of Arévalo's return, but demonstrations broke out both for and against it. Also, rebels responded by attacking army installations. On 25 March Ydígoras declared a state of seige. According to Kennedy (1971:166–167), Arévalo sneaked back into Guatemala on 29 March. The next day there were wholesale arrests to find out how he had done it and where he was hiding. Early the next morning, 31 March 1963, the army rose up and arrested Ydígoras and sent him and his wife into exile in Nicaragua on an air force plane. This event ushered in the three-year dictatorship of Colonel Enrique Peralta Azurdia, the ex-president's defense minister.

When Ydígoras landed in Nicaragua, he remarked, "What is going on in Guatemala is for her own good and for the good of the rest of Central America" (Rodríguez 1966:340). Most observers interpreted this statement to mean that the ex-president encouraged the coup. Many people speculated that Ydígoras had arranged the return of Arévalo in hope of beating him in an open election. Peralta Azurdia could have agreed to the scheme if only to capture Arévalo or to give him an excuse to topple the government of Ydígoras. Some people believe that the latter was the case but that it was executed with Ydígoras's connivance to give the old general an out, an auto-coup, or *auto-golpe* (Melville and Melville 1971:153). As Rodríguez (1966:340) notes, the evidence appears to support this contention, but as time passed, Peralta found it expedient to disassociate himself from the ex-government in order to gain popularity with the people. Eventually, the official reason for the coup became graft and corruption, an accusation in which Ydígoras was charged with having robbed more than $10 million from the national treasury. Consequently, the new government made "Operation Honesty" its major slogan.

General Peralta continued Ydígoras's state of siege for his first year in office. He also threw out the 1956 constitution and ruled by decree (Rodríguez 1966:341). Under his leadership, efforts to improve the condition of the poor were mostly abandoned. He heavily militarized the country and eased the way for the military's becoming the senior partner in an alliance with the bourgeoisie, a trend that largely had grown out of response to the guerrilla challenge of the early 1960s (Gleijeses 1983:188). His specially trained troops kept the rebels on the run and inflicted many casualties. He refused, however, persistent U.S. offers of Green Berets trained in guerrilla warfare to fight the rebels. Although his forces murdered hundreds of anti-government activists, they never completely wiped out the movement of insurgents (Schlesinger and Kinzer 1983).

Some advances were made in Peralta's government in public works, education, public welfare, and civic action programs. The economy took an upward swing in part due to better prices for export commodities such as coffee and sugar. Also, the military regime cooperated in forming the Central American common market. Both foreign and domestic investors were attracted to the economy, and a modified income tax was introduced. Peralta permitted a return to elections for select deputies to the constituent assembly in March of 1964, even though the state of siege meant that the elections turned out to be a sham. Guatemalans, nevertheless, welcomed a return to some semblance of a constitutional government, and the press was again free to discuss the pros and cons of various issues raised in the assembly (Rodríguez 1966).

The military openly revealed that it was more political than it pretended when it formed the Partido Institucional Democrático (PID). In addition to taking out page-sized advertisements in the papers to publicize its achievements, the Peralta government ran feelers in the press to the effect that the members of the *de facto* government should be allowed to run for office. When the democratic element responded negatively, another state of siege was called, and sycophants of the military passed Article 174, which made it possible for military men to run for office (Rodríguez 1966:342).

Keeping his word, Peralta allowed presidential elections on 6 March 1966. The candidate for the PID, representing the military government, was Col. Juan de Dios Aguilar, and the candidate of the MLN was Col. Miguel Angel Ponciano. The government refused to allow the Democracia Cristiana Guatemalteca (DC, Guatemalan Christian Democracy, a Christian democratic party) to run its candidate, presumably because the DC had fallen from grace when it refused to participate in Peralta's Congress (Melville and Melville 1971:185–186). The PR, made up of liberals and anti-military activists, ran Mario Méndez Montenegro, a centrist politician who had survived by cooperating with the government and allowing his party to join the rubber-stamp Congress of Peralta and by stating that Arévalism was something of the past since he had opposed Ydígoras for the presidency in 1957 and 1958 (Rodríguez 1966; Melville and Melville 1971).

On 31 October 1965, four months before the election, Mario Méndez was found by his wife and son shot to death. The government claimed that a paraffin test confirmed the bullet in his head was from his own gun. But his brother, Julio César Méndez Montenegro, ex-dean of the University of San Carlos Law School, claimed that the death was another murky political murder (like those of Castillo and Arana) (Rodríguez 1966; Melville and Melville 1971; Schlesinger and Kinzer 1983).

The campaign was a bitter one, and it reached a high pitch when Julio César Méndez, who was running in his brother's place, accused the military government of trying to assassinate him, of burning seven small planes used by the PR for campaigning, and of imprisoning a number of his bodyguards without the benefit of legal charges or court trials. The PID, the ruling party, denied the accusations and responded that it would take Méndez to court for his calumnies (Melville and Melville 1971:186). In turn, the PID charged that the PR was Communist-controlled. The PR's vice-presidential candidate, Clemente Marroquín Rojas, was not even a member of the party, and he was chosen for his vehement attacks on all institutions in his own newspaper, *La Hora*. It was a good choice because his newspaper was an effective medium for propaganda against the opposing parties. On 6 March 1966 Julio César Méndez M. won the election. However, the shocked military government immediately tried to oust Méndez and backed down only when the U.S. embassy issued a statement indicating support for Méndez (Melville and Melville 1971; Schlesinger and Kinzer 1983).

Nevertheless, the military allowed Méndez to assume office only after signing a written guarantee that the armed forces would effectively rule the country during his tenure (Gleijeses 1983:191). According to Schlesinger and Kinzer (1983:245), this capitulation made it possible for American defense officials to place U.S. Green Berets in Guatemala. Thus, although the Méndez government was the first civilian one in 16 years, it signaled the demise of civilian government. By the end of its administration in 1969, civilian government was on a clear path to being replaced by raw military power (Torres-Rivas 1983:38).

When Méndez took over the government, the military had a clear understanding that it would be free of civilian government controls in its pursuit of the guerrillas. Under pressure from his military commanders, Méndez named a tough colonel, Arana Osorio, commander of the Zacapa province. U.S. Green Berets did much of the instructing of Arana's troops, and the U.S. gave $17 million in aid and equipment, at least some of it apparently coming from the Alliance for Progress funds (Melville and Melville 1971:282; Gordon 1983:65).

Under Ydígoras, the guerrillas were not considered much of a threat, and little was done to counter them. Peralta publicly called them bandits rather than guerrillas. But Turcios, operating in Izabal and Alta Verapaz and occasionally Guatemala City, and Yon Sosa, struggling among the peasants in the Sierre de las Minas region, were developing their plans of action. As noted above, they participated in some joint actions, but eventually they went separate ways. Yon Sosa began to follow more of a Trotskyist orientation organized under the name of the MR-13 (13 of November Movement), and Turcios Lima's group called itself the Fuerzas Armas Rebelde (FAR). The FAR aligned itself with the PGT. Then it subsequently broke off again and reunited with Yon Sosa. The difficulties seemed to revolve more around tactics than objectives, because all three groups' main objective was to give land to the peasants. Both guerrilla bands emphasized a *foco* strategy (small groups establishing themselves in the countryside and awakening the people by setting an example of how to struggle by confronting the army). Turcios worked more, however, at what he considered to be a fifteen-to-twenty-year struggle and tried to indoctrinate the peasants. For that reason, he seemed to have more success (Adams 1970:268; Melville and Melville 1971:176; Fried et al. 1983:259).

According to Pablo Monsanto (1983:261), the current commander in chief of the FAR, the first attack of the FAR to initiate hostilities and announce itself publicly was at Río Hondo. It was carried out on 30 June 1964. The second attack took place in Panzós in October of the same year. During a confrontation at Panzós with the army, the FAR withdrew in disarray. After a year of hiding in the mountains, only five of the original twenty-one guerrillas remained.

During the campaign of Méndez, the FAR was persuaded to participate and carried out armed propaganda in which it occupied villages with arms and gave political talks to encourage the people to vote for Méndez. When Méndez won, the government called on the armed movement to lay down its arms and rejoin civil activity in peace. The government announced it would carry out a progressive program including agrarian reform, allowing campesinos workers' organizations, and so on. Also, a general amnesty for all political prisoners and guerrillas was declared. The condition was for the armed forces to hand in their arms, but the FAR refused, although it committed itself to not attacking the army as long as the army did not attack it.

At the same time FAR began to participate openly in organizing the peasants. Everyone knew who the guerrillas were and who helped them. At the same time *La Mano Blanca* (The White Hand), a clandestine right-wing group, began to appear in Zacapa. Members painted a white hand on the doors of the houses of all the associates of the FAR that they had discovered at that time. The white hand was a signal, and a few days later the person would be assassinated or captured, tortured, and killed. On 2 October 1966, the same day that Turcios was killed in an auto accident in Guatemala City, the army launched a new operation in the mountains in which they occupied the towns and organized the people into militias to fight the guerrillas. Some of the guerrillas were lynched in the Río Hondo marketplace by the same colleagues they had organized earlier. Again the guerrillas were reduced to a small group. In 1971 they concluded they would have to organize the populace (Monsanto 1983:261–263).

Adams (1970:214–215) sums up this period by saying that true insurgency in Guatemala against the post-revolutionary regimes began after the failure of the 13 of November Movement. During the previous five years there had been random acts of terrorism, usually scattered bombings in Guatemala City. Since the guerrillas were classified as bandits, their activities were kept out of the newspapers, especially their successes. They had to publish their own newsletters and manifestos to drum up support and get wider publicity. Their plan was to gradually create loyal units in the countryside, first in the north, where they were then operating, and then in the south and east. If this activity could not be controlled by the government, the U.S.

marines would have to be brought in, and their presence would neutralize the Guatemalan military and contribute to its breakdown as an effective organization and then bring about the collapse of the government. The guerrillas found the Indian west to be not particularly hospitable and the Ladino east to be irregular in support.

Following the 13 of November Movement, the military had taken measures to extend its control more directly over the campesino and provincial populations. To gain more knowledge about political affairs and security interests, the army revised the role of the *comisionado militar* (military commissioner), who until this time was an army reserve appointee in each municipality and on each large farm. The military commissioner was usually an ex-noncommissioned officer whose main function was to round up and deliver a quota of conscripts for the army. They were responsible to the chief of reserves in the capital city of each department, and in turn the *jefe* (head) of the reserves was responsible to the chief of the military reserves. Campesino organizations had already perceived the military commissioners as a threat and had requested the transfer of those who resisted agrarian reform or officials of the National Confederation of Campesinos (Adams 1970:271).

The change in the *comisionado* system was to convert what had been a local controlling device into a widespread, active spy network. The commissioners reported both military and political activity of the local people. Under Peralta, the information that the commissioners collected went directly to the chief of state's general staff. However, in some instances, the commissioners were sympathetic to the political concerns of the campesinos and gave the army little useful information (Adams 1970:272).

By the time Méndez came to power in 1966, the military again was taking the guerrilla movement more seriously. The insurgents had raised some $500,000 from ransoms of wealthy individuals, and they had escalated their killings from military officers, landowners linked directly to repression, and numerous military commissioners to private citizens who they thought were a threat to their safety (Adams 1970:268; Torres-Rivas 1983).

The counterinsurgency campaign, dubbed Operation Guatemala, that began in 1966 and lasted until 1970 has been compared to Operation Phoenix in Vietnam, which was conceived in 1967, made fully operational by November 1968, and lasted until 1971. Both programs were conceived by the CIA, and each claimed the lives of thousands of innocent civilians—Operation Guatemala an estimated 2,800 to 10,000 (Gordon 1983:65; Schlesinger and Kinzer 1983:246; Simons 1983a:129), and Operation Vietnam an estimated 20,587 to 60,000 (Sharckman 1974:200; MacLear 1982:262; Karnow 1983:602). In the case of Vietnam the deaths came after an estimated 37,000 people had already been killed for opposing the guerrillas and an unknown number of peasants had been caught in the cross fire. Simons (1983a:129) cited a state department report that concluded that the counterinsurgency program in Guatemala escalated into indiscriminate terror in which, to eliminate a few hundred guerrillas (according to Davis and Hodson 1982:29, no more than 500 combatants), the government killed as many as 10,000 people. Although Karnow (1983:602) cites new information indicating that the Phoenix program was effective against Communist leaders, there were numerous examples of excessive destruction, such as a B-52 strike wiping out a whole village because an operative reported that one person living there was suspected of being Viet Cong (Stein in MacLear 1982:264). While there were no B-52 raids in Guatemala, there were reported napalm bombings of guerrilla regions (Sharckman 1974:198). And, according to a reporter's interview with Marroquín Rojas, vice-president under Méndez, some of the bombs were dropped from aircraft flying from U.S. bases in Panama without landing on Guatemalan soil (Schlesinger and Kinzer 1983:247). As in Vietnam (MacLear 1982:263), probably 99 percent of the peasants in Guatemala just hoped the war would go away and leave them alone.

Nevertheless, in Guatemala during this period insurgency and counter-insurgency spread deep into every corner of life. Most sources implicate the right-wing death squads as taking the greater number of lives. In 1967 a right-ist gang mutilated and killed Rogelia Cruz Martínez, Miss Guatemala of 1959, who was critical of the government. Leftists responded by killing Colonel John Webber, who was thought to have directed the counter-terror strategy against the guerrillas in Zacapa-Izabel, and his aide, Lt. Commander Ernest Murno. The leftists also killed John Gordon Mein, the U.S. ambassador, when he resisted being kidnapped (Sharckman 1974:196; Schlesinger and Kinzer 1983:248).

By the end of the Méndez administration, the repressive apparatus had grown far beyond civilian control. It assassinated guerrillas, friends and fam-ily of guerrillas, and finally anyone who was suspected of democratic sympa-thies (Torres-Rivas 1983:42). Schlesinger and Kinzer (1983:249) cite reports that, during Arana's first three years in office, murders and disappearances claimed 3,500 to 15,000 victims, depending on the source. Meanwhile, the military had begun to buy up private companies to establish an independent economic base with businesses such as the Bank of the Army (Fried et al. 1983:85).

In the elections of 1974 despairing liberals and leftists who wanted so-cioeconomic change rather than bloodshed supported a moderate, reformist coalition that backed General Efraín Ríos Montt as the candidate of the Chris-tian Democrats. Although Ríos won the election, the military installed Arana's favorite, Kjell Eugenio Laugerud García (1974–1978). U.S. diplomats in Guatemala admitted that an embarrassing and counterproductive fraud had taken place, but Washington did not answer their pleas to protest it. Some analysts believe this was a major turning point that sent young people underground, disillusioned with the possibility of peaceful change through the electoral process (Simons 1983a; *The New York Times* 1982b).

In the spring of 1975 a small band of guerrillas that had been organizing since 1972 in northern Quiché, announced themselves publicly as the Ejér-cito de los Pobres (EGP) with the execution of a landlord named Luis Arenas Barrea. This group of guerrillas had separated from the FAR over a dispute on the policy toward Indians. The landlord they killed was known as the Jaguar of Ixcán because of his reputation of land seizures and crimes since the 1954 coup. Discouraged with the lack of progress in the urban areas and with the failure of the *foco* theory of revolution, the EGP had a new goal of win-ning the support of the Indians. Thus, when the band shot Arenas, an Ixil member explained what had happened in their own language, and the guer-rillas were careful not to touch any of the money of the payroll (Payeras 1983).

The EGP had carefully planned to appear in a region of endemic land disputes and police brutality (*Latin American Regional Reports Mexico & Central America* 1980a) and where church-sponsored organizations were strongest (Melville 1983). With the overthrow of Arbenz, unions, peasant leagues, and cooperatives had been halted. During the regime of Castillo Armas only the church was allowed to organize cooperatives, and these were limited to credit unions. However, Ydígoras signed a decree in 1959 that allowed the Ministry of Agriculture to promote and control agricultural cooperatives. Some native and international Catholic clergy encouraged their catechists to organize cooperatives. But as cooperatives became more successful, they were intimidated when they affected vested economic and political interests of large landowners needing migrant workers during the harvest (Melville 1983:24) and when retail services to their members conflicted with those of local businessmen who were accustomed to receiving the profits of most commercial activity (Adams 1970:201).

Such intimidation heightened an awareness among church personnel of Guatemala's social structure. In 1967, when a group of U.S. missionaries discussed with guerrilla leaders the implications of structural violence for Christians in Guatemala, they were expelled from the country. In 1968, at a continental meeting of church leaders in Medellín, Colombia, "structural violence" became an official code word for much of Latin America's social problems. Also, the view of a minority of strong leaders prevailed, and a declaration of the church's preference for the poor was made. However, Cardinal Mario Casriego of Guatemala did not sympathize with the poor (Melville 1983).

In cooperation with the government, the church encouraged a program of colonization in the remote jungles of Petén in 1967. In the early 1970s bishops were encouraging and supporting another program of colonization in the northern Indian provinces of Huehuetenango and Quiché. However, these programs had barely gotten off the ground when participants were denied land that had been previously promised to them and others were expelled from lands that they had laboriously cleared in the belief that they had been given to them. These lands went to military officers and large landowners with government connections. When the Indians protested, they were met with violence and death (Melville 1983:24).

Melville (1983) notes that many of the original leaders of the EGP, who had worked in church-sponsored programs of literacy and preventive medicine of the middle 1960s among the highland Indians, left the country because of fear of persecution and the conviction that peaceful change was impossible. The Indians, who were devout Catholics, had received leadership training in the church for two decades.

Following the successful counterinsurgency tactics of the 1960s, the government flew in army personnel, who began kidnapping and murdering uninvolved cooperative members. In the next five years, as the army occupied the Ixil-speaking villages of Chajul, Cotzal, and Nebaj, and the Quiché-speaking village of Uspantán, more than 100 peasants disappeared. Finally, in 1980, 89 cooperative members went to the capital to protest, and later 30 of them occupied the Spanish embassy, where they were attacked by the police. A lone survivor of the burning embassy was later killed as he recuperated in a hospital (*Latin American Regional Reports Mexico & Central America* 1980a).

The February 1976 earthquake and its aftershocks, which killed 22,915 individuals, wounded 77,310 others, and made more than a million Guatemalans homeless, brought a generous response of international developmental aid. Although there were some reports that the rich got the lion's share of this aid and thereby exacerbated the discrepancies between the rich and poor (Davis and Hodson 1982:15), and that the government provided scant relief and persecuted foreign missions that brought in outside aid, much of this aid was used to start self-help organizations throughout the country, especially in urban slums and Indian communities. Even though the Laugerud government was dismantling the cooperative movement in Ixcán, where it perceived a guerrilla threat (Melville 1983:25), in other areas of the country it seemed to be encouraging modest social reforms in allowing cooperatives to receive national and foreign financial assistance (Gleijeses 1983:192). And Laugerud seemed to be responding to the demands of the growing trade union and cooperative movement to have more participation in the national process of reconstruction and development. However, the Guatemalan government tried to impose military control of the reconstruction effort, and it established a counterinsurgency program in El Quiché and the northern part of the country (Plant in Davis 1983b:33). In the first month after the earthquake, over 50 assassinations took place. But Laugerud, like his predecessors, claimed that the death squads were not officially sanctioned. Still, according to Melville (1983:25), no one was ever accused or even investigated for such activities.

René de León Schlotter tried to explain the unimaginable terror that had engulfed Guatemala. De León, who was in 1976 (the time of his statement) the leader of the Democracia Cristiana Guatemalteca and secretary-general of the worldwide Christian Democrats, said:

> One of the characteristics of violence in my country is that it comes basically from political groups. Quite apart from the violence that comes from normal, ever-present social and economic factors, this phenomenon of violence is political, carried out for political reasons: the establishment of terror for the general purpose of eliminating an adversary.
>
> Another feature of this phenomenon is that it is mainly from the right. . . . (De León in Schlesinger and Kinzer 1983:250).

In 1977 Amnesty International reported that since 1966 over 20,000 Guatemalans, mainly political dissidents, had disappeared or been killed, mostly as a result of government action or by semi-governmental officials (Bacheller 1980:581). When President Jimmy Carter imposed human rights requirements for U.S. military aid, the Laugerud administration promptly refused to accept aid (Associated Press 1982b; Riding 1982; Rohter 1982; Sancton 1982). On 1 November of the same year, Carter signed a foreign assistance appropriation bill that specifically barred military credit sales to Guatemala (United Press International 1977).

Even though Laugerud was repressing the cooperative movement in Ixcán, his surprising tolerance of unions and support of cooperatives elsewhere gave hope to some Guatemalans that his government might be a transition from the harsh years of the Arana regime to an open political system in the next government. Laugerud seemed to be taking the first steps toward depolarization of political forces by forging a moderately conservative coalition of the PR and PID with General Romeo Lucas García (1978–1982) as president and liberal-minded politician Dr. Francisco Villagrán Kramer as

vice-president. General Laugerud's decision split the ranks of his own administration with the right-wingers of the MLN, who put up their own candidate,
Enrique Peralta Azurdia. Lucas won the presidency, and the party that was
most affected by abstention was the DC (Crawley 1980:163).

Unfortunately, the hope of opening up the political system turned out
to be a naive one. The government's modernizing effort had assumed that a
limited number of circumscribed reforms along with less repression would
co-opt opposing sectors of the population. Instead, the reforms were too modest to allow for a significant degree of co-optation. And the slackening of
repression, the number of successful strikes, and the hopes awakened by the
government's timid steps as well as the frustration resulting from their shal-
low character all contributed to radicalizing large sectors of the population.
By early 1978, the trade unions, however small, had reached their highest
numbers since 1954. In the countryside the militant and politically conscious
Comité de Unidad Campesina (CUC), which had been established in 1978,
gained strength rapidly. It did not turn out to be a meek, government-con-
trolled cooperative movement. And guerrilla activities were picking up
(Gleijeses 1983:192).

Instead of pursuing more meaningful but painful social and economic
reforms that might successfully assimilate disaffected segments of the population, the Guatemalan ruling class unleashed a wave of terror to suppress
the movement for socioeconomic reforms and protect their vested interests.
Thus, the last months of the Laugerud regime marked yet another period of
fierce repression, which, according to Piero Gleijeses (1983:192), demonstrated that the alternating cycles of extreme and moderate violence were
hardly influenced by personal attitudes of the men in power. However, other
observers link Laugerud more closely to the brutal repression, suggesting
that despite denials it was officially sanctioned (Melville 1983:25; Davis
1983b:33). They point specifically to the unprecedented massacre at Panzós
of 115 Kekchí Indian campesinos who were mowed down in May of 1978, two
months before Lucas took office, over protest of the government's denying
them clear title to their land.

In addition to being one of the locations where the FAR made its armed
appearance in 1964, Panzós was part of a larger area that was named the
Northern Transversal Strip, where there was a project to open territory to
the settlement of landless peasants and to increase the country's production
of grains. In cooperation with the government and in the framework of the
Instituto Nacional de Transformación Agraria (INTA), Maryknoll priests began resettling landless peasants from Huehuetenango and El Quiché on agricultural cooperatives in the Ixcán area of the strip. Also, investors from
Guatemala City began establishing cattle ranches in the Panzós region incor-
porating land that had traditionally been cultivated by local campesinos,
mainly Kekchí Indians (Aguilera P. 1983:311; Peckenham 1983:203).

As Peckenham (1983) notes, by the 1970s the region of the strip had
become a hotbed of construction and development for oil. Aguilera P. (1983)
adds it was also important for its deposits of nickel and copper. In addition,
oil pipelines and a highway were being constructed with financing from the
U.S. Agency for International Development (USAID). With multinational
corporations such as Basic Resources and Exmibal taking keen interest in
northern Guatemala, many Guatemalans did likewise, including General Lucas García, whose family owned a 100,000-acre estate along the path of a

pipeline near Sebol (Peckenham 1983:202). Bank of America also extended a
personal loan to General Lucas to purchase a 7,000-acre cattle estate in the
oil-rich Northern Transversal Strip (Nairn 1983:102).

Since FAR's initial attack in 1964, the army had occupied many of the
towns and villages of the region (*Latin America Regional Reports Mexico &
Central America* 1980a). By the late 1970s campesinos were being dispos-
sessed of their land in increasing numbers, and tensions had grown.

Some of the campesinos applied to INTA to legalize their claims to
small plots of land. They received promises of provisional titles or permission
to plant and harvest, but none received permanent title to the property. The
large landowners were threatening campesinos living on land that was
claimed by both parties, and the campesinos continued to appeal to officials
in Guatemala City for settlement (Peckenham 1983:203). Thus, as Aguilera P.
(1983:313) points out, the usual tactic to intimidate the campesinos would
have been the kidnapping, torture, and murder of a few leaders by *desconocidos* (unknown men). However, Peckenham (1983:204) reports that a mass
grave outside of Panzós was dug on 27 May, and that on 29 May the people
of Cahaboncito, near Panzós, came into the town on a summons to make some
decisions about their land rights. The men, who were carrying machetes,
apparently for their afternoon work in the fields, were accompanied by
women and children. Peckenham (1983:203), who reconstructed the episode
from eyewitnesses, reports that a campesino who could not understand Spanish began arguing with a soldier. The campesino thought that he was being
insulted and attacked the soldier, who fell to the ground wounded. Then all
the soldiers [who Davis (1983b) said were a special forces unit but Aguilera
said were regular army units], opened fire on the civilians. And plainclothes
individuals (who Aguilera said were armed landowners), local policemen, and
a local government official joined the military in the shooting spree. The terrified campesinos fled, but they were shot in the parks, streets and fields.
Some tried to escape by plunging into the river, but the current carried them
away. Two municipal trucks picked up the corpses and took them to the previously dug mass grave.

As Davis (1983b:33) writes, Panzós was to become the first in a long list
of massacres of Indian communities by the army. The Lucas regime, which
took over in July of 1978, was to become the most infamous of the brutal
military dictatorships. But the repression was not restricted to Indian peasants struggling to gain title to land in areas labeled "zones of conflict." Amnesty International directly linked the Lucas regime to the killings, which
included the assassination of opposition political party leaders, journalists,
professors, students, doctors, lawyers, priests, missionaries, and trade union-
ists. Between July 1978 and February 1981 more than 5,000 people were
reported to have been seized and killed by government security forces (Amnesty International 1981; Davis and Hodson 1982; Falla, S.J., 1983).

Melville (1983:25) suggests that Lucas's repression might have been
partly motivated by an unprecedented demonstration by 100,000 people who
marched in the streets of the capital shortly before his election shouting, "We
do not want elections—we want revolution!" A group of miners of Ixtahuacán,
Huehuetenango, had begun the march to protest the closing of a mine in
order to break the miners' union. It was led by catechists with local ecclesi-
astical blessing. By the time it reached the capital, it had gained national
attention. Melville (1983:27) also adds that, although the Catholic Church did

not shift its loyalties from the privileged to the poor until the late 1960s, it was not until Lucas took over in 1978 that the Catholic Church was considered an enemy of the state.

Ríos Montt Takes Control

By August of 1981, the Guatemalan government had declared that the official candidate for president of the PID, the ruling party, would be General Aníbal Guevara. The Reagan administration tried to persuade the Lucas government to run a civilian candidate with less bloodied credentials. As the scope of the atrocities attributed to right-wing elements widened, relations between the National Palace and Washington deteriorated. Even staunch Reaganite Vernon Walters had changed his position from viewing the Guatemalan government as mildly repressive to acknowledging that corruption and indiscriminate repression were only strengthening the forces of revolution. In response the Lucas government saw signs of creeping Carterism. Nevertheless, the U.S. state department thought a civilian would provide a better image for its policy of emphasizing the importance of the March 1982 elections.

Although in the last 12 months 120 prominent leaders of the DC had been murdered, Cerezo Arévalo stated that it was unlikely that the party would abstain from the elections and thereby deny the Lucas government some semblance of credibility of a free election. He said this even though the party had closed its Guatemala City headquarters and he was in semi-hiding because of two attempts made on his life. Party activists of the DC feared that, if the party refused to participate, the government would have an excuse to step up the repression and destroy the party's organization. (The reader can recall that when Ignacio tried to quit the PID he was warned that he would be taken for a Communist and killed.) Party members of the DC did not wish to go underground or take up arms. According to Cerezo, civil war was inevitable unless social and economic reforms were introduced in the near future. However, the party felt that it had to do everything possible to avoid civil war because it would lead to an internationalization of the whole Central American conflict, which in turn would only promote conservative interests (*Latin America Regional Reports Mexico & Central America* 1981c).

The Reagan administration was hoping for a fair election on 7 March 1982 in order to convince reluctant members of the U.S. Congress to approve a renewal of military aid to Guatemala, and the $250,000 it was requesting might be just the beginning of such aid (Press 1982a).

For the first time since 1966, three civilian candidates would be running, along with the official candidate. In Guatemala the campaign raised hopes of curbing violence by both the left and the right. Such violence had created a climate of fear in the country. Although most sources implicated most of the violence to the right, in Guatemala City and the northwest sections of the country, guerrillas were stepping up their attacks against the police, soldiers, and civilians suspected of working against the guerrillas (Press 1982a).

By U.S. standards, all four presidential candidates appeared to be rightists, but by Guatemalan standards, the candidates ranged from left to right. Attorney Maldonado Aguirre, considered a moderate in Guatemala, was backed by a coalition of the DC and the PNR; architect Gustavo Anzueto

Vielman, supported by CAN, was said to have been the Reagan administration's favorite (Gleijeses 1983); General Angel Aníbal Guevara Rodríguez, who was President Lucas's defense minister before resigning to run for office, was backed by a coalition of the PID and PR, both conservative parties; and attorney Mario Sandoval Alarcón, a rightist and former vice-president who was a leader in the 1954 overthrow of the Arbenz government, was supported by the MLN. It was not likely that any of the candidates would receive a majority. In such a case, the National Congress of Guatemala would elect one of the top two candidates (Press 1982a; Montealegre and Arnson 1983:294).

General Guevara's campaign centered on dealing effectively with the guerrillas and paying attention to the social inequalities that spawn revolution. Sandoval, who believed Carter's human rights policy contributed to the growing guerrilla problem and that the U.S. paid too little attention to the guerrillas' human rights violations, stated that his top priority was to crack down harder on guerrilla activity by giving the military better training and equipment and making the national police more efficient. Maldonado, whose centrist DC party had suffered some 200 assassinations in the previous two years, believed the police were conspiring with the right-wing death squads, and he wanted to end the government's involvement in political violence. Cerezo, the party secretary and Maldonado's main strategist, believed that the military had growing doubts about the war against the guerrillas and that the guerrillas were losing popular support. He hoped the DC's coalition with the PNR would influence the military to ease off involvement with the police and death squads. Anzueto Vielman advocated a Reagan-type approach to government with tax reform and reduction of the size of the government (Press 1982a).

Because guerrilla forces had been attacking municipal halls and destroying records, it might have been difficult for some people to obtain documentation for voter identification. Since party symbols are used on the ballots, illiterates could vote, and failure to vote is punishable by fines and jail sentences (Press 1982a).

When the Central Elections Council declared Guevara the winner with 37 percent of the total vote, the three losing candidates formed a spontaneous coalition and set out marching to the National Palace to present documents they claimed would prove fraud. However, riot police blocked their path at gunpoint. The police took the candidates to police headquarters, where Police Chief General Germán Chupina lectured them for almost an hour (Sancton 1982). Government troops and secret police with automatic arms dispersed demonstrators in the capital who had defied a government ban to protest the election results (Associated Press 1982b).

The three defeated candidates for president overcame their political rivalries to protest collectively the fraud and to challenge the military regime to repudiate its own candidate. They also ordered their deputies to boycott the congressional session called by Lucas to confirm Guevara's victory (Press 1982b; Sancton 1982:25).

Although Guevara was challenged by the losing candidates, he expected his victory to hold, and he promised to increase development in the countryside, which both U.S. and Guatemalan experts saw as a key to reducing the attraction of the guerrillas to increasing numbers of poor Indian farmers. The Lucas government had taken some steps toward rural development with aid from the U.S. Some of the projects included building rural hospitals and health clinics, building and improving roads, terracing and irrigating farmlands, building schools and municipal facilities, and launching a literacy campaign. Ignacio noted all three of the last activities in San José. However, the Lucas government's steps toward rural development to eliminate rural poverty as a root cause of insurgency were charged with corruption and mismanagement and even violence toward rural community workers. Apparently the new defense minister, General Luis René Mendoza Paloma, had called for an end to such terrorism and had begun investigating allegations of abuse against rural community leaders, but it seems he was acting on his own (Press 1982:4).

Just 100 days before the end of his term, junior army officers, who called themselves the "Young Officers Movement," staged a coup on 23 March 1982 to oust President Lucas García. Colonel Jaime Rabanales, army public relations chief at the time, broadcast on radio and television that a military junta had been named to rule the country. He declared that the junta would be run by retired General Ríos Montt, who had unsuccessfully run for president in 1974 with the backing of the DC. The other two ruling members of the junta would be General Horacio Maldonado and Colonel Francisco Gordillo. Apparently the coup had the backing of Alejandro Maldonado, the most moderate of the four conservative candidates for president, and Mario Sandoval, the most conservative (Associated Press 1982b).

The Associated Press (1982b) cites the following three reasons the junior officers gave for staging the coup: (1) General Angel Aníbal Guevara's winning with President Lucas's support was fraudulent, and they promised to restore peace and authentic democracy to Guatemala; (2) Guatemala was in the midst of hunger and misery, subjugated through the use of terror by a corrupt minority; and (3) a government needed to be formed for all Guatemalans. A fourth reason was discontent with the counterinsurgency strategy advocated by Army Chief of Staff Benedicto Lucas García. Junior officers, who found themselves in the front lines, were taking a high number of casualties, and the doctrine of occupational force and burnt land was thought to be counterproductive. Although some younger officers favored a strictly military solution in an all-out war with both the left and right, others in the middle ranks of major and colonel believed that the current civil strife in Guatemala has been caused by an outdated social structure in which a few possess most of the country's wealth (Goodsell 1982b; *Latin America Regional Reports Mexico & Central America* 1982d; Davis 1983b:34; Montealegre and Arnson 1983:295).

The state department estimated that political violence had claimed the lives of about 300 persons a month in the previous year and that in early months of 1982 the level of violence had risen (Associated Press 1982b). Also, Amnesty International's report of political murder run from an annex of the National Palace was making it difficult for Guatemala to obtain foreign aid credits for both economic and military purposes. Tourism, which was previously the third leading source of foreign revenue next to coffee and cotton, was nearly dead. Along with fear of getting caught in a cross fire, an international boycott on travel to protest human rights abuses dissuaded tourists from traveling to Guatemala (Montealegre and Arnson 1983:295).

While an increasing number of junior officers found themselves in the thick of action, eight leading generals (there are about 27 to 28 generals in total) were accused of running an arms-buying racket in which they overvalued the cost of weapons purchased and placed the difference in private bank accounts in the Cayman Islands. According to junior officers, the eight generals had enriched themselves with $250 million. In another case, five junior officers were said to have been murdered on orders of the high command because they wanted to expose army involvement in the rape and murder of a university student (Montealegre and Arnson 1983:295, 306–307).

After the coup the DC and the MLN, who had previously been at odds, agreed on several political demands, including: (1) elections within six months; (2) a declaration by the junta that the military rule was transitional; (3) the creation of a new national electoral commission with equal representation from each party, and (4) the revision of the electoral laws. Vinicio Cerezo stated that the DC would not join the post-coup government and that it would press for elections and an investigation into human rights violations (Montealegre and Arnson 1983:296).

In addition to wanting an end to corruption in government, the junior officers who staged the coup called for elections within 60 days and with military personnel ineligible to run. However, Ríos Montt ignored their plans and gradually relegated them to the role of advisers.

Ríos Montt did dry up corruption in the government, and he removed several officials identified with repression in the Lucas regime, including Chief of Police Ruiz and Interior Minister Alvarez Ruiz (Russell 1983:35). He also retired seven generals and some colonels, although the armed forces otherwise remained nearly intact. Army Chief of Staff General Benedicto Lucas García, brother of the deposed president, was placed under house arrest and replaced in office by General Héctor López Fuentes. However, Benedicto later emerged as head of counterinsurgency operations in the Petén (Gleijeses 1983:206). Within several weeks of the 23 March coup, at least 20 officials had been arrested and charged with corruption, including the former attorney general, prison director, officials of the ministry of finance, and the security chief of the Guatemalan Telecommunications Enterprise. They were charged with embezzlement, extortion, fraud, and abuse of authority (Montealegre and Arnson 1983:298).

Ríos Montt flooded the country with blue-and-white posters proclaiming his favorite slogan, "I do not rob, I do not lie, I do not steal." While he definitely had an effect on drying up corruption, his main goal was to eradicate the left-wing insurgents.

General Ríos Montt had successfully offered amnesty to many gue--rillas in the earlier civil strife of the 1960s (Goodsell 1982b). The amnesty that he declared after taking over the junta that ousted Lucas was for 30 days for members of the armed forces who had committed human rights violations while carrying out their duties against insurgency, and for subversives if they would turn in their guns and ammunition to army posts or the Guatemalan Red Cross by 30 June. Although the rebels officially rejected the offer of amnesty, military authorities claimed that 430 to 1,800 guerrillas took advantage of the offer (Associated Press 1982c). Following the expiration of amnesty, Ríos Montt declared a state of siege, initially for 30 days, but which was extended until March of 1983.

In addition to suspending constitutional freedoms that were already limited by the March coup, the decree introduced a number of draconian laws that gave the army even greater powers: (1) the death penalty was introduced for subversive acts such as burning buses, planting bombs, and kidnapping; (2) military courts, or special tribunals, were set up, and those found guilty were shot by firing squad; (3) controls were placed on the press, radio, and television; (4) public services were militarized; and (5) as the army prepared for a big counterinsurgency offensive, all reservists between 18 and 30 were subject to recall to bolster Guatemala's 17,000-man army (Associated Press 1982c; *Latin America Regional Reports Mexico & Central America* 1982c; Russell 1983:35; Montealegre and Arnson 1983:298).

Among the severest critics of the measure were the Christian Democrats, whose leader, Vinicio Cerezo, called it an overreaction. Even the MLN was ambiguous, although they had called for similar measures in the past and had allies in the high command of the army, including General Mejía and General López, two of the most prominent hard-liners. Many of the MLN feared the state of siege would further strengthen the military at the expense of the civilian politicians (*Latin American Regional Reports Mexico & Central America* 1982c).

Ríos, who ousted co-members of the junta and declared himself head of state on 9 June 1982, defended the state of siege and special tribunals by claiming that his administration was merely making legal what was going on before. "People who were murdered before, we now jail and hold for trial," he said (Torgerson 1982a). "We declared a state of siege so that we could kill legally" (Simons 1982a). Ríos told a CBS crew, "We don't hang subversives; that would be barbaric. Here we shoot them" (Associated Press 1982d; Nelson 1983). "Many people are being killed, but we have also lost many officers" (Simons 1982a).

On 23 May 1982 Ríos demonstrated his resolve by executing six men convicted of subversive activities on the eve of the papal visit, even though Pope John Paul asked for clemency (Russell 1983). After receiving considerable criticism for lack of respect for the pope, Ríos claimed that he had not received the message asking for clemency.

Along with cleaning up corruption in the government, Ríos Montt brought about a marked decline in the violence in Guatemala City. He disbanded the Cuerpo de Detectives (detective bureau) of the Policía Nacional, whose members were reputed gunmen who executed intellectuals and professionals suspected of subversion on orders of right-wing political and military powers. He also pressured these forces to disband private armies. Although Ríos was able to claim that violence had declined by 90 percent, making Guatemala City as safe as New York or Chicago (Torgerson 1982a), according to Gleijeses (1983:206) the detective bureau simply reappeared under another name. Also, violence in the rural areas was soon exceeding the levels reached in the last months of the Lucas regime, with the Indians remaining the main victims.

Military Tactics and Civilian Patrols

In August of 1981 landowning interests were severely criticizing the army for not preventing raids by the guerrillas, who were using scorched-earth tactics to disrupt agricultural operations. Under General Benedicto Lucas García, who had been promoted to army chief of staff by his brother the president in the same month, the army responded with new aggressiveness against the guerrillas, but the main victims were unarmed peasants who allegedly supported the guerrillas. Rather than just *desconocidos* coming into their towns and killing suspected sympathizers in lots of 20 and 30, some 4,000 soldiers with strong air and artillery support now confronted the peasants. The unarmed peasants suffered because of a deliberate strategy to destroy the social and economic base of the guerrillas and because the army rarely managed to engage the rebels themselves (*Latin America Regional Reports Mexico & Central America* 1982b).

Despite Benedicto's dynamism, President Lucas was unable to impose firm leadership on the army, and many local commanders did as they pleased. The young officers who had planned the coup and formed a seven-man advisory council to Ríos corrected this situation. They streamlined military intelligence and claimed to get more accurate information on guerrilla activities. The army began choosing its targets much more selectively, but massacres of guerrillas and their suspected supporters increased sharply and were characterized as clinical savagery. Sometimes only community leaders such as teachers or church activists and their families were singled out. In other instances, whole villages were wiped out, depending on the perception from military intelligence on the degree of support for the guerrillas. In several cases, it was reported that civil defense units and the army masqueraded as guerrillas and killed indiscriminately and then returned in uniform to rescue the survivors and organize them into civil defense units (*Latin American Regional Reports Mexico & Central America* 1982d).

The extent to which the guerrillas had actually penetrated the traditionally passive and politically conservative Indians remains unclear (Sanders 1982). According to Benjamin Colby (1981), the Indians who have been politicized have become so not so much, as Frazier (1980) claims, from exposure to consumer goods and clandestine radio, but from the action of the government against the populace and the murder by the military of Catholic priests whose Indian constituency is deeply devout.

Some refugees say that their troubles began with visits by rebels. One refugee who was a farmer in Quiché said that in January of 1982 armed guerrillas suddenly appeared and forced all 115 families into the local school. When the guerrillas finished their armed propaganda and left the village, the people reported the incident to the army, which in turn told the villagers not to worry. However, in May the army returned and kidnapped three men and a woman from an evangelical church. Thus, the villagers fled. "We're all Christians and expect to die," the campesino said, "but who wants to die so soon?" (Schuster 1983:1).

In practice the counterinsurgency strategy used by Ríos Montt was little different than that of Lucas García, with the exception that under Ríos the massacres of Indians were more systematic. In many regions the army's scorched-earth policy was driving peasants away from their homes and burning their crops, forests, and whole villages. As Nelson (1983) reports, fragile Indian cultures were uprooted wholesale and herded into refugee camps and forced to work to deprive guerrillas of support. Such activity was unweaving irretrievable remnants of Mayan civilization (Torgerson 1982a).

The Asociación de Periodistas Democráticas, which was freer to speak out under the Ríos regime than under the Lucas regime, claims that in the first 63 days of the Ríos administration more than 4,000 peasants were killed in a program of pacification and eradication first drawn up in 1976. But other sources blame the massacres on dissidents in the army aligned with the far-right MLN or the displaced Lucas García clique, which was trying to undermine the reformist plans of Ríos (*Latin America Regional Reports Mexico & Central America* 1982b).

By October 1982 a number of coups had been attempted on the Ríos Montt regime, most of which were efforts of unhappy officers wishing to oust the president. One group of several officers was dissatisfied with the political and military progress against counterinsurgency in the Chimaltenango and El Quiché provinces. They contended that there had not been any real progress and that the high command had overemphasized the purely military aspects of the "beans and rifles" strategy without tackling the underlying causes of the war. The dissident officers were concerned about the same burnt-land strategy used by Lucas García, especially against the Indian communities. They were also concerned about the toll the guerrillas were taking on the army, such as ORPA's shooting down a helicopter near Sololá. They also preferred U.S. weapons to Israeli ones such as the Galil rifle, which has less firepower than the M-16. Finally, they worried that Ríos's ruling out a return to civilian rule would damage their relations with the U.S.

Nevertheless, Ríos's strategy (which in many ways was similar to the program used in Vietnam called CORDS, or Civil Operations and Revolutionary Development Support, which included the Phoenix program of assassinating the Viet Cong) was having enough military success that it was also being advocated for El Salvador (Torgerson 1983). The armed forces, bolstered by reservists and the civil militia, which was estimated to be 25,000 strong, saturated the rural areas with small anti-guerrilla patrols that chased the rebels from their bases of support. Under the "beans and guns" policy, rural villagers and townspeople were organized into Patrullas de Autodefensa Civil (PAC), or defense patrols, designed to aid the counterinsurgency efforts. Those peasants who joined were rewarded with food, public works, jobs, and housing. Some who refused to join the patrols were summarily shot. Others therefore joined from fear of being labeled subversives (Russell 1983; Simons 1982a; *Latin America Regional Reports Mexico & Central America* 1983c).

The second stage of the counterinsurgency program involved a resettlement and pacification program. Many of the estimated 250,000 to 1 million persons displaced by the violence were being resettled into model villages where security was organized by the armed forces and guaranteed by the local civil defense militia. The Comité Nacional de Reconstrucción, initially set up after the 1976 earthquake but now controlled by the army, was working with the United Nations World Food Program to provide emergency relief and revive food production. The Programa de Ayuda de Areas en Conflicto (PAAC) was initiated to boost food production by giving resettled families agricultural credits in exchange for promises not to support the guerrillas. Under a program that replaced the "beans and rifles" strategy and that was called "*techo, tortilla y trabajo*" (roof, tortilla, and work, or TTT), the ministries of agriculture, employment, public health, and education were trying to redevelop social and economic institutions by carrying out such projects as building 173 schools, repairing 80 in 9 departments, and helping to replace

399 schools that were destroyed in Huehuetenango alone between 1980 and 1982 (Russell 1983; *Latin America Regional Reports Mexico & Central America* 1983c).

In part of a major effort to change tactics, Ríos had given the army strict orders to pay fairly and promptly for food supplies, to respect the customs and traditions of the Indians, and to prevent civilian deaths. The policy was effective against the guerrillas, who were surprised at how quickly their support evaporated in some areas. The guerrillas also had to worry about not being able to protect friendly villages from army reprisals. The EGP admitted that it mistakenly thought that greater insurrection against Lucas García was imminent and that it was not prepared to defend or evacuate its peasants supporters from the areas of conflict.

The FAR and ORPA were badly mauled by the army's fierce counter-insurgency campaign. The FAR's front in Chimaltenango was destroyed, and it suffered setbacks in Petén, its traditional stronghold. And ORPA never recovered from the destruction of its urban network in late 1981. An unidentified guerrilla spokesman said that the guerrillas were short of weapons and would concentrate on the annihilation of army units and confiscation of weapons. Less attention would be paid to armed propaganda, which had provoked army reprisals against the local population. According to *Latin America Regional Reports Mexico & Central America* (1982d, 1983c), ORPA would most likely concentrate on sabotage of economic targets, especially export crops, since attacks on electric pylons, post offices, and similar targets have alienated supporters in the past. But this new emphasis could also alienate migrant workers by denying them needed means of livelihood.

As usual, the Indians were receiving the worst of the increased violence in the countryside. The Episcopal Conference of Guatemala states that the murders in the rural area were genocide and that never in history had Guatemala come to such extremes. Amnesty International reports that Guatemalan security forces killed 2,186 from from March to June, the majority of whom were Indian noncombatants. Although the defense department believed the figures were inflated, Krueger and Smith (1983) say that other sources report an estimated 8,000 to 10,000 deaths, mostly from March through December. The army's claim that massacres of Indians were carried out by guerrillas was confirmed by the U.S. embassy, which based its information on the local press (which had been censored since the July state of siege), the army, the police, and its own intelligence. Indeed, it is difficult to determine who is responsible (*Latin America Regional Reports Mexico & Central America* 1982e).

Both the guerrillas and the army have been blamed for the massacre at Saquiyá Dos. Twenty-five children, 3 men, and 15 women, 3 of them pregnant, all Indians, were killed. Witnesses who saw their bodies said that their throats were slashed and some had been shot through the head. Spent cartridges from Israeli-made Galil assault rifles were found. When Jorge Carpio Nicolle condemned the killings in an editorial of *El Gráfico*, the paper he publishes, he indirectly pointed a finger at the government. Ríos indicated that this was a kind of Guatemalan freedom of the press that had not been possible under Lucas. Nevertheless, the next day the army paid for advertisements in *El Gráfico* and other newspapers stating that the army had not been responsible for the killings. Instead, according to the army, subversives were wearing uniforms similar to the national army to confuse the public and undermine the confidence of the armed forces. Some outsiders supported the Ríos regime and pointed out that the more flexible government of Ríos was causing the guerrillas to change tactics. Still others found the situation confusing and doubted that the army would change course so quickly and that the guerrillas would cut themselves off from their base of support (Bonner 1982c; Vasquez 1982a).

Despite denials, Ríos's counterinsurgency campaign had cost the lives of thousands of innocent noncombatants. Of the estimated one million made homeless by the fighting (about 14 percent of the population), most are Indians. Of the one million displaced persons, an estimated 150,000 to 250,000 left the country as refugees to Mexico, the United States, Canada, Honduras, Belize, and Puerto Rico. About twice that number have swelled the population in and around Guatemala City; thousands have moved from outlying villages to municipal capitals; scores have moved from the highlands to coastal areas where they had previously done seasonal work; and several thousand were reported wandering malnourished in the mountain forests (Krueger and Smith 1983).

An estimated 30,000 to 70,000 campesinos have escaped to refugee camps inside Chiapas along the border with Mexico. In the camps refugees have been killed by armed Guatemalans crossing the border. While the refugees claimed Guatemalan plainclothes soldiers were doing it, the Guatemalan government blamed it on guerrillas. Some analysts side with the refugees believing that the Guatemalan government feared that the camps would be staging grounds for guerrillas because of the hatred the refugees have for the government. In addition to reports that Guatemalan troops and helicopters have made incursions into the refugee camps in Mexico, there were reports that refugees who were enticed or forced to return to Guatemala to build a new country were killed by the army. Although Guatemalan officials have said that the refugees are either guerrillas or sympathetic to them, the Mexican government believed the refugees and decided to let them stay in 27 camps along the border. Mexican officials have said that Guatemala wants to eliminate the camps because they help the guerrillas and are a blemish on their international image. And United Nations refugee officials fear for the safety of any Guatemalan Indians repatriated against their will. As camps grow in size, relations between Guatemala and Mexico have turned extremely cold (Aguilar Zinser 1983; *Latin America Regional Reports Mexico & Central America* 1983a; Schuster 1983; Simons 1983b).

When Vasquez (1982b) interviewed refugees in Mexico, none of them believed that the guerrillas had turned to killing great numbers of campesinos or burning their villages. Some acknowledged that not the army itself but the war between the army and guerrillas was responsible for the destruction and turmoil. However, one informant stated, "Both sides killed people. If you side with the guerrillas, you get screwed by the army. If you side with the army, or if people think you do, you get screwed by the guerrillas."

In the summer of 1981 the guerrillas took numerous actions against military patrols and people they considered military collaborators (Vasquez 1982b). On 23 July 1982, the night I arrived in Guatemala City, a clandestine organization of the left exploded a powerful bomb early in the morning a few blocks away from my hotel. The group blew up the office of Servicios Aérecs de Honduras, Sociedad Anónima (SAHSA), to protest the presence of the Honduran army in El Salvador (*El Imparcial* 1982). In August of 1982 a new guerrilla group calling itself the Movimiento Revolucionario del Pueblo exploded a leaflet bomb in Guatemala City. And on 17 September 1982 four members of the EGP were executed after being found guilty by a special court of charges of attempted murder and robbery (*Latin America Regional Reports Mexico & Central America* 1982d).

By August 1982 more evidence was surfacing that guerrillas were changing tactics against Indians who either volunteered or were forced to participate in the civil defense patrols and who were suspected of being sympathizers with the army. Torgerson (1982a:15) cited a survivor of a massacre in a western village as saying, "We are getting slaughtered by both sides." However, another survivor countered, "I know they were soldiers. They were well fed and had no running sores. The guerrillas are always thin and sick." Nevertheless, foreign diplomats said that both sides were killing Indians—the army makes an example out of a village which cooperates with the rebels, and then the rebels make an example out of those who cooperate with the army. When Ríos Montt was pressed by Torgerson (1982a) on this issue, the president said that he did not deceive, lie, or steal and that the army was not massacring Indians.

In a follow-up story on 19 September Torgerson (1982b) reports how the bloody battle for the Guatemalan highlands has become a new type of war, with both sides changing tactics. He reports that a year ago it was the guerrillas who were trying to get the peasants to join them and the army which was accused of massacring civilians. Now, the army was trying to avoid civilian deaths and win back the population, and the guerrillas were accused of killing civilians. The guerrillas were turning their wrath on the civil defense forces and the pro-government towns that the army had armed. Village leaders and church pastors in the war zone told of the killings by the guerrillas of whole families suspected of having pro-government sympathies.

Foreign military experts told Torgerson (1982b) that the army's barring of killing civilians seemed to be working and was remarkably different from the previous year, when the army would kill a bunch of civilians as an example if a convoy was ambushed. However, there were still reports that soldiers wearing civilian clothes were killing civilians. But there were also reports of guerrillas dressed as soldiers killing peasants. "It can be as hard to tell who is winning as it is who is killing," Torgerson (1982b:1) writes.

However, a captain told Torgerson (1982b) that the army had changed its policy. Instead of going to a village to fight the guerrillas, it fights only groups that are armed. Instead of fighting villages which have guerrillas, it goes to help the people who will accept assistance, including help to form militias to protect themselves. The people were recognizing that the army was helping them with materials to rebuild their homes, with food, and with guns and training to form militias to protect themselves. The people were recognizing that the army was doing things to help them and were changing their minds about the guerrillas. According to the captain, more towns were asking for civil defense groups, and in one month the army had organized more than 1,300 such groups. The civil defense groups, he pointed out, were not just to fight the guerrillas but also to develop the villages with schools, health centers, and the distribution of food.

By September 1982 the government claimed that as many as 40,000 men had joined the patrols (Torgerson 1982b), but officials of the U.S. embassy estimated that 500,000 men were in the patrols with 5 percent of them armed. The patrols included virtually all the adult population in the western highlands, including the Verapaces, and the system was being extended to areas of new and anticipated conflict, especially the south (Krueger and Smith 1983; *Latin America Regional Reports Mexico & Central America* 1984a). Although there have been reports of campesinos joining the groups from coercion or fear, military experts believe the success of the program can be measured by the number of people who join the groups and by the fierceness of the guerrilla attacks against the patrols and their villages. Apparently more people are now being killed in fire fights between patrols and the guerrillas than between the army and the guerrillas (Torgerson 1982b).

An estimated 20,000 military commissioners are in charge of the civil patrols at the local level (*Latin America Regional Reports Mexico & Central America* 1983f). Depending on the number of eligible men (18 to 55 years of age) available and the personality of the military commissioner in charge, duty periods vary from several hours to an entire 24-hour shift from once every four days to once a month. Patrol duty includes monitoring activity along the sides of roads, weekly training exercises, and excursions into surrounding territory to keep it free from guerrillas. Patrols report to the military commissioners, who in turn report to local army officers (Krueger and Smith 1983).

There is widespread criticism of the civil patrol system. Men are not paid for their time, and it takes them away from the economic activities needed for subsistence for their families. Families left behind by the patrols are not protected when men go out in search of guerrillas. Trips to the coast may be reason enough to be excused from patrol duty, but permission may be obtained in various ways—bribery, just informing the military commissioner, or getting someone to serve in one's place (Krueger and Smith 1983).

One of Torgerson's (1982b) informants stated that the guerrillas massacre whole families of members of civil patrols if they can. Torgerson (1982b) also cited a priest in a town in Chimaltenango province who said that the guerrillas at first tried to convince the people to join their cause by spray-painting their slogans on the walls (similar to what happened in San José). Then about two years ago they began to kill individuals they thought were sympathetic to the government as an example to the others. Now the guerrillas were killing "whole groups, the heads of houses and also relatives and friends in a campaign of terror to try to frighten people from supporting the civil patrols" (Torgerson 1982b:10).

The same priest, who wished not to be identified, stated that last year the army killed 39 people in his area, but that this year he had heard of only a handful of people being killed by the army, usually in fights in the villages. He went on to say that this year the guerrillas had killed hundreds of persons in their anger over the civil patrols. Most of the 600 widows lost their husbands to the guerrillas, who are the new widow-makers.

In September of 1982 the Guatemalan army numbered about 20,000 men, including reservists called up for six months' active duty for the offensive against the guerrillas. Experts estimated that there were 3,000 armed guerrillas who fought full-time, with perhaps as many as 60,000 sympathizers, at least as long as guerrilla forces maintained control over the areas of the sympathizers (Torgerson 1982b).

Extensive death and destruction had taken place in the departments of Chimaltenango, Sololá, El Quiché, and Huehuetenango, especially in the final six months of 1982. Extensive military operations of aerial bombardment and army sweeps resulted in widespread death of noncombatants and destruction of homes and crops, particularly in northern Huehuetenango and El Quiché. Guerrilla activity in these areas was reported to be sporadic, but the guerrillas themselves apparently suffered few casualties (Krueger and Smith 1983).

Torgerson (1982b) cites a pastor in Santiago Atitlán who said that last year the guerrillas were fighting at the end of a cobblestone street at the foot of a nearby volcano. Now, he said, the guerrillas are gone because the people did not support them. The guerrillas burned the plantations and put many men out of work—work that had been critical in raising their standard of living in a region of acute land shortage (Early 1982). The pastor pointed out that, with the guerrillas gone, the army had gone. Because the army was very heavy-handed before the change of government, it was the government that the people did not like last year. Now it is the guerrillas that the people do not like.

❧References Cited

Abramson, Rudy, and Paul Houston
 1983 "Reagan Names Stone As Central America Envoy." *Los Angeles Times*, April 29:1, 6.

Adams, Richard Newbold
 1970 *Crucifixion by Power: Essays on Guatemalan National Social Structure, 1944–1966*. Austin: University of Texas Press.

Aguilar Zinser, Adolfo
 1983 "Mexico and the Guatemalan Crises." In *The Future of Central America: Policy Choices for the U.S. and Mexico*, Richard R. Fagen and Olga Pellicer, editors. Stanford University Press.

Aguilera P., Gabriel
 1983 "The Massacre at Panzós and Capitalist Development in Guatemala." In *Revolution in Central America*, Stanford Central America Action Network, editors. Boulder: Westview Press.

Amnesty International
 1981 "Guatemala: A Government Program of Political Murder." Reprinted in *Revolution in Central America*, Stanford Central America Action Network, editors. Boulder: Westview Press, 1983.

Armas, Daniel
 1971 *Diccionario de la Expresión Popular Guatemalteca*. Tipografía Nacional de Guatemala, Centro América.

Arriola, Jorge Luis
 1973 *El Libro de las Geonimias de Guatemala*. Guatemala City: Seminario de Integración Social Guatemalteca.

Associated Press
 1982a "American Missionary Found Dead in Guatemalan Town." *The Sun*, February 15:7.
 1982b "Army Takes Over in Guatemala." *Los Angeles Times*, March 24:1, 8.
 1982c "Guatemala Declares War on Rebels." *Arizona Star*, July 2.
 1982d "CBS Offers Look at Guatemala." *The Sun*, September 1:14.

1983a "Goldwater Urges Stronger Role in Central America." *The Sun*, May 23:2.

1983b "New Ruler Vows to Wipe Out Leftist Rebels." *The Sun*, August 9:10.

Bacheller, Martin A.
1980   *The Hammond Almanac*. Maplewood, New Jersey: Hammond Almanac, Inc.

1983   *The Hammond Almanac*. Maplewood, New Jersey: Hammond Almanac, Inc.

Beck, Melinda, et al.
1982   "Distrust and Dissent." *Newsweek*, March 1:18–19.

Bonner, Raymond
1981   "In Guatemalan Politics, Death Is a Daily Danger." *The New York Times*, December 6:10.

1982a "Why Guatemala? Some Answers to the Question." *The New York Times*, January 3:2E.

1982b "The Mayan War God Is Under New Management." *The New York Times*, March 14:4E.

1982c "Giving Is No Picnic in Guatemala." *The New York Times*, June 6:2E.

Brecher, John, et al.
1982   "The Fire Next Door." *Newsweek*, March 1:16–24.

Brown, Andrea
1983   "Land of the Few: Rural Land Ownership in Guatemala." In *Revolution in Central America*, Stanford Central America Action Network, editors. Boulder: Westview Press.

Butterfield, Fox
1983   "The New Vietnam Scholarship." *The New York Times Magazine*, February 13:26–35, 45–61.

Buttinger, Joseph
1968   *Vietnam: A Political History*. New York: Frederick A. Praeger, Publishers.

Chavez, Lydia
1983a "Violence Weakens Guatemala Regime." *The New York Times*, November 13:1, 11.

1983b "Guatemala Tries to Win Over 5,000 Indian Refugees." *The New York Times*, November 20:8.

Church, George J.
1983   "A Big Stick Approach." *Time*, August 8:18–25.

Cockburn, Alexander
1983   "Sharing Responsibility for Guatemalan Horrors." *The Wall Street Journal*, February 24:29.

Colby, Benjamin
1981   "What Politicized Guatemala Indians?" *The Wall Street Journal*, January 6:33.

Colom Argueta, Manuel
1983   "Behind the Facade of Democracy: A Liberal Politician's Last Interview." In *Guatemala in Rebellion: Unfinished History*, Jonathan L. Fried et al., editors. New York: Grove Press, Inc.

Crawley, Eduardo, editor
    1980   *Latin America & Caribbean 1980.* Essex, England: World of Information, Rand McNally.

Davis, Shelton
    1983a "The Social Roots of Political Violence." *Cultural Survival Quarterly* 7(1):4–11.
    1983b "The Social Consequences of 'Development' Aid in Guatemala." *Cultural Survival Quarterly* 7(1):32–35.

Davis, Shelton H., and Julie Hodson
    1982 *Witnesses to Political Violence in Guatemala: The Suppression of a Rural Movement.* Boston: Oxfam America.

Dirección General de Estadísticas
    1980 Guatemala City, Guatemala.

Dombrowski, John, et al.
    1970 *Area Handbook for Guatemala.* Washington, D.C.: U.S. Government Printing Office.

Early, John D.
    1982 *The Demographic Structure and Evolution of a Peasant System: The Guatemalan Population.* Boca Raton: University Presses of Florida.

El Imparcial
    1982 "Destrozos en SAHSA por Bomba Terrorista." July 23:1.

Fagen, Richard R., and Olga Pellicer, editors
    1983 "Introduction." In *The Future of Central America: Policy Choices for the U.S. and Mexico*, Richard R. Fagen and Olga Pellicer, editors. Stanford: Stanford University Press.

Falla, S.J., Ricardo
    1983 "The Massacre at the Rural Estate of San Francisco–July, 1982." *Cultural Survival Quarterly* 7(1):43–44.

Farnsworth, Clyde H.
    1983 "Third World Debts Mean Fewer Jobs for Peoria." *The New York Times*, December 11:3E.

Frank, Allan Dodds
    1982 "Guatemala: The Ultimate Prize." *Forbes* 129:111–113.

Frank, Louisa
    1974 "Resistance and Revolution: The Development of Armed Struggle in Guatemala." In *Guatemala*, Susanne Jonas and David Tobis, editors. New York: North American Congress on Latin America.

Frazier, Steve
    1980 "Violence Stirs Polarized Guatemala." *The Wall Street Journal*, December 18:33

Fried, Jonathan L., Marvin E. Gettleman, Deborah T. Levenson, and Nancy Peckenham, editors
    1983 *Guatemala in Rebellion: Unfinished History.* New York: Grove Press.

García-Pelayo Y Gross, Ramón, and Micheline Durand, directors
    1976 *Diccionario Moderno: Español-inglés, English-Spanish.* New York: Larousse.

Girling, Robert Henriques, and Luin Goldring
    1983   "U.S. Strategic Interests in Central America: The Economics and
            Geopolitics of Empire." In *Revolution in Central America*, Stan-
            ford Central America Action Network, editors. Boulder: West-
            view Press.
Gleijeses, Piero
    1983   "Guatemala: Crisis and Response." In *The Future of Central
            America: Policy Choices for the U.S. and Mexico*, Richard R. Fa-
            gen and Olga Pellicer, editors. Stanford: Stanford University
            Press.
Goodsell, James Nelson
    1982a   "Guatemala Rebels: Attacks Intensify, But Support Lags: Guer-
            rillas Besiege Officials, Neither Side Very Popular." *The Chris-
            tian Science Monitor*, January 22:1, 10.
    1982b   "Army Coup Shifts Guatemala . . . Toward the Center." *The
            Christian Science Monitor*, March 25:1, 8.
Gordon, Max
    1983   "A Case History of U.S. Subversion: Guatemala, 1954." In *Gua-
            temala in Rebellion: Unfinished History*, Jonathan L. Fried et al.,
            editors. New York: Grove Press, Inc.
Gossen, Gary H.
    1983   Review of *Symbolism of Subordination: Indian Identity in a Gua-
            temalan Town*. *Ethnohistory* 29:227–230.
Gwertzman, Bernard
    1983   "The Company It Keeps Puts U.S. on the Spot Once Again." *The
            New York Times*, March 27:3E.
Hanley, Charles J.
    1983   "Ties to Central America in a State of Flux." *Los Angeles Times*,
            September 25:2, 23.
Houston, Paul
    1983   "Democrats Fear a Vietnam-Type Latin Quagmire." *Los Angeles
            Times*, April 28:1, 16.
The Institute for Policy Studies
    1983   "Behind Guatemala's Military Power." In *Guatemala in Rebellion:
            Unfinished History*, Jonathan L. Fried et al., editors. New York:
            Grove Press, Inc.
Isaacson, Walter
    1983   "Harsh Facts, Hard Choices." *Time*, May 9:20–28.
Jonas, Susanne
    1974a   "'The Democracy Which Gave Way': The Guatemalan Revolu-
            tion of 1944–1954." In *Guatemala*, Susanne Jonas and David To-
            bis, editors. New York: North American Congress on Latin
            America.
    1974b   "Anatomy of an Intervention: The U.S. 'Liberation' of Guate-
            mala." In *Guatemala*, Susanne Jonas and David Tobis, editors.
            New York: North American Congress on Latin America.
    1974c   "'Showcase' for Counterrevolution." In *Guatemala*, Susanne
            Jonas and David Tobis, editors. New York: North American Con-
            gress on Latin America.

Kaiser, Philip M.
    1983   "Central America Unready for Massive Aid." Letter to *The New Times*, March 13:20E.
Karlstrom, LeRoy
    1983   "Crises in Our Backyard: What Next?" Paper presented at the Social and Behavioral Science College Colloquium, Northern Arizona University, November 2.
Karnow, Stanley
    1983   *Vietnam: A History.* New York: The Viking Press.
Kelly, James
    1983   "From Preacher to Paratrooper." *Time*, August 22:37.
Kennedy, Paul
    1971   *The Middle Beat: A Correspondent's View of Mexico, Guatemala, and El Salvador.* New York: Teachers College Press.
Kohan, John
    1983   "Central America: To Share the Pain." *Time*, March 14:34–39.
Krueger, Chris, and Carol A. Smith
    1983   "Interim Report of the Advisory Panel on Guatemala." *Anthropology Newsletter* 24(8):20, 3, 4.
LaFeber, Walter
    1982   "Inevitable Revolutions." *The Atlantic Monthly*, June:74–83.
Latin America Regional Reports Mexico & Central America.
    1980a   "Guatemala Massacre Points to Growing Peasant Resistance." February 15:1–3.
    1980b   "A Sharp Twist to the Right." November 28:3.
    1981a   "Corporate Guatemala Under Fire." July 10:7–8.
    1981b   "Fighting in the Streets." August 14:3–4.
    1981c   "Cerezo Gets an Invitation to the Party." August 14:6–7.
    1981d   "Agonising Over Military Sales: Guatemala." September 18:3.
    1982a   "Guatemala: Army Steps Up Action Against Guerrillas." February 12:3.
    1982b   "Counter-insurgency at a Crossroads." June 4:6.
    1982c   "State of Siege Decree Dismays Civilian Parties." July 9:3–4.
    1982d   "Ríos Montt Faces Problems on the Right . . . But Has Some Success Against the Left." September:6–7.
    1982e   "Army Discontent Threatens Ríos Montt." October 29:2.
    1983a   "Guerrillas Win Breathing Space." February 18:8.
    1983b   "Ríos Montt: The Unlikely Survivor." March 25:7.
    1983c   "The Guerrillas Change Tack." March 25:8.
    1983d   "Ríos Montt's Opponents in Disarray." May 6:3.
    1983e   "Ríos Montt Survives But Threats Remain." July 15:5.
    1983f   "A Risky Step to the Right." August 19:6–7.
    1983g   "Mixed Reception for Mejía in U.S." August 19:1.
    1983h   "Transforming the Indian Highlands." May 6:8.
    1984a   "Army's Reforms Strengthen Mejía." January 13:6.
    1984b   "'Disappearances' Are Up to Argentine Levels." March 23:8.
    1984c   "Military Will Back MLN-CAN Alliance." June 8:6.
    1984d   "Military-CD 'Truce' in Guatemala As Left Dismisses Election Results." July 13:1.

LeoGrande, William
    1983   "A Splendid Little War: Drawing the Line in El Salvador." In *Revolution in Central America*, Stanford Central America Action Network, editors. Boulder: Westview Press.

Lewis, Anthony
    1983   "Who Among Us?" *The New York Times*, May 1:21E.

Lewis, Flora
    1982   "Vietnam and Salvador–A Battle for Hearts and Minds." *The New York Times*, February 21:19.

Long, William R.
    1984   "Guatemala's Leader Terms Vote a Success." *Los Angeles Times*, July 2:1, 10.

MacLear, Michael
    1982   *The Ten Thousand Day War: Vietnam: 1945–1975*. New York: Avon Books.

Maira, Luis
    1983   "The U.S. Debate on the Central American Crisis." In *The Future of Central America: Policy Choices for the U.S. and Mexico*, Richard R. Fagen and Olga Pellicer, editors. Stanford: Stanford University Press.

McManus, Doyle
    1984   "U.S. Points to Gains in El Salvador: Progress Against Death Squads Is Closely Watched." *Los Angeles Times*, Jan. 8:1, 6–7.

Melville, Thomas
    1983   "The Catholic Church in Guatemala, 1944–1982." *Cultural Survival Quarterly* 7(1):23–27.

Melville, Thomas, and Marjorie Melville
    1971   *Guatemala: The Politics of Land Ownership*. New York: Free Press.

Monsanto, Pablo
    1983   "The Foco Experience: The Guerrillas' First Years." In *Guatemala in Rebellion: Unfinished History*, Jonathan L. Fried et al., editors. New York: Grove Press, Inc.

Montealegre, Flora, and Cynthia Arnson
    1983   "Background Information on Guatemala, Human Rights, and U.S. Military Assistance." In *Revolution in Central America*, Stanford Central America Action Network, editors. Boulder: Westview Press.

Moore Lappé, Frances, and Nick Allen
    1983   "Guatemalan Victims." In *Guatemala in Rebellion: Unfinished History*, Jonathan L. Fried et al., eds. New York: Grove Press, Inc.

Nairn, Allan
    1983   "Guatemala: Central America's Blue Chip Investment." In *Guatemala in Rebellion: Unfinished History*, Jonathan L. Fried et al., editors. New York: Grove Press, Inc.

Nelson, Anne
    1983   "In Guatemala, a Buffo Jefe Falls As U.S. Attache Patrols the Halls." *Los Angeles Times*, August 14:3.

The New York Times
    1960   "Guatemala Fights Revolt; State of Siege Is Imposed." Nov. 14:1, 3.

1962 "Guatemala's President Reports Crushing of Bananera Rebels." February 6:1.
1981 "Excerpts From Haig's Remarks at First News Conference as Secretary of State." January 29:10A.
1982a "Land Reform's Big Spenders." July 4:2E.
1982b "Central American Politics at a Glance." December 5:10.
1983a "Rights Group Asserts Guatemala Is Killing Indians." May 8:8.
1983b "State of Alert, Days of Alarm." July 3:2E.
1983c "Another Linguist Is Reported Seized." November 20:8.
Newbold, Stokes (Richard N. Adams)
1956 "Receptivity to Communist Fomented Agitation in Guatemala." *Economic Development and Cultural Change* 5:338–361.
Partido Guatemalteco del Trabajo
1982 "El genocidio y la dictadura del ejército continuan la lucha del pueblo avanza." *Prensa Libre*, August 11:6. (Manifesto published for humanitarian reasons for the family of Señor Méndez Ruiz Valdés, who was kidnapped by the PGT.)
1983 "A fortalecer la unidad revolucionaria para contribuir a detener la intervención imperialista y derrotar a la dictadura militar en Guatemala!" *Prensa Libre*, October 12:25–27. (Manifesto published for humanitarian reasons for the family of Pedro Julio García, who was kidnapped by the PGT.)
Pastor, Robert A.
1982 "Our Real National Interests in Central America." *The Atlantic Monthly* 250(1), July:27–39.
Payeras, Mario
1983 "The Tiger of Ixcán." In *Guatemala in Rebellion: Unfinished History*, Jonathan L. Fried et al., eds. New York: Grove Press, Inc.
Peckenham, Nancy
1983 "Fruits of Progress: The Panzós and Spanish Embassy Massacres." In *Guatemala in Rebellion: Unfinished History*, Jonathan L. Fried et al., editors. New York: Grove Press, Inc.
Prensa Libre
1983 "Sin aclarar muerte de padre franciscano." November 26:4, Guatemala.
Press, Robert M.
1982a "Guatemala Vote Marked by Ballots–and Bullets." *Christian Science Monitor*, March 5:1, 6.
1982b "Guatemala Dilemma: How to Revive Economy During War." *Christian Science Monitor*, March 15:4.
Preston, Julia
1981 "Guatemala: The Muffled Scream: A Field Report on the Unthinkable Revolution." *Mother Jones* 6(9):40–49.
Riding, Allan
1982 "U.S. General Urges Aid to Guatemala." *The New York Times*, August 22:6.
Robb, Louis A.
1980 *Diccionario de Términos Legales*. Mexico: Editorial Limusa.
Roderick, Lee
1984 "White: Salvadoran Facts Hidden." *The Sun*, January 9:8.

Rodríguez, Mario
    1966 "Guatemala in Perspective." *Current History* 50–51:338–343.
Rohter, Larry
    1982 "Guatemala: No Choices." *Newsweek*, March 1:24.
Rosénthal, Mario
    1962 *Guatemala: The Story of an Emergent Latin-American Democracy.* New York: Twayne Publishers, Inc.
Russell, George
    1983 "Guatemala: Surprise in the Sermon." *Time*, May 23:35.
Sancton, Thomas A.
    1980 "Central America: The Land of the Smoking Gun; Terrorism and Turmoil Imperil U.S. Hopes for Moderate Reform." *Time*, August 18:34–43.
    1982 "Terror, Right and Left." *Time*, March 22:24–32.
Sanders, Sol W.
    1982 "The 'Battle for Central America' May Be in Guatemala." *Business Week*, March 22:50–54.
Schlesinger, Stephen, and Stephen Kinzer
    1983 *Bitter Fruit: The Untold Story of the American Coup in Guatemala.* New York: Anchor Press/Doubleday.
Schuster, Lynda
    1983 "Flight From Fear: Guatemalan Refugees Jam Mexican Camps, Tell Stories of Terror." *The Wall Street Journal*, May 18:1, 26.
Schwartz, Norman
    1983 "Ethnicity, Politics and Cultural Survival." *Cultural Survival Quarterly* 7(1):20–23.
Sexton, James D.
    1972 *Education and Innovation in a Guatemalan Community: San Juan la Laguna.* Los Angeles: Latin American Studies Series, Vol. 19.
    1978 "Protestantism and Modernization in Two Guatemalan Towns." *American Ethnologist* 5:280–302.
    1979a "Modernization among Cakchiquel Maya: An Analysis of Responses to Line Drawings." *Journal of Cross-Cultural Psychology* 10:173–190.
    1979b "Education and Acculturation in Highland Guatemala." *Anthropology and Education Quarterly* 10:80–95.
    1982 "Ignacio Bizarro Ujpán: Thematic Analysis of a Tzutuhil Maya's Life Story." Paper presented at the Annual Meeting of the American Folklore Society, Minneapolis, Minnesota.
Sexton, James D., editor
    1981 *Son of Tecún Umán: A Maya Indian Tells His Life Story.* Tucson: University of Arizona Press.
Sexton, James D., and Clyde M. Woods
    1977 "Development and Modernization among Highland Maya: A Comparative Analysis of Ten Guatemala Towns." *Human Organization* 36:156–177.
    1982 "Demography, Development and Modernization in Fourteen Highland Guatemalan Towns." In *The Historical Demography of Highland Guatemala*, Robert M. Carmack, John Early, and Christopher Lutz, editors. Institute for Mesoamerica Studies, SUNY at Albany, Pub. No. 6, p. 189–202.

Sharckman, Howard
    1974   "The Vietnamization of Guatemala: U.S. Counterinsurgency Pro-
           grams." In *Guatemala*, Susanne Jonas and David Tobis, editors.
           New York: North American Congress on Latin America.
Simons, Marlise
    1982a "Guatemalans Are Adding a Few Twists to 'Pacification.'" *The
           New York Times*, September 12:3E.
    1982b "Latin America's New Gospel." *The New York Times Magazine*,
           November 7:45–47, 112–117, 120.
    1983a "Guatemala: The Coming Danger." In *Revolution in Central
           America*, Stanford Central America Action Network, editors.
           Boulder: Westview Press.
    1983b "Guatemala Asks Refugees to Return." *The New York Times*,
           June 12:3L.
Skelton, George
    1984   "More El Salvadoran Arms Aid Urged: Central America Is Vital
           to U.S. Security, Kissinger Panel Finds." *Los Angeles Times*, Jan-
           uary 12:1, 8, 13.
Stevens Point (Wis.) Journal
    1982   Award Memorializes Brother Miller." December 23:8.
Time
    1984   "First Step: Guatemala Opts for Moderation." July 16:40.
Tobis, David
    1974   "The Largest U.S. Corporations in Guatemala." In *Guatemala*,
           Susanne Jonas and David Tobis, editors. New York: North Amer-
           ican Congress on Latin America.
Torgerson, Dial
    1982a "Life Is a Little Less Deadly in Guatemala." *Los Angeles Times*,
           August 1:1, 15.
    1982b "New Tactics Mark War in Guatemala." *Los Angeles Times*, Sep-
           tember 19:1, 10, 20.
    1983   "El Salvador Regime to Shift Tactics." *Los Angeles Times*, April
           10:1, 17.
Toriello Garrido, Guillermo
    1983   "Introduction." In *Guatemala in Rebellion: Unfinished History*,
           Jonathan L. Fried et al., editors. New York: Grove Press, Inc.
Torres-Rivas, Edelberto
    1983   "Guatemala: Crisis and Political Violence." In *Revolution in Cen-
           tral America*, Stanford Central America Action Network, editors.
           Boulder: Westview Press.
Toth, Robert C.
    1983   "Reagan Says Security of Americas Is at Stake: Speech Seen As
           Warning to Democrats." *Los Angeles Times*, April 28:1, 15.
Tuohy, William
    1983   "War Similarities: El Salvador Faces Ghost of Vietnam." *Los An-
           geles Times*, March 20:1, 24–25.
United Press International
    1977   "Carter Signs Aid Bill; Some Nations Barred." *The New York
           Times*, November 2:14A.
    1984   "Election Results Contested." *The Sun*, July 11:10.

U.S. News & World Report
   1960   "Castro Tries Again: Another Flop." November 28:62–63.
Vasquez, Juan M.
   1982a   "New Regime Faces Test–Guatemala Killings Go On." *Los Angeles Times*, June 3:1, 16.
   1982b   "Guatemalan Aliens Pour Into Mexico." *Los Angeles Times*, November 14:1, 24, 15.
   1983   "General Ousts Guatemala Leader; 8 Reported Slain." *Los Angeles Times*, August 9:1, 6.
Vietnam: A Television History
   1983   "The Roots of War." Public Broadcasting Corporation. WGBH, Boston.
Walsh, Edward
   1983   "Strategic Guatemala: Next Red Plum in the Hemisphere?" In *Guatemala in Rebellion: Unfinished History*, Jonathan L. Fried et al., editors. New York Grove Press, Inc.
Weinraub, Bernard
   1983a   "Mrs. Kirkpatrick Urges U.S. to Adopt Latin Marshall Plan." *The New York Times*, March 6:1, 10.
   1983b   "Mrs. Kirkpatrick Critical of Dodd." *The New York Times*, May 1:9.
Whetten, Nathan L.
   1961   *Guatemala: The Land and the People*. New Haven: Yale University Press.
Whitaker, Mark, et al.
   1983   "The Battle for Hearts and Minds." *Newsweek*, May 9:20–22.
White, Robert E.
   1982   "Central America: The Problem That Won't Go Away." *The New York Times Magazine*, July 18:20–33.
Wilkie, James W.
   1983   "The Management and Mismanagement of National and International Statistical Resources in the Americas." In *Statistical Abstract of Latin America*, Volume 22, James W. Wilkie and Stephen Haber, editors. UCLA Latin American Center Publications, University of California.
Wilkie, James W., and Stephen Haber, editors
   1983   *Statistical Abstract of Latin America*, Volume 22. Los Angeles: UCLA Latin American Center Publications, University of California.
Woods, Clyde M.
   1975   *Culture Change*. Dubuque: Wm. C. Brown Company, Publishers.
Woods, Clyde M., and Theodore D. Graves
   1973   *The Process of Medical Change in a Highland Guatemalan Town*, Los Angeles: Latin American Studies Series, Vol. 21.

❧ Acknowledgments

I should like to express my appreciation to Kathleen Newman and my wife, Marilyn, for editorial suggestions. I should also like to thank two Guatemalans (whose names I shall not reveal), currently living in the U.S., for aiding in translating a number of Guatemalan expressions. Thanks also go to several of my students who read *Son of Tecún Umán* and gave me feedback that I have used in *Campesino*. Special thanks go to Noel Logan, Chris Beard, Heather Cooper, and Arlene Haber, members of my spring 1984 seminar on life histories, who read *Campesino* and gave me invaluable constructive criticism. Throughout this project, the Committee for Organized Research at Northern Arizona University has generously supplied financial support. Also, I am grateful to Gary Buckley, former dean of the College of Social and Behavioral Science at NAU, who provided part of my cost of transportation to Guatemala in the summer of 1982. Finally, I should like to thank my young son Randy for exercising considerable patience with a dad who often refused to leave his computer terminal when requested.

J.D.S.

✌ Index

441

bombas, 103
bomberos, 161, 214, 331
boundary markers, 136–37, 152–54
bravo, 110
bread, sold by Ignacio, 294–98
breastfeeding, 116
bribery, 23, 96, 173, 217, 262, 321, 365, 366, 369, 401, 403, 427
brujo, 43, 126, 145, 330, 332. *See also* witchcraft
business interests, U.S., 3, 6, 7. *See also* coup, of 1954

Cacíque Inn, 121. *See also* guerrillas
café pergamino, 299, 351
calumnias, 24, 72, 83, 89, 92, 94, 97, 167, 409; against cooperative, 351–58; against guerrilla, 180; against Ignacio, 122; against Ignacio and Andrés, 121; against Ignacio Puzul, 312; against the mayor, 173; against Protestants, 119–20; against student, 259–60
canoj, 116
caporal, 149, 175
Caritas, 25–26, 42–45, 250
Carter administration, 391 n. 22, 392 n. 24, 414, 417–18
Castillo Armas, Col. Carlos, 22, 401–4, 413
Castro, Fidél. *See* Cuba
catechist, 110, 276, 290
Catholic Action, 80, 84, 110, 195, 224, 256, 303; and collecting Holy Friday offerings, 297; and education, 281; and Ignacio's role as head of cofradía, 254, 276; influence of, on campesinos, 205; and local politics, 319; as policy maker, 362
Catholic church, 88, 104, 110, 168, 175, 296, 302, 417; activities of priests in, 129, 247–50, 361; aid from, 380; confirmations in, for income, 195; factions in, 242, 361–65, 377; and guerrillas, 379; and Holy Week, 361–65; and killing of clergy, 247–50, 393 n. 27; and local politics, 230, 257, 320, 322, 345; and Protestants, 119, 346–49; as teachers of literacy, 277, 413
Catolicos Antiguos, 100
caución juratoria, 84
cayetes, 18
cédula de ciudadanía, 176
cédula de vencidad, 139, 176, 205
celebrations. *See costumbres;* customs
Central America, importance of, 3–9
Central American Church, 168, 172, 281, 349

Cerezo Arévalo, Vinicio, 377, 379, 381, 390, 417, 418, 420, 421
chamarra, 132
charity, 49, 302
chicharrones, 161
chicote, 232
chipilín, 191
chirimía, 268
chirmol, 111
chuchito, 237
chupa, 256
CIA, 10, 397, 401, 404–5, 407, 411
citación, 152
climate and weather, 45–46, 51, 56–58; difficulties due to, 130–31, 173, 199; drought, 140; hail, 109
coffee prices, 194, 195–96, 299; and quotas, 299, 351–59
cofrades, 67, 69
cofradía, 13, 33, 67, 69, 145, 274, 302, 317; and Christmas, 210, 281; and community affairs, 349; duties of, 270–72; and fiesta of Cristo de Esquipulas, 283; and fiesta of Holy Week, 281, 295–96, 362; and fiesta of San Pedro, 242–43; and grave-digging, 283; and Holy Week, 317; of María de Concepción, 13, 254, 300, 349; and San Juan Bautista celebration, 333
Colom Argueta, Manuel, 95–96, 387, 389
colonization, 413
comadre, 24
comedor, 152
comienda, 398
comisionado militar, 19, 411. *See also* military commissioners
comisión de vigilancia, 106, 226
Comité de Defensa Nacional Contra el Comunismo, 402
Comité de Unidad Campesina (CUC), 415
Comité Nacional de Reconstrucción, 423
commissioners, military. *See* military commissioners
Communism, 96, 175; doctrine of, on radio, 185; spreading of, 397, 407
Communists, 397, 399–401, 404, 407; being labeled as, 189, 234, 250, 258, 282, 286, 319, 330, 381, 390–91 n. 21, 395 n. 29; influence of, in Guatemala, 4,5; problems among, 234; suspected, 248–50, 257–58
community, working for, 110, 111
compadre, 35, 146
compassion, Ignacio's, 176
Congress of the Republic, 161

midwife, 163

military, 178–80; antagonism of, for
other factions, 401; and Arbenz regime, 400, 402; bombardment by, 428;
against Communists, 245, 249; confrontation of, with guerrillas, 211–12,
275, 289, 395 n. 21, 409–10; in control
of government, 402, 405; fear of, 238,
282, 289; and juntas, 319–20, 322,
375; kidnappings by, 259–62, 413; killing by, 211–12, 256, 393 n. 26, 413,
422; and landowners, 421; and peasants, 426; as political force, 408–9; reserves of, 336; search by, 181, 205;
strafing by, near San José, 182; against
Ydígoras, 407. *See also* military
commissioners

military aid, 8, 392 n. 24, 393 n. 27, 417;
from China and Soviet-bloc countries,
392 n. 26

military commissioners, 189, 193, 234–
35, 256–57, 259–60, 282, 302, 314,
319, 427; *jefe* of, 320–21, 411; killing
by, 330, 336–45; newly appointed,
345; persecution by, 192; wrongdoing
by, 365–69

mill (at cooperative), 106, 128, 129

milpa, 27, 32, 107, 309

miracle, 200

molinos, 105

monte, 140

mordida, 132. *See also* bribery

mosh, 159

Mother's Day, 47

Movimiento de Liberación Nacional
(MLN), 404

mozos, 91–92, 155

municipal corporation, 174

municipal registry, 144

nagual, 315–16, 330

national coffee association, 351–59

national institute of cooperatives. *See*
INACOP

national police, 140, 318, 365

natural resources, 3, 6, 10

New Year's customs, 37

naval de la marina de guerra, 343

Nicaragua, 55, 109, 390 n. 21, 391 n. 22,
393 n. 26, 407. *See also* Sandinistas

nixtamal, 39, 105

notificatión, 83, 90

Nueva España Sembradores de Maíz, 50

Nuevo Mundo, 95

nutrition, 159–60

omen, 61

Operation: Guatemala, 411; Honesty,
408; Phoenix, 411; Vietnam, 411–12

oppression, 153–54, 164, 314

Organización del Pueblo en Armas
(ORPA). *See* ORPA

ornato, 144, 212

ORPA, 171–72, 206, 232, 335, 368, 390
n. 21, 392 n. 26, 423–24

overols, 169

PAC. *See autodefensa civil*

pacification program, 4, 423

Padre Pablo, 247–49, 306

padrinos, 146

panela, 60

panteón, 164

Panzós, massacre at, 415–16

parasites, 109

Partido Frente Unido de la Revolución,
95

Partido Guatemalteco de Trabajo (PGT),
386, 400

Partido Institucional Democrático (PID),
40, 165, 408

Partido Revolucionario (PR), 112; candidate of, for mayor, 112

patrulla de autodefensa civil. *See autodefensa civil*

paxte, 307

peasant unions, 399

Peralta Azurdia, Col. Enrique, 407–8,
415

personería jurídica, 353

pesquiza, 94

pílon, 30

pipa, 108

policía judicial, 78, 96, 289, 312, 375,
387 n. 17

police, national, 140, 318, 365

political parties, 374, 387–89 n. 18 and
n. 20, 390 n. 21, 402, 408–9

politics, 10, 40–42, 45, 135, 165–69, 385
n. 6, 414–15; Ignacio's involvement in,
230, 285, 317; and reforms, 398; in
support of Lucas, 189

ponchos, 49. *See also chamarra*

prayer, 110, 111, 284

pre-cooperative, 27, 59, 139

premonition, 77, 197, 200, 215, 220

Prensa Libre, 318

Prince of Peace Church, 361

principales, 89, 91, 122, 230, 242–43,
272–74, 276–77, 296, 300, 362. *See
also cofradía*

proceso, 74, 104